The Development of Russian Verse explores the Russian verse tradition from Pushkin to Brodsky, showing how certain formal features are associated with certain genres and, at times, specific themes. Michael Wachtel's basic thesis is that form is never neutral: poets can react to the work of their predecessors positively by means of stylization and development or negatively by means of parody or revision, but they cannot ignore it. Keeping technical terms to a minimum and providing English translations for all Russian quotations, Wachtel offers close readings of individual poems of more than fifty poets. His aim is to help English-speaking readers reconstruct the strong sense of continuity Russian poets have always felt, that transcends any individual epoch or ideology. Ultimately, his book is an inquiry into the nature of literary tradition itself, and how it coalesces in a country that has always taken so much of its identity from its written legacy.

Michael Wachtel is Professor of Slavic Languages and Literatures at Princeton University. He is author of *Russian Symbolism and Literary Tradition: Goethe, Novalis, and the Poetics of Vyacheslav Ivanov* (1994) and he has written articles on Russian Symbolism and poetics in English, German, and Russian.

CAMBRIDGE STUDIES IN RUSSIAN LITERATURE

THE DEVELOPMENT OF RUSSIAN VERSE

THE DEVELOPMENT OF
RUSSIAN VERSE

Meter and its Meanings

MICHAEL WACHTEL

CAMBRIDGE
UNIVERSITY PRESS

PUBLISHED BY THE PRESS SYNDICATE OF THE UNIVERSITY OF CAMBRIDGE
The Pitt Building, Trumpington Street, Cambridge CB2 1RP, United Kingdom

CAMBRIDGE UNIVERSITY PRESS
The Edinburgh Building, Cambridge, CB2 2RU, United Kingdom   http://www.cup.cam.ac.uk
40 West 20th Street, New York, NY 10011–4211, USA   http://www.cup.org
10 Stamford Road, Oakleigh, Melbourne 3166, Australia

First published 1998

Printed in the United Kingdom at the University Press, Cambridge

Typeset in Baskerville 11/12.5 pt   [CE]

A catalogue record for this book is available from the British Library

Library of Congress cataloguing in publication data
Wachtel, Michael.
The development of Russian verse : meter and its meanings / Michael Wachtel.
p.   cm. – (Cambridge studies in Russian literature)
Includes bibliographical references and index.
ISBN 0 521 62078 3 (hardback)
1. Russian poetry – History and criticism.
2. Russian language – Versification.
I. Title.   II. Series.
PG3041.W33   1998
891.71'009 – dc21   98–20052   CIP

ISBN 0 521 62078 3 hardback

For my parents

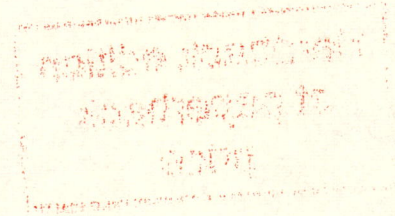

Contents

Acknowledgments

This book has been several years in the making, and I have benefited throughout from the advice of friends and colleagues. My brother Andrew Wachtel was instrumental in determining the book's overall shape and even its cover. Elena Alekseeva, David Bethea, my tireless colleague Caryl Emerson, Stephanie Sandler, and Barry Scherr took time out of their already overburdened schedules to read the manuscript (in some cases, more than once) and to supply me with detailed and challenging commentary. Annette Pein and Kirill Postoutenko generously shared with me their own unpublished and otherwise inaccessible works. Nikolai Bogomolov, Lazar Fleishman, Roman Timenchik, and Alexander Zholkovsky gave suggestions that I have gratefully incorporated.

Having written this book in part as a pedagogical aid, I find it particularly appropriate to acknowledge the contributions of my own teachers. John Malmstad, Omry Ronen, and Igor Smirnov introduced me to many of the poets discussed in these pages, and their influence on my specific readings is incalculable. Though I have never sat in his classroom, I consider Mikhail Gasparov both a mentor and a guardian angel. This manuscript developed under his watchful eye and would have been much the poorer were it not for his careful criticisms. I take this opportunity both to express my gratitude for his unfailing generosity and to absolve him of any responsibility for my judgments.

Much of this material was presented and discussed in my graduate seminars on "The Evolution of Russian Poetic Form" at Princeton University. For helping me not only to formulate the essential questions, but also to answer them, I thank the participants in those courses: Sharon Lubkemann Allen, Mirande Bissell-Siders, Sarah Clovis, Craig Cravens, Thomas Cunningham, Eugene Gurarie, Maryl Hallett, Firoozeh Khazrai, Nina Khrushcheva, Sarah Kube,

Inessa Medzhibovskaya, Nicole Monnier, Anthony Prather, Tricia Rattigan, Naomi Rood, Eva Rottmann-Kalenskij, Gabriella Safran, Ludmila Shleyfer, Heather Smith, and my colleague Charles E. Townsend. Special thanks go to Nicole Monnier for proofreading and for compiling the index to this book.

At Cambridge University Press, editors Katharina Brett and Linda Bree deserve encomiums for both efficiency and patience. I am truly grateful to them and to the anonymous readers they selected, who taught me – among other things – the dangers of making generalizations about Anglophone cultures. Series editor Catriona Kelly went far beyond the call of duty by closely reading my manuscript and offering extensive suggestions for its improvement. Karen Anderson Howes was a superlative copy-editor.

I cannot sufficiently thank my wife, who dealt patiently with all manner of manuscript crises and deadlines, and my parents, to whom I dedicate this book.

The following people and organizations have kindly permitted me to quote material under their copyright: Walter Arndt, the translator of Aleksandr Pushkin's poem "Echo"; Indiana University Press, the publisher of Dmitrii Prigov's "Kogda ia v Kaluge po sluchaiu byl," in Gerald S. Smith (ed.), *Contemporary Russian Poetry: A Bilingual Anthology*; Oxford University Press, the present publisher of James Falen's translation of Aleksandr Pushkin's *Eugene Onegin*. I am particularly indebted to Farrar, Straus & Giroux, Inc. and the Brodsky estate for allowing me to cite Joseph Brodsky's poem "Ostanovka v pustyne" in its entirety in Russian and to use my own translation of it.

Note on translations and transliterations

In this book, I have used two different types of translation: prosaic and equimetrical. The former, which aims for literal accuracy, needs no introduction, as it is standard practice among American and British Slavists. The latter, in which semantic precision is sacrificed in order to retain formal elements of the original, is generally deemed inappropriate for scholarly writings. However, in a study such as this one, which is based on the premise that meter has meaning, the equimetrical approach has a definite advantage. Whatever semantic freedoms it may entail and however inadequately it may function as poetry, it reproduces the sound of the verse, thereby making my argumentation more accessible to the non-Slavist.

Equimetrical translations can be found in the introduction, throughout the second chapter, in most of the fourth chapter, and where possible in the third chapter and the afterword. I have relied exclusively on prosaic translations in the first chapter (where my own abilities were not equal to the task of equimetrical renderings) and in the fifth chapter, where it was not essential for my purposes to preserve elements like rhythm and rhyme. Except where otherwise noted, the translations are my own. For the convenience of students, translations have been placed wherever possible beside the original Russian text.

When writing Russian names, I use a simplified system of transliteration in the text and expository sections of the notes (essentially that found in Victor Terras [ed.], *A Handbook of Russian Literature* [New Haven: Yale University Press, 1985], p. xix) and the more exact, but less readable British system in the bibliography and the non-expository parts of the notes. In this way, I hope to simplify pronunciation for readers who do not know Russian without sacrificing the precision necessary for specialists.

Introduction

Продолжающиеся по вечерам разговоры о Пушкине . . .
Как много зависело от выбора стихотворного размера!
Борис Пастернак, *Доктор Живаго*[1]

Continuous evening conversations about Pushkin . . . How
much depended on his choice of meter!
Boris Pasternak, *Doctor Zhivago*

The French Symbolist Stéphane Mallarmé once said that "poetry is
made not with ideas, but with words."[2] This statement should be
understood less as a blanket condemnation of ideas than as an
attempt to define a hierarchy of poetic values. Mallarmé merely
shifts emphasis from ideas as such to the way they are expressed in
verse. When viewed in this way, his claim seems eminently reason-
able and considerably clearer than more technical yet ultimately
kindred explanations, e.g., "the poetic function projects the principle
of equivalence from the axis of selection into the axis of combination."[3] Put most simply, we might say that poetry relies on the
rhythmic and phonic organization of language to strengthen an
utterance and make it memorable. In this crucial regard it resembles
numerous other forms of communication, from prayer to political
slogan to advertising jingle to popular song. For example, while there
is nothing inherently profound about the sentiment "Yesterday all
my troubles seemed so far away," it has left an indelible mark on the
otherwise porous Anglophone cultural memory. If confronted with
the phrase "Yesterday all my troubles seemed very distant," English
speakers would overwhelmingly disapprove. Thanks to Paul
McCartney, the first version now seems inevitable; the second,
though essentially identical in meaning, sounds incorrect. If asked to
continue McCartney's song beyond its first line, some people might
falter, but few would have difficulty recalling the melody, the rhythm,
and even the next rhyme word ("stay").

I

Strange as it may seem, the non-semantic elements of language are what prove to be most persistent. The *sound* of words (be it melody, rhythm, or rhyme) outlasts their meaning. Anyone who has ever recited a poem or sung a song should know the sensation when, at some point, uncertainty sets in. The next phrase suddenly proves elusive, yet its rhythm remains. This common experience indicates that the memory of sound patterns is more durable than the memory of their specific verbal realization. On closer consideration, it can be seen that the hegemony of aural memory verges on tyranny. Not only does sound remain long after meaning has dissipated; sound can even disfigure meaning. Such a claim may appear to come directly from the manifestos of the most radical Russian Futurists, yet it is vindicated by everyday language use. Numerous Americans unwittingly demonstrate this phenomenon when they change the perfectly logical (if redundant) phrase "for all intents and purposes" into the semantically absurd (yet rhythmically equivalent) "for all intensive purposes." Granted, it is a large step from "for all intensive purposes" to a Shakespeare sonnet, yet both testify – the latter with infinitely more subtlety, variety, and profundity – to the power of sound to shape verbal utterance.

I begin with these general reflections because they offer the most obvious reason why a study of verse should carefully consider formal elements. All poetry functions by structuring words in accordance with aural principles. Rhyme, rhythm, meter, and stanza have defined poetry for centuries, and in Russia (where free verse has never achieved more than marginal status) they continue to define poetry today.[4] Any attempt to determine "what the poem means" must necessarily consider how the poet chooses to express this meaning. Questions of verse technique, in short, are not tangential to a poet's concerns. Rather, they *are* the poet's concerns and therefore – whether this is consciously recognized or not – they become the reader's concerns.

In this book, I seek to demonstrate the interpretive value of studying Russian poetic form – and to do so in a way both accessible and meaningful to an English-speaking reader. My study is by no means the first attempt to acquaint a non-Russian audience with this subject. The books of Boris Unbegaun and Barry Scherr offer clear presentations of basic and sometimes even arcane aspects of Russian prosody.[5] Both Unbegaun and Scherr provide a wealth of information on rhyme, on various meters, on the caesura, on laws governing the stress patterns in the iambic line, yet they are essentially taxonomical in approach. Their goal – and achievement – is to explain the terminology, to clarify and summarize decades of scholarship. However, they only rarely consider how such formidable conceptual knowledge can be applied pragmatically.[6]

It is my conviction that formal study of verse justifies its existence only when it can be brought to bear on semantic questions. To identify a poem's meter is, in and of itself, useless. The true task is to transform this observation into a meaningful interpretive tool. The Western reader in particular needs not so much an arsenal of terminology as a general framework for comprehending why such terminology exists. Until it can be shown that there is a significant reason why iambs should be distinguished from trochees, then – following in the illustrious footsteps of Pushkin's Eugene Onegin – we might as well go ahead and confuse them.

Why *should* one know the difference between an iamb and a trochee or, for that matter, between a sonnet and an Onegin stanza? Such basic questions deserve to be taken seriously. For the poet – and therefore for the knowledgeable reader – specific poetic meters and strophic forms carry with them associations and expectations. Consider the following verses:

> I sat in the theater above you
> And sensed what that biblical dove knew,
> When high on the ark,
> It saw land through the dark.
> I, too, saw the light: How I love you!

As the last line makes clear, this is a love poem. A certain pathos is introduced through a biblical allusion. Gazing at his beloved from a distance in a theater, the poet compares himself to Noah's dove, which saw land after forty days of floods. This "sighting" implies the end of disaster, the beginning of a new life. On a strictly thematic level, then, the poem can be understood as a sincere hymn to the beloved.

However, the reader should immediately sense that something is amiss. A fundamental problem becomes apparent if one (momentarily) ignores the theme and concentrates exclusively on the form:

$$\smile\smile\acute{}\smile\ \ \smile\smile\acute{}$$
$$\smile\acute{}\smile\ \ \smile\smile\acute{}\smile\ \ \smile\acute{}\smile$$

The poem contains five lines of amphibrachs, with rhyme scheme A-A-b-b-A (capital letters designate feminine rhymes). Lines 1, 2, and 5 are trimeter and lines 3 and 4 dimeter, the latter with an anacrusis. Even without (perhaps *especially* without) this technical description, the English-speaking reader should recognize this pattern, for it can be found in numerous poems. For example:

> There once was a lady from Niger,
> Who smiled as she sat on a tiger,
> They finished the ride
> With the lady inside
> And the smile on the face of the tiger.

Any schoolchild would without difficulty identify these verses as a limerick, a form which, ever since it was championed by Edward Lear in the nineteenth century, has been extremely popular in Britain and America. The limerick has a wide range of potential themes, but a specific genre: light verse. In direct contrast to our first-person example, it is invariably written in the third person. Even more importantly, outside the sphere of comic (often bawdy) poems, it is simply not used. Thus, when confronted with a declaration of love in the form of a limerick, a reader should be aware of an incongruity between form and content. Whether intended or not, the effect is comic, because a single poem – with rare exceptions[7] – is not sufficiently powerful to offset a century of firm associations. For this reason, we can say that a heartfelt love limerick is doomed to failure. The poet may be sincere, but his form is not. On a perhaps subconscious level, the reader's response to the new poem is largely determined by a set of *metrical* expectations.

An important question arises from these considerations: are the comic associations inherent in the meter of a limerick, or are they essentially arbitrary, the result of historical coincidence? Numerous poets and philosophers have insisted on the former, yet modern comparative poetics suggests the latter.[8] There is nothing intrinsically comic about amphibrachs, truncated lines, or five-line stanzas. Were our love limerick to be translated into Russian, maintaining the semantics, serious tone, and formal features, most readers would be untroubled by inappropriate associations.[9] In short, metrical associations are not psychological invariants or a part of mankind's "collective unconscious." Often, they are specific to a national literature and do not cross geographical boundaries.

At times, of course, a poetic form occurs with the same semantic associations in any number of national literatures. This does not mean that these literatures developed the identical form independently. On the contrary, it generally indicates that one has influenced the other or that both originate from a common ancestor. For example, Dante's *Divine Comedy* is written in *terza rima*, three-line stanzas in which the second line takes its rhyme from the first and third lines of the preceding stanza. This form stands out graphically and is thus particularly easy to recognize and remember. Because Dante's example was so powerful, subsequent poets in various languages used the form as a way to hark back to the *Divine Comedy*, usually writing narratives and often consciously borrowing Dantesque themes. Among the works of the major Russian poets, one could name Pushkin's "I dale my poshli" ("And we went further") and "Telega zhizni" ("The Cart of Life") or Blok's "Pesn' ada" ("Song of Hell").

At this point, a legitimate objection may be raised. If the connection of a given meter and a specific semantic content is completely arbitrary, how do forms such as the *terza rima* or the limerick arise in the first place? Is it a matter of utter coincidence that a limerick has come to convey a humorous effect rather than being the favored vehicle for epics? Both the limerick and *terza rima* owe much of their effect to the triple repetition of rhyme. Would Dante's *Divine Comedy* have achieved such renown had it been written in stanzas of limericks? Likewise, had *terza rima* first been used for bawdy anecdotes, might it have proved as effective a form as the limerick? Absurd as they may seem, these are not simple questions. Certainly one senses that the limerick, if only because of its brevity, is better suited to pithy statements than to philosophical speculation. Likewise, *terza rima*, with a structure that incessantly pushes forward, is probably more appropriate for narratives than, say, for nature poetry. The fact that, in both cases, these forms have kept such strict associations for so many years suggests that they were well suited to their original purposes. (In many instances, specific meters and stanzas fall out of favor entirely or change associations in the course of time.) In short, there may well be certain characteristics that make the limerick appropriate for comic subject matter or the *terza rima* appropriate for narratives of grand scale, but there is no reason to believe that such characteristics make these forms *uniquely* suited to those purposes. The longevity of a form's semantic associations relates first and foremost to the power of its example. Unsuccessful poems will be quickly forgotten; successful ones enter the cultural memory and remain "alive" for generations of subsequent poets, who draw on them in a variety of ways.

The fact that the limerick is probably the sole poetic form familiar to the average native speaker of English does not weaken the general theory that various meters have specific semantic (or generic) associations. If we agree that meaning is not *inherent* in the meter, then it would be peculiar indeed if readers poorly acquainted with the tradition could "sense" the associations of a form they were encountering for the first time. A trained musician who hears the first two movements of a Haydn string quartet "automatically" expects a minuet to follow, while a listener unfamiliar with the history of classical music does not anticipate anything of the sort. The presence or absence of such associations has nothing to do with genius or clairvoyance, but is simply the result of exposure and education. If an Anglophone reader, without any training whatsoever, can understand the metrical and generic associations of the limerick, then it stands to reason that poets, who consciously and constantly think about form, have a far more developed sense of the subtle interplay between meter and meaning.

Always aware of a larger tradition, poets express their relationship to it through their choice of form. Certain movements have an almost religious awe of their precursors (in Russia, one thinks of the Symbolists and Acmeists), while others deny their existence or profess a disdain for them (e.g., Russia's Cubo-Futurists). As one might expect, poets of the former category tend to choose forms that align them with the tradition, while those of the latter grouping prefer to confront the tradition head-on, often claiming (with considerable bombast) to repudiate it entirely. However, whether the basic impulse is reverent or destructive, each movement *necessarily* regards past practice as its point of orientation. As Arnold Schoenberg, the radical innovator of twentieth-century music, wrote: "It is seldom realized that a hand that dares to renounce so much of the achievements of our forefathers has to be exercised thoroughly in the techniques that are to be replaced by new methods."[10] Whether seeking to affirm or to polemicize, any artist looks back to his predecessors.

It may be helpful to give examples of two radically different types of creativity, both of which must be understood in terms of tradition. Pushkin, generally considered the greatest Russian poet, represents the "borrower"; Mayakovsky, self-styled "poet of the revolution," exemplifies the "destroyer."

Boris Tomashevsky, one of the first and finest Russian scholars to examine the connection of meter and meaning, convincingly demonstrated Pushkin's predilection for borrowing poetic forms. For all of Pushkin's stanzas, Tomashevsky sought – and usually found – models in Russian or Western European literature. He concluded that "Pushkin associates a poem's emotional and thematic content with its strophic form."[11] Of Tomashevsky's many examples, it will perhaps be most instructive to begin with one which he himself discovered in the work of a previous scholar.[12] In the late 1820s, Pushkin began (in earnest, and with obvious difficulty) to study English poetry in the original language.[13] From a modern standpoint, his tastes were peculiar. Of all English poets contemporary to him, Pushkin favored the now forgotten Barry Cornwall (pseudonym of Bryan Waller Procter). In an anthology of English verse, he discovered "A Sea-Shore Echo":

> I stand upon the wild sea-shore –
> I see the screaming eagle soar –
> I hear the hungry billows roar,
>   And all around
> The hollow answering caves out-pour
>   Their stores of sound.
>
> The wind, which moaneth on the waves,
> Delights me, and the surge that raves,
> Loud-talking of a thousand graves –
>   A watery theme!
> But oh! those voices from the caves
>   Speak like a dream!
>
> They seem long hoarded, – cavern-hung, –
> First uttered ere the world was young,
> Talking some strange eternal tongue
>   Old as the skies!
> Their words unto all earth are flung:
>   Yet who replies?
>
> Large answers when the thunders speak
> Are blown from every bay and creek,

And when the fire-tongued tempests speak
  The bright seas cry,
And when the seas *their* answer seek
  The shores reply.

But Echo from the rock and stone
And seas earns back no second tone;
And Silence pale, who hears alone
  Her voice divine,
Absorbs it, like the sponge that's thrown
  On glorious wine!

Nymph Echo, – elder than the world,
Who wast from out deep chaos hurl'd,
When beauty first her flag unfurl'd,
  And the bright sun
Laugh'd on her, and the blue waves curl'd,
  And voices run.

Like spirits on the new-born air,
Lone Nymph, whom poets thought so fair,
And great Pan wooed from his green lair,
  How love will flee!
Thou answeredst *all*; but none now care
  To answer thee!

None–none: Old age has sear'd thy brow;
No power, no shrine, no gold hast thou:
So Fame, the harlot, leaves thee now,
  A frail, false friend!
And thus, like all things here below,
  Thy fortunes end![14]

For reasons perhaps mysterious to a modern reader, these verses
made a profound impression on Pushkin, who responded to them in
1831 with a poem called "Ekho" ("Echo"):

Ревет ли зверь в лесу глухом,
Трубит ли рог, гремит ли гром,
Поет ли дева за холмом –
  На всякий звук
Свой отклик в воздухе пустом
  Родишь ты вдруг.

Ты внемлешь грохоту громов,
И гласу бури и валов,
И крику сельских пастухов –
  И шлешь ответ;

Тебе ж нет отзыва . . . Таков
И ты, поэт![15]

Pushkin's verses have been translated by Walter Arndt, who pre-
serves the form of the original:

> Where beasts in deepest forests wail
> Where horns intone, where thunders flail,
> Or maiden chants in yonder vale –
>   To every cry
> Through empty air you never fail
>   To speed reply.
>
> You harken to the thunder knells,
> The voice of gales and ocean swells,
> The shepherd's hail in hills and dells
>   And you requite;
> Yet unrequited stay. . . This spells
>   The poet's plight.[16]

A comparison reveals Pushkin's extraordinary closeness to his
model. He not only reproduces the unusual form exactly (maintaining the position of the truncated lines as well as the exclusively
masculine rhyme scheme), he even takes with it the larger themes:
echo and the lack of echo. These indisputable similarities force one
to ask the question: what makes Pushkin a major poet and Cornwall
a minor one?

The answer is, in a word, structure. Pushkin condenses the rather
unfocused "Sea-Shore Echo" into a work of extraordinary precision.
Cornwall's first four stanzas contain a lengthy description of the
sounds of a storm as they echo back from the caves, while the final
four stanzas elaborate the concept of lack of echo, relying on a series
of mythological (and allegorical) figures. Everyone was attracted to
"Nymph Echo" in her youth, and she answered them all, but, now
that she has become old, no one answers her. On the basis of this
ephemeral quality, Echo becomes representative of the fleeting
nature of beauty and love. In terms of the poem as a whole, however,
it is difficult to ascertain any logical reason for Cornwall's excursus
into myth. Indeed, extraneous detail abounds throughout. The
"lyrical I" supplies an impressive opening anaphora, yet it quickly
(and inexplicably) disappears. "Fame, the harlot," suddenly makes
an appearance in the final stanza (much as "Silence pale" did three
stanzas earlier), yet her presence does not add focus to the poem. On
the contrary, these allegorical figures become a series of loose ends.

In creating his own "Echo," Pushkin borrows the form, the phonological richness, specific motifs, rhetorical devices, and even syntactic constructions from Cornwall, yet he improves on the original a hundredfold. First of all, by limiting himself to two stanzas, he removes the rambling quality entirely. Secondly, he extends the notion of echo to a point that Cornwall could not have fathomed (and that Arndt's translation is incapable of reproducing). Cornwall's verses have an undeniably sonorous quality, largely the result of reiterated rhymes, anaphora, and alliteration. Pushkin applies these same techniques, but develops them, putting an echo into every nook and cranny of poem – beginning with the phonological level, e.g., anagrams ("*Rev*et li *zver'*," line 1), assonance and consonance ("*les*u/*gl*ukhom," line 1; "*gr*emit li *gr*om," line 2). The lists of sounds he includes in the first stanza may seem to have been chosen randomly (a wild animal in the forest, a horn sounding, a maiden singing), yet they have subtle "equivalents" in the second stanza (the rumble of thunder, the voice of the storm and waves, the shouting of shepherds). In each case, the first two lines describe threatening sounds of untamed nature (what might be called the *locus horridus*), while the third suddenly shifts to a pastoral setting (the traditional *locus amoenus*). In the fifth line of each stanza one finds, respectively, the synonyms "otklik" and "otzyv" (in English, both words could be rendered as "response"), which resonate with the poem's title. Even the insistent interrogative particle "li" of stanza 1 serves a poetic function: it prepares the anaphoric "i" of stanza 2, creating repetition on yet another level. In short, Pushkin uses stanzaic form *meaningfully*; in numerous ways, the second stanza represents an echo of the first.

Following Cornwall's example, Pushkin also depicts the lack of echo. Once again, however, he elaborates on his model, altering Cornwall's motif and using form to express it in an unprecedented way. In Pushkin's poem, Nymph Echo is dispensed with entirely, but the poet himself takes on her role.[17] He answers everything, yet remains "echo-less" himself. Pushkin expresses this fundamental paradox through the enjambment in the poem's penultimate line. In ordinary language use, the words "Such are you, poet" (rendered loosely by Arndt as "This spells / The poet's plight") would belong together as a single phrase in a single line of verse. Indeed, Pushkin himself testifies to this in another poem written at approximately the same time:

Гордись: *таков и ты, поэт,*
И для тебя условий нет.[18] (Emphasis added.)

Be proud: *such are you, poet,*
And for you there are no conditions.

However, in "Echo," he breaks that very phrase, creating a deliberate tension between the intonation indicated and the natural
intonation:

Тебе ж нет отзыва . . . *Таков*
И ты, поэт! (Emphasis added.)

For you there is no response . . . *Such*
Are you, poet!

This enjambment marks the semantic crux of the entire poem. The
"unnatural" stop in the middle of a sentence ("Such / Are you")
accompanies the introduction of the concept of "non-echo." In
short, this break occurs simultaneously on both the semantic and
formal levels. It could be argued that Pushkin even found a model
for this enjambment in Cornwall's lines ("but none now care / To
answer thee").[19] Yet Pushkin's enjambment (in which the adjective is
separated from the noun that it modifies) ruptures a much firmer
syntactic link than Cornwall's (where a conjugated verb is separated
from a second verb).[20] This is, in fact, not the first time that Pushkin
had taken his syntactic cue from Cornwall. A comparison of the first
stanzas of each poem reveals a striking similarity (the first three lines
are composed of a number of short sentences, while the final three
form a single run-on sentence). However, only in Pushkin's poem are
the syntactic features incorporated into the larger poetic structure.
In other words, Pushkin's closing enjambment is so striking because
it breaks both the syntactic and the thematic pattern that the first
stanza leads us to expect. Cornwall's poem includes a rich variety of
themes, images, syntactic constructions, and phonetic echoes, yet
they come at random points and serve no overarching function.

It should be clear that, for Pushkin, Cornwall's form and theme
were inseparable; when he borrowed one, the other inevitably
followed along.[21] Nonetheless, even when taking both form and
theme, Pushkin showed himself to be considerably more imaginative
than his model. One must therefore be cautious about applying
terms like "indebtedness" or "influence" to this type of literary
reception. By comparing "Echo" with its indisputable source, one

becomes cognizant of an extraordinarily significant aspect of Pushkin's art: his ability to recognize and realize the *potential* of another
poet's verses. Through judicious borrowing, radical reorganization,
and subtle changes, he makes a foreign text his own, creating a
poem in which every element (from theme to syntax to punctuation)
is carefully balanced against every other one.

In direct contrast to Pushkin, Mayakovsky is generally considered
a radical innovator, an iconoclast with no respect for or interest in
tradition. "Knigi? Chto knigi!" ("Books? What are books!") exclaims
the speaker of "Oblako v shtanakh" ("A Cloud in Trousers"), a
thinly disguised version of Mayakovsky himself.[22] In his 1926 essay
"Kak delat' stikhi" ("How to Make Verses"), in a disingenuous
passage suspiciously reminiscent of Pushkin's *Eugene Onegin*, 1, 7, he
claims: "Honestly speaking, I know neither iambs nor trochees,
never differentiated between them and never will."[23] Yet Mayakovsky's verse teems with both metrical and semantic allusions to his
predecessors. The 1924 "Iubileinoe" ("Anniversary Poem") takes the
form of a monologue that Mayakovsky addresses to none other than
Pushkin himself, whose 125th birthday was being celebrated
throughout Russia. It begins in prose, with the "poet of the revolution" introducing himself and offering his hand to Pushkin's statue.
The remainder of the poem, with a few notable exceptions, is
written in trochees. Throughout, Mayakovsky emphasizes his soli-
darity with Pushkin. Carried away by this spirit of collaboration,
Mayakovsky at one point suddenly shifts to iambs, which he explains
in the following way:

(Я даже	(I even
ямбом подсюсюкнул,	joined in now by lisping iambs,
Чтоб только	So I
быть	would be
приятней вам.)[24]	more pleasing to you.)

Iambs, of course, were commonly used by all Russian poets from
Pushkin's predecessors to Mayakovsky's contemporaries (and successors), but they were so dominant in Pushkin's metrical repertoire
that Mayakovsky justifiably associated them with him. Most interestingly, Mayakovsky here interrupts the poem's trochaic flow, suddenly
switching to iambic tetrameter for these two lines. By uttering a
"servile" sentiment to Pushkin in Pushkin's own favorite rhythm,
Mayakovsky indicates that – subsequent claims notwithstanding – he

is well aware of traditional Russian versification and that he recognizes the semantic associations of meter.

This passage merely makes obvious a more subtle connection between iambs and Pushkin that Mayakovsky had exploited two years earlier. In a poem entitled "Neobychainoe prikliuchenie" ("An Unusual Adventure," sometimes called simply "Solntse" ["The Sun"]), Mayakovsky had related how, during a heat wave, he had turned to the sun and invited it to come to tea. To his astonishment, the sun complied, leading Mayakovsky the host to suggest that they join forces as poets. Curiously, this entire poem is written in iambs and, once again, the meter is semantically motivated. It is used to tip off the (attentive) reader to the presence of numerous Pushkin allusions.[25] After all, since his death, Pushkin was constantly referred to as the "sun of Russian poetry." In a gesture at once realistic and metapoetic, Mayakovsky identifies "Pushkino" as the village where his "unusual adventure" supposedly took place. Moreover, the motif of inviting the sun to tea (and the subsequent acceptance of that offer) clearly recalls a Pushkinian subtext – the drama "Kamennyi gost'" ("The Stone Guest"), in which Don Juan invites a statue to dinner only to have it accept.[26] (This statue motif is developed in the subsequent "Anniversary Poem.") Of course, one is struck by numerous incongruities in the circumstances and consequences of this invitation. Traditionally, the Commendatore comes to avenge his own death by killing Don Juan. In both "An Unusual Adventure" and "Anniversary Poem," the visit leads to close, life-affirming friendships. The handshake motif concludes "The Stone Guest," where it seals the protagonist's fate; Don Juan begs the statue to release his hand from its heavy grip. In "Anniversary Poem," however, the same motif occurs at the *beginning* and leads to very different results. Mayakovsky shakes hands with the enormous statue, hugs him, and asks colloquially (and – for those who recognize the subtext – ironically), "Stisnul? Bol'no?" ("Did I squeeze too hard? Does it hurt?"). This is one of the numerous ways in which Mayakovsky takes potentially serious (and traditionally tragic) situations from Pushkin's works and turns them upside-down, into scenes of utter harmony. I would emphasize that these allusions are both semantic *and* metrical. The fact that Mayakovsky is using his sources parodically in no way lessens their significance. Indeed, his dependence on the tradition proves to be no less than that of Pushkin.[27]

Parody, as Iurii Tynianov has shown, is one of the most effective means of evolving tradition.[28] It is not limited to the work of the "destroyers," but can frequently be found in the "borrowers" as well (for example, in Pushkin himself). Perhaps more explicitly than any other type of poem, it affirms the fundamental link between form and meaning. Consider the following verses, published anonymously in 1886:

Ночь (подражание Фету)	Night (An Imitation of Fet)
Шепот, грозное бряцанье	Whispers and a threat'ning grating
Сабель, звуки шпор, –	Sounds of spurs and swords, –
Обыск, тягость ожиданья.	Searches and the weight of waiting.
Тихий разговор;	Quiet, furtive words;
Свет ночной, – поодаль тени	Light of night, – afar impressions,
Матери, отца, –	Mother's, father's trace, –
Смена быстрых выражений	Sudden changes of expressions
Бледного лица;	Of a pallid face;
В вечность канувшие грезы,	Daydreams, now forever dying
Бед в грядущем тьма,	Sadness without fail,
И прощание, и слезы –	And the parting, and the crying
И тюрьма, тюрьма! . . .[29]	And the jail, the jail! . . .

This "imitation of Fet" has a very specific referent:

Шепот, робкое дыханье,	Whispers, breathing, timid quaking,
Трели соловья,	Nightingale and rook,
Серебро и колыханье	Silver and the gentle shaking
Сонного ручья,	Of a sleepy brook,
Свет ночной, ночные тени,	Light of night and night's impressions,
Тени без конца,	Shadows in a race,
Ряд волшебных изменений	Changing magical expressions
Милого лица,	Of a dearest face,
В дымных тучках пурпур розы,	Smoky clouds with purple dyeing,
Отблеск янтаря,	Amber shadows drawn,
И лобзания, и слезы,	And the kisses and the crying,
И заря, заря! . . .[30]	And the dawn, the dawn! . . .

Famed for its verblessness, this untitled Fet poem of 1850 is considered one of the most subtle and musical in the entire Russian lyric tradition. It consists of a single extended sentence, which reflects – rather than narrates – a series of fleeting impressions. Nothing is stated directly: the people involved are named only metonymically ("whisper," "face"). The scene itself takes place during the evanescent boundary between night and dawn. Fet repeats words and sounds in such a way as to make the poem seem like an incantation. So mysterious and understated is the verse that one easily overlooks its traditionality of genre: an alba (a love poem devoted to the theme of parting at daybreak).

The author of the parody borrows Fet's meter, rhyme, intonation, poetic devices, and specific motifs (e.g., the whisper, the tears, the moment of parting) to create a poem with diametrically opposed thematics. Like Fet, the parodist describes a world traditionally associated with darkness and secrecy. However, he sketches not the atmosphere of love, but the furtive existence of the political criminal. Since Fet's preference for personal lyricism and distaste for civic themes enraged numerous contemporary critics, it may be assumed that the parodist was seeking to hit an already sore spot.[31]

It is possible to delineate three discrete categories of potential readers and their responses. The first, entirely unaware of Fet's relevance, reads the parody as a univocal, serious statement about the plight of the political revolutionary. The second, knowing Fet's reputation as an apolitical, art-for-art's-sake poet, senses the generic incongruity between the original and the "imitation." The third understands this general context, but also recognizes the specific Fet poem alluded to and thus reads the new text as a succession of references. For this reader, the effect is richest, for every word is "double-voiced."

A parody succeeds maximally when it can draw attention to the specific work that it is attacking. The less familiar the target, the less effective the parody. Sumarokov's so-called "Vzdornye ody" ("Nonsense Odes"), for example, written at the end of the eighteenth century, were directed at the solemn odes of his contemporaries.[32] It is not difficult to explain why they are far less amusing to us than they were when first written. Except for a handful of specialists, today's readers belong to the second category: they understand these poems as parodies of a genre. However, the original audience (third category) recognized not merely the generic affinities, but even knew the *specific* odes that were under attack. Of course, if the target remains completely unrecognized, the parody fails.[33] For a reader of the first category (with no previous exposure to the Russian solemn ode), these "Nonsense Odes" are simply incomprehensible.

Parody is only one possible means of developing tradition. However, it is for my purposes highly significant and even paradigmatic, because it so palpably testifies to the need for a diachronic (historical) approach to literary analysis. Scholars who seek to understand a poem in isolation (the ideal of certain "new critics" and structuralists) are powerless when confronting parody, which unequivocally demands the context of a previous work. Moreover, because it operates so insistently with formal echoes, parody highlights the significance of the non-semantic elements of verse. Poetic parodists invariably repeat the stanzaic and metrical features of the poems they are attacking. Without such formal repetition, it is unlikely that readers would recognize the function of the new poem.

Parody allows us to observe *in extremis* a fundamental principle of literary tradition. Tradition, commonly misconstrued as stasis and therefore evaluated negatively, is an essentially dynamic process which includes periods of formation, continuity, deformation, and renewal. Certain influential theoretical movements (e.g., early Russian Formalism or the Konstanz school of "aesthetics of reception") have tended to privilege the third element, suggesting that the greatest writers were those who broke most radically from the inherited norms. This seems to me a grave error. Pushkin's example alone – to which we will frequently have recourse in the following chapters – serves as eloquent testimony that the greatest poets are not necessarily the most radical innovators. Any artistic work reflects the influence of conservative and innovative impulses. Too much repetition leads to epigones, too much novelty to chaos. It behooves the scholar to investigate a literary text as a balance of heterogeneous elements – variants and invariants, continuity and change. It is important, but not sufficient, to note that a given writer borrows a form, genre, or theme from his predecessor(s). Equally significant are the features that he rejects and adds.

By looking beyond isolated poems to the poetic context from which they emerged, one can observe the way that form guides tradition. On a microcosmic level, an individual poet's formal decisions reflect both his sense of connectedness and his creative ideals. On the macrocosmic level, the evolution of form offers a record of tradition as it developed. In a vibrant poetic culture – as Russia's has always been – poets expect their readers to recognize and *to understand* their metrical and stanzaic choices. My approach is aimed at "recovering" for Western readers this sense of form, and thereby allowing them to reconstruct the dynamics of literary tradition. In the course of this book, questions of literary evaluation will inevitably arise (e.g., Pushkin is a "better" poet than Cornwall). I do not shirk them, but neither do I consider them central to my enterprise. My purpose is less to insist on qualitative differences between poems than to point out the fundamental formal and semantic elements that link them.

A few words are in order about the structure and methodology of the chapters that follow. The meaning of Russian verse form has been studied by some of the foremost scholars of the twentieth century, and I have not hesitated to draw selectively on their work.[34] The first systematic investigation in this area was done in the early 1960s by Kirill Taranovsky.[35] By tracing the reception of a highly influential Lermontov poem written in the relatively rare meter of trochaic pentameter, Taranovsky argued that a given metrical (and even rhythmic) pattern can exert a palpable *semantic* influence. A poet's choice of meter, he contended, was predetermined by the practice of his predecessors, which was in turn influenced by a certain inherent "synesthetic" quality of the rhythm itself. Relying on extensive empirical evidence (hundreds of poems written by dozens of poets), Taranovsky seemed to offer a straightforward explanation of a phenomenon that had generally been considered important, yet unclassifiable.

Subsequent scholars have developed Taranovsky's fundamental insight while trying to avoid a certain Procrustean tendency in his essay. Mikhail Gasparov has disputed Taranovsky's synesthetic notions about a rhythm's "natural" meaning, but has shown that poetic meter nevertheless carries semantic overtones which are determined by prior poetic practice.[36] In his own essays, Gasparov guides the reader with extraordinary thoroughness through a dizzying number of poems and poets in an effort to delineate "metrical aura"[37] – that is, the variety of semantic possibilities that a given meter possesses. An encyclopedic command of the Russian poetic tradition lends Gasparov's work an impressive sense of completeness.

My approach is greatly indebted to Gasparov, but I part company from him in one significant respect. Gasparov insists that any investigation of the semantic associations of a meter should try to consider every single poem in which that meter is used. This conviction, for all of its obvious logic, can lead to unwieldy results. When maximum completeness is the ideal, individual poems quickly turn into statistics. The interpreter is forced to reduce them to a single question: do they or do they not conform to the larger generic/formal pattern(s)? In each of my five main chapters, I trace the evolution of a specific poetic form through a series of exemplary texts. While this leaves me open to charges of sins of omission (to a greater or lesser extent, depending on the popularity of the form in question), it offers me the time and space to pay close attention to individual poets and poems. This methodological decision is in part determined by pedagogical experience: it seems to me that Western audiences will benefit more from sustained analysis of representative works than from fleeting observations on an enormous number of poems, most of which are unfamiliar to them. In short, I seek to preserve the essential diachronic dimension of Gasparov's work, but focus more intently on interpretive questions. Keeping in mind the needs of a non-Russian reader, I make a considerable effort to situate the poets and poems in a cultural, historical, and – when appropriate – biographical context.

With the exception of the final chapter (which focuses on the visual aspect of verse), all of the work in this book could fit under the rubric of "metrical semantics," i.e., the way meter conveys meaning. Each chapter is devoted to a different form and its generic and thematic tendencies. While my methodology remains constant throughout, the nature of the material ensures that the conclusions to the individual chapters vary considerably. The specific genres have been selected in order to achieve maximum breadth (short and long forms, ancient and modern forms, odic, elegiac, balladic, epigrammatic, and even "epic" verse) and thus to allow me to cover the gamut of Russian poetic styles and movements. At one point or another, I draw upon the work of most of the leading poets from the age of Pushkin through the twentieth century (including both official Soviet and émigré verse). With the exception of Pushkin, however, I have made no conscious attempt to allot poets space in direct proportion to their stature. As a result, certain minor poets get more attention than they would warrant in a traditional literary history, while some indisputably major ones are relegated to a footnote. Unfair as this may be from an evaluative point of view, it is crucial to my approach, in which lesser works provide the essential context for understanding the genuine masterpieces. Throughout the book, then, interpretive principle takes precedent over exhaustive coverage. My primary aim is to demonstrate how an awareness of form can enrich our understanding both of individual poems and of literary tradition as a whole.

CHAPTER I

The Russian ballad: passion, betrayal, revenge, and the amphibrachic tetrameter line

Нас было два брата – мы вместе росли
И жалкую младость в нужде провели . . .
Но алчная страсть овладела душой,
И вместе мы вышли на первый разбой.
                Пушкин, "Братья разбойники"[1]

We were two brothers – we grew up together
And spent our wretched youth in need . . .
But greedy passion took hold of [our] souls,
And together we set out on our first robbery.
                Pushkin, "Brigand Brothers"

In Russia, the emergence of the ballad as an important poetic genre was to a large extent influenced by prior Western European developments. Decades before their Russian counterparts, English and German Romantics had turned their attention to the richness of folklore. In their search for "unschooled" creativity, they discovered the ballad – a narrative poem set in a remote, vaguely defined past. The ballad featured a limited number of simple characters whose actions were governed more by emotion than by rationality. The plot revolved around a single fateful moment and was related in a straightforward manner, with metaphor and digression kept to a minimum.[2]

Given its origins in oral culture, the ballad might seem an unlikely place to situate a study of literary form. However, folkloric genres were never as "pure" and "primitive" as readers were encouraged to think. The image of the enthusiastic scholar/poet roaming the countryside, collecting and faithfully transcribing stories and poems, was largely mythical. To the extent that this happened at all, the collector tended to edit and embellish the material in accordance with a written standard.[3] The widespread infatuation with a folk culture that relatively few readers had actually experienced led to a

20

proliferation of adaptations or imitations that left their sources far behind and whose authenticity could not be easily verified. Ultimately, the Romantic poet was not concerned whether his ballad conformed with actual folklore. His primary goal was to create a work that satisfied the criteria of this genre as established by *literary* predecessors.[4]

If the Western European educated classes learned their folk ballads through highly literate intermediaries, then Russian readers found themselves at an additional remove. Just as Russia's Slavophiles derived their ideas about national identity from German philosophers, so Russian poets, too, imported their folk ballads from Germany. The "original" became doubly distorted – but the results, interestingly enough, were extraordinarily successful. In the course of a few years (beginning in 1808), the German-style ballad became a fixture of the Russian poetic repertoire. In this process of domestication, no name was more significant than that of Vasily Zhukovsky. A prolific poet and celebrated translator from several languages, Zhukovsky bridged the gap between the Russian public and the European verse tradition. The popularity of his ballad translations created an enormous demand among readers, leading him and his fellow poets to create their own original works in this genre. So, for example, Gottfried August Bürger's celebrated German ballad "Lenore" (1773) inspired three different Russian incarnations from Zhukovsky alone – "Liudmila" (1808), "Svetlana" (1808–12), and finally "Lenora" (1831).

From a formal point of view, Russian ballads departed in an obvious way from their German sources. German folk poetry (and literary imitation thereof) was characterized by rhythmic variation. Otherwise regular lines were often interrupted by the addition or subtraction of a syllable. The opening couplet of Ludwig Uhland's ballad "Die Rache" ("Revenge") exemplifies this tendency (my *rhythmically* faithful English translation follows the original German):

> Der Knecht hat erstochen den edeln Herrn,
> Der Knecht wär' selber ein Ritter gern.

> The servant just murdered his noble lord
> The servant envied his master's sword.

This meter (in Russian terminology, a *dol'nik*) belongs to the category of accentual verse. Each line has a set number of stresses (four), which are separated by an interval of either one or two unstressed syllables. It would be a simple matter to alter these verses and make them conform to a stricter pattern, as the following variant demonstrates (emendations are noted in italics):

> Der Knecht hat erstochen den *sehr* edeln Herrn,
> Der Knecht wär*e* selber ein Ritter *und* gern.

> The servant just murdered his *most* noble lord,
> The servant *had* envied his *own* master's sword.

The result is syllabo-tonic verse, in which the pattern of stressed and unstressed syllables is completely predictable. In this "corrected" version, the meter has become amphibrachic tetrameter. The basic foot, which repeats four times per line (truncated the fourth time), consists of three syllables, of which only the second is stressed ($\smile \acute{\ } \smile$).

The unpolished effect of accentual verse (variant 1) appealed to German poets, who eagerly incorporated it into their own stylized ballads for folkloric flavor.[5] However, Russian nineteenth-century poetry was written almost exclusively in syllabo-tonic verse (variant 2). To the Russian poet, the expressive rhythmical peculiarities of German folk-influenced verse simply sounded like mistakes. In their renderings of German ballads, therefore, they assiduously removed these rhythmical "lapses." The Russian translations no longer resembled their German source texts, but Russian readers – unaware of such rhythmic sleight of hand – nonetheless equated these new Russian meters with folk poetry. From the point of view of historical accuracy, this association was fundamentally incorrect. Yet, from the standpoint of literary tradition, it proved to be highly influential.

The example from Uhland's "Revenge" (written in 1810) was not chosen randomly. For in an odd and circuitous fashion, this ballad engendered an entire series of Russian poems. The most curious aspect of this idiosyncratic tradition was that – with the notable exception of Zhukovsky – the Russian participants apparently had no inkling that Uhland was their source. By tracing the trajectory of this single poem from Zhukovsky's time to the present day, we can observe the semantic power of a metrical example.[6]

The first step of the process occurred in 1816, with Zhukovsky's translation of "Revenge" into Russian:

Мщение

Изменой слуга паладина убил:
Убийце завиден сан рыцаря был.

Свершилось убийство ночною порой –
И труп поглощен был глубокой рекой.

И шпоры и латы убийца надел
И в них на коня паладинова сел.

И мост на коне проскакать он спешит:
Но конь поднялся на дыбы и храпит.

Он шпоры вонзает в крутые бока:
Конь бешеный сбросил в реку седока.

Он выплыть из всех напрягается сил:
Но панцирь тяжелый его утопил.[7]

(Revenge: A servant killed his lord through betrayal: / The murderer
envied the rank of the knight. // The murder took place at night – / And
the corpse was swallowed by the deep river. // The murderer donned the
spurs and the armor / And sat himself on the lord's steed. // And he
hurried to gallop across the bridge, / But the steed reared and snorted. //
He plunged his spurs into its sleek sides; / The furious steed cast the rider
into the river. // He tried with all his strength to swim out, / But the heavy
armor drowned him.)

Zhukovsky's translation is in amphibrachic tetrameter couplets
with exclusively masculine rhymes. The couplet structure, masculine
rhymes, and number of lines are taken directly from Uhland, but the
amphibrachs, of course, represent a simplified version of German
accentual verse (variant 2 as shown above). In terms of the Russian
literary tradition, Zhukovsky's form was strikingly innovative. Before
about 1810, amphibrachs had rarely been used in Russian poetry,
and meters consisting of only masculine rhymes were equally
infrequent. Both of these elements began to appear in Russian
poetry in attempts to render recent Western European (in particular,
German and English) verse.[8]

In its semantics, Zhukovsky's translation remains largely faithful
to the original.[9] As in Uhland's ballad, the narrative structure is
extremely simple: a brief sequence of events is described in chronological order by an omniscient observer. These events are related
with only the most rudimentary consideration of psychology and
without any extraneous detail. A servant, prompted by envy, kills his
lord; yet no sooner does he attempt to emulate his master than he

himself is killed. The moral, while not spelled out explicitly, is
nevertheless hard to miss: to envy is evil, and evil deeds will be
punished. The only shade of ambiguity is found in the title
("Revenge"), which might first be construed as the motive behind
the crime, but which, upon closer consideration, appears to describe
the punishment meted out by fate to the servant.

Neither Uhland's poem nor Zhukovsky's translation of it need be
considered outstanding art. Both ballads conformed to the rather
one-dimensional Romantic expectations of the ballad and were
presumably appreciated by their readers for precisely that reason.
These poems would belong entirely to the dustheap of literary
history were it not for the reaction of a single influential reader. In
February 1820, Zhukovsky first published his translation of
"Revenge." In November of that same year, Pushkin "responded"
with a poem entitled "Chernaia shal'" ("The Black Shawl"):

Черная шаль
(Молдавская песня)

Гляжу как безумный на черную шаль,
И хладную душу терзает печаль.

Когда легковерен и молод я был,
Младую гречанку я страстно любил.

Прелестная дева ласкала меня;
Но скоро я дожил до черного дня.

Однажды я созвал веселых гостей;
Ко мне постучался презренный еврей.

"С тобою пируют (шепнул он) друзья;
Тебе ж изменила гречанка твоя."

Я дал ему злата и проклял его
И верного позвал раба моего.

Мы вышли; я мчался на быстром коне;
И кроткая жалость молчала во мне.

Едва я завидел гречанки порог,
Глаза потемнели, я весь изнемог . . .

В покой отдаленный вхожу я один . . .
Неверную деву лобзал армянин.

Не взвидел я света; булат загремел . . .
Прервать поцелуя злодей не успел.

Безглавое тело я долго топтал,
И молча на деву, бледнея, взирал.

Я помню моленья . . . текущую кровь . . .
Погибла гречанка, погибла любовь!

С главы ее мертвой сняв черную шаль,
Отер я безмолвно кровавую сталь.

Мой раб, как настала вечерняя мгла,
В дунайские волны их бросил тела.

С тех пор не целую прелестных очей,
С тех пор я не знаю веселых ночей.

Гляжу как безумный на черную шаль,
И хладную душу терзает печаль.[10]

(The Black Shawl [A Moldavian Song]: I look like a madman at the black shawl / And sadness tears at my cold soul. // When I was young and quick to believe, / I was passionately in love with a young Greek woman. // The charming girl caressed me; / But soon I lived to regret it. // Once when I called together my joyous friends, / A despicable Jew knocked at my door. // He whispered, "Your friends are celebrating with you, / But your Greek girl has betrayed you." // I gave him some gold and cursed him, / And called for my loyal servant. // We set off; I rushed off on my quick steed, / And meek pity was silent within me. // Hardly had I glimpsed the Greek girl's threshold, / When my eyes darkened, I felt completely exhausted . . . // I entered the isolated chamber alone . . . / An Armenian was kissing the unfaithful girl. // I was beside myself; steel sounded forth . . . / The villain did not have time to interrupt his kiss. // I stamped on the headless body at length, / And, becoming pale, glared without a word at the girl. // I remember [her] entreaties, the flow of blood . . . / The Greek girl perished, love perished! // Having taken the black shawl from her lifeless head, / I silently wiped the bloody steel with it. // As soon as the evening haze appeared, / My servant tossed their bodies into the waves of the Danube. // Since that time I have not kissed charming eyes, / Since that time I have not known joyous nights. // I look like a madman at the black shawl / And sadness tears at my cold soul.)

Boris Tomashevsky was the first to recognize that "The Black Shawl" reproduces precisely the metrical and stanzaic model found in Zhukovsky's "Revenge."[11] The fact that Russia's greatest poet was in general a fanatic borrower – and that this exceedingly rare form occurs only once in his entire poetic output[12] – leaves little doubt that Pushkin was conscious of his metrical source.

But what was the purpose of this formal allusion? Composed in the first months of exile in the 1820s, "The Black Shawl" reflects Pushkin's early infatuation with Romanticism (understood at the time primarily as exoticism) and anticipates in a number of ways his "Southern Poems."[13] In "The Black Shawl," he portrays a group of distinctly non-Russian characters who are ruled by emotion. Without exception, these *dramatis personae* reflect crude Russian stereotypes of "the other": the loose woman (a Greek), the evil lover (an Armenian), the greedy gossip (a Jew), and, last but certainly not least, the brutal hero (presumably a Moldavian). Ever the careful craftsman, Pushkin sought a poetic form that would convey convincingly the poem's "uncivilized" milieu, so distanced from his own cultured persona. Since, generically speaking, "The Black Shawl" possessed virtually all the qualities of a ballad (simple plot, limited number of uneducated characters, vaguely defined setting), it was only logical that Pushkin should have selected a balladic meter – and Zhukovsky's recently published text obviously provided a convenient model.[14] It is, of course, ironic that a poetic form adapted from the German should have become the vehicle for a "Moldavian Song" (as the poem was designated by Pushkin himself). However, such incongruities were lost on readers before Tomashevsky. Indeed, generations of fanatic Pushkinists, convinced that the poem had its origins in popular culture, scrutinized Moldavian folklore in a misguided search for its source.[15]

A comparison of "The Black Shawl" with "Revenge" reveals numerous parallels as well as striking differences. In addition to the formal borrowings and the common genre, the poems share central themes (betrayal and revenge) and even a seemingly minor motif (a corpse ends up in the river). On the level of plot, Pushkin expands considerably on his model, adding a love triangle and changing the motivation behind the murder from envy to jealousy. He replaces the heavy suit of armor with a light shawl and shifts the vague medieval setting to the recent past (or, quite possibly, the present).[16] Yet it is in narrative technique that Pushkin makes his most radical alterations. In "Revenge," a detached third-person narrator tells the tale in chronological order, that is to say, in the order in which the events actually "happened."[17] In contrast, "The Black Shawl" is narrated by the emotionally involved protagonist, who, in his first two lines, presents the text's final chronological moment. As a result, the reader confronts the symbolically burdened shawl immediately, but understands its importance only at the poem's conclusion (i.e., the refrain). By filtering the entire tale through the perception of the protagonist, Pushkin eschews authorial commentary. Zhukovsky's clearly expressed moral judgment is replaced by an eerie silence in regard to ethical questions. The protagonist has achieved his revenge, but it is difficult to say whether justice has been served.

Today's readers may not immediately recognize why "The Black Shawl" is considered the work of a major poet. By twentieth-century standards, Pushkin's theme seems hackneyed and his stereotyped cast of characters distasteful. The narrative innovations fail to impress a reader familiar with Nabokov, Bely, and Joyce. However, in the context of the Russian literature of 1820, Pushkin's morally ambiguous poem stood out as a creation of unusual boldness and originality. The impulsive southern hero, virtually unprecedented in Russian poetry of the time, immediately captivated the imagination of the public. Indeed, the poem quickly achieved a life beyond the printed page: it was recited dramatically in theaters and set to music, and it even "returned" to its supposed folk origins in a series of primitive "lubok" drawings.[18] So famous was Pushkin's poem that, more than a century later, the newly minted communist hack Sergei Gorodetsky (erstwhile Acmeist poet) could entitle a story "The Black Shawl" and assume that the Soviet mass readership would recognize in this detail a symbol of loose morals.[19] Popularity, needless to say, is hardly a reliable measure of artistic quality. Nonetheless, it is a significant factor in literary history, because well-known and more assimilatable works enter the culture in a way that lesser-known ones do not. The fact that Pushkin's poem was committed to memory by countless admirers marked it as a cultural landmark, an immediately recognizable touchstone that could be utilized by subsequent poets in a variety of ways.

One reflection of the immediate success of "The Black Shawl" is found in a poetic "response" that appeared within a few months of the work's initial publication.[20] The new poem's author, Sergei Aksakov, was not even acquainted with Pushkin.[21] His work, entitled "Ural'skii kazak" ("The Cossack of the Urals"), bore the subtitle "Istinnoe proisshestvie" ("A True Occurrence"), but it betrays the influence less of "real life" than of Pushkin's powerful example:

Уральский казак
(Истинное происшествие)

Настала священная брань на врагов
И в битву помчала Урала сынов.

Один из казаков, наездник лихой,
Лишь год один живши с женой молодой,

Любя ее страстно и страстно любим,
Был должен расстаться с блаженством своим.

Прощаясь с женою, сказал: "Будь верна!"
"Верна до могилы!" – сказала она.

Три года за родину бился с врагом,
Разил супостатов копьем и мечом.

Бесстрашный наездник всегда впереди,
Свидетели – раны, и все на груди.

Окончились битвы; он едет домой,
Все страстный, все верный жене молодой.

Уже достигают Урала брегов
И видят навстречу идущих отцов.

Казак наш объемлет отца своего;
Но в тайной печали он видит его.

"Поведай, родимый, поведай ты мне
Об матери милой, об милой жене!"

Старик отвечает: "Здорова семья;
Но, сын мой, случилась беда у тебя:

Тебе изменила младая жена;
Зато от печали иссохла она.

Раскаянье видя, простили мы ей;
Прости ее, сын мой; *мы* просим об ней!"

Ни слова ответа! Идет он с отцом;
И вот уже входит в родительский дом.

Упала на грудь его матерь в слезах,
Жена молодая лежала в ногах.

Он мать обнимает; иконам святым,
Как быть, помолился с поклоном земным.

Вдруг сабля взвилася могучей рукой . . .
Глава покатилась жены молодой!

Безмолвно он голову тихо берет,
Безмолвно к народу на площадь идет.

Свое преступленье он всем объявил,
И требовал казни, и казнь получил.[22]

(The Cossack of the Urals [A True Occurrence]: There arose a holy war
against the enemy, / And it hurried to battle the sons of the Urals. // One
of the Cossacks, a dashing horseman, / Had lived only a year with his
young wife. // Loving her passionately and being passionately loved, / He
was forced to part with his bliss. // Bidding his wife farewell, he said, "Be
faithful!" / "Faithful to the grave!" she replied. // For three years he
fought with the enemy for the motherland, / He smote his foes with sword
and lance. // As his chest wounds testified, / The fearless horseman was
always in front. // The battles ended; he set off for home, / Still passionate,
still true to his young wife. // They reached the shores of the Urals / And
saw their fathers coming to meet them. // Our Cossack embraced his
father, / But saw in him a secret sadness. // "Tell me, my dear one, /
About my beloved mother and my beloved wife!" // The old man
answered: "Your family is healthy, my son; / But a misfortune has befallen
you: // Your young wife has betrayed you; / For this she has withered from
sadness. // Seeing her regret, we pardoned her; / Pardon her, my son; *we*
beg for her!" // Not a word in answer! He went with his father; / And
entered his parents' house. // His mother fell in tears on his breast, / And
his young wife lay at his feet. // He embraced his mother; prostrating
himself, / He prayed to the holy icons for advice. // Suddenly the saber
was raised by a powerful hand . . . / The young wife's head rolled off! //
Without a word he calmly took the head, / Without a word he went out to
the central square to the people. // He announced his crime to everyone /
And asked for his own execution – and he was executed.)

In addition to its distinctive meter and stanzaic form, Aksakov's
poem recalls Pushkin's text through its basic theme – passionate
love, a young woman's betrayal, her lover's bloody revenge. To be
sure, there are changes, both thematic (Pushkin's enigmatic hero
becomes a concrete personage who confesses and is punished for his
crime) and "narratological" (Aksakov uses a third-person narrator
and a simplified temporal scheme reminiscent of Zhukovsky). Yet it
is the repetition of details that makes clear the derivative nature of
Aksakov's poem. For example, Aksakov maintains the specific motif
of beheading, going so far as to repeat Pushkin's metonymic depiction of the murder (which emphasizes the weapon rather than the
murderer) and allowing the actual deed to occur during an ellipsis.[23]
Pushkin writes, "I was beside myself: steel sounded forth . . ." ("Ne
vzvidel ia sveta; bulat zagremel . . . ") and Aksakov "answers" with:

"Suddenly the saber was raised by a powerful hand . . ." ("Vdrug sablia vzvilasia moguchei rukoi . . . "), even repeating the distinctive Russian phonemic cluster "vzvi." Moreover, lexical echoes abound; entire lines can be traced without difficulty to Pushkin's model. In Pushkin's poem, the Jew tells the hero, "But your Greek girl has betrayed you" ("*Tebe* zh *izmenila* grechanka tvoia"), while in Aksakov's poem the father tells the hero, "Your young wife has betrayed you" ("*Tebe izmenila* mladaia zhena"). Since Pushkin had referred to the heroine as "young Greek" ("mladaia grechanka") (line 4: "I fell passionately in love with a young Greek woman" ["mladuiu grechanku ia strastno liubil"]), one can easily identify the raw material for Aksakov's choice of the marked word for "young" ("mladaia" rather than, for example, the synonymous "molodaia"). Another telling echo occurs in the penultimate couplet. In terms of both sound and sense, Aksakov's "Without a word he calmly took the head" ("*Bez*molvno on *golovu* tikho beret") recalls Pushkin's "I stamped on the headless body at length" ("*Bezglavoe* telo ia dolgo toptal"). Aksakov even repeats "without a word" ("bezmolvno") at the beginning of the next line. (It is the sole occurrence of anaphora, which, as in Pushkin's poem, is found only in the penultimate couplet.) While "bezmolvno" occurs only once in the text of "The Black Shawl" as we know it today, it figured prominently in the initial publication, a "pirate" edition that was obviously Aksakov's source.[24]

Aksakov's poem is a minor work, but it allows us to draw several important conclusions about metrical semantics. To begin with, one finds an excellent illustration of the power of Pushkin's example. Shortly after its publication, "The Black Shawl" inspired an imitation. It cannot be doubted that the most obvious link between the poems is metrical. Were one to rely entirely on English prose translations, it is possible that the poems' numerous resemblances would be overlooked. However, in the context of the rare meter that they share, other similarities are accentuated. A metrical model, in short, is inextricably linked to decisions about genre, theme, lexicon, and even stylistic devices.

It is noteworthy that Aksakov himself never included "The Cossack of the Urals" in his collected verse. In his memoirs, written more than three decades after the poem, he called it a "weak and pale imitation of Pushkin's 'Black Shawl.'"[25] Nonetheless, his evaluation was not shared by the public at large. Like Pushkin's poem, Aksakov's "Cossack" became a great success, eventually finding its way (anonymously) into various compilations of Russian songs.[26] Its dependence on Pushkin's model appears to have gone unnoticed, or, if recognized, seems not in any way to have lessened its popularity. Indeed, Aksakov's poem itself became the subject of an imitation, Aleksandr Polezhaev's "Kazak" ("The Cossack," 1830). This poem need not detain us, as it is imitative in the extreme. However, it serves as yet another example of the semantic influence of a metrical model. Using couplets of amphibrachic tetrameter with exclusively masculine rhymes, Polezhaev tells the story of a Cossack who leaves his young wife to go off to battle and returns to discover that he has been betrayed. One couplet should suffice to demonstrate the derivative (and unintentionally comical) nature of this poem:

> Он прямо в светлицу к жене молодой
> И кто же там с нею? . . . Казак холостой![27]

(He steps directly into his young wife's chamber / But who should be there with her? A Cossack bachelor!)

Minor alterations in plot and strophic form notwithstanding, this poem is blatantly modeled on Aksakov.[28]

Pushkin dated "The Black Shawl" November 14, 1820, and numerous facts (e.g., the very existence of Aksakov's imitation) make clear that it quickly became widely known. On March 23, 1821, from his exile in Kishinev, Pushkin wrote to Del'vig ("my friend Del'vig, brother on Parnassus") in St. Petersburg:

In your absence my heart remembered you and your muse – [your] journals. You're still the same – a talent wonderful and indolent. Do you plan to keep joking around, to keep swapping your genius for pocket money? Write a glorious poem, only not [about] the four times of day and not [about] the four seasons – write your "Monk." Gloomy, heroic, powerful, Byronesque poetry – this is your true calling. Destroy the old man within you, but don't kill the inspired poet. As concerns me, my dear [friend], let me say that I have finished a new narrative poem, "The Prisoner of the Caucasus," which I hope to send you soon. You'll be not entirely satisfied with it and you'll be right. Let me also say that still other narrative poems are roaming around in my head, but I'm not writing anything now.[29]

In this often-quoted letter, Pushkin announced to Del'vig that he had taken a new direction (that of Byron) and urged his fellow poet to follow him. As he insisted, it was Del'vig's destiny to write Romantic narrative poems.

Del'vig, of course, differed from Pushkin in both temperament and style. The Byronic hero and his colorful adventures had little attraction for this most phlegmatic of Russian poets.[30] Indeed, while Pushkin was composing his southern poems, Del'vig continued to write in the genres of the "lyceum" period (idylls, elegies, romances, album verse, etc.). His own formal experiments went in very different directions, e.g., stylizations of classical verse, imitations of Russian folklore, sonnets. In short, Del'vig was not destined to write the type of Romantic poem that Pushkin desired. Yet Del'vig did not completely ignore his friend's challenge. While his letters to Pushkin have been lost, one poem – if read in the context of metrical semantics – suggests his response:

Луна

Я вечером с трубкой сидел у окна;
Печально глядела в окошко луна;

Я слышал: потоки шумели вдали;
Я видел: на холмы туманы легли.

В душе замутилось, я дико вздрогнул:
Я прошлое живо душой вспомянул!

В серебряном блеске вечерних лучей
Явилась мне Лила, веселье очей.

Как прежде, шепнула коварная мне:
"Быть вечно твоею клянуся луне."

Как прежде, за тучи луна уплыла,
И нас разлучила неверная мгла.

Из трубки я выдул сгоревший табак,
Вздохнул и на брови надвинул колпак.[31]

(The Moon: I sat at the window in the evening with my pipe; / The moon looked sadly through the window. // I heard how the [river's] currents sounded in the distance. / I saw how fog covered the hills. // My soul became troubled, I shuddered wildly: / In my soul I remembered the past vividly! // In the silver radiance of the beams of the moon, / Lila, the joy of my eyes, appeared to me. // As before, she whispered to me in her nefarious way: / "I swear to the moon to be yours eternally." // As before, the moon disappeared behind the clouds, / And the unfaithful haze separated us. // I blew the burned tobacco from my pipe, / Sighed and donned my nightcap.)

Written in 1821 or 1822, "The Moon" is the only poem that Del'vig ever wrote in amphibrachic tetrameter couplets with exclusively masculine rhymes. Such unusual formal details leave little doubt that the poem is meant as a rejoinder to Pushkin's "Black Shawl." Indeed, Del'vig's verses not only share the unusual meter with Pushkin's, but even borrow words and the basic motif of lost love. In Pushkin's opening couplet, we find the key concepts "to look" ("gliadet'") and "sadness" ("pechal'").

> *Гляжу* как безумный на черную шаль,
> И хладную душу терзает *печаль.*

(I *look* like a madman at the black shawl / And *sadness* tears at my cold soul.)

These words, in the context of the amphibrachic tetrameter meter are, of course, strongly marked and would have been immediately recognizable to a Russian reader of 1821 or 1822. It is therefore telling that Del'vig combines them in his own opening couplet:

> Я вечером с трубкой сидел у окна;
> *Печально глядела* в окошко луна.

(I sat at the window in the evening with my pipe; / The moon *looked sadly* through the window.)

Like Pushkin, Del'vig brings the narrator into the poem with the very first word.[32] In a similar way, he introduces the theme of the beloved indirectly, using a noun of feminine gender (in Pushkin a metonymic shawl, in Del'vig the metaphoric moon) to adumbrate her actual appearance.[33] Indeed, Del'vig makes a point of using the exact lexicon that Pushkin has placed at his disposal. In "The Black Shawl," the servant waits for the "evening haze" ("vecherniaia mgla") to dispose of the bodies. In "The Moon," the separation occurs during the "unfaithful haze" ("nevernaia mgla"). The missing Pushkinian adjective "evening" ("vecherniaia") appears in Del'vig's phrase "evening lights" ("vechernikh luchei," translated above as "beams of the moon"), which in turn rhymes with "joy of my eyes" ("vesel'e ochei"). "Joy of my eyes" creates yet another intertextual allusion, this time through rhyme, since Pushkin had used the rhyme pair "charming eyes" ("prelestnykh *ochei*") and "joyous nights" ("veselykh *nochei*"). As the poem continues, one recognizes still other basic ingredients of Pushkin's text: the themes of a woman's betrayal and the hero's remembrance of her. Yet while Pushkin's poem concludes with the verbatim repetition of the first couplet (thereby suggesting that these memories continue to torment the speaker), Del'vig's poem ends on a note of quiet resignation.

Rather than recounting a scene of passion and murder, the speaker empties his burnt-out pipe, sighs, and puts on his nightcap.[34]

Aksakov's poem was an imitation of Pushkin, but Del'vig's is something quite different: a parody.[35] In his fourteen-line poem, Del'vig insistently refers to Pushkin's "Black Shawl" through meter, rhyme, lexicon, structure, and theme. The fact that his poem was written within a year or so of the appearance of Pushkin's immensely popular ballad makes their connection yet more obvious. Two elements deserve emphasis. First, it is surely the meter that calls attention to the textual associations. The thematic links (love and betrayal) and common lexicon would not be sufficient to allow us to posit an intertextual link. However, in the context of this rare a form (used only once by Pushkin and only once by Del'vig), one may safely assume that Del'vig was consciously modeling his own poem on Pushkin's enormously successful example. Secondly, Del'vig's poem should be understood not simply as a mockery of Pushkin's, but as a true literary polemic, a direct response to Pushkin's challenge that he write a heroic narrative poem. Del'vig takes all the requisite elements, but combines them in such a way as to spell a complete rejection of this type of poetry. Like his hero in "The Moon," he considers the clichés of Romanticism and ultimately dismisses them. He does this, first and foremost, by selecting a meter which, for his contemporaries, immediately created a thematic expectation. By using the same lexicon and even the same theme, but replacing the climax with an anticlimax, Del'vig changes Pushkin's Romantic tale of betrayal and revenge into a harmless lament, an elegy of sorts (ironically, the very genre that Pushkin sought to escape in the poems of his southern exile).

It is not surprising that parody, which functions by furnishing a recognizable form with an unexpected (and contrary) content, should rely on metrical allusion. However, the association of meter and thematics need not serve a parodic (Del'vig) or strictly imitative (Aksakov) purpose. Among the handful of nineteenth-century Russian poems written in the "Black Shawl" meter (amphibrachic tetrameter couplets with masculine rhyme), one finds a single example in Lermontov's verse:

Баллада

Над морем красавица-дева сидит;
И, к другу ласкаяся, так говорит:

"Достань ожерелье, спустися на дно;
Сегодня в пучину упало оно!

Ты этим докажешь свою мне любовь!"
Вскипела лихая у юноши кровь,

И ум его обнял невольный недуг,
Он в пенную бездну кидается вдруг.

Из бездны перловые брызги летят,
И волны теснятся, и мчатся назад,

И снова приходят и о берег бьют,
Вот милого друга они принесут.

О счастье! он жив, он скалу ухватил,
В руке ожерелье, но мрачен как был.

Он верить боится усталым ногам,
И влажные кудри бегут по плечам . . .

"Скажи, не люблю иль люблю я тебя,
Для перлов прекрасной и жизнь не щадя,

По слову спустился на черное дно,
В коралловом гроте лежало оно. –

Возьми!"– и печальный он взор устремил
На то, что дороже он жизни любил.

Ответ был: "О милый, о юноша мой!
Достань, если любишь, коралл дорогой."

С душой безнадежной младой удалец
Прыгнул, чтоб найти иль коралл, иль конец.

Из бездны перловые брызги летят,
И волны теснятся, и мчатся назад,

И снова приходят и о берег бьют,
Но милого друга они не несут.[36]

(Ballad: A beautiful maiden sat by the sea / And, caressing her friend, said, // "Dive down to the bottom and fetch my necklace. / This morning it fell into the depths! // In this way you will prove your love to me!" / The youth's daring blood became heated. // And an involuntary ailment came over his reason. / He leapt suddenly into the foaming abyss. // From the abyss flew pearl-like gusts of water, / And the waves crowded together and rushed back, // And again they came and beat against the shore, / And they carried with them the dear friend. // O joy! He's alive, he has grasped the rock, / His hand holds the necklace, but he is gloomy. // He is afraid to trust his exhausted legs, / And his wet curls rush along his shoulders . . . //

"Tell me if I love you or not; / For the pearls of my beloved, risking death, // I descended at your command to the black bottom. / It was lying in a grotto of coral. // Take it!" – And he fixed his saddened gaze / On the one whom he loved more dearly than his own life. // She answered: "O my dear youth! / If you love me, fetch me the precious coral." // With a hopeless soul the daring youth / Leapt to find either the coral or his death. // From the abyss flew pearl-like gusts of water, / And the waves crowded together and rushed back, // And again they came and beat against the shore, / But they did not carry with them the dear friend.)

Dating from 1829, this poem belongs to the earliest period of Lermontov's work. Although nominally part of a small group of translations from Schiller, this "Ballad" is quite distant from the poem it purports to translate. The original, Schiller's "Der Taucher" ("The Diver," 1797), is indeed a ballad, but it is 162 lines long. Lermontov's truncated version dispenses with all of the descriptive passages (for which the original is famous) as well as much of the plot. The most radical semantic change concerns the cast of characters. In Schiller's poem, a king throws a golden goblet into the raging sea and urges his knights and vassals to fetch and keep it. The knights prove too scared, but one daring squire plunges into the depths and miraculously returns with the goblet. The king then throws in a golden ring and bids the same youth to fetch it. This prompts the king's daughter to intercede and urge an end to his cruel game. The king responds to her plea by raising the stakes: he promises his daughter to the squire should he succeed. The youth again leaps into the sea, never to return.

In Lermontov's version, one is immediately struck by the thematic changes. Most significantly, there is no king. His role is taken over by the female protagonist (a "krasavitsa-deva" – "beautiful maiden"), no longer the virtuous woman depicted by Schiller. Rather than seeking to save the youth from her father's cruel challenge, she herself assumes the role of temptress. The hero is not simply an obscure and unknown member of the king's retinue, but the maiden's "dear friend," who loves her "more dearly than his own life."

On the level of meter, Lermontov's translation is equally puzzling. Like many German ballads, Schiller's poem is a *dol'nik*, which, it will be recalled, proved to be an extremely complicated form for nineteenth-century Russian translators. Lermontov clearly recognized this problem when he undertook his Schiller translations. His rendering of "Der Handschuh" ("The Glove," 1797), for example, is one of a handful of nineteenth-century Russian attempts to mirror the accentual verse of the German original. In his version of "The Diver," however, Lermontov makes no effort to reflect the form of the original. Not only does he substitute regular amphibrachs for the accentual *dol'nik*; he even sacrifices Schiller's six-line stanzas (with a-b-a-b-C-C rhyme scheme), opting instead for masculine rhyming couplets.

How is one to explain such sweeping formal and semantic changes? Boris Eikhenbaum, in his detailed commentary to the 1936 Academy edition, grapples with these issues. In regard to the thematic changes, he suggests that Lermontov "contaminates" the plot of two Schiller ballads – "The Diver" and "The Glove." In the latter, a nefarious female protagonist drops her glove into a lion's den and forces her admirer to fetch it in order to prove his love. Eikhenbaum thus offers a plausible model for the heroine of Lermontov's "Ballad." Yet two factors call his claim into question. First, except for the motif of the evil beloved, Lermontov's "Ballad" has little to do with Schiller's "Glove" (in which the protagonist, having miraculously succeeded in his task, hurls the trophy at his lady and storms away). Secondly, Lermontov was working at this very time on a translation of "The Glove," which he obviously understood as a separate entity. (No elements of "The Diver" intrude into this translation.) In regard to the question of metrics, Eikhenbaum emphasizes that the drafts of Lermontov's poem indicate that, "in certain verses, under the influence of Schiller's original, he attempted the change the anacrusis, [thereby] shifting to an anapest."[37] This observation is intriguing, since individual lines of Schiller's poem can be read as anapests, while other lines can be read as amphibrachs. Nonetheless, it must be remembered that most lines of Schiller's ballad are accentual, that is, *neither* amphibrachic *nor* anapestic. Moreover, even if Lermontov had at one point felt that a mixture of ternary meters best rendered the German *dol'nik*, he clearly rejected this idea, since his final version contains no trace of any such experiment.

In short, Eikhenbaum's conclusions, ingenious as they are, cannot be accepted. In this instance, metrical semantics allows us an alternative – and rather obvious – explanation. When Lermontov decided to use the extremely unusual form of amphibrachic couplets with masculine rhymes, he did not do so randomly. Seeking to render the "clumsy" German *dol'nik* into Russian verse, he opted for the identical solution that Zhukovsky had reached several years earlier in his translation from Uhland. However, Zhukovsky's choice of amphibrachic tetrameter couplets was an innovation. By the time the young Lermontov used this strophic and metrical constellation, the situation had changed considerably. As the Aksakov and Del'vig poems indicate, the extraordinary popularity of Pushkin's "Black Shawl" had canonized this form, providing it with a genre (the ballad) as well as a specific semantic realization (love, betrayal, a brutal murder).[38] In other words, for a poet as "tradition-conscious" as Lermontov, the choice of this distinctive a form was necessarily accompanied by a predetermined theme.[39]

In this context, it is worth returning to Lermontov's semantic changes. His poem, a tale of love, deception, and murder, fits neatly into the horizon of expectations created by Pushkin's "Black Shawl." Pushkin's poem provides certain motifs (the unfaithful beautiful young woman, the dead body in the water) and, once the connection is recognized, even specific word choice. Thus, one can observe, aside from the obvious repetitions demanded by the plot (forms of the verb "to love," "sadness"), other words not entirely necessary (e.g., "waves," forms of the verbs "to rush" and "to caress"), and even the subtle phonological echo of Pushkin's "until a black day" ("do chernogo dnia," translated above as "But soon I lived to regret it") in Lermontov's phrase "to the black bottom" ("na chernoe dno"). Most importantly, Lermontov's central plot change (whereby Schiller's merciful heroine becomes deceitful) brings his poem further away from his German (semantic) source and closer to his Russian (metrical) model.[40]

The derivative nature of most of Lermontov's early poetry has long been noted.[41] However, insufficient emphasis has been placed on his early achievements, in particular, his experimental use of meter. In his translation of Schiller's ballads, Lermontov's approach to translation indicates an extremely subtle understanding of diachronic poetics. In rendering the accentual verse of "The Glove," he attempted to recreate the "identical" meter (a radical, almost unprecedented solution for the time). In his "Ballad," he opted for an entirely different approach, which might be termed the "equivalent" meter (a meter that – through repeated usage or a single powerful example – has come to be associated with a given content). Genetically speaking, his form is completely unrelated to that of

Schiller. Yet, for a reader familiar with Russian poetry, Lermontov's meter conveys a ballad far more convincingly than a direct imitation would have. On a perhaps subconscious level, the Russian reader was expected to perceive Schiller's poem as a variation on a Pushkinian theme. A final, unanswerable question arises: was Lermontov conscious of the Zhukovsky translation that inspired Pushkin's "Black Shawl"? If so, the meter may serve yet another purpose: to point indirectly to his poem's German origin.[42]

The youthful "Ballad" demonstrates Lermontov's ability to take advantage of previous models.[43] It also makes abundantly clear the need for metrics as a means of understanding individual poems. In the final analysis, Pushkin's metrical model affords the only plausible explanation for Lermontov's formal decisions and, ultimately, for his semantic changes. Once again, form is not only linked to genre; it *demands* overarching themes, specific motifs, and even lexical choices. Lermontov thus "translates" the foreign (Schiller) in terms of the familiar (Pushkin). The fact that this precise metrical and strophic form appears only once in all of Lermontov's poetic output – and only once in Pushkin's – should silence any suspicion that coincidence was at work.

The handful of poems discussed above represents virtually the only Russian poems written before 1830 in masculine couplets of amphibrachic tetrameter.[44] All are ballads and all point back to Pushkin's poem (with the exception, of course, of Zhukovsky's "Revenge," which preceded it). In short, while Pushkin was not the "inventor" of this metrical/generic nexus, his example was far more influential than Zhukovsky's.

The few poems in this meter from the 1830s indicate that the generic associations of the meter remained, as well as certain specific motifs. Even a decade after its creation, Pushkin's poem had lost none of its popularity; in fact, in 1831, it was (once again) adapted for the stage, this time as a ballet entitled "The Black Shawl, or Punished Infidelity."[45] In that same year, a new parody of Pushkin's poem appeared. Del'vig had structured his parody by creating a protagonist whose resigned response to his beloved's betrayal contradicted the impulsive and bloody actions of Pushkin's hero. The anonymous author of the 1831 parody reverses more than just the protagonist's reaction. Written from the point of view of a woman, the poem uses Pushkin's lexicon and phraseology to tell a tremendously un-Byronic tale:

Гляжу я безмолвно на белый султан,
И душу терзает любовь и обман.[46]

(I look silently at the white plume, and love and deceit tear at my soul.)

This opening couplet suffices to demonstrate the poem's basic strategy. The parodist borrows vocabulary and plot (love and betrayal) from Pushkin's model. However, he reverses the main characters and their behavior. In the opening lines (which, as in Pushkin, repeat as a refrain at the poem's conclusion), a white plume replaces the black shawl. Aside from the obvious color change, this substitution reflects a subtle understanding of Pushkin's text, in which the grammatically feminine noun "shawl" serves as a metonymy for the murdered heroine. In the parody, the "plume," a grammatically masculine noun, takes the place of the hero, who (as the female narrator laments) absconds to the Caucasus immediately after setting eyes upon her. Using mock seriousness and anticlimax, the poem reduces Pushkin's violent tale to harmless absurdity.

Two other minor poems of the 1830s deserve attention in the context of our study, Dmitri Oznobishin's "Chudnaia bandura" ("The Magical Bandura," 1835) and Fedor Koni's "Chudnaia arfa" ("The Magical Harp," 1838).[47] These poems are close enough in theme (and even in title) to lead one to believe that the second was based on the first. More importantly, both can be easily traced – metrically, generically, and motivically – to Pushkin's model. Like "The Black Shawl," they are ballads, set in exotic places (one in the Don region, one in a stylized medieval England), and their plots revolve around love and betrayal. In each, we find even the familiar motif of the beloved's corpse in the water. Yet these deaths come about not through the faithlessness of the lovers themselves, but through evil external influences. In Oznobishin's poem, a "rusalka"[48] snatches away the bride on her wedding day. In Koni's poem, the heroine is drowned by her treacherous sister shortly before her wedding. In terms of the thematic associations of this meter, the most remarkable innovation occurs at the end. In both poems, the death proves temporary, when, through music, the beloved is brought back to life. This "happy ending" suggests that the poets in question were following Pushkin's model more in a generic way than as a specific master-plot. Direct lexical echoes of Pushkin are infrequent in Oznobishin, but nonetheless present: e.g., "When I was a carefree child" ("Kogda ia rebenkom bespechnym byla"; cf. "When I was young and quick to believe" ["Kogda legkoveren i molod ia byl"]). In Koni, however, there are no specific lexical echoes and even the meter is not strictly maintained.[49]

After these popular, but somewhat formulaic poems, the form of "The Black Shawl" – never widely used – went into virtual oblivion for the remainder of the century.[50] Nikolai Nekrasov, the only major poet to use rhyming couplets with frequency, appears never to have written a complete poem in amphibrachic rhyming couplets with masculine rhymes. In fact, the most influential poem from the latter part of the nineteenth century in the meter of "The Black Shawl" was surely the so-called "Romans" ("Romance," 1884) of Russia's parodic master Koz'ma Prutkov:[51]

> На мягкой кровати
> Лежу я один.
> В соседней палате
> Кричит армянин.
>
> Кричит он и стонет,
> Красотку обняв,
> И голову клонит,
> Вдруг слышно: пиф-паф! . . .
>
> Упала девчина
> И тонет в крови . . .
> Донской казачина
> Клянется в любви . . .
>
> А в небе лазурном
> Трепещет луна;
> И, с шнуром мишурным,
> Лишь шапка видна.
>
> В соседней палате
> Замолк армянин.
> На узкой кровати
> Лежу я один.[52]

(On a soft bed / I lie alone. / In the neighboring room / An Armenian screams. // He screams and moans, / Having embraced a beautiful woman, / And he bends his head, / Suddenly a "piff-paff" sound is audible! . . . // The young woman has fallen / And is covered in blood . . . / An enormous Cossack from the Don / Swears his love . . . // And in the azure sky / The moon trembles; / And, with its tinsel string, / Only a hat is visible. // In the neighboring room / The Armenian has fallen silent. / On the narrow bed / I lie alone.)

Its title and four-line stanzas notwithstanding, this poem explicitly looks back to "The Black Shawl" and its various imitations. Not only is the form transparently derived from this tradition (the amphibrachic tetrameter lines of "The Black Shawl" are simply divided into two, with additional rhymes added at the hemistichs), but even the love triangle and the specific *dramatis personae* represent a pastiche of Pushkin (the Armenian), Aksakov (the Cossack), and Del'vig (the moon). Most curious, of course, is the speaker, who – in direct contrast to the first-person heroes of Pushkin and Del'vig – is a calm observer rather than an active participant. Precisely his lack of emotional involvement renders the poem's refrain absurd. (The passion and brutality affect the speaker only to the extent that his "soft" bed becomes a "narrow" one.) Even the symbolic shawl of Pushkin's text is reduced to a meaningless hat (another noun of feminine gender, but here without any metaphoric or metonymic function). Prutkov's somewhat enigmatic genre designation of "romance" is probably derived from the "Moldavian song" of Pushkin's subtitle. However, the balladic nature of this verse remains indisputable. In one redaction, the poem was even called "The Cossack and the Armenian (A Ballad)" and was accompanied by the author's explanatory footnote: "The music of my own invention will be published for the pleasure of readers in the complete edition of my works."[53] This music was surely a mystification, but it served to remind the reader of the numerous musical incarnations of Pushkin's popular poem. For subsequent poets, the deliberate absurdity of Prutkov's "Romance" might have spelled the end for any further allusion to or creative application of "The Black Shawl." However, Russian poetic tradition was to prove itself quite resourceful.

In Russian cultural history, the twentieth century ushered in an extraordinary renaissance often called the "Silver Age."[54] After the hegemony of prose fiction in the latter half of the nineteenth century, poetry again came to occupy a central position. With a rich knowledge of tradition and a renewed interest in declamation, craft, and metrical diversity, the poets of the "Silver Age" sought consciously to revive and develop the work of their "Golden Age" predecessors, in particular that of Pushkin. According to the formulation of Boris Gasparov, "The inhabitant of the Silver Age lived in a world where the reincarnated 'Pushkin principle' was omnipresent."[55] In this atmosphere of imitation and experimentation, the form of "The Black Shawl" reappeared. However, the direct connection between Pushkinian form and content was no longer so predictable.

The very first reappearance of this distinctive form coincides with the new century, in Konstantin Fofanov's "Rusalka," published in his book *Illiuzii* (Illusions, 1900). As the title implies, the poem is based on a folkloric theme:

> Вечерней порою при тусклой луне
> Мечтательный витязь скакал на коне.
>
> И слышит, у речки, в густом тростнике,
> Русалка рыдает в глубокой тоске.

(In the evening by the dim light of the moon / A dreamy knight galloped on his horse. // He heard at the river's edge, in the thick reeds, / A rusalka was sobbing in deep anguish.)

There is little reason to cite the remainder of the ballad, for it follows a predictable course. Imitation outweighs innovation in a highly derivative version of the corpse-in-the-water motif. Diana Burgin has recognized that both the theme and the meter recall Lermontov's "translation" of Schiller.[56] In other words, Fofanov clearly harks back to the Pushkin tradition not only in his choice of genre, but even in his orientation on a specific text that was itself directly influenced by Pushkin's poem.

Things get more complicated when we turn to the work of the leading Symbolists. In the first years of the twentieth century, Andrei Bely wrote a number of poems in amphibrachs. Not unlike Fofanov, though with much greater freedom, Bely used amphibrachs to evoke an atmosphere of folklore and myth. A remarkable consistency of theme and spirit makes clear that he systematically linked this meter to a single semantic field. His amphibrachic tetrameter poems with exclusively masculine rhymes were all devoted to a single subject: centaurs. The relevant poems are "Kentavr" ("The Centaur"), "Pesn' kentavra" ("The Song of the Centaur"), and "Son" ("The Dream").[57] Only in the last of these, however, do we find the visually distinctive couplet stanzas of "The Black Shawl":

Сон

> И стены распались . . . И все отнеслось . . .
> И лес проступил сквозь обои; лилось –

Сплетение линий: струей ручейка;
Прордели мельканием два мотылька . . .

Двурогий кентавр из сосновых стволов
Мохнатой рукою распугивал сов . . .

Двурогий кентавр незабудок дождем
Мохнатой рукою рассыпал кругом.

Я слышал раскатистый хохот его;
И счастья не мог позабыть своего.

Но солнца сломалась громовая ось . . .
И стены – вернулись: и все – пронеслось.[58]

(The Dream: And the walls disintegrated . . . And everything was carried
away . . . / And the forest appeared through the wallpaper; there poured
forth – // The interlacing of lines: like the flowing of a brook; / Two
butterflies glowed as they fluttered by . . . / A two-horned centaur with its
hairy arm / Scared away owls from the pine trunks . . . // A two-horned
centaur with its hairy arm / Poured out a rain of forget-me-nots
everywhere. // I heard its booming laughter; / And I could not forget my
happiness. // But the sun's thunderous axle broke . . . / And the walls –
returned: and everything – rushed by.)

A full interpretation of this poem would entail a discussion of
Bely's fascination with centaur depictions in the work of the German
Symbolist painter Franz von Stuck, as well as a host of private
associations shared by the group of Bely's friends known as the
Argonauts.[59] For present purposes, however, it is sufficient to
consider the poem on its own terms. "The Dream" depicts a
characteristically Symbolist theme – an otherworldly vision that
temporarily removes the speaker from quotidian reality. This vi-
sionary moment concludes with daybreak ("the sun's thunderous
axle" – presumably a reference to the mythical chariot of the sun).
While Bely's poem lacks the plot development characteristic of most
ballads, it shares certain features with the subgenre of "magic nature
ballads."[60] In these poems (Goethe's "Erlkönig" being the best-
known example), a mortal comes into contact with superhuman
forces. However, this encounter traditionally leads to a mysterious
death, while in Bely's poem it has no lasting effect ("and everything
– rushed by"). As regards the specific balladic tradition of "The
Black Shawl," connections are few. The treacherous woman is
replaced by a frolicking centaur; in lieu of murder and vengeance we
find laughter and mirth. The only structural link is the refrain. In

"The Dream," the first and last couplets rhyme with each other and share the essential word "walls," which serves as a literal and figurative frame.[61] In short, while careful comparison reveals certain points of contact between "The Dream" and the ballad tradition, one should not overestimate them. Bely displays considerable independence from the trajectory that began with Zhukovsky and Pushkin, and his poem demonstrates that "The Black Shawl" no longer had a monopoly on thematic (or even generic) incarnations of amphibrachic tetrameter couplets with masculine rhyme.

Aleksandr Blok, whose "cult of Pushkin"[62] was recognized even by his contemporaries, wrote two poems in the form that concerns us: "Po beregu plelsia bol'noi chelovek" ("The sick man dragged himself along the shore," 1903) and "Angel-khranitel'" ("Guardian Angel," 1906). The former is a ballad, but shares only its genre with Pushkin's poem. The plot concerns a gypsy woman who picks up a dying wanderer in her cart and delivers his corpse to his wife. The latter, the poet's direct address to his "Guardian Angel," bears virtually no resemblance – beyond meter (and even this does not remain constant) – to Pushkin's poem. In terms of theme, "Guardian Angel" is far closer to the civic rhetoric of Nekrasov than to Pushkin.[63]

However, a third poem, while not written in amphibrachs, bears more than a passing resemblance to Pushkin's "Black Shawl." I have in mind the first poem of the cycle "Chernaia krov'" ("Black Blood," 1914). In this case, already the coincidence of titles leads one to expect similarities. Not only is the word "black" repeated (in Russian, the gender remains the same), but the specific substitution of "blood" for "shawl" reflects the spirit of Pushkin's text, where the protagonist had used the shawl ("shal'") to wipe his beloved's blood ("krov'") from his sword. Blok even closes his poem with the rhyme "krov'"/"liubov'" ("blood"/"love") – a hackneyed combination that can be excused largely because it had previously appeared in "The Black Shawl."[64] Like Pushkin's model, Blok's poem is written in the first person:

> Вполоборота ты встала ко мне,
> Грудь и рука твоя видится мне.
>
> Мать запрещает тебе подходить,
> Мне – искушенье тебя оскорбить![65]

(You stood up facing me at an angle, / I see your breast and hand. //

[Your] mother forbids you to come close to me, / For me it is a temptation to offend you!)

These verses may not formally coincide with Pushkin's poem, but they most definitely recall it. They are written in a four-foot ternary meter (dactylic rather than amphibrachic), in couplets with exclusively masculine rhyme. In terms of theme, they introduce a familiar set of characters: a malevolent and excitable speaker with a potentially fatal attraction to a young woman. While betrayal and murder remain only hints, this brief introductory poem contains numerous passages that resonate with Pushkin's model. For example, Blok repeatedly emphasizes the motif of looking:

> Взор мой горит у тебя на щеке,
> Трепет бежит по дрожащей руке . . .
>
> Ширится круг твоего мне огня,
> Ты, и не глядя, глядишь на меня!

(My glance burns on your cheek, / A shudder runs along [my] trembling arm . . . // The circle of your fire spreads out to me, / You look at me even when you are not looking!)

The emphatic repetition of the verb "gliadet'" ("to look") strongly recalls the very first word of Pushkin's ballad ("gliazhu" – "I look").[66] Moreover, the ellipsis after the phrase "trembling arm" suggests (particularly for the reader who recalls its function in "The Black Shawl") an act of violence that does in fact occur later in the cycle. Perhaps the most important reason for recognizing the Pushkinian echoes, however, is generic. Ballads tend not to be autobiographical poems: just as Pushkin's bloodthirsty hero was not to be confused with Pushkin himself, so Blok's first-person speaker should not be identified with the poet. "Black Blood" is not a confession; rather, Blok models his unappealing protagonist on one of the famous villains in Russian poetic history.[67] It is not the last time we will observe this phenomenon.

Anna Akhmatova's reception of Pushkin's text is remarkably akin to Blok's. Her famous early poem "Seroglazyi korol'" ("The Grey-Eyed King," 1910), uses the same meter as "Black Blood." Despite the substitution of dactyls for amphibrachs, Akhmatova's poem recalls "The Black Shawl" in form (couplets with exclusively masculine rhyme), genre (a ballad), and theme (love, betrayal, murder):

Сероглазый король

Слава тебе, безысходная боль!
Умер вчера сероглазый король.

Вечер осенний был душен и ал,
Муж мой, вернувшись, спокойно сказал:

"Знаешь, с охоты его принесли,
Тело у старого дуба нашли.

Жаль королеву. Такой молодой! . . .
За ночь одну она стала седой."

Трубку свою на камине нашел
И на работу ночную ушел.

Дочку мою я сейчас разбужу,
В серые глазки ее погляжу.

А за окном шелестят тополя:
Нет на земле твоего короля.[68]

(The Grey-Eyed King: Glory to you, inescapable pain! / The grey-eyed
king died yesterday. // The autumn evening was stuffy and crimson, / My
husband, upon returning, said calmly: // "You know, they brought him
back from the hunt, / They found his body by an old oak." // A pity for
the queen. [The king] was so young. / In a single night she turned grey."
// He found his pipe on the fireplace / And went off to his night's work. //
Now I will wake my daughter, / I will look in her little grey eyes. // But
beyond the window the poplars rustle: / Your king is no longer on this
earth.)

Akhmatova achieves a subtlety rare to the genre by leaving the
plot in the background and shifting the focus to emotion. Writing in
the first person, the poet only vaguely suggests the murder and the
motive behind it. As in Pushkin's example, the poem gains psychological richness by beginning with the chronologically final moment.
The "inescapable pain" is mentioned immediately, but explained
only in the subsequent verses. Curiously, Akhmatova seems to blend
Pushkinian themes and techniques with a model more distant
semantically, but more precise metrically: Nekrasov's lighthearted
hunting poem, "Psovaia okhota" ("The Hunt with Dogs," 1846).
One can trace the intonation of Akhmatova's opening line to
Nekrasov's paean to the hunting dogs: "Слава тебе, неизменный
Нахал . . . Слава тебе, резвоножка Победка!" ("Glory to
you, unchanging Rascal . . . Glory to you, fleet-footed Victory!") in

the dactylic couplets of the fifth section of his poem.[69] Here one recognizes what might be termed a "reverse parody."[70] Akhmatova turns Nekrasov's jocular scene from folk culture into a serious and enigmatic ballad, retaining certain folk elements and the crucial theme of the hunt. In short, Akhmatova responds to "The Black Shawl" like Blok, in a poem that is formally close, but not identical. She ultimately moved away from the balladic associations of Pushkin's amphibrachic meter and – probably inspired by Nekrasov – replaced them with civic rhetoric. The second epilogue of "Requiem" (1940) is written in the precise meter and stanzaic pattern of "The Black Shawl," yet has no thematic connection whatsoever to Pushkin's model.

The 1924 novel in verse "Razboinik Van'ka-Kain i Son'ka-Mani-kiurshchitsa" ("The Brigand Van'ka Kain and Son'ka the Manicurist") of the Cubo-Futurist poet Aleksei Kruchenykh indicates that Pushkin's poem continued to exert an influence – in terms of form, genre, and semantics – on poets of the most varied schools. Kruchenykh prided himself on his irreverent attitude to tradition (at one point proclaiming that a certain Mr. Krysiun's six-item laundry list was stylistically superior to eight lines of *Eugene Onegin*),[71] yet his works evince manifold links to the poetry of his nineteenth-century predecessors. Kruchenykh himself recognized the irony of this situation when in his 1921 programmatic essay "Sdvigologiia russkogo stikha" ("The Shiftology of Russian Verse"), he exclaimed: "Strange as it may be, it falls to the lot of the Futurists (largely destroyers) to be the guardians of verse craft and poetic technique!"[72]

Kruchenykh's approach to tradition is most clearly reflected in a work contemporaneous with "Van'ka Kain," a 1924 essay entitled "500 novykh ostrot i kalamburov Pushkina" ("500 New Witticisms and Puns of Pushkin"). In this essay, building on the basic ideas of his earlier work on "shiftology," he uses Pushkin's verse to demonstrate the frequency and significance of the "zvukovoi sdvig" ("sound shift").[73] In brief, Kruchenykh's method consists in focusing attention on the way that sound can alter meaning. Thus, in the word "стихотворения" ("verses"), Kruchenykh recognizes the phrase "стих от варения" ("[he] fell silent from jam").[74] When applied to Pushkin's poetry, as Kruchenykh himself emphasizes, the possibilities are almost endless. Under Kruchenykh's guidance, the reader becomes aware of numerous puns and double-entendres that had previously gone unnoticed. To give a single example, Kruchenykh takes a line from Pushkin's early "Poslanie Lide" ("Epistle to Lida"):

> Но с бочкой странствуя пустою
> ("But wandering with an empty barrel").

By "shifting" the third letter of this line to adjoin it to the second, he creates the phonologically similar, but semantically Gogolian phrase:

> Нос бочкой странствуя пустою
> ("The nose, wandering like an empty barrel").

A minor shift in sound thus engenders a radical change in meaning. Needless to say, the new reading considerably alters (obscures) the traditional understanding of Pushkin's line. (In its original context, the passage obviously refers to Diogenes, yet Kruchenykh passes over this detail in order to maximize the incongruous comic effect. According to him, the line refers to the poem's heroine and dedicatee: "Lida has a nose like a barrel, and an empty one at that!")[75] What is important here is not the scholarly value of "shiftology," but its creative potential: what does it offer to the poet? For Kruchenykh, the word is primarily the spoken word. By concentrating on the aural component of verse, he allows "hidden" meanings and associations to surface. While Kruchenykh recognized the necessity of writing poetry down – indeed, today he is primarily remembered for his numerous experiments in graphic layout and book design[76] – his intention was to foreground the aural aspect of language, to realize the virtually untapped communicative potential of old words and to create new ones (neologisms and "trans-rational language" ["zaum'"]). For a true Futurist poet, then, sound becomes the driving force of verse. An elaborate system of phonological and rhythmical echoes takes priority over logical, thematic, or motivic development.

This approach to poetry is evident already in the generic designation of the novel in verse "The Brigand Van'ka Kain and Son'ka the Manicurist": Kruchenykh calls it a *"foneticheskii* roman" (*"phonetic* novel"). In this work, plot motivation is reduced to a minimum, while sound organization becomes central. Kruchenykh includes substandard Russian, speech impediments, thieves' cant, and neologisms to create an appropriately rich linguistic texture. The title characters of Kruchenykh's work would have been familiar to readers of the 1920s, for Van'ka Kain and "Son'ka-Zolotaia ruchka" ("Son'ka Golden-hand") were the subjects of numerous popular crime novels.[77] Even the basic plot belongs to the genre of boulevard fiction: it concerns Van'ka Kain's escape from prison, which is abetted by the beautiful Son'ka – against the wishes of her husband, the warden, who witnesses her treachery.[78] In Kruchenykh's handling, however, these characters behave in ways that increasingly defy the demands of logic. In the background of this bewildering triangle of love, betrayal, and ultimately murder lurks the powerful example of Pushkin's "Black Shawl."

The very beginning of the novel prepares the reader for a tale of crime and passion (the typographical peculiarities are all in the original):

> В полночь
> в черном
>   кружевном
>   шарфе
> **когда желанья**
>   **жгут**
>   **кожу**
> Пре-кра-сная Ме-р-се-дес
> девушка со своим восьмым мужем
> начальником Саратовской тюрьмы –
>   порывистее, чем авто,
>   тоньше, чем ось,
>   гиб
>   че
>   чем
>   луч,
> спустилась
>   в подземелье.[79]

(At midnight / in a black / lace / scarf / **when desires / burn / the skin** / Beau-ti-ful Mer-ce-des / a young woman together with her eighth husband / the head of the Saratov jail – / more impulsive than an auto, / thinner than an axle, / more malleable / than / a ray of light / descended / into the dungeon.)

This opening passage brings the reader *in medias res*, with the heroine descending to the underground cell of Van'ka Kain. While the poem's title has identified her as "Son'ka" (a common Russian diminutive), she suddenly is given the improbable appellation "Mercedes."[80] In terms of plot, this is gratingly illogical, as the action unambiguously takes place in the Russian backwater Saratov. However, it is a telling detail, for the new name has exotic "southern" and therefore (according to age-old Russian stereotypes accepted by Pushkin and now by Kruchenykh) sensual associations.[81] Mercedes is the archetypal "loose woman," and she even wears the literary emblem of infidelity: a black scarf.[82] As if this were not enough, we learn that this young woman is already on her *eighth* husband. So strong is her erotic aura that the midnight hour is depicted – in boldface – as the time "when desires burn the skin." Clearly, this is a fickle woman, ready to fall for any rake who crosses her path. As it turns out, however, the rake does not even need to cross her path: Mercedes seeks him out. Yet she betrays her husband not by becoming Kain's lover (as the opening leads us to expect), but by assisting in his escape from her husband's jail.[83]

When, after numerous digressions, Mercedes performs this ultimate act of infidelity, she makes the seemingly gratuitous plea that Kain take her Spanish shawl (a sudden metamorphosis of the black scarf of the opening lines). She exclaims:

> "Беги!
> Для тебя все готово!
> Да захвати вот испанскую шаль!"[84]

("Run! / Everything is prepared for you! / And grab this Spanish shawl!")

It is remarkable that the all-important word "shawl" makes its appearance in a passage of regular ternary rhythms, the first two lines scanning as amphibrachic trimeter, the third line as dactylic tetrameter. In the texture of Kruchenykh's novel, which is written in unpredictable accentual verse in a "stepladder-style" layout (see the opening passage quoted above), these lines stand out.[85] Each is derived from Pushkin's "Black Shawl": the first takes the amphibrachic rhythm, the second the tetrameter line and masculine line ending. That such an association was intended is clear from two comments of the husband, who, as an observer, functions as a semicoherent Greek chorus (a speech defect makes him incapable of differentiating between the sounds "s," "z," and "sh"). Even before his wife gives the Spanish shawl to Kain, the warden invokes Pushkin's authority in one of his moralistic ramblings:

> шрамота! шрамота! . . .
> Чтоб вам пошмотреть на Пушкина![86]

(Shame! Shame! / You should look at Pushkin!)

Toward the end of the novel, after bizarre twists of plot too numerous to recount, he observes his wife cut off Kain's tongue with a razor. At this point, the jubilant warden taunts the criminal:

"Эй, рашгони тошку-печаль,
Будешь ты помнить про крашную шаль."[87]

("Hey, chase away anguish and sadness, / Now you'll remember 'bout the red shawl.")

This rhyming couplet is the closest one gets in Kruchenykh's novel to a regular meter. As in the earlier passage when Mercedes gives Kain the shawl, the word "shawl" is the final word of a line of strict dactylic tetrameter. Here the reference to "The Black Shawl" is blatantly obvious, since the "pechal'/shal'" rhyme is taken directly from the first (and final) stanza of Pushkin's poem. The allusion is, of course, intentionally mangled – metrically (the lines are a parody of Pushkin's amphibrachic tetrameter couplets), semantically (red[88] [Spanish] shawl vs. black [Greek?] shawl), and even phonetically (thanks to the warden's speech impediment, the crucial sibilant "sh" recurs with absurd frequency).

In keeping with this parodic spirit, the novel ends with yet another surprising reversal: instead of the wronged husband murdering the adulterous couple (Pushkin's version), the adulterer Kain murders Son'ka (his savior and admirer), leaving her husband to observe the proceedings. In the final lines, he rushes off to the Volga with her dead body slung over his shoulder (an adumbration, it would seem, of the familiar corpse-in-the-water motif, but the text ends too abruptly to allow any definitive conclusions).

Kruchenykh's interest in "The Black Shawl" deserves attention for several reasons. When composing his own highly idiosyncratic triangular constellation of lust, treachery, and murder, Kruchenykh returned to Pushkin's master-text. On the basis of plot alone, one would hardly be able to recognize Pushkin's ballad in this "criminal novel." However, Kruchenykh draws attention to these similarities by borrowing symbols, sounds, and even rhythms from the earlier text. In short, when the thematic subtext is "overdetermined" by the plot, Kruchenykh brings out the resemblance through obvious *metrical* allusions. Far from tossing Pushkin off the steamship of modernity (as he and his comrades-in-arms had advocated in the 1912 Futurist manifesto "Poshchechina obshchestvennomu vkusu" ["A Slap in the Face of Public Taste"]),[89] Kruchenykh recognized in Pushkin a model for the Futurist murder novel.

If, in his "novel in verse," Kruchenykh returned to Pushkin's poem as an archetype of the sordid criminal tale, the work of

Kruchenykh's contemporary, the official Soviet poet Mikhail Svetlov, offers an alternate adaptation of "The Black Shawl." A prolific and enthusiastic follower of the party line, Svetlov was ultimately – even by his own admission – remembered as the author of a single poem: "Grenada." Written in 1926, this poem depicts a Ukrainian communist who marches off to battle inspired by the melodious sound of the word "Grenada." With its unquestioning (and unintellectual) commitment to revolutionary ideals, the poem clearly could receive the blessing of the authorities. However, an enormous number of Soviet poems praised revolution, yet few achieved this kind of genuine popularity. Indeed, the poem received the highest compliment that any Soviet poet could have wished for: Mayakovsky himself recited it on numerous occasions, deeming it "an enormous accomplishment of Soviet proletarian poetry."[90]

"Grenada" is written in eight-line stanzas which, on first glance, appear quite distant from the couplets of Pushkin's "Black Shawl":

> Я хату покинул,
> Пошел воевать,
> Чтоб землю в Гренаде
> Крестьянам отдать.
> Прощайте, родные!
> Прощайте, семья!
> "Гренада, Гренада,
> Гренада моя!"[91]

(I left my hut / I set off to fight / In order to give land / To the peasants in Grenada. / Farewell, relatives! / Farewell, family! / "Grenada, Grenada, / My own Grenada!")

Yet one need only rearrange these verses to recognize that this form is metrically identical to that of Pushkin's "Black Shawl":

> Я хату покинул, пошел воевать,
> Чтоб землю в Гренаде крестьянам отдать.
>
> Прощайте, родные! Прощайте, семья!
> "Гренада, Гренада, Гренада моя!"

Moreover, for all of its civic sentiment (Svetlov later described it as an expression of his nascent "internationalist" world-view), the poem recalls in uncanny ways Pushkin's master-text. To begin with, the key word "Grenada" (repeated numerous times in the course of the poem) sounds suspiciously like "grechanka" ("Greek woman"): both are amphibrachic in rhythm and have distinctly foreign (and therefore exotic) connotations. The fact that both are feminine in gender is significant, for they represent the object of the male subject's longing. The fatal sexual attraction so central to Pushkin's poem is thus reflected (sublimated?) in the Ukrainian patriot's ardent quest for the frequently personified Grenada ("Krasivoe imia, / Vysokaia chest'," ["Beautiful name, / Great honor"] in the words of Svetlov's hero, who, in fact, dies with the name of his "beloved" on his lips: "Grena . . . ").

In addition, many of Svetlov's lines appear to draw on Pushkin's poem either lexically or rhythmically:

> Pushkin: "Мы вышли; я мчался на быстром коне"
> Svetlov: "Мы мчались, мечтая / Постичь поскорей"
> Pushkin: "We set off; I rushed off on my quick steed"
> Svetlov: "We rushed off, dreaming / To understand quickly"

> Pushkin: "Безглавое тело я долго топтал"
> Svetlov: "Пробитое тело / Наземь сползло"[92]
> Pushkin: "I stamped on the headless body at length"
> Svetlov: "The punctured body / Fell to the ground"

> Pushkin: "С тех пор не целую прелестных очей"
> Svetlov: "С тех пор не слыхали / Родные края"
> Pushkin: "Since that time I have not kissed charming eyes"
> Svetlov: "Since that time / The native lands have not heard"

> Pushkin: "Погибла гречанка, погибла любовь!"
> Svetlov: "Прощайте, родные! / Прощайте, семья!"
> Pushkin: "The Greek girl perished, love perished!"
> Svetlov: "Farewell, dear ones! / Farewell, family!"

Finally, and most importantly, one recognizes a fundamental generic continuity. Both poems are ballads: they use simple (non-Russian) characters to tell a story of unhappy love. Of course, Svetlov rewrites Pushkin's tale in consonance with the dictates of Soviet culture. Betrayal, so central to the "Black Shawl," is replaced by unflagging loyalty. Lust and revenge give way to revolutionary fervor.[93]

A work of the contemporary conceptualist poet Dmitri Prigov serves as an appropriate coda to this chapter:

> Когда я в Калуге по случаю был
> Одну калужанку я там полюбил
>
> Была в ней большая народная сила
> Меня на руках она часто носила

А что я? – москвич я, я хрупок и мал
И вот что однажды всердцах ей сказал:

Мужчина ведь мужественней и сильней
Быть должен – на том и расстаилися с ней.[94]

(When I chanced to be in Kaluga, / I came to love a Kalugan girl // There was the great strength of the people in her, / She often would carry me in her arms // But what about me? – I'm a Muscovite, I'm brittle and small / And here's what I said to her in a rage once: // The man should be more manly and powerful [than the woman] – // And with that we parted.)

Prigov's poetry is based on the appropriation of another's words, be they official bureaucratese, political slogan, newspaper jargon, or poetic cliché. Simple in terms of syntax and lexicon, his work presupposes a familiarity with Soviet everyday life and a broad, if not particularly profound, knowledge of Russian literature. In this case, the reader/audience is expected to recall the meter, theme, and rhyme scheme of Pushkin's lines:

Когда легковерен и молод я был,
Младую гречанку я страстно любил.

(When I was young and quick to believe, / I was passionately in love with a young Greek woman.)

Like Pushkin, Prigov tells a love story in the first person. However, he substitutes inexpressive lexical choices for the words that gave Pushkin's poem its atmosphere of exoticism and impulsiveness. Pushkin chose a Greek woman because of the sensual stereotypes associated with southern peoples. Prigov selects a Kaluga woman precisely because she lacks such passionate associations. Moreover, he carefully avoids all adjectives and adverbs that might give his ballad a psychological foundation. Pushkin's protagonist, "young and quick to believe," was "passionately" in love with the "young" Greek woman. Prigov's hero, when he "chanced to be" in Kaluga, "came to love" a nondescript woman there (Prigov opts for the neutral phrase "tam poliubil" rather than Pushkin's unambiguously passionate – and rhythmically equivalent – "strastno liubil"). Having called attention to his source, Prigov immediately distances himself. Formally, his second stanza departs from the model by using feminine rhymes. Semantically, it departs through the sheer absurdity of the scene described. (The Soviet cliché "power of the Russian people" is realized literally as physical strength.) The third stanza returns formally to the meter supplied by Pushkin, yet it recalls through rhyme Akhmatova's "Grey-Eyed King":[95]

Prigov:

> А что я? – москвич я, я хрупок и мал
> И вот что однажды всердцах ей сказал:

(But what about me? – I'm a Muscovite, I'm brittle and small / And here's what I said to her in a rage once:)

Akhmatova:

> Вечер осенний был душен и ал,
> Муж мой, вернувшись, спокойно сказал:

(The autumn evening was stuffy and crimson, / My husband, upon returning, said calmly:)

Because of the striking semantic differences, the echoes in rhythm, rhyme, and grammatical form (the two short adjectives at the end of the first line) produce a comic juxtaposition. The incongruities between the two poems stand out yet more markedly because Prigov's hero (who is apparently afraid of being dropped to the ground) speaks in a fit of rage, in contrast to the husband in Akhmatova's poem, who, although he has seemingly been involved in a murder (this ambiguity is fundamental to her poem's effect), speaks calmly. Like the other parodies we have seen (Del'vig's "The Moon," the anonymous parody of 1831), the poem ends with an anticlimax.[96] In the final lines, Prigov's hero, a classic Soviet male, cannot accept that a woman is stronger than he. This necessarily leads to their separation, at which point the poem ends.

This chapter allows us to make several conclusions about the persistence of poetic memory. In translating a minor German poet, Zhukovsky created for the Russian reader a firm association between a poetic form (amphibrachic tetrameter couplets with exclusively masculine rhyme), genre (the ballad), and plot (betrayal and revenge). Upon acquainting himself with that poem, Pushkin adapted this complex for his own poetic practice, keeping the associations intact but adding a love intrigue to the plot. The success of Pushkin's "Black Shawl" completely eclipsed Zhukovsky's poem, which was soon forgotten. For contemporaries, Pushkin's model became so powerful that his realization of the meter influenced their own use of this form – not only in regard to genre and plot, but even concerning details of lexicon and poetic devices. The "Black Shawl" meter invariably inspired ballads on the theme of love and betrayal, often with specific textual allusions to Pushkin's model. In the twentieth century, these echoes were no longer so predictable, yet "The Black Shawl" continued to exert a palpable influence. Blok and Akhmatova clearly remembered Pushkin's poem, yet, in contrast to earlier poets, they no longer felt the connection between his meter and his thematics as an imperative. Alternative models (most likely Nekrasov's frequent use of amphibrachs and ternary meters in general) allowed for other semantic and generic realizations of Pushkin's meter. However, as the works of Kruchenykh, Svetlov, and Prigov indicate, the metrical and generic model supplied by Pushkin continued to operate even in the Soviet era, fed by vastly different social and ideological presuppositions.

Poets do not simply "pour out their souls." Rather, they write with a keen awareness of tradition. Something of what I have in mind is suggested by the German poet and theoretician Lessing, who, in his work on the fable, stressed the notion of "Bestandheit der Charaktere" (which might best be rendered in English as "unchangeable personalities"). "One hears: *Britannicus and Nero.* How many people know what they are hearing? Who was the former? Who was the latter? What was their relationship to each other? – But one hears: *the wolf and the lamb*; everyone immediately knows what he is hearing and how the one relates to the other."[97] In other words, the fox of fables is always sly, the donkey always dumb. Such invariance can be constricting, yet it also possesses a distinct advantage; the fable writer knows that his audience is familiar with his characters. Without any time wasted on introductions, the story can simply begin. One might argue that the roles in the fable are not arbitrary, for they developed from actual observation of animals: donkeys really are stupid, foxes are sly. In the case of meter and semantics, we enter the realm of pure convention, for it is difficult to claim a necessary, *a priori* link. There is nothing "natural" about the fact that amphibrachic tetrameter poems should be ballads. It should be recalled that, in the German tradition (the putative "source" of the Russian ballad), this association does not exist. Moreover, English Romantics often used the amphibrachic tetrameter in elegies.[98] Yet Pushkin observed this connection in the work of his friend and mentor Zhukovsky and wrote a poem so popular as to ingrain it in the Russian poetic memory for the next 150 years.

How crucial is it that the *reader* recognize the generic/thematic implications of a given meter? Generations of Russians loved Aksakov's "Cossack of the Urals" and decades of Soviets were captivated by Svetlov's "Grenada," yet it is unlikely that they were aware of these poems' connection to Pushkin. No one has *ever* explicitly stated that Lermontov's "Ballad" (from Schiller) is formally indebted to Pushkin. Nonetheless, in a poetically rich culture such as Russia's, it is certainly conceivable that readers sense the semantic associations of meter on a subconscious level. When these links are recognized and consciously brought to the surface, the interpretation gains an entirely new dimension. Just as poetry is not produced in a vacuum, so it should not be read in isolation. Against a background of similarity (metrical, generic, thematic, etc.), differences become more pronounced. By changing the model, the individual poet consciously moves against the tradition. In some cases (e.g., Del'vig or Prigov), the recognition of differences is essential to understanding a poem's message.[99] In others (Lermontov), a poet's creativity first becomes evident when the metrical echo is noted and conceptualized. In all poems, however, meter becomes not merely a means for classifying verse along technical lines, but also a subtle indicator of content and thus, for the reader, an entry into a whole kingdom of poetic interconnectedness and craft.

CHAPTER 2

The blank verse lyric: ". . . Again I visited" revisited

Если бы во времена Софокла и Горация появилась трагедия или ода с рифмами, чтó сказали бы Греки и Римляне, эти превосходные ценители изящного в мире чувственности, к которой относится и рифма? . . . Нет сомнения, что тонкий слух этих народов, столь хорошо понимавший все таинственные прелести *ритма*, содрогнулся бы от рифмы, как от непростительного варваризма!

Барон Розен, "О рифме"

If a rhymed tragedy or ode had appeared in the times of Sophocles and Horace, what would the Greeks and Romans have said, those superlative connoisseurs of elegance in the world of the senses, to which rhyme also belongs? . . . There is no doubt that the delicate ear of these peoples, which understood so well all the mysterious charms of *rhythm*, would have shuddered from rhyme as from an unpardonable barbarism!

Baron Rozen, "On Rhyme" (1836)[1]

PUSHKIN'S EVOLUTION

Pushkin's lyric meditation ". . . Vnov' ia posetil" (". . . Again I visited") is generally regarded as one of the masterpieces of his last years. It has repeatedly attracted attention for numerous reasons: the overtly autobiographical references (to people, places, and things), the "realistic" style (concrete description and uncomplicated syntax), the philosophical dimensions (Pushkin's understanding of his place in the universe). My interest concerns the link between Pushkin's form and thematics, where this link originated and to what extent it proved influential for subsequent poets. This approach seeks to reconstruct a broad context for understanding Pushkin's creative method as well as the method of Russian poets in general, from Zhukovsky to Brodsky.

". . . Again I visited" is written in what is commonly known as blank verse, that is, unrhymed iambic pentameter. In English literary history, this form has a venerable place, beginning with Shakespeare's plays and Milton's epic poems. In the Russian tradition, however, it is a relative newcomer, first appearing with regularity in the nineteenth century. In drama, Shakespeare's model (seconded by Schiller's plays) had a decisive effect on the Russians. Beginning with Zhukovsky's translation of Schiller's "Die Jungfrau von Orleans" ("The Maid of Orleans") and Pushkin's "Boris Godunov," it quickly became the form of choice. Yet blank verse was not limited to drama – it also took the form of lyric meditation, both in the West (e.g., Wordsworth's "Tintern Abbey" and Byron's "The Dream") and in Russia. ". . . Again I visited," while not the first Russian poem in this form, is the cornerstone of the Russian lyric tradition of blank verse.

A word is in order as to why Russia did not "discover" blank verse until the nineteenth century. In contrast to their Western counterparts, Russia's eighteenth-century poets were still struggling to domesticate syllabo-tonic poetry and thereby create an immediately recognizable poetic idiom. Their ideal was a language as distant as possible from prose. For their purposes, blank verse had an obvious disadvantage: poetry without rhyme lacked one of the most distinctive markers of modern verse. Unrhymed verse did appear in eighteenth-century Russian poetry, but with very specific functions. It was used either in imitations – of Greek and Latin poets (high style) or folk poetry (low style) – or in translations.[2] Thus, a poet's avoidance of rhyme could be construed as a signal to his audience that his work was derivative rather than "original." Only when syllabo-tonic poetry had been firmly implanted on Russian soil could poets enjoy the relative freedom of blank verse.

In 1816, Zhukovsky translated two poems in blank verse by the distinctly minor Swabian poet Johann Peter Hebel.[3] As a rule, Zhukovsky felt no compunction to retain the formal characteristics of the poems he translated. However, in this case, he faithfully reproduced the meter. Both of these poems ("'Tlennost'" ["Perishability"] and "Derevenskii storozh v polnoch'" ["The Village Guard at Midnight"]) were meditations on the theme of mortality. The former, more significant for present purposes, bears the subtitle "Conversation on the Road Leading to Basel, in View of the Ruins of the Röttler Castle." It takes the form of a dialogue between a young boy and his grandfather, with the former asking naive questions and the latter answering them at great length. The basic theme is sounded in the very first lines, as the grandson explains his uneasiness whenever he walks past the dilapidated Röttler castle. What, he asks, if this same fate were to befall their own little house?:

> Послушай, дедушка, мне каждый раз,
> Когда взгляну на этот замок Ретлер,
> Приходит в мысль: что, если то ж случится
> И с нашей хижинкой? . . . Как страшно там!
> Ты скажешь: смерть сидит на этих камнях.
> А домик наш? . . . Взгляни: как будто церковь,
> Светлеет на холме и окна блещут.
> Скажи ж, как может быть, чтобы и с ним
> Случилось то ж, что с этим старым замком?[4]

> Oh, grandpa, listen: ev'ry time I look
> Upon that Röttler castle over there,
> A thought comes to me: what if this should happen
> To our own little hut? . . . How terrifying!
> You'll say that death is sitting on those stones.
> But what of *our* house? . . . Look: just like a church,
> It's light upon the hill, the windows shine,
> Oh, tell me, could that very fate befall
> Our little house, just like the ancient castle?

In response, the grandfather pours out the wisdom his many years have given him. The Röttler castle, he explains, is an apt symbol for the glory of this world, for it is the nature of all earthly things to decay:

> Как может быть? . . . Ах! друг мой, это будет.
> Всему черед; за молодостью вслед
> Тащится старость: все идет к концу
> И ни на миг не постоит. Ты слышишь:
> Без умолку шумит вода; ты видишь:
> На небесах сияют звезды; можно
> Подумать, что они ни с места . . . нет!
> Все движется, приходит и уходит.
> Дивись, как хочешь, друг, а это так.
> Ты молод; я был также молод прежде,
> Теперь уж все иное . . . старость, старость!
> И что ж? Куда бы я ни шел – на пашню,

В деревню, в Базель – все иду к кладбищу!
Я не тужу . . . и ты, как я, созреешь.
Тогда посмотришь, где я? . . . Нет меня!
Уж вкруг моей могилы бродят козы;
А домик, между тем, дряхлей, дряхлей;
И дождь его сечет, и зной палит,
И тихомолком червь буравит стены,
И в кровлю течь, и в щели свищет ветер . . .
А там и ты закрыл глаза; детей
Сменили внуки; то чини, другое;
А там и нечего чинить . . . все сгнило!
А поглядишь: лет тысяча прошло –
Деревня вся в могиле; где стояла
Когда-то церковь, там соха гуляет.

How could it be? Oh, my good friend, it *will* be!
There is a time for all things; after youth
Old age sets in: all things move toward their end,
They never even pause. You hear the way
The water sounds incessantly. You see:
There in the heavens shine the stars. You'd think
They move not from their places yon – but no!
Like everything, they move, they come, they go.
You may be shocked, my friend, but it is so.
You're young, yet I myself was also young.
And now it's different. Oh, old age, old age . . .
And so? Wherever I may go – to village,
Or field, or Basel – all leads to the grave!
I don't lament . . . like me, you will mature.
And then you'll wonder where I've gone. I've left!
Around my grave a herd of goats will wander
And all the while our little house will age,
The rain will lash it; then the sun will beat it,
And slow and steady worms will gnaw the walls,
The ceiling leaks, the wind blows through the holes
And now you too have shut your eyes – grandchildren
Replace the children; fix this, then that happens.
And then there's nothing left to fix – all's rotted!
You look around – a thousand years have passed.
The village now is in the grave; where once
A church had stood, a plow now roams the fields.

Indeed, destruction will befall the grandson's generation and, ultimately, even the mighty city of Basel. The grandfather goes on to envision the lament of a future passerby:

ДЕДУШКА

И много, много лет спустя, быть может,
Здесь остановится прохожий: взглянет
Туда, где нынче город . . . там все чисто,
Лишь солнышко над пустырем играет;
И спутнику он скажет: "В старину
Стоял там Базель; эта груда камней
В то время церковью Петра была . . .
Жаль Базеля."

ВНУК

Как может это статься?

GRANDFATHER

And many, many years from now perhaps,
A passerby will stop and look upon
The place where now a city stands . . . all empty,
The sun above the wilderness will play;
He'll say to his companion: "On that place
Stood Basel once: the heap of stones beyond,
Was then the Church that bore Saint Peter's name . . .
Poor Basel."

GRANDSON

O, how could it come to pass?

The conversation continues (at length) in this vein, with the grandfather placing emphasis on the fleeting nature of all things. Yet the poem concludes with an element of hope, as the grandfather explains to his grandson that good deeds will assure him a place in heaven:

Посмотри: там светят звезды;
И что звезда, то ясное селенье;
Над ними ж, слышно, есть прекрасный город;
Он невидим . . . но будешь добр, и будешь
В одной из звезд, и будет мир с тобою;
А если Бог посудит, то найдешь
Там и своих: отца, и мать, и . . . деда.
А может быть, когда идти случится
По Млечному Пути в тот тайный город, –
Ты вспомнишь о земле, посмотришь вниз
И что ж внизу увидишь? *Замок Ретлер.*
Все в уголь сожжено; а наши горы,
Как башни старые, чернеют; вкруг

Зола; в реке воды нет, только дно
Осталося пустое – мертвый след
Давнишнего потока; и все тихо,
Как гроб. Тогда товарищу ты скажешь:
"Смотри: там в старину земля была;
Близ этих гор и я живал в ту пору,
И пас коров, и сеял, и пахал;
Там деда и отца отнес в могилу;
Был сам отцом, и радостного в жизни
Мне было много; и Господь мне дал
Кончину мирную . . . и здесь мне лучше."

Look above us, where the stars shine.
Where there's a star, there's a clear settlement;
Above them, it is said, there is a city
Invisible, yet splendid . . . if you're good
You'll be at peace upon a star up there.
And if the Lord should grant it, there you'll find us
Your father, mother, dear ones, and . . . your grandpa.
And then perhaps, when you will go along
The Milky Way into that secret city –
You'll think about the earth and glance below.
And what will you then see? *The Röttler castle.*
But all is burned to charcoal; and our mountains,
Like ancient towers, darken; everywhere
Is ash; the river holds no water, only
The bottom is still empty – the dead trace
Of ancient flooding: all around it's quiet
Like in a grave. You'll say to your companion:
"Behold! In olden times here was a land.
Close to those mountains I myself once lived,
And herded cows, and planted fields and plowed.
I buried there my grandpa and my father.
I too became a father and enjoyed
Much happiness in life; and God gave me
A peaceful death . . . and here it's better still."

In these final lines, traditional Christian beliefs in an afterlife
(simplified for the benefit of the child who is listening) serve as the
consolation for the destruction that will inevitably befall all earthly
things.

When read today, "Perishability" does not make much of an
impression. It is long, rambling, and easily forgotten. Yet it was a
source of striking novelty and even amusement to Zhukovsky's
contemporaries, who ordinarily had great respect for this master of
poetic translation. In 1819, Konstantin Batiushkov teased Zhukovsky

in a letter, saying: "I ask you to write me; how much work can it be, when you have time to write to all the young ladies and still manage to translate some Pindar of Basel into some sort of pentameter verses . . . ?"[5] Its light tone notwithstanding, this passage indicates that Batiushkov questioned not simply Hebel's quality as poet (the hyperbolic epithet "Pindar of Basel"), but also the poem's unusual form ("some sort of pentameter verses"). Clearly, blank verse did not fall within the accepted limits of Russian versification.

Pushkin's reaction was similar. In 1818, he more or less dismissed the poem with a parody:

> Послушай, дедушка, мне каждый раз,
> Когда взгляну на этот замок Ретлер,
> Приходит в мысль: что, если это проза,
> Да и дурная? . . .

> Oh, grandpa, listen: ev'ry time I look
> Upon that Röttler castle over there,
> A thought comes to me: what if this is prose,
> Bad prose at that?

Pushkin quotes the opening lines verbatim, but adds a metapoetic commentary. Instead of posing the expected question about the poem's *theme* (perishability), he asks about the poem's *form* ("What if this is prose?"). This parody deserves to be taken seriously. Pushkin's comment indicates the extent to which unrhymed iambic penta-meter (often considered a "natural" meter) was perceived as some-thing altogether foreign to poetry (that is, as prose). It should be recalled that, in the Russia of 1818, prose was not a viable literary form. What Pushkin seems to be saying is that Zhukovsky's "Perish-ability," in dispensing with rhyme, caesura, and strophic form, no longer has sufficient organization to qualify as verse. Indeed, in the context of the (unwritten) poetics of his time, Zhukovsky had attempted something quite radical – he had pared poetry down to two constituent elements: iambic rhythm and a pentameter line. Pushkin's parody, with its truncated fourth line, eliminated even the pentameter, thereby removing one of the two remaining predictable elements in Zhukovsky's already streamlined form.

In 1818, Pushkin rejected "Perishability" and, it would seem, the very possibility of lyric poetry in blank verse. However, in character-istic fashion, he was to reassess his judgment. In 1828, he returned to the subject obliquely in a fragmentary critical essay conventionally called "O poeticheskom sloge" ("On Poetic Style"). His discussion focused on the poetry of Wordsworth and Coleridge (presumably *Lyrical Ballads*, although this is never explicitly stated), lavishing praise on their use of simple poetic means:

> In Russia the time is not yet ripe . . . the so-called language of the gods is [so] new to us that we call anyone a poet who is capable of writing a dozen rhymed iambic verses. We not only have not yet thought to bring poetic style closer to noble simplicity, but we even attempt to endow prose with pomposity. We do not yet understand poetry that is freed from conventional poetic adornments. The experiments of Zhukovsky and Katenin were unsuccessful not in and of themselves, but because of the effect they produced. Few, extremely few people understood the value of the translations from Hebel. [6]

In this extraordinary passage, Pushkin the parodist has been replaced by Pushkin the champion of Zhukovsky's daring innovations. In complete seriousness, Pushkin laments that no one had appreciated the very poems that he himself had mocked. Clearly, his attitude had changed, but why?

In the decade that separated Pushkin's parody of "Perishability" from his impassioned defense of it, Russian poetry had developed rapidly. Forms once new and unexpected had become increasingly familiar, forcing Russia's leading poets to seek new poetic means. For Pushkin, this meant a move away from the ubiquitous iambic tetrameter to less conventional forms. One of the possibilities was, of course, blank verse, which he had used to great effect in his play *Boris Godunov* (written in 1825).[7] And while this type of drama (in particular, the numerous soliloquies) may well have paved the way for the blank verse lyric, several more years of poetic evolution were necessary before Pushkin would take this seemingly inevitable next step.

Typically slow to follow metrical innovation, Pushkin began experimenting with the blank verse lyric only in 1829–30. Interestingly enough, these attempts are found not in original poems, but in unfinished renderings from the English poet Robert Southey. Now remembered primarily as the target of Byron's attacks (e.g., "He had written much blank verse, and blanker prose, / And more of both than anybody knows"),[8] Southey was in his day considered one of the major British poets, ultimately even attaining the dubious honor of Poet Laureate. Along with Wordsworth and Coleridge, Southey was considered one of the "Lake Poets," and thus it comes as no surprise that Pushkin praises him highly, if obliquely, in the pre-

viously mentioned critical fragment "On Poetic Style."[9] Pushkin's
two incomplete translations – from "Hymn to the Penates" (1796)
and "Madoc" (1805) – have rarely been studied, yet they are
essential if we are to understand the trajectory that led to ". . .
Again I visited." For present purposes, it will be sufficient to cite
excerpts, beginning with the "Hymn to the Penates" (Pushkin
translated only a small fraction of this lengthy work):

Southey's original:

> Yet one Song more! one high and solemn strain,
> Ere, Phoebus! on thy temple's ruin'd wall
> I hang the silent harp: there may its strings,
> When the rude tempest shakes the aged pile,
> Make melancholy music. One Song more!
> Penates! hear me! for to you I hymn
> The votive lay; whether, as sages deem,
> Ye dwell in inmost Heaven, the Counsellors
> Of Jove; or if, Supreme of Deities,
> All things are yours, and in your holy train
> Jove proudly ranks, and Juno, white-arm'd Queen,
> And wisest of Immortals, the dread Maid
> Athenian Pallas. Venerable Powers!
> Hearken your hymn of praise! Though from your rites
> Estranged, and exiled from your altars long,
> I have not ceased to love you, Household gods![10]

Pushkin's translation:

> Еще одной высокой, важной песни
> Внемли, о Феб, и смолкнувшую лиру
> В разрушенном святилище твоем
> Повешу я, да издает она,
> Когда столбы его колеблет буря,
> Печальный звук! Еще единый гимн –
> Внемлите мне, пенаты, вам пою
> Обетный гимн. Советники Зевеса,
> Живете ль вы в небесной глубине,
> Иль, божества всевышние, всему
> Причина вы, по мненью мудрецов,
> И следуют торжественно за вами
> Великий Зевс с супругой белоглавой
> И мудрая богиня, дева силы,
> Афинская Паллада, – вам хвала.
> Примите гимн, таинственные силы!
> Хоть долго был изгнаньем удален

От ваших жертв и тихих возлияний,
Но вас любить не остывал я, боги.[11]

(English rendering of Pushkin's translation: O Phoebus! Listen to one more
lofty, important song / And then I will hang / My silenced lyre in your
ruined temple. / Let it make a sad sound / When the storm shakes the
pillars! / One single hymn more – / O listen to me, Penates, to you I sing /
My votive hymn. Advisers of Zeus, / Whether you live in the heavenly
depths, / Or if you, highest gods, / Are the cause of everything, in the
opinion of sages, / And you are followed solemnly / By the great Zeus and
his white-headed wife / And the wise goddess, the maiden of power, /
Pallas Athena, – praise to you. / Accept my hymn, mysterious powers! /
Though I have for a long time been distanced by exile / From your
sacrifices and quiet libations / I have not cooled in my love for you, gods.)

It is on first glance puzzling why this particular passage should
have caught Pushkin's attention, for it hardly seems characteristic of
the poetry "freed from conventional poetic adornments" that
Pushkin so admired in English Romanticism. True to its genre
designation, this hymn uses a relatively high stylistic register as it
celebrates the Penates, or household gods. In Russian literature, the
theme of the Penates was hardly new; Batiushkov had devoted a
celebrated poem ("Moi Penaty" – "My Penates") to this subject
almost two decades earlier. But while the Russian poet had persona-
lized his theme in a friendly epistle, Southey brings it closer to
antiquity, including all manner of Greek and Roman deities and even
abstruse questions about the hierarchy of gods. (Southey went so far
as to include footnotes on this subject, which Pushkin seems to have
ignored.) Pushkin's translation is unquestionably nothing more than
a rough draft, and it would be unfair to judge it by the standards of a
finished work. Nonetheless, one cannot but be struck by a few serious
shortcomings in his knowledge of English (most notably, his confusion of the preposition "ere" with the imperative "hear!").

Underneath the neo-classical trappings, two features seem likely to
have attracted Pushkin. The first is simply the curious resemblance of
Southey's first line (when rendered into Russian) to the first line of
Pimen's famous monologue from Pushkin's own *Boris Godunov* ("Esche
odno poslednee skazan'e" – "Just one last story"). More important
for the present purposes is Pushkin's slight alteration of the final lines
I have cited. Southey writes: "Though from your rites / Estranged,
and exiled from your altars long, / I have not ceased to love you,
Household gods!" In the English, the word "exiled" is nothing more

than a figure of speech, a paraphrastic substitute for separation. Particularly since it parallels the previous verb "estranged," its importance is secondary. In his translation, however, Pushkin omits this first verb and thus places emphasis on the word "exile." Now a concrete noun (rather than an abstract participle), it serves a new function, offering a precise reason for the poet's lengthy absence: "Though I have for a long time been distanced by exile / From your sacrifices and quiet libations / I have not cooled in my love for you, gods." The notion of exile, considerably more pronounced in the translation than in the original, gives a convincing (if inexact and unanticipated) explanation for the speaker's earlier departure and for his joy upon returning. In terms of biography, of course, exile had considerably greater meaning for Pushkin than for Southey.

The motif of a return that follows a lengthy absence leads neatly to Pushkin's next experiment in lyric blank verse: his second rendering from Southey. In 1830, Pushkin turned to the hundred-page narrative poem "Madoc," translating only the first twenty-six lines. I quote lines 4–22:

Southey's original:

> What feelings then
> Filled every bosom, when the mariners,
> After the peril of that weary way,
> Beheld their own dear country! Here stands one
> Stretching his sight toward the distant shore,
> And as to well-known forms his busy joy
> Shapes the dim outline, eagerly he points
> The fancied headland and the cape and bay,
> Till his eyes ache o'erstraining. This man shakes
> His comrade's hand, and bids him welcome home,
> And blesses God, and then he weeps aloud:
> Here stands another, who in secret prayer,
> Calls on the Virgin and his patron Saint,
> Renewing his old vows of gifts and alms
> And pilgrimage, so he may find all well.
> Silent and thoughtful and apart from all
> Stood Madoc; now his noble enterprise
> Proudly remembering, now in dreams of hope,
> Anon of bodings full, and doubt and fear.[12]

Pushkin's translation:

> Многим
> Наполнилася грудь у всех пловцов.

Теперь, когда свершен опасный путь,
Родимый край они узрели снова;
Один стоит, вдаль устремляя взоры,
И в темных очерках ему рисует
Мечта давно знакомые предметы,
Залив и мыс, – пока недвижны очи
Не заболят. Товарищу другой
Жмет руку и приветствует с отчизной,
И [Г]оспода благодарит, рыдая.
Другой, в безмолвии творя молитву
Угоднику и деве пресвятой,
И милостынь и дальних поклонений
Старинные обеты обновляет,
Когда найдет он всё благополучно.
Задумчив, нем и ото всех далек,
Сам Медок погружен в воспоминанья
О славном подвиге, то в снах надежды,
То в горестных предчувствиях и страхе.[13]

(English rendering of Pushkin's translation: The breasts of all the sailors became full of many things. / Now that the dangerous journey was completed, / They again saw their native land; / One man stands, casting glances afar, / And in dark outlines his dream draws for him / Long-familiar objects, / The gulf and the cape, – until his unmoving eyes / Begin to hurt. Another / Shakes the hand of his comrade and welcomes him home, / And thanks the Lord, sobbing. / Another, making a prayer in silence / To the saint and the holy Virgin, / Renews his old vows / Of charity and distant adorations, / If he'll [only] find all well. / Pensive, mute and distant from the others, / Madoc himself is deep in recollections / About the glorious deed, at times in dreams of hope, / At times in grievous forebodings and fear.)

This surprisingly literal – and rather accurate – Russian rendering of Southey's verses seems to typify the simplicity that Pushkin had praised in his critical prose fragment of 1828. In English (as in Russian), the language is shorn of traditional poetic adornment: no rhyme, no tropes, no classical allusions, no complicated syntactic constructions. In contrast to his translation of "Hymn to the Penates," Pushkin here finally removes the caesura after the second foot, an organizing principle that Zhukovsky had already dispensed with in his versions of Hebel.[14] By limiting himself to the opening passage, Pushkin utterly removes the fundamental narrative element from Southey's poem.[15] Rather than depicting scenes of action, he concentrates on a single lyrical moment, depicting the varied reactions of sailors as they approach their native country. One of them stares into the distance in order to recognize "long-familiar objects" (Pushkin's version of "well-known forms"), one congratulates another and "welcomes him home," while the hero (Madoc) loses himself in recollections. These repeated references to a homecoming – combined with the motif of exile from "Hymn to the Penates" – are remarkable insofar as they recur five years later in Pushkin's sole lyric masterpiece in blank verse, ". . . Again I visited."

By 1830, of course, "Madoc" hardly represented the most surprising direction in Pushkin's creative development. At this point, Pushkin was writing blank verse dramas without caesura (the "Little Tragedies") and, yet more radically, prose fiction. His growing fascination with blank verse and with the potential of literary prose was accompanied by an apparent dissatisfaction with the limitations of rhymed verse. In approximately 1833, he predicted that Russian poetry would eventually dispense with rhyme altogether:

I think that in time we will turn to blank verse. There are too few rhymes in the Russian language. One calls forth the next. *Plamen'* [flame] inevitably drags after itself *kamen'* [stone]. From behind *chuvstvo* [feeling], *iskusstvo* [art] always peeps out. Who is not tired of *liubov'* [love] and *krov'* [blood], *trudnyi* [difficult] and *chudnyi* [wonderful], *vernyi* [true] and *litsemernyi* [hypocritical], etc.[16]

Shortly after making this prediction, Pushkin produced his only two original poems in blank verse: "Он между нами жил" ("He Lived Among Us," 1834) and ". . . Вновь я посетил" (". . . Again I visited," 1835). The former, Pushkin's recollections of his erstwhile friend, the Polish poet Mickiewicz, is obviously unfinished, breaking off in mid-sentence in the twenty-first line. The latter, meditative and explicitly autobiographical, was to become one of his most celebrated lyrics:

> . . . Вновь я посетил
> Тот уголок земли, где я провел
> Изгнанником два года незаметных.
> Уж десять лет ушло с тех пор – и много
> Переменилось в жизни для меня,
> И сам, покорный общему закону,
> Переменился я – но здесь опять
> Минувшее меня объемлет живо,
> И, кажется, вечор еще бродил
> Я в этих рощах.

                    Вот опальный домик,
Где жил я с бедной нянею моей.
Уже старушки нет – уж за стеною
Не слышу я шагов ее тяжелых,
Ни кропотливого ее дозора.

      Вот холм лесистый, над которым часто
Я сиживал недвижим – и глядел
На озеро, воспоминая с грустью
Иные берега, иные волны . . .
Меж нив златых и пажитей зеленых
Оно синея стелется широко;
Через его неведомые воды
Плывет рыбак и тянет за собою
Убогий невод. По брегам отлогим
Рассеяны деревни – там за ними
Скривилась мельница, насилу крылья
Ворочая при ветре . . .
                          На границе
Владений дедовских, на месте том,
Где в гору подымается дорога,
Изрытая дождями, три сосны
Стоят – одна поодаль, две другие
Друг к дружке близко, – здесь, когда их мимо
Я проезжал верхом при свете лунном,
Знакомым шумом шорох их вершин
Меня приветствовал. По той дороге
Теперь поехал я и пред собою
Увидел их опять. Они всё те же,
Всё тот же их знакомый уху шорох –
Но около корней их устарелых
(Где некогда всё было пусто, голо)
Теперь младая роща разрослась,
Зеленая семья, кусты теснятся
Под сенью их как дети. А вдали
Стоит один угрюмый их товарищ,
Как старый холостяк, и вкруг него
По-прежнему всё пусто.

                          Здравствуй, племя
Младое, незнакомое! не я
Увижу твой могучий поздний возраст,
Когда перерастешь моих знакомцев
И старую главу их заслонишь
От глаз прохожего. Но пусть мой внук
Услышит ваш приветный шум, когда,

С приятельской беседы возвращаясь,
Весёлых и приятных мыслей полон,
Пройдет он мимо вас во мраке ночи
И обо мне вспомянет.[17]

           . . . Again I visited
That corner of the earth, where I once spent
Two years of exile, by the world unnoticed.
Since then a decade has passed by – and much
Has changed in life for me, and I myself,
According to the general law of things,
Have changed also – but here again
The past itself surrounds me vividly,
Indeed, it seems that only yesterday,
I wandered through these groves.
         And here's the house
Of exile, where I lived with my poor nanny.
She now has passed away – behind the wall
I do not hear her heavy footsteps, nor
Detect her as she eavesdrops carefully.

And here's the tree-lined hill, above which often
I used to sit not stirring – and would gaze
Upon the lake, while sadly recollecting
Some other distant shores, some other waves . . .
Among the golden crops and greening pastures
The lake shows blue and stretches broadly onward;
A fisherman along its unknown waters
Sails on and drags behind, dilapidated
His net. Along the sloping shores are spread
The villages – behind them is the windmill
Now crooked, with its wings so heavily
Pushed when the wind blows on them . . .
         On the border
Of grandfather's estate, the very place
At which the road ascends into the mountain,
Eroded by the rains, there stand three pine trees,
The one is set apart, while the two others
Are close to one another, – here, whenever
I'd ride by, on my horse on moonlit evenings
The rustling treetops with familiar sounds
Would welcome me. Along that very road
Just now I rode and right before my eyes
Again I saw them standing, without change.
They greeted me with their familiar rustling.
Yet next to their so ancient roots I noticed

(Where formerly it had been empty, naked),
A youthful grove of plants had issued forth,
A family of green, new bushes crowded
Under the cover of the old like children.
Afar still stood their lonely, sullen comrade,
An ancient bachelor, as before; around him,
It was deserted, empty.

       Hail, o clan
Still young, unknown! For I'll not be the one
Who sees your powerful, late growth, when you'll
Outgrow and overgrow my former friends
And block their ancient heads from view of those
Who pass you by. But may my grandson hear
Your noise of welcome, when, returning from
A meeting with a friend, with thoughts of pleasure
And joy, he'll pass you by in darkest night
And will remember me.

As the poem's first lines make clear, Pushkin describes his return to a place where, a decade earlier, he had spent two years in isolation. Biographically speaking, he means the estate Mikhailovskoe, where he had lived in exile from 1824 to 1825. A letter that Pushkin wrote to his wife on September 25, 1835, makes clear the extent to which this poem draws on actual experience:

In Mikhailovskoe I found everything as it had been except that my nanny is no longer there and that, in my absence, near the familiar old pine trees, a young family of pines has arisen. I find it annoying to look at them, just as it is sometimes annoying for me to look at young horse-guardsmen at balls at which I no longer dance. But there's nothing to be done; everything around me says that I am aging, sometimes even in straightforward Russian. For example, yesterday I ran into an old peasant woman I know and I couldn't help saying that she had changed. And she said to me: "You too, my benefactor [kormilets], have gotten older and uglier." Although [to that] I could say, together with my late nanny: "I never was beautiful, but [at least] I was young."[18]

This letter is a dream come true for biographically minded critics, for it contains virtually all of the poem's raw material: the people and things (the nanny, the old and new groves of pines), the larger themes (aging and change), even specific words or phrases (e.g., the Russian verb "peremenit'sia" ["to change"], the anthropomorphic "family of pines"). In shifting genres from letter to lyric, Pushkin's attitude changed from annoyance to acceptance, from a somewhat petty and individualistic view of the world to a more contemplative, almost pantheistic one.[19] Of course, this is more or less what most readers expect from poets – that they reorganize and reconsider the material that life has placed before them. What the biographical critic cannot begin to explain, however, is why Pushkin should have chosen to write his poem in blank verse. This decision, I would argue, was independent of personal experience and directly related to literary tradition.

For Pushkin, it will be recalled, blank verse was a move toward simplicity. And, indeed, one recognizes in the language of this poem the kind of realism for which Soviet critics never tired of praising Pushkin. Details of everyday life (places, things – the windmill, the hill, the lake, etc.) are placed before the reader as if for inspection. In the repeated colloquial "vot" ("here") one almost hears the intonation of the tour guide, directing our attention as we follow along. In keeping with an ideal of unadorned simplicity, Pushkin dispenses with caesura and uses stanzas (paragraphs) of varying lengths.[20] Through repeated ellipses, he creates an unstructured, "unpremeditated" effect, a sensation of incompleteness. Thus, the poem begins with an ellipsis, giving the impression that we have entered midway. Rhythmically speaking, we have; for the first word actually occupies the position of the sixth syllable of the line. (The fact that the first five syllables are missing only becomes evident a few lines later, once the iambic pentameter has had time to establish itself.) This "incomplete" opening line is mirrored in the truncated final line of only six syllables. Moreover, Pushkin makes frequent use of enjambment, intentionally violating the line boundary and forcing a "run on" effect (e.g., in the opening passage, lines 1, 2, and especially 4). Finally, he employs graphic elements of verse to create additional unpredictability. Within the stanzas, sentences frequently end in the middle of lines, creating additional shifts and breaks (e.g., an ellipsis leads to a skipped line which begins with the symbolically weighty phrase "on the border"). This effect is not unusual in drama, where one character stops speaking and another begins. Indeed, Zhukovsky employs it this way in the dialogue of "Perishability" (e.g., the grandfather says "Zhal' Báselia" ["Poor Básel"], and his grandson fills out the pentameter line with "Kak mózhet eto stát'sia?" ["O?, how cóuld it cóme to páss?"]). Yet it has a more striking effect in a lyric monologue, which is, in principle, the voice of a single speaker. In this case, the skipped lines suggest sudden changes in the direction of the poet's thoughts.[21] In short, in his realization of blank verse, Pushkin makes no effort to limit its "prosaic" (i.e., formally unpredictable) qualities, but rather exploits these very qualities to their fullest extent. The connection between blank verse and prose that Pushkin made in his 1818 parody still held true for the Pushkin of 1835. However, his evaluation of the literary potential of prose had itself changed radically in the intervening years.

What is most remarkable about Pushkin's poem is how it transforms Zhukovsky's banal dialogue into a powerful autobiographical monologue while retaining so much of the earlier poem's form, theme, and imagery. In Zhukovsky's translation of Hebel, the setting (a walk past a familiar place) inspires a discussion between child and grandfather about time and its destructiveness, about the fleeting quality of things and, ultimately, people. In Pushkin's poem, a visit to a familiar place leads to very similar meditations. The poet ponders the way that time has changed his surroundings and himself and ultimately welcomes the future generations, thus recognizing his own mortality. The generational motif (grandfather/grandson) so fundamental to Zhukovsky's poem is revived and developed by Pushkin.[22] First, in a seemingly minor autobiographical detail, he refers to the land as his grandfather's ("on the border / of grandfather's estate"), thus establishing his own role as grandson.[23] In the poem's final lines, this detail gains in significance when the poet shifts position from grandson to grandfather, imagining how his descendant will gaze upon this same scene in the future. It will be recalled that Zhukovsky's poem uses similar motivic material: there is repeated emphasis on the generational shift (e.g., children replaced by grandchildren) and the identical image of the impressions of an imaginary future passerby.

It should be evident that Pushkin did not arbitrarily select blank verse for ". . . Again I visited." He had lived with this form for almost two decades before deciding to apply it to lyric poetry. When he did so, he drew – whether consciously or subconsciously – on Zhukovsky's model *not only* for the form, but also for the genre (lyric meditation), the theme (death), the setting (repeated visits to a familiar place), and even specific motifs (grandfather/grandson, the future observer).

These numerous borrowings in no way impinge on Pushkin's originality. Pushkin took the material at his disposal and reworked it thoroughly. In Zhukovsky's poem, for example, time is an unrelentingly linear, destructive, even apocalyptic force which can be countered only by an unquestioning faith in God. The dilapidated Röttler castle serves as a *memento mori*, an appropriate emblem for this world-view. In contrast, Pushkin's central symbol of transience is not a man-made structure (though he does begin by noting a building: "here's the house of exile"), but rather nature itself: the two old pine trees and the new life springing forth at their roots. According to such a view, time is cyclical. The passage of generations is understood not as a succession of helpless victims, but as a constant process of growth, maturation, and renewal. Moreover, Pushkin does not treat nature in isolation to man, but, through personification, constantly emphasizes its link to humanity. The trees are described as a "a family of green," their isolated "sullen comrade" stands "like an ancient bachelor," the new bushes crowd around them "like children."

Instead of introducing a Christian moral, Pushkin closes the poem by putting his faith in memory. In fact, memory serves as the poem's fundamental organizing principle. Already in the opening passage, the poet's recollections are so powerful that they transform ten years into a single day: "Indeed, it seems that only yesterday, / I wandered through these groves." The first part of the poem is essentially a list of impressions, all of which call forth memories and thus force the poet to compare the present with the past. The poet acknowledges that things have changed (e.g., the nanny's death), yet he is still inextricably linked to the earlier time: "but here again / The past itself surrounds me vividly." While memory is only implicit in the opening passage, it becomes increasingly foregrounded as the poem develops: "And here's the tree-lined hill, above which often / I used to sit not stirring – and would gaze / Upon the lake, while sadly recollecting / Some other distant shores, some other waves . . ." In these lines, the poet describes a memory *of* memory; a scene from the past comes alive precisely because it recalls an *earlier* past.[24] In the second half of the poem, memory is linked to the generational theme. The poet recalls his moonlight rides (as grandson) past trees that welcomed him with their rustling. (The passage is one of the few examples of a "heavily orchestrated" line in a poem that generally eschews "poeticisms": "Znakomym *shumom shorokh ikh* ver*sh*in / Menia privetstvoval"). In the final passage, repeating the very same words, the poet envisions his own grandson, who will walk past the next generation of trees and hear their "noise of greeting" ("pri-

vetnyi shum"). Most important, of course, is the conclusion: the
trees' noise will inspire in the grandson a memory of the grandfather
(the final line: "And will remember me"). If Zhukovsky's poem
ended with literal immortality (a life after death in heaven), Pushkin's
poem concludes with immortality achieved through memory. Such a
conception of memory, wholly absent from "Perishability," is frequently found in Pushkin's late poetry (the most conspicuous
example being his version of Horace's "Exegi monumentum"). Its
centrality to ". . . Again I visited" indicates that Pushkin had no
qualms about departing from Zhukovsky's model when his convictions demanded it.

Pushkin's achievement in ". . . Again I visited" was to demonstrate to the Russian reader (and poet) the literary potential of a
poetic form. Borrowing liberally from Zhukovsky's "Perishability,"
he created a firm constellation of meter, genre, theme, and style.
Blank verse, already comfortably established in Russian drama, now
found a lyric incarnation as a first-person meditation on questions of
permanence, death, and memory. These questions arose through a
visit to a familiar place and – in keeping with the unrhymed and
caesura-less form – tended to be phrased in a language of simplicity.
Before Pushkin's masterpiece, lyric blank verse had not been entirely
neglected, but it had no particular associations.[25] After its appearance, poets had something to respond to and build upon. Of course,
they did not *necessarily* have to follow Pushkin's semantic realization
of this meter, but there was a powerful impulse to do so.

PUSHKIN'S LEGACY

". . . Again I visited" was published posthumously (as poetic justice
would have it, by Zhukovsky) in 1837. In the next decade, this
heretofore rare lyric form suddenly began appearing in the work of a
number of lesser poets. Nikolai Ogarev, the most prolific practitioner
of unrhymed iambic pentameter, published the following untitled
verses in 1843:

> Стучу – мне двери отпер ключник старый.
> Я знал, что нет хозяйки, что давно
> Она уже уехала далеко
> И странствует теперь под небом чуждым;
> Но мне на дом хотелось посмотреть.
> Как все знакомо! Зала длинная,
> Где поздним вечером, при слабом свете,

Какие-то таинственные тени
Уныло бродят; кабинет безмолвный,
Где часто мы вдвоем сидели близко . . .
Я молча темным локоном играл
Иль говорил, что было на душе,
А на душе тогда так было полно!
И всё на том же месте, как и было:
Диван в углу, перед камином кресло,
Цветы на окнах, на стенах портреты,
А на столе развернутая книга.
Я взял и пыль с нее обтер рукой,
Скамейку шитую толкнул к дивану
И у окна гардину белую
Расправил. Солнце зимнее светило
Печально . . . Уходя, спросил я: есть ли
Оттуда письма? – Нет-с, не получаем. –
Она меня теперь забыла, верно;
А я? – и у меня любви нет в сердце,
Одно воспоминанье![26]

I knock upon the door – the old steward opens.
I know the mistress is not there, that she
Already left from here for distant climes
And now is traveling in foreign countries.
But it's the house itself I want to see.
And how familiar it all is! The room,
Where late at night, with scant illumination,
Some sort of enigmatic shadows seem
To wander dolefully; the silent study,
Where we would sit, the two of us, so closely . . .
Without a word I'd play with [her] dark ringlet
Or speak of that which weighed upon on my soul,
And at that time my soul was overfull!
And everything is just as it had been:
The sofa and the armchair by the fire,
The flowers on the sill, the portraits hanging,
The open book that lay upon the table.
I picked it up and wiped the dust away,
Then pushed the small embroidered bench aside,
Adjusted the white curtain at the window.
The winter sun came shining through so sadly . . .
On my way out, I asked a question, whether
They'd been receiving letters. "No, Sir, nothing."
She's now forgotten me, that much is certain;
And I? – in my heart too there is no love,
But only memory.

Ogarev is remembered primarily for his decades of work with Aleksandr Herzen and therefore through the prism of his political views. However, there is no social or political message here. Rather, we find a poem with extraordinary debts to Pushkin: in form (a first-person blank verse meditation), theme (time and memory), and setting (a return after a long absence to a once familiar place). Within this context, echoes of motivic minutiae also sound suspiciously similar. When Ogarev introduces the "old steward" in the first lines of the poem, one recalls Pushkin's mention of his old servant (his nanny) at the beginning of ". . . Again I visited." Ogarev wishes to look at the house ("But it's the house itself I want to see"), just as Pushkin immediately recognized his "house of exile."[27] Most obviously, Ogarev truncates his final line and ends emphatically on a "marked" word: "vospominan'e" ("memory"). In both sound and meaning, this word ineluctably calls to mind "vspomianet" ("will remember"), the concluding word of Pushkin's poem. This is not to minimize the differences: Ogarev emphasizes the stability (unchangeability) of the house in order to underscore the enormous change in human relationships. For him, recollection is not the key to uniting past, present, and – through projection – future (as it is for Pushkin), but rather an obviously inadequate substitute for prior experience. The pained final exclamation in Ogarev's poem contrasts sharply to the spirit of reconciliation that characterizes Pushkin's concluding lines. Yet this difference especially stands out within the context of so many similarities. Ogarev models his poem on Pushkin's verses, retaining the form, genre, and setting, while introducing the theme of lost love (an invariant of Ogarev's poetry of this period). Like most of Ogarev's lyrics, this poem had little influence on subsequent Russian poets. Yet it is significant insofar as it reflects the way Pushkin's poem became a model.

Another indication of the sudden popularity of Pushkin's form can be found in the poetry of the young Ivan Turgenev, who was later to achieve fame as one of Russia's great realist novelists. In 1844, Turgenev wrote an untitled meditation that begins "Odin, opiat' odin ia" ("Alone, again I am alone"). The entire poem is cast as a first-person lyric monologue. A brief excerpt should suffice to give a sense of the whole (the ellipses are in the original):

> . . . Потом
> Лет через пять, в том городе далеком,

Наставника я встретил . . . Поклонились
Друг другу мы неловко, торопливо
И тотчас разошлись. Но я заметить
Успел его смиренную походку,
И робкий взгляд, и старческую бледность . . .
То, наконец, я вижу дом огромный,
Заброшенный, пустой, – мое гнездо,
Где вырос я, где я мечтал, бывало,
О будущем, куда я не вернусь . . .
И вот я вспомнил: я стоял однажды
Среди высоких гор, в долине тесной . . .[28]

          . . . Then in
That distant city, five years afterwards
I met that teacher . . . And uncomfortably
We bowed to one another; hurriedly
We parted ways at once. But I had time
To recognize his humble way of walking,
His timid glance, his old and pale complexion . . .
Now, finally, I see a house: enormous,
Neglected, empty . . . and this is my nest,
Where I grew up and used to dream about
The future. To this house I won't return . . .
And then did I recall: I once was standing
Among high mountains, in a narrow valley . . .

Scholars have generally read these verses autobiographically, trying to identify the teacher whom Turgenev mentions.[29] Biographical prototypes may well lurk in the background, yet the poem seems more a stylization than a confession. Elements both formal (the frequent enjambments and ellipses) and motivic (the passing of years, the remembrance of an earlier home and its natural surroundings, the temporal shifts from past to future) make abundantly clear that Turgenev derived and adapted his monologue from Pushkin.

Shortly after Ogarev and Turgenev, another poet experimented with the blank verse lyric, leaving a more decisive mark on the genre. Apollon Grigor'ev, known to posterity primarily as a literary critic, wrote two youthful blank verse meditations. In keeping with much of Grigor'ev's verse (and, for that matter, his world-view), an atmosphere of gloom pervades these poems. The first, "Prizrak" ("The Phantom"), describes a recurring vision, in which the poet encounters a terrifying yet beautiful ghostlike woman whom he vainly tries to breathe life into. The second, more important in terms of the subsequent development of the Russian blank verse

lyric, is called "Vopros" ("The Question") and deserves to be quoted
in full (all ellipses are in the original):

Вопрос

. . . .
. . . .
Уехал он. В кружке, куда, бывало,
Ходил он выливать всю бездну скуки
Своей, тогда бесплодной, ложной жизни,
Откуда выносил он много желчи
Да к самому себе презренья; в этом
Кружке, спокойном и довольном жизнью,
Собой, своим умом и новой книгой,
Прочтенной и положенной на полку, –
Подчас, когда иссякнут разговоры
О счастии семейном, о погоде,
Да новых мыслей, вычитанных в новом
Романе Санда (вольных, страшных мыслей,
На вечер подготовленных нарочно
И скинутых потом, как вицмундир),
Запас нежданно истощится скоро, –
О нем тогда заводят речь иные
С иронией предоброй и преглупой
Или с участием, хоть злым, но пошлым
И потому нисколько не опасным,
И рассуждают иль о том, давно ли
И как он помешался, иль о том,
Когда он, сыну блудному подобный,
Воротится с раскаяньем и снова
Придет в кружок друзей великодушных
И рабствовать, и лгать . . .
                        Тогда она,
Которую любил он так безумно,
Так неприлично истинно, она
Что думает, когда о нем подумать
Ее заставят поневоле? – То ли,
Что он придет, склонив главу под гнетом
Необходимости и предрассудков,
И что больной, но потерявший право
На гордость и проклятие, он станет
Искать ее участья и презренья?
Иль то, что он, с челом, подъятым к небу,
Пройдет по миру, вольный житель мира,
С недвижною презрительной улыбкой
И с язвою в груди неизлечимой,

С приветом ей на вечную разлуку,
С приветом оклеветанного гордым,
Который первый разделил, что было
Едино, и подъял на раменах
Всю тяжесть разделения и жизни?[30]

The Question

. . . .
. . . .

He left. And in the circle where before,
He'd gone to pour out an abyss of boredom
Of his own false and fruitless life, from where
He brought forth so much spleen and even scorn
Directed toward himself; now in that circle,
All calm and fully satisfied with life,
And with themselves, their minds, and the new book
They'd read and placed again upon the shelf, –
When now and then the conversation stops,
About the weather and the family,
When unexpectedly the source dries up of
New thoughts, which had been read in a new novel
By Sand (those free and terrifying thoughts,
Prepared intentionally for the evening
And then discarded like a uniform) –
Just then do they begin to speak of him
With irony so kind and yet so stupid
Or with a sympathy, both mean and vulgar
And for this reason fully without danger,
And they discuss if he had long ago
Gone mad, or else if he'd return once more,
Repenting like a prodigal son, and then if
He'd visit his forgiving friends, that circle,
Again to be a slave and lie . . .
                                    Then she,
The one whom he had loved so ardently
Loved truly as was not the custom there,
What would she think, when they would force her now
Against her will to think of him? – Perhaps
That he would come and place his head beneath
The weight of prejudice, necessity,
That being ill he'd lost the right to pride
And curses, and that he'd begin to seek
Her sympathy and scorn? Or that with forehead
Raised heavenwards, he'd wander through the world
A free inhabitant of earth, with an

Unwavering and scornful smile, and with
An abscess in his chest that cannot heal,
While greeting her before eternal parting,
The haughty greeting of a man accursed
Who first had separated that which once
Had been united, taking on his shoulders
The heavy weight of parting and of life?

Like Turgenev's imitation of Pushkin, these verses stand out through insistent enjambment and ellipses (the first of which creates an opening that is not, strictly speaking, a beginning, while the second breaks a line in two, indicating a shift in direction of the poet's thought). On a thematic level, Grigor'ev's poem is also concerned with the passing of time, with departure and return. Yet "The Question" departs from the model of ". . . Again I visited" in several striking ways. Where Pushkin praises continuity in the natural world, Grigor'ev bemoans the alienation of modern society. Where Pushkin shows the interconnectedness of the individual and his environment, Grigor'ev depicts "eternal parting." Pushkin's speaker is consoled by memory and internalizes past, present, and future, while Grigor'ev's protagonist relives the painful past and can only hypothesize an equally bleak future. If Pushkin endowed time with the power to reconcile and even unify, then Grigor'ev views time as a force that intensifies the separation inherent in life itself. This overwhelming sense of alienation is reflected both in the question that ends the poem (and is already suggested in the title)[31] and in the impersonal style. Like Pushkin's meditation, Grigor'ev's poem has strong autobiographical elements (the uneasy relationship between the individual and the group mirrors Grigor'ev's unhappy experiences with the Korsh family, whose daughter he had wooed unsuccessfully),[32] yet it is related in the third person. This creates an impression less of soliloquy (interior monologue) than of omniscient narration and indirect discourse (*style indirect libre*).

Ogarev had also supplied a variation in a minor key to Pushkin's life-affirming meditation. Like Grigor'ev, his poem depicted a failed romance. However, the emotion of the speaker had been covered by a veneer of propriety (reflected in the polite conversation between the protagonist and the servant). Grigor'ev's poem, the third-person narration notwithstanding, has a histrionic, overly emotional quality (e.g., the closing lines recalling Atlas, who bears the world of suffering on his shoulders),[33] which is foreign to Pushkin's meditative poetry as a whole and ". . . Again I visited" in particular.

One may safely assume that Grigor'ev was familiar with ". . . Again I visited." As an aspiring poet, he was thoroughly acquainted with the work of his immediate predecessors. In fact, he especially prized Pushkin (Grigor'ev would later pen the oft-quoted dictum "Pushkin – nashe vsë" ["Pushkin is our everything"]).[34] In writing "The Question" – and, to a lesser extent, "The Phantom" – Grigor'ev was obviously seeking to transform his model, to give a new direction to the Russian blank verse lyric as canonized by Pushkin. According to this new conception, time would stand forth in all its destructiveness, leaving the individual a helpless victim. In contrast to the minor variations on a Pushkinian theme of Ogarev and Turgenev, Grigor'ev can be said to have produced an alternative, genuinely polemic response to Pushkin's model.

As it happened, Grigor'ev's "challenge" to Pushkin was slow to bear fruit. Subsequent nineteenth-century poets tended to avoid blank verse, as did Grigor'ev himself in his later lyric poetry. Even if the next generations of poets *had* sought a model, however, it is unlikely that they would have fastened on Grigor'ev. Grigor'ev always led a precarious and impecunious existence, and he was to die an alcoholic in a debtor's prison. Only one book of his poetry appeared during his lifetime (published at the author's expense), and it had a print run of fifty copies. Such poetry therefore had only a minimal chance of being known at all.

Yet Grigor'ev eventually found his reader, and it proved to be one of the towering figures of twentieth-century Russian poetry: Aleksandr Blok. Indeed, Grigor'ev's posthumous poetic reputation is intimately connected to the great Symbolist poet. In 1915, to commemorate the fiftieth anniversary of Grigor'ev's death, Blok prepared the first serious edition of his verse.[35] As contemporaries quickly recognized, the work had a twofold significance: it brought Grigor'ev to the attention of the reading public, and it revealed Blok's enormously high evaluation of this neglected figure. In a lengthy introduction, Blok emphasized in Grigor'ev's work certain inchoate stirrings that would come to full expression only in the twentieth century: "*Struggle, struggle* – repeats Grigor'ev in all of his verses, using the word symbolically, giving it a number of meanings."[36] This edition was not the beginning, but rather the culmination of a fascination with Grigor'ev's poetry, which left its mark in a number of ideas, symbols, and even formal features of Blok's own poetry.[37]

It was Blok who rejuvenated the blank verse lyric poem, making it a productive vehicle for a number of major twentieth-century poets. What is remarkable is that Blok did so by drawing simultaneously on the models of both Pushkin and Grigor'ev. In 1907, at a transitional point in his development, Blok wrote a cycle of poems entitled "Vol'nye mysli" ("Free Thoughts"). This phrase, of course, is a borrowing from Grigor'ev's "The Question."[38] Yet now it describes not the "free and terrifying thoughts" inspired by a George Sand novel, but Blok's own thoughts. In accordance with the title – and with the examples of Pushkin and Grigor'ev – Blok chose a correspondingly "free" meter. For the first time in his career, he turned to unrhymed iambic pentameter without caesura. Like Pushkin, he maximized the form's unpredictability, using stanzas of varying lengths, often breaking lines off before the final foot and allowing thoughts to trail off into ellipses. In fact, Blok took even greater liberties, occasionally including lines with three, four, six, or seven feet and, at one crucial moment, shifting to rhyme. Taken as a whole, these poems depart in obvious ways from Pushkin's model. Yet, in equally obvious ways, they reveal the power of Pushkin's influence. As Lidiia Ginzburg has remarked: "The world of objects of the cycle 'Free Thoughts' is wide and unexpected in its concreteness. But then it is created under the sign of Pushkin . . . Pushkin's intonation, the intonation of ' . . . Again I visited' insistently penetrates these verses, illuminating in advance everything depicted in them."[39]

"Free Thoughts" is a cycle of four poems, linked by a first-person narrator who is at least loosely based on Blok himself. Not only are the poems set in the vicinity of St. Petersburg (the site of Blok's own lengthy wanderings), but they depict the speaker's isolation from and caustic attitude toward bourgeois society (a trait that would later endear Blok to Soviet critics). The present discussion will focus on "O smerti" ("About Death"), the first poem in Blok's cycle and the most influential. It is curious that, like Pushkin's ". . . Again I visited," the poem's central episode is adumbrated in a letter from the poet to his wife. On May 27, 1907, Blok wrote (in his inimitable epistolary fashion):

And I was in Lesnoi recently and saw a squirrel on a pine tree. Besides that, when I walked up behind the fence of the racetrack, a yellow jockey fell while galloping at full speed. People ran up to him and lifted some sort of pitiful and absolutely [motionless] dead hands and legs which flopped around all yellow. He fell into the green grass – with his face to the sky. There you have all my recent impressions of life.[40]

As was the case with Pushkin, much of Blok's "realia" (the fallen jockey, the people who rush up to him, the yellow body against the green background of nature) can be found in the prose excerpt. On the other hand, one confronts a number of motifs foreign to the letter, yet familiar from the Russian tradition of blank verse:

> Всё чаще я по городу брожу.
> Всё чаще вижу смерть – и улыбаюсь
> Улыбкой рассудительной. Ну, что же?
> Так я хочу. Так свойственно мне знать,
> Что и ко мне придет она в свой час.[41]

> More frequently I wander through the city.
> More frequently I gaze on death – and smile
> A calculating smile. Well, so what?
> That's how I want it. That's my way of knowing
> That death will come to me when it is ready.

As in Pushkin's poem, the first-person protagonist is a wanderer who is obsessed with the thought of his own death. Even the repeated visit implicit in the first word of Pushkin's poem ("vnov'" – "again") is echoed in Blok's opening phrase ("vse chashche" – "more frequently"). Yet together with these Pushkinian elements, one also senses in Blok's alienated yet smiling wanderer the presence of Grigor'ev's "vol'nyi zhitel' mira s nedvizhnoiu prezritel'noi ulybkoi" ("free inhabitant of earth, with an unwavering and scornful smile").

Blok's "free thoughts" are reflected in a loosely structured poem, which gains continuity through the repeated verbs "brodit'" (to wander) and "prokhodit'" (to walk past/along), usually at the beginning of a stanza:

> line 1: Всё чаще я по городу брожу
> (More frequently I wander through the city.)
> line 6: Я проходил вдоль скачек по шоссе
> (I wandered on the highway near the racetrack.)
> line 16: Я шел и слышал быстрый гон коней
> (I walked and heard the rapid race of horses.)
> line 62: Однажды брел по набережной я
> (I once was wandering along the shore.)

line 112: Пойду еще бродить.
(I'll go and wander further.)

In the course of his wanderings, the poet encounters two scenes of death. In Pushkin's poem, death had been present only obliquely, as the necessary consequence of time's passing. Whether in people (e.g., the nanny) or nature (e.g., the trees), old age led ineluctably to death. In Blok, however, death is neither so subtle nor so predictable: before the poet's gaze, two young men perish. Their deaths are obviously parallel, and Blok repeats a number of words to under-score these similarities. In the first (the scene described in the letter), a jockey is thrown off his racehorse; in the second, a drunkard falls into the water. In both cases, the poet observes and evaluates the death quite differently from other eyewitnesses. While the others scream out in horror ("Upal! Upal!" – "He fell! He fell!") and rush toward the fallen man, the poet keeps his distance and calmly reflects on the events. After describing the fallen jockey, he concludes:

> Так хорошо и вольно умереть.
> Всю жизнь скакал – с одной упорной мыслью,
> Чтоб первым доскакать. И на скаку
> Запнулась запыхавшаяся лошадь,
> Уж силой ног не удержать седла,
> И утлые взмахнулись стремена,
> И полетел, отброшенный толчком . . .
> Ударился затылком о родную,
> Весеннюю, приветливую землю,
> И в этот миг – в мозгу прошли все мысли,
> Единственные нужные. Прошли –
> И умерли. И умерли глаза.
> И труп мечтательно глядит наверх.
>
> Так хорошо и вольно.

In this way does one die both well and freely.
His whole life with one stubborn thought he galloped –
To finish first. And as he galloped onward,
His panting horse tripped up, and he went flying,
Hurled forth, without the strength to hold the saddle,
His fragile stirrups shaking to and fro . . .
He struck his head against the native earth
The vernal earth, which welcomed him back to it.
And at this moment thoughts went through his mind,
The only necessary thoughts went through
And died. And at this point his eyes died also.

And now the corpse glanced, meditating, upward.

So good and free.

In ". . . Again I visited," it will be recalled, the poet sought to reconcile himself with the inevitability of his own death by thinking of the continuity in nature. In Blok's poem the emphasis is different. The jockey's death is viewed in unambiguously positive terms ("good and free") as a return to the "native, vernal, friendly" earth. The moment of death becomes a moment of mystical initiation during which "the only necessary thoughts" come to the dying person. In describing these thoughts, Blok repeats the verbs "proshli" ("passed by") and "umerli" ("died"), thereby subtly drawing a parallel between his own activities (a wanderer who observes and muses on death) and the moment of death itself.

The second scene of dying contains no detailed description of the dead man or of a mystical initiation into death. Instead, the poet offers a caustic dismissal of the onlookers, reporting their "stupid questions" as well as a (drunken) worker's "authoritative" lecture on the dangers of drinking. The poet turns inward, setting himself off from the agitated crowd. He urges himself once again to observe death "with a smile" while enjoying life – which he explicitly associates with alcohol. Memory and immortality, so central to Pushkin's poem, play no role whatsoever in Blok's verses. Rather, the poet comes to terms with the inevitability of his own death through a mystical closeness to nature and an epicurean attitude to life (signaled by the traditional triad of wine, women, and song):

> Сердце!
> Ты будь вожатаем моим. И смерть
> С улыбкой наблюдай. Само устанешь,
> Не вынесешь такой веселой жизни,
> Какую я веду. Такой любви
> И ненависти люди не выносят,
> Какую я в себе ношу.
>
> Хочу,
> Всегда хочу смотреть в глаза людские,
> И пить вино, и женщин целовать,
> И яростью желаний полнить вечер,
> Когда жара мешает днем мечтать
> И песни петь! И слушать в мире ветер!
>
> O, heart!
> You be my guide. And with a smile look

At death. You will yourself get tired, for
You simply cannot bear this carefree life,
This life that I am leading. Such a love
And such a hatred people cannot bear,
Like that I bear within myself.

> I want,
I always want to look in people's eyes,
I want to drink the wine and kiss the women,
And fill the evening with desires' ardor
When in the afternoon the heat disturbs
My dreaming, singing, listening to the wind.

If Pushkin's meditation concluded with the poet addressing a future visitor, so in Blok's final passage, the poet speaks directly to his heart. The poem closes on an exclamatory note with powerful (and clearly connected) symbols of wind and song. In keeping with images of sound, the unrhymed iambic pentameter switches unexpectedly to rhymes in the last four lines (not preserved in the translation).

To return to the larger issues, it should be emphasized that Blok's poem shares with Pushkin's a number of significant features: meter (blank verse), genre (lyric meditation), theme (death), protagonist (first-person narrator), and setting (repeated visits to familiar places). It is, of course, against this familiar background that Blok's changes stand out. The poem "On Death" contains a mystical and willfully destructive element utterly foreign to Pushkin. The calm resignation of Pushkin's verses gives way to repeated exclamation in Blok. Some of these new elements appear to be derived from Grigor'ev. Not only do essential words ("vol'nyi" ["free"] being the most striking) recur, but larger themes (such as the opposition between the protagonist and the rest of humanity) have been incorporated into this verse. Other aspects, such as Blok's conclusion, seem to be without a direct literary source. If Pushkin reconciled himself with death by projecting himself into the memory of his descendants, Blok sees death as a reminder that one must live life to the fullest in order to die "freely."

In "Free Thoughts," Blok revived the blank verse lyric and brought it into the twentieth century. After Blok, many leading poets would experiment with the form, drawing not simply on Pushkin, but also on Blok (and thus, indirectly, on Grigor'ev). One of the first was Nikolai Gumilev, in a 1917 poem entitled "Ezbekieh":

Как странно – ровно десять лет прошло
С тех пор, как я увидел Эзбекие,

Большой каирский сад, луною полной
Торжественно в тот вечер освещенный.
Я женщиною был тогда измучен,
И ни соленый, свежий ветер моря,
Ни грохот экзотических базаров,
Ничто меня утешить не могло.
О смерти я тогда молился Богу
И сам ее приблизить был готов.

Но этот сад, он был во всем подобен
Священным рощам молодого мира:
Там пальмы тонкие взносили ветви,
Как девушки, к которым Бог нисходит;
На холмах, словно вещие друиды,
Толпились величавые платаны,
И водопад белел во мраке, точно
Встающий на дыбы единорог;
Ночные бабочки перелетали
Среди цветов, поднявшихся высоко,
Иль между звезд, – так низко были звезды,
Похожие на спелый барбарис.

И, помню, я воскликнул: "Выше горя
И глубже смерти – жизнь! Прими, Господь,
Обет мой вольный: что бы ни случилось,
Какие бы печали, униженья
Ни выпали на долю мне, не раньше
Задумаюсь о легкой смерти я,
Чем вновь войду такой же лунной ночью
Под пальмы и платаны Эзбекие."

Как странно – ровно десять лет прошло,
И не могу не думать я о пальмах,
И о платанах, и о водопаде,
Во мгле белевшем, как единорог.
И вдруг оглядываюсь я, заслыша
В гуденьи ветра, в шуме дальней речи
И в ужасающем молчаньи ночи
Таинственное слово – Эзбекие.

Да, только десять лет, но, хмурый странник,
Я снова должен ехать, должен видеть
Моря, и тучи, и чужие лица,
Все, что меня уже не обольщает,
Войти в тот сад и повторить обет
Или сказать, что я его исполнил
И что теперь свободен . . .[42]

How strange – precisely ten years have now passed
From when I first laid eyes on Ezbekieh
The sprawling Cairo garden which that evening
The moon so solemnly illuminated.

At that time I was tortured by a woman,
And not the salty, fresh air of the sea, nor
Cacophony of the exotic markets –
Nothing could then have possibly consoled me.
I prayed to God at that point for my death
And was myself prepared to help it come.

But then that garden – it resembled fully
The holy groves of the young universe.
The palm trees raised their fine and subtle branches
They seemed like girls, whom even God descends to;
Upon the hills, just like prophetic druids,
Enormous plane-trees clustered all around,
A waterfall showed through the darkness whitely;
It looked as though a unicorn had reared.
Nocturnal butterflies were flying round
Among the flowers which were raised up high
Or in the stars themselves – so low the stars were –
They looked like ripened fruits of barberry.

And I recall exclaiming: "Life itself is
Above all sorrow, more profound than death.
Accept, O Lord, my freely given vow –
Whatever happens, if humiliation
Or sadness falls my lot, I will not dream
About an easy death until again
Under the selfsame moonlit night I enter
Among the palms and planes of Ezbekieh."

How strange – precisely ten years now have passed
And I cannot but think of palm and plane trees,
And of a waterfall, that in the darkness,
Gleams with white color like a unicorn,
When suddenly I look around and hear in
The evening's hum, the sound of distant speech, in
The horrifying silence of the night –
That word so enigmatic – Ezbekieh.

Yes, ten years only now, yet I must travel,
Always the sullen pilgrim, I must see
The ocean, rainclouds, and the foreign faces,
No longer captivating. I must enter
Into that garden to repeat my vow

Or else to say that I have now fulfilled it.
And that I now am free . . .

In these autobiographical verses, Gumilev recalls his journey(s) to Africa as well as (obliquely, in stanza 2) his relationship with Anna Akhmatova. The title refers to a park in Cairo and in this respect recalls a number of poems on African themes that Gumilev had written at an earlier stage in his career (in the 1908 book *Romanticheskie tsvety* – Romantic Flowers). As in those poems, Gumilev takes advantage of the exotic setting, using words uncommon to a Russian ear (most obviously, Ezbekieh itself, that "mysterious word," which – repeated numerous times – becomes a kind of mantra). However, whereas those earlier poems had concentrated on exoticism for its own sake, the later poem uses the exoticism to introduce abstract, even metaphysical considerations. In terms of the present study, the central question concerns Gumilev's use of blank verse: why should he have chosen this particular form to record his personal experiences?

"Ezbekieh" is Gumilev's only extended lyric poem in blank verse. It is therefore particularly telling that it should bear striking resemblances to the previously discussed poems of Pushkin and Blok. Like his predecessors, Gumilev divides his poem into stanzas of varying length. In the final line, he not only truncates the pentameter to trimeter (following Pushkin's example), he even adds an ellipsis, giving the poem an unresolved quality.[43] In addition to such formal markers, one finds a striking similarity of genre, theme, setting, and even lexicon. Once again, an anonymous (yet clearly autobiographical) speaker describes a visit to a once familiar place. The speaker combines a nature description with the thought of time passing and, ultimately, of his own death ("I prayed to God"). In the context of such similarities, lexical echoes stand out. For example, Gumilev repeatedly emphasizes that ten years have passed since his visit. On the one hand, this is presumably biographical detail; on the other, Gumilev phrases his statement as a deliberate echo of Pushkin. Pushkin writes "Уж десять лет ушло с тех пор," while Gumilev repeats the phrase "Как странно – ровно десять лет прошло / С тех пор." The ten-year interval was in Pushkin a simple matter of fact, but in Gumilev it offers a deliberate link to Pushkin and, as such, serves as a striking coincidence ("how strange").[44] Likewise, Gumilev uses words that are strongly marked from Blok's poems (via

Grigor'ev): e.g., Gumilev's "vol'nyi obet" ("free vow") recalls the title of the cycle "Vol'nye mysli" ("Free Thoughts").

Working within the metrical/semantic nexus he inherited from Pushkin and Blok, Gumilev creates a unique atmosphere. It is characteristic that, if Pushkin sets his poem in Mikhailovskoe and Blok places his speaker in the environs of St. Petersburg, Gumilev's "homecoming" should be to distant Cairo. Pushkin had described a typical natural scene on a Russian estate. Blok depicted events – horseracing, dock workers – that were in and of themselves mundane. (Only the speaker's *interpretation* of these events was mystical. Indeed, interpreters generally understand the cycle "Free Thoughts" as a move by Blok to a more realistic type of poetry.)[45] In contrast, Gumilev emphasizes the *peculiarity* of his surroundings and his circumstances. From the outset (e.g., the title as well as the first phrase), the scene described is not simply unfamiliar to the reader, but even otherworldly. In the third line, Ezbekieh is described as a garden ("сад"). In the context of Gumilev's verses, it clearly functions as a second garden of Eden, to which the poet seeks return. In fact, the poem's lexicon teems with words either overtly religious ("holy," "God," "vow," "pilgrim," "Lord") or mythical ("druid," "unicorn"). Even the opening phrase "Kak *stranno*" ("how strange"), reiterated in the beginning of the penultimate stanza, leads – through paranomasia and false etymology – to the final, religiously tinged depiction of the poet as "*strannik*" ("pilgrim").

Like Pushkin's ". . . Again I visited," Gumilev's "Ezbekieh" is a poem concerned almost exclusively with memory and the passing of time. Like Blok's "Free Thoughts," it examines life and death from a fundamentally mystical perspective. Yet Gumilev expresses ideas that differ significantly from those of his predecessors. Rather than *experiencing* a return visit, Gumilev *anticipates* it. The poem is therefore located in a peculiar temporal moment, a type of limbo between past (recollection) and future (projection). If Blok's wanderer is aimless, Gumilev's has a very precise – if mythical and even ritualized – destination. Yet in both cases, the ultimate goal of wandering is spiritual freedom (significantly, Gumilev's poem trails off after the word "svoboden" ["free"]).

Perhaps the most important and certainly the most frequent twentieth-century visitor of Pushkin's ". . . Again I visited" was Vladislav Khodasevich. Khodasevich's boundless admiration for Pushkin

comes across clearly in the diction and form of his own verses as well
as in numerous critical essays he devoted to his beloved precursor.
Between the years 1918 and 1920, Khodasevich turned to lyrics in
blank verse, writing seven major poems. As numerous scholars have
remarked, these poems are clearly modeled on Pushkin.[46] Not only
are Pushkin's works both named and alluded to, but Pushkin himself
is twice mentioned explicitly. For example, in "2-go noiabria" ("The
Second of November"), Khodasevich describes a city in the aftermath of a cataclysmic event (Moscow in the days immediately
following the October Revolution) using phrases and imagery taken
wholesale from the depiction of another city after a different sort of
calamity (St. Petersburg after the flood in Pushkin's "Bronze
Horseman"). In the concluding lines, Khodasevich names two of
Pushkin's works, noting:

> Но, впервые в жизни,
> Ни "Моцарт и Сальери," ни "Цыганы"
> В тот день моей не утолили жажды.[47]

> But, for the first time in my life,
> Not "Mozart and Salieri," nor "The Gypsies,"
> Could satisfy my thirst on that one day.

While Khodasevich does not name ". . . Again I visited" in any of
these poems, its presence is ubiquitous.[48] The poem "Epizod" ("An
Episode"), for example, begins with an obvious graphic allusion – an
ellipsis and a truncated line: ". . . Eto bylo" (". . . It happened"). In
the context of unrhymed iambic pentameter, such an opening
obviously recalls Pushkin's model. Blok's "Free Thoughts" also leave
their mark on Khodasevich's blank verse poems, both formally and
motivically. In "An Episode," the poet encounters death in the form
of his own "Doppelgänger," who visits him and suddenly topples
over:

> Вдруг откачнулся, и вздохнул, и умер.
> Лицо разгладилось, и горькая улыбка
> С него сошла.[49]

> He suddenly reeled back, breathed in, and died.
> His face smoothed out, and from it disappeared
> A bitter smile.

The depiction of a sudden death before the eyes of a calm narrator
(together with the motif of the smile, here transferred from observer
to observed) surely has its origin in Blok's "On Death."

To treat all the relevant Khodasevich poems would require a chapter in itself, but a few general points can be made. Without exception, these poems are meditations of a first-person narrator. The language is generally "prosaic," with an emphasis on realistic description. While the events described in these poems vary considerably, one motivic invariant stands out: as in Pushkin and Blok, the speaker's meditations are triggered by a walk:[50]

> На соседней даче
> Кричал петух. Я вышел за калитку. ("Обезьяна")
> At the neighbor's dacha
> A rooster crowed. I went out past the gate. ("The Monkey")

> И поздним вечером, когда я шел
> К себе домой . . . ("Встреча")
> And once in the late evening as I walked
> Toward home . . . ("The Meeting")

> У Благовещенья на Бережках обедня
> Еще не отошла. Я выхожу на двор. ("Музыка")
> At the Berezhki church, Annunciation mass
> Had not yet finished. I went out to the courtyard.[51] ("Music")

> К моим друзьям в тот день пошел и я.
> Узнал, что живы, целы, дети дома, –
> Чего ж еще хотеть? Побрел домой. ("2-го ноября")
> I too on that day set off to my friends
> To learn that they were safe and sound, their kids, too –
> And what more could one want? I set off homewards.
> ("The Second of November")

> Теперь мне любо приходить сюда
> И долго так сидеть, полузабывшись. ("Полдень")
> I find it pleasant now to come here and
> In half-forgetfulness, sit a long while. ("Noon")

In all of the poems, the walk sparks the speaker's observations (of a physical nature), which in turn inspire philosophical speculation.

I choose to concentrate on "Dom" ("The House") because it resonates so obviously with earlier poems in the blank verse tradition, most clearly with that of Pushkin. True to expectation, it is a first-person narrator's meditation brought about by a visit to a familiar place. These observations lead Khodasevich (as they had Pushkin) to broader questions of transience and human memory:

> Дом
> Здесь домик был. Недавно разобрали

Верх на дрова. Лишь каменного низа
Остался грубый остов. Отдыхать
Сюда по вечерам хожу я часто. Небо
И дворика зеленые деревья
Так молодо встают из-за развалин,
И ясно так рисуются пролеты
Широких окон. Рухнувшая балка
Похожа на колонну. Затхлый холод
Идет от груды мусора и щебня,
Засыпавшего комнаты, где прежде
Гнездились люди . . .
Где ссорились, мирились, где в чулке
Замызганные деньги припасались
Про черный день; где в духоте и мраке
Супруги обнимались; где потели
В жару больные; где рождались люди
И умирали скрытно, – всё теперь
Прохожему открыто. О, блажен,
Чья вольная нога ступает бодро
На этот прах, чей посох равнодушный
В покинутые стены ударяет!
Чертоги ли великого Рамсеса,
Поденщика ль безвестного лачуга –
Для странника равны они: всё той же
Он песенкою времени утешен;
Ряды ль колонн торжественных иль дыры
Дверей вчерашних – путника всё так же
Из пустоты одной ведут они в другую
Такую же . . .

          Вот лестница с узором
Поломанных перил уходит в небо,
И, обрываясь, верхняя площадка
Мне кажется трибуною высокой.
Но нет на ней оратора. А в небе
Уже горит вечерняя звезда,
Водительница гордого раздумья.

Да, хорошо ты, время. Хорошо
Вдохнуть от твоего ужасного простора.
К чему таиться? Сердце человечье
Играет, как проснувшийся младенец,
Когда война, иль мор, или мятеж
Вдруг налетят и землю сотрясают;
Тут разверзаются, как небо, времена –

И человек душой неутолимой
Бросается в желанную пучину.

Как птица в воздухе, как рыба в океане,
Как скользкий червь в сырых пластах земли,
Как саламандра в пламени – так человек
Во времени. Кочевник полудикий,
По смене лун, по очеркам созвездий
Уже он силится измерить эту бездну
И в письменах неопытных заносит
События, как острова на карте . . .
Но сын отца сменяет. Грады, царства,
Законы, истины – преходят. Человеку
Ломать и строить – равная услада:
Он изобрел историю – он счастлив!
И с ужасом и с тайным сладострастьем
Следит безумец, как между минувшим
И будущим, подобно ясной влаге,
Сквозь пальцы уходящей, – непрерывно
Жизнь утекает. И трепещет сердце,
Как легкий флаг на мачте корабельной,
Между воспоминаньем и надеждой –
Сей памятью о будущем . . .

                                                Но вот –
Шуршат шаги. Горбатая старуха
С большим кулем. Морщинистой рукой
Она со стен сдирает паклю, дранки
Выдергивает. Молча подхожу
И помогаю ей, и мы в согласье добром
Работаем для времени. Темнеет,
Из-за стены встает зеленый месяц,
И слабый свет его, как струйка, льется
По кафелям обрушившейся печи.[52]

The House

There was a house here. Recently they broke
The roof for firewood. Only stone remains,
The raw foundation. To this place I come
With frequency at evening-time. The sky
And green trees of the courtyard rise so young
From out behind the ruins. And the outline
Of window-bays is clearly drawn. A beam
That broke resembles now a column. Musty coldness
Comes from a pile of trash and gravel, poured
Upon the rooms where people used to nest
In times gone by . . .

Where people quarreled, and made peace, where they
Placed soiled money in a sock in case
Hard times should come; where couples in the darkness
And stuffiness embraced; where sickly people
All feverish did sweat; where people, all concealed,
Were born and died – this all is now wide open
To the passerby. O blessed is he whose foot
Steps happily and freely on this dust, whose
Indifferent staff beats on these walls deserted!
The walls might be a pharaoh's palace or
The hovel where some unknown worker lived.
It is no matter to the pilgrim, who
Finds consolation in the song of time.
If they be rows of solemn columns or
The holes that yesterday were doors – whatever –
They lead the pilgrim from one empty space
Into another . . .

              Here the patterned staircase
Of broken rails leads upwards, to the sky
And where it breaks, the upper landing seems
To me a lofty tribune – but devoid
Of orator. And in the sky shows forth
The evening star, the leader of proud thought.

Yes, you're a good one, time. It's good to breathe
The air from your so horrible expanse.
What's there to hide? The heart of man is wont
To play just like an infant when awoken –
When war or pestilence or revolution
Descends and strikes the earth without a warning.
Then time – just like the sky – will open wide
And man with his unsatiated soul
Will leap into the depths he so desires.

Like birds in air, like fishes in the ocean,
Like slippery worms in dampest layers of earth,
Like salamanders in a flame – is man
In time. He is a nomad, a half-savage.
At each new moon, according to the stars,
He tries to measure the abyss before him
And in uncertain letters he jots down
Events of life, like islands on a map . . .
But son replaces father. Cities, kingdoms,
And laws and truths – these things all pass. To build
Or to destroy gives equal joy to man.
He has invented history – he's happy.

With horror and with secret lust the madman
Observes the way life flows away unceasing,
How in between the future and the past
It slips away, much like transparent liquid
Through fingers. All the while the heart is trembling
Like floating banners hanging from a mast,
Between man's recollection and his hope,
That memory of future time . . .

                          But here –
Some footsteps sound. An old and hunch-backed woman
Appears, capacious sack in hand. She strikes
With wrinkled hands the oakum from the wall.
And pulls out wooden laths. I silently
Approach and help. In happy harmony
We work for time. As it gets dark, there rises
From out behind the wall a moon of green,
And like a stream it pours its pallid light
Along the tiles of the ruined oven.

Formally speaking, it is remarkable to what extent Khodasevich draws on the techniques of his predecessors. As in Pushkin, we find truncated lines, stanzas of uneven length, ellipses. Enjambment – used frequently by Pushkin and Blok – becomes a virtual obsession for Khodasevich (e.g., eight times in the first twelve lines). Line boundaries only rarely coincide with syntactic periods, forcing the reader to pause in unexpected places. To add yet more unpredictability, Khodasevich takes advantage of a Blokian innovation; he interrupts the flow of iambic pentameter by including lines of more or less than five feet (hexameter and even dimeter, the latter appearing only once in Blok – as the closing line of the entire cycle).

Khodasevich's conscious orientation toward his predecessors is particularly evident in a series of details. Beyond the overarching thematic, generic, and formal similarities, one finds specific lexical echoes. For example, Pushkin had repeatedly underlined the act of observation with the word "vot" ("here"). Set off and indented at the end of the eleventh line of ". . . Again I visited" is the phrase: "Vot opal'nyi domik" ("Here's the house of exile"). Five lines later, a new stanza begins with the words: "Vot kholm lesistyi" ("Here's the tree-lined hill"). Blok had himself borrowed this locution when describing the corpse of the jockey (not surprisingly, indented and at the beginning of a stanza): "I vot povisla" ("And there was hanging"). In Khodasevich, the word "vot" again appears as an indented beginning of a new stanza: "Vot lestnitsa s uzorom" ("Here the patterned staircase"). Later in the poem, the indented phrase "No vot" ("But here") again introduces a stanza. If, in Pushkin, this phrase served to draw the reader closer to the objects being described, then, in Khodasevich – and, to a lesser extent, in Blok – it has a double function. It points both to an object *and* to a previous poet's intonation. Another detail provides an equally telling link to tradition. Early in his poem, Khodasevich writes: "Zatkhlyi kholod / Idet ot grudy musora i shchebnia" ("Musty coldness / Comes from a pile of trash and gravel"). On first glance there is nothing remarkable about this line. In the context of the Russian iambic pentameter lyric, however, one recognizes a curious coincidence: in "On Death," Blok had written (line 6): "Den' zolotoi dremal na grudakh shchebnia" ("The golden day had dozed on piles of gravel"). In Khodasevich, then, the pile of gravel is at once a realistic detail and a signal that points the reader toward a prior literary work.[53]

Like any major poet, Khodasevich alludes to his predecessors not simply to claim kinship, but also to allow differences to stand out more starkly. "The House" cannot be considered imitative, its myriad links to previous poems notwithstanding. Written shortly after the October Revolution, it provides a profound philosophical commentary on the recent events. While Khodasevich was soon to become an émigré, it would be overly simplistic to consider this an anti-Soviet poem. Rather, it is an expression of a characteristically "modern" world-view, in the sense that it attributes the unremitting destructiveness less to man than to time itself. Khodasevich does not point an accusing finger at the Bolsheviks; instead, he views his circumstances as part of an unceasing pattern of decay, ultimately including even himself as a participant in this process.

There is a certain irony to the poem's title. One ordinarily associates a house with physical stability or family life. Yet in the very first line it becomes clear that this house warrants attention because it lacks precisely these elements. It is relegated to the past tense and transformed into a diminutive.[54] As the matter-of-fact speaker states (eschewing all explanation and evaluation), the roof has been stripped off for firewood, leaving only the stone skeleton intact. In short, the house has become part of history, a ruin ("razvaliny") which opens up to onlookers what once was private.[55] This realization leads the speaker to praise the individual who can observe such decay without despair: "O blessed is he whose foot /

Steps happily and freely on this dust, whose / Indifferent staff beats
on these walls deserted!"

The motif of the wanderer (passerby), familiar from Zhukovsky,
Pushkin, and Blok, is particularly significant for Khodasevich.
Indeed, "The House" is structured around a series of visits. It begins
with the speaker himself (line 4), who describes how, in the evenings,
he frequently comes to the house. The next visitor is the St.
Petersburg citizenry (line 19), anyone who wanders by what used to
be the house. From this passerby Khodasevich moves to a more
generalized pilgrim/wanderer (lines 25 and 28), who does not
distinguish between Ramses' palace and an insignificant worker's
hovel. The reference to the Egyptian king opens up the temporal
and spatial scheme beyond the confines of post-revolutionary St.
Petersburg. This is reflected in the next image of a passerby, which
reaches the highest level of abstraction – man himself, "a nomad, a
half-savage" (line 50). In the final stanza, a final visitor appears: a
mysterious old woman, who returns the poet's thoughts from
philosophical abstractness to concrete reality. She has come to
scavenge shards of wood left behind the tiles of the walls. In her
activity, she functions as both a personification of time and a pitiful
echo of the wanderer whose "indifferent staff beats on these walls
deserted."

Previous poets found salvation – or at least recompense – in
Christianity (Zhukovsky), in nature and memory (Pushkin), in life
itself (Blok), or in mystical repetition (Gumilev), yet Khodasevich
sees only the inevitability of decay. His sole conclusion is that time is
man's element, that destruction is natural: "To build / Or to destroy
gives equal joy to man." Pushkin, drawing on Zhukovsky, had used a
generational metaphor of child and grandfather in order to emphasize a fundamental continuity. Khodasevich uses a similar image, but
with an unambiguously negative evaluation: "But son replaces
father. Cities, kingdoms, / And laws and truths – these things all
pass." In the final stanza, two generations – the speaker and the old
woman – "work for time," patiently breaking apart what little is left
of the house. Ironically, this continuity between generations produces rupture – a sharp contrast to the sort of spiritual community
that Pushkin had celebrated. Like the revolutionary forces (which
are never explicitly mentioned in Khodasevich's poem), the speaker
and the old woman hasten time's destruction. In the haunting final
image, a moon pours its faint light on the tiles of a destroyed oven.

This inundation of green light is compared to a stream and, when taken with the numerous maritime images that preceded it, can be understood as a flood (a recurring scourge in the history of St. Petersburg and a central theme in the poetic tradition of that city). This watery intrusion, combined with the figure of the old woman (realistic, yet also conceivably an allegorical figure of death) suggests a scene of apocalypse. The oven, once a symbol of warmth, solidity, domesticity, and life itself, has become a relic from a lost civilization, devoid of value.

In "The House," Khodasevich's view of the human condition is unremittingly bleak. Man has developed a historical sense ("invented history"), but is incapable of true comprehension of time. While he attempts to jot down events in his "uncertain letters," life slips through his fingers "like transparent liquid" (again one finds the underlying water imagery). The fundamental instability of his position in time is evident in the comparison of his heart beating "like floating banners hanging from a mast." Only in this already compromised context does the all-important word "memory" appear: "Between man's recollection and his hope / That memory of future time . . ." The combination of hope and memory leads the poet to an aporia. His highly metaphorical musings come to a sudden end, interrupted by the concreteness of the final stanza and its scene of silent yet willful destruction.

In 1966, Joseph Brodsky, meditating on problems of cultural continuity, chose to write a lengthy poem in blank verse. "Ostanovka v pustyne" ("A Halt in the Desert," from a collection of the same name) is both a central poem for understanding early Brodsky and a magnificent example of the way poets build on the work of their predecessors:

Остановка в пустыне

Теперь так мало греков в Ленинграде,
что мы сломали Греческую церковь,
дабы построить на свободном месте
концертный зал. В такой архитектуре
есть что-то безнадежное. А впрочем,
концертный зал на тыщу с лишним мест
не так уж безнадежен: это – храм,
и храм искусства. Кто же виноват,
что мастерство вокальное дает

сбор больший, чем знамена веры?
Жаль только, что теперь издалека
мы будем видеть не нормальный купол,
а безобразно плоскую черту.
Но что до безобразия пропорций,
то человек зависит не от них,
а чаще от пропорций безобразья.

Прекрасно помню, как ее ломали.
Была весна, и я как раз тогда
ходил в одно татарское семейство,
неподалеку жившее. Смотрел
в окно и видел Греческую церковь.
Всё началось с татарских разговоров;
а после в разговор вмешались звуки,
сливавшиеся с речью поначалу,
но вскоре – заглушившие ее.
В церковный садик въехал экскаватор
с подвешенной к стреле чугунной гирей.
И стены стали тихо поддаваться.
Смешно не поддаваться, если ты
стена, а пред тобою – разрушитель.
К тому же, экскаватор мог считать
ее предметом неодушевленным
и, до известной степени, подобным
себе. А в неодушевленном мире
не принято давать друг другу сдачи.
Потом – туда согнали самосвалы,
бульдозеры . . . И как-то в поздний час
сидел я на развалинах абсиды.
В провалах алтаря зияла ночь.
И я – сквозь эти дыры в алтаре –
смотрел на убегавшие трамваи,
на вереницу тусклых фонарей.
И то, чего вообще не встретишь в церкви,
теперь я видел через призму церкви.

Когда-нибудь, когда не станет нас,
точнее – после нас, на нашем месте
возникнет тоже что-нибудь такое,
чему любой, кто знал нас, ужаснется.
Но знавших нас не будет слишком много.
Вот так, по старой памяти, собаки
на прежнем месте задирают лапу.
Ограда снесена давным-давно,
но им, должно быть, грезится ограда.

Их грезы перечеркивают явь.
А может быть земля хранит тот запах:
асфальту не осилить запах псины.
И что им этот безобразный дом!
Для них тут садик, говорят вам – садик.
А то, что очевидно для людей,
собакам совершенно безразлично.
Вот это и зовут: "собачья верность".
И если довелось мне говорить
всерьез об эстафете поколений,
то верю только в эту эстафету.
Вернее, в тех, кто ощущает запах.

Так мало нынче в Ленинграде греков,
да и вообще – вне Греции – их мало.
По крайней мере, мало для того,
чтоб сохранить сооруженья веры.
А верить в то, что мы сооружаем
от них никто не требует. Одно,
должно быть, дело нацию крестить,
а крест нести – уже совсем другое.
У них одна обязанность была.
Они ее исполнить не сумели.
Непаханное поле заросло.
"Ты, сеятель, храни свою соху,
а мы решим, когда нам колоситься."
Они свою соху не сохранили.

Сегодня ночью я смотрю в окно
и думаю о том, куда зашли мы?
И от чего мы больше далеки:
от православья или эллинизма?
К чему близки мы? Что там, впереди?
Не ждет ли нас теперь другая эра?
И если так, то в чем наш общий долг?
И что должны мы принести ей в жертву?[56]

A Halt in the Desert

There are in Leningrad so few Greeks now
that we've destroyed the Greek church, to free space
to build a concert hall. There's something hopeless
in architecture of this type. But then –
a concert hall that seats a thousand plus
is not so very hopeless. It's a temple –
a temple of the arts. And who's to blame
that singers' virtuosity now draws

a bigger crowd than banners of belief?
It is a pity, though, that now afar
we will not see a normal cupola,
but just a line that's hideously flattened.
But as concerns such hideous proportions,
mankind depends on them far less than on
proportions of the hideous in others.

I well remember how it was destroyed.
It was in spring, and I would often go
to see a certain Tatar family
that lived nearby. And through their window I
looked out upon the Greek church that still stood.
It all began with Tatar conversations.
And then some sounds disturbed the conversation.
They mixed in with the speech in the beginning,
but soon thereafter drowned them out completely.
A power crane drove into the church garden,
an iron wrecking ball hung from its boom.
And quietly the walls began to yield.
It would be funny *not* to yield if you're
a wall – and right in front is a destroyer.
Besides, the power shovel could consider
the wall to be inanimate, an object
that to a large extent was similar to
itself. And in the world inanimate
it's hardly customary to strike back.
And then they sent in dump trucks, bulldozers . . .
and thus one evening late I sat upon
the ruins of an apse. And night itself
yawned widely in the altar's gaping holes.
And I – through these same altar's holes – looked out
upon the trams that ran off in the distance,
upon the row of streetlights that were dim.
And what you'd never see inside a church
I now saw clearly through the church's prism.

Sometime when we ourselves will be no longer
or more exactly – after us, there will
arise something to take our place so awful
that anyone who knew us will be shocked.
But there won't be too many who had known us.
In this same way do dogs, by memory,
raise up their leg upon a spot they knew.
The fence was razed already long ago.
Yet they, it seems, still dream about the fence.

Their dreams can cancel out reality – or
perhaps the earth itself retains that smell.
The asphalt cannot cover scent of dogs.
And what to them is this new ugly building!
For them a garden's here – you hear, a garden.
And that which seems so evident to people
for dogs is absolutely unimportant.
That's why it's called "the loyalty of dogs."
And should it ever fall my lot to speak
about the relay race of generations,
then I believe in that sole relay race
or better still – in those who sense that smell.

There are in Leningrad so few Greeks now,
so few outside of Greece in general.
At least, there are too few of them to help
maintain the buildings of their ancient faith.
But no one asks them to believe in that
which we now build. It is one thing, that is,
to bring the cross and Christianize a nation.
To bear the cross – that is another thing
Entirely. They had a single duty
which they have proved unable to fulfill.
And thus the unplowed field is overgrown.
"Oh, sower, keep at hand thy faithful plow,
and we shall tell thee when the grain is ripe."
But they themselves failed to maintain the plow.

Tonight again I look out through the window
and think about that point to which we've come,
and then I ask myself: from which are we
now more remote – the world of Hellenism,
or Orthodoxy? Which is closer now?
What lies ahead? Does a new epoch wait?
And, if it does, what duty do we owe? –
What sacrifices must we make for it?[57]

Numerous elements encourage one to read Brodsky's poem as a conscious sequel to Khodasevich's. If Khodasevich was commenting on destruction in the immediate aftermath of the October Revolution, Brodsky could continue the discussion with the added authority of five decades of observation. In both cases the "victim" is a building: in Khodasevich, a house; in Brodsky, a church. Whereas the house creates associations of physical warmth and comfort, the church symbolizes spiritual shelter. Like Khodasevich, Brodsky avoids creating a narrowly anti-Soviet statement. Rather than viewing the destruction of a church as an example of a specifically Soviet hostility toward spirituality (which would have been entirely justified), Brodsky chooses to examine it as part of a broader phenomenon. The "desert" of the poem's title is not simply the USSR but, more generally, the contemporary world. Ultimately, Brodsky is less interested in the peculiarities of Soviet policy than in overarching questions of history, culture, and memory.

In terms of meter and genre, "A Halt in the Desert" fits neatly into the pattern of blank verse lyrics that we have established.[58] In stanzas of varying length, a first-person narrator describes his observations and then reflects on them. The theme is that of time and death (in this case, the death of a civilization). As so often, a walk brings the meditation about: "It was in spring, and I would often go / to see a certain Tatar family / that lived nearby." From his vantage point among the Tatars, the poet witnesses the destruction of a Greek church. In the context of Russian history, of course, Brodsky's choice of Tatars and Greeks ineluctably calls forth associations. Beginning in the tenth century, the Greeks had supplied Russia with a rich spiritual tradition. A few centuries later the Tatars had invaded, doing their utmost to erase the Byzantine influence. Interestingly, Brodsky does not replay this ancient animosity. The Tatars are in no way responsible for this new phase of destructiveness – like the poet, they sit by passively as it takes place. And, according to the penultimate stanza, the responsibility for the church's demolition lies to some extent with the Greeks themselves, who are no longer numerous enough to sustain it.

Ancient hostilities between nations thus yield to a subtler and more generalized conflict between secular and spiritual culture: in place of the church, a concert hall is built. On the one hand, as the speaker suggests in the first stanza, such a replacement is not disastrous: a concert hall is, after all, itself a "temple of the arts." On the other hand, the destruction of the church results in a loss of sacred space. Sitting among the ruins of the church, the poet looks out into the secular world of streetlights and trams. "And what you'd never see inside a church / I now saw clearly through the church's prism."

These thoughts lead the poet to familiar motifs: the future passerby and subsequent generations. In contrast to Pushkin's grandson, who will look upon a serene landscape and recall his predecessors, Brodsky envisions a nightmarish picture of succession:

anyone who knew us will look with horror at what has replaced us. Brodsky can envision the "relay race of generations" (i.e., continuity) only when it is reduced to the level of the canine world. Though the churchyard has been replaced by a concert hall, the dogs will still return because their sense of smell reminds them of what was formerly there. However, such loyalty is in no way romanticized. The dogs, devoid of spirituality, recall the church only metonymically – because its fence was a favorite place for urinating.

In Khodasevich's poem, the speaker ultimately joins in the destruction by helping to tear apart the already ruined house. In Brodsky's poem, the speaker's degree of complicity is ambiguous. Throughout, there is a curious and significant wavering between the pronouns "I" and "we." At times, the poet speaks as if part of the collective, explaining that "we" have torn down the church, that no one asks the Greeks to believe in what "we" build. At other moments, he speaks as an individual. It is the "I" who looks, thinks, recalls, and reflects: he observes the actual demolition, he sits among the ruins of the church. Closer examination suggests that the pronoun "we" represents the voice of Soviet society, the "I" that of the poet as individual. In the final stanza, the "I" asks a series of questions about the "we." Briefly summarized, these questions concern the passage of time: what have we come to and where are we going? Contemporary Russia, he implies, has severed all ties with both Orthodoxy (Greek Christianity, the spiritual tradition that came to Russia in the tenth century) and the Hellenistic period that preceded it (an age of extraordinary artistic, philosophical, and scholarly achievement).[59] A new era may be beginning and, if so, what are our obligations to the past? And what will have to fall victim to the future?

As a rule, the poems examined in this chapter conclude with a passage in which the poet unambiguously states his views. The series of questions that constitutes the final stanza of "A Halt in the Desert" thus represents a striking departure from that tradition.[60] These questions, precisely because they concern the future, are unanswerable. However, insofar as they are derived from the preceding meditation, they comment (albeit indirectly) on the recent past and thus contain hints of a response. Throughout the poem, the speaker has questioned the possibility of progress and of memory. As the title itself makes clear, Brodsky has little faith in contemporary society, which can so easily dispense with its past. One of the clues to understanding the poem, it would seem, is to be found in the contrast between linearity and circularity. Circularity, it will be recalled, was the "solution" to Pushkin's metaphysical deliberations in ". . . Again I visited." Brodsky, commenting on the replacement of the church (symbol of spiritual values) with the concert hall (symbol of contemporary civilization), writes: "It is a pity, though, that now afar / we will not see a normal cupola, / but just a line that's hideously flattened." While Brodsky's poem describes the unceasing and unstoppable forward motion of civilization (the line), its structure and themes contain myriad instances of continuity and repetition (the circle). The first line recurs almost verbatim as the first line of the penultimate stanza. The repeated verb "smotret'" ("to look") accompanies the poet through the second, third, and final stanzas. Most importantly, memory itself is a form of circularity, a link between past and future. While the poet has doubted memory in his fellow man (seemingly relegating it to the world of dogs), he himself clearly possesses it. It is he who recalls past civilizations (Orthodoxy and Hellenism) and, most obviously, it is he who remembers the church. "Prekrasno pomniu, kak ee lomali" (literally: "I beautifully recall how they destroyed it") he states, using a standard expression ("prekrasno pomnit'") with an ironic twist, for there is nothing "beautiful" about this recollection.

Under these circumstances, the poet becomes the repository of historical and cultural memory. Incapable of stopping the forces of "civilization," he is at least capable of recognizing them. His poem confers a certain immortality on a church that, in every other way, has been consigned to oblivion. It is in this regard that one can best understand Brodsky's decision to write about time, memory, and transience using blank verse. Had he wished only to recall the demolition of a church, he could have chosen any meter. However, by deciding on blank verse, he creates a subtle link to the Russian poetic tradition and makes a statement in favor of continuity, of remembering. Speaking of the autodidactic poets of his generation, Brodsky once said:

When I left school, when my friends quit work or college and started in on poetics, the people we read – and we read a lot – we chose by instinct, by intuition. We had no feeling that we were continuing any sort of tradition, or that we had any mentors or spiritual fathers, or anything like that. We were, if not the black sheep of the family, then orphans. And it is a marvelous thing when an orphan begins to sing in his father's voice.[61]

"A Halt in the Desert" reflects a poet-orphan's discovery of a number of spiritual forebears. By fastening on to the Russian blank verse tradition, the young Brodsky lay claim to a strikingly non-Soviet (though by no means anti-Soviet) inheritance.

This chapter has been devoted to meditative and philosophical lyrics that were derived, to a greater or lesser extent, from the poets' genuine personal experiences. The Pushkin and Blok poems can be understood as reworkings of scenes witnessed by the poets themselves (and even attested to in their letters). Gumilev's "Ezbekieh" reflects on his much-publicized earlier visit to Africa, Khodasevich's meditations are set in the bleak post-revolutionary Russia that he himself inhabited, Brodsky's "Halt in the Desert" contains an eye-witness account of the actual demolition of a Greek church in Leningrad. I emphasize this autobiographical element because it so clearly sets these poems off from those examined in the first chapter. Within the highly stylized genre of the ballad, the poet envisioned a world quite distinct from that of himself and his readers. He created this distance by selecting characters who belonged to another class (generally uneducated), to some other cultural group or even historical era. A successful ballad should appear to have its origins in oral culture. If present at all, the first-person narrator should be perceived as a fictional construct, in no way resembling the poet himself. Only the most naive of readers could mistake Pushkin the poet for the bloodthirsty protagonist of "The Black Shawl." In contrast, numerous biographical and realistic details from Pushkin's life (e.g., the reference to his beloved nanny, the landscape of Mikhailovskoe) encourage the reader of ". . . Again I visited" to identify the poet Pushkin with that poem's "lyric I." This speaker is a genuine thinker, not the impulsive caricature of "The Black Shawl."

It cannot be said with certainty whether ". . . Again I visited" truly reflects the precise thoughts that went through the poet Pushkin's mind during his 1835 visit to Mikhailovskoe. However, the poem clearly asks to be understood as such – and generations of readers have indeed read it in this way. What deserves emphasis is that, in this seemingly most personal of genres (lyric meditation), Pushkin is no less dependent on tradition than in the obviously and intentionally stylized "Black Shawl." Moreover, this very indebtedness is hardly unique to Pushkin's meditation – it is characteristic of

all of the poems we have examined in this chapter. Scholars have
generally read these long, unrhymed, philosophical lyrics as the
expression of a poet's individuality at a unique historical moment.
Yet, when viewed as a series, it becomes clear to what extent these
poems depend on each other, in terms of form, genre, theme, and
specific motifs.

As in the case of "The Black Shawl," Pushkin's example was not
the first, but it became canonic. For subsequent Russian poets,
unrhymed iambic pentameter seemed a "natural" vehicle for first-
person meditations on the subject of time, death, and memory. That
these poems are linked to Pushkin (or to each other) in no way
diminishes their effect. Rather, this linkage adds to the sense of
tradition by creating, as it were, a dialogue between speakers
separated by time and space. A common form provides a point of
departure for poets with very different perspectives and intentions. A
brief glance at three additional poems in this form demonstrates the
rich possibilities of this process of borrowing and departure.

In 1930, the émigré poet Dovid Knut devoted a long poem in
blank verse to the subject of a Jewish funeral in Kishinev. Already
the title of this poem, "Vospominanie" ("A Recollection"),[62] recalls
the central theme of Pushkin's ". . . Again I visited." Indeed,
Pushkin is explicitly mentioned in the first lines:

> Я помню тусклый кишиневский вечер:
> Мы огибали Инзовскую горку,
> Где жил когда-то Пушкин. Жалкий холм.

> I recollect dim night in Kishinev,
> We went around the little Inzov hillock,
> Where Pushkin had once lived. A wretched hill.

For the Russian-language poet, Kishinev itself is inextricably linked
to Pushkin, for this was the place where he began his southern exile.
Knut's opening reference is therefore to the young Pushkin, to the
early period of exile. Yet his formal and generic reference is to the
older Pushkin, to the memory-poem ". . . Again I visited." If that
later Pushkin poem focused on the revisitation of a scene of youth,
then Knut's variation offers a revisitation not simply of an émigré
poet's earlier life in Russia, but also of the lost world of Jewish
Russia. The movement of Knut's poem (the verb "to go" is repeated
frequently) describes a Jewish funeral procession and, in particular, a
woman "iz Knigi Bytiia" ("from the Book of Genesis") who leads it

with her dirge. This singing transcends time and place, becoming a song of mourning for the entire Jewish people:

> О, как прекрасен был высокий голос!
>
> Не о худом еврее, на носилках
> Подпрыгивавшем, пел он – обо мне,
> О нас, о всех, о суете, о прахе.
>
> O, how magnificent her voice sang forth!
>
> It sang not of the Jew emaciated,
> Who tossed about the bier they held; it sang
> Of me, of us, of dust, of vanity.

Knut's depiction of the scene transforms the misery of a nameless toiler's funeral into a celebration of humanity and spiritual community. As in Pushkin, the process of recollection leads to an acceptance of mortality and a sense of connectedness with all things. The poem ends with two lines set off as a separate stanza:

> . . . Особенный, еврейско-русский воздух . . .
> Блажен, кто им когда-либо дышал.
>
> . . . There was that special Jewish–Russian air . . .
> O, blessed is the man who ever breathed it.

A quite different religiously tinged reinterpretation of Pushkin's blank verse form can be found in the work of Vera Bulich, another émigré poet. Her 1938 book *Plennyi veter* (The Captive Wind) concludes with an explicit homage to Pushkin. This final sequence begins with the brief poem entitled "1837." Writing of Pushkin's fatal duel of that year, Bulich expresses the conviction that Pushkin's arm, falling into the snow, was fated "to bless Russia for centuries" ("veka blagoslavliat' Rossiiu").[63] By naming this twelve-line poem "1837" (i.e., using only numerals) and conspicuously dating it "1937," Bulich unambiguously marks the passage of that first century. In a similarly conscious fashion, she returns to Pushkin in the poems that immediately follow "1837," the cycle "Iz dnevnika" ("From [My] Diary").

"From [My] Diary" consists of three blank verse meditations. As the title suggests, these poems are intimate and to a significant extent autobiographical.[64] However, as so often in the blank verse we have examined, the personal is closely linked to the Pushkinian. Like Pushkin, Bulich uses unrhymed iambic pentameter to write about a return or, more precisely, a series of returns: in nature, in memory,

and, ultimately, in spirit. These poems present a variety of epipha-
nies, the first of which is experienced in nature:

> И вдруг с внезапной силой ощутить
> От шума сосен, от сырого ветра,
> Качнувшего сухой бурьян шуршащий.

> And suddenly with instant force to sense
> From noise the pine trees make, from the rough wind
> That shakes the rustling, dry, tall weeds.

It should be recalled that Pushkin had also been struck by the
"noise" of pine trees and had even accompanied this sound with the
onomatopoetic sibilant "sh" (cf. Pushkin's "*sh*umom *sh*orokh ikh
ver*sh*in" and Bulich's "*sh*ur*sh*ash*ch*ii"). More significant, however, is
that – in Bulich as in Pushkin – these natural images are ultimately
linked to the essential concept of "memory." In the final lines of the
first part of Bulich's poem, this word sounds forth repeatedly:

> И молнией блеснет воспоминанье
> О дивном знании первоначальном,
> Забытом позже, искаженном, смытом
> Волною повседневных мелочей,

> Воспоминание о том, что́ небо
> Дает земле, о смысле нашей жизни.

> And then as lightning memory will shine,
> A memory of our ancestral knowledge,
> Which was forgotten later, changed, erased
> By waves of daily trivialities,

> A memory of what the sky above gives
> To earth, about the meaning of our life.

Already in the opening section of "From [My] Diary," the
repeated word "memory," the sound of rustling pine trees, the
reflections on the passing of time combine with the blank verse form
to recall Pushkin's ". . . Again I visited." In the final two parts,
Bulich maintains these associations, but aligns them with music (part
II) and Russian Orthodoxy (part III). Both of these parts begin with a
formal allusion (an ellipsis and a truncated pentameter line) and the
theme of a visit:

> . . . На скалах, по дороге в Му́нкснэс,
> В сырое, пасмурное воскресенье. (part II)

> . . . On cliffs, along the road to Muknäs,
> A damp and gloomy Sunday afternoon.

. . . И снова Пятница страстная.
В весеннем небе год смыкает круг.
И главное не то, что было за-год,
А то, что вновь стою у Плащаницы,
И в чаще свеч горит моя свеча. (part III)

. . . And once again Good Friday comes.
The year concludes its circle in spring's sky.
What matters isn't what occurred last year,
But that I stand again before the icon,[65]
My candle burning in the candles' thicket.

In the course of Bulich's second poem, this dreary Sunday ("voskresen'e") is transformed (or "transfigured" – she herself uses this religiously marked word) by nature and music. In the third part, "voskresen'e" returns, not as the day of the week, but as its Russian homonym ("resurrection"). In a striking manner, Bulich takes Pushkin's motifs of memory and return (even the marked Pushkinian "vnov'" ["again"] appears in line 4) and synthesizes them with Russian Orthodox ritual. Much of this final poem is devoted to a description of the Good Friday church ceremony. As the service progresses, the poet loses her individuality, becoming one with the multitude of worshipers (the opening "I" is subsumed in the "we" of the second stanza). The poet describes a series of sensory experiences (hymns, churchbells, incense), all of which "vkhodit v dushu svetloiu pechal'iu" ("enter the soul with a light sadness"). The epithet "light sadness," of course, is an unmistakable reference to one of Pushkin's most celebrated love poems ("Na kholmakh Gruzii lezhit nochnaia mgla" – "The night's darkness lies on Georgia's hills," 1829). The entire religious experience thus seems to take place under Pushkin's guiding hand. In the final stanza, even the "we" disappears, leaving the concept of return to the realm of suprapersonal religious mystery:

Пройдут, забудутся, остынут чувства,
Изменит радость, притупится боль,
Но навсегда останется лишь это:
Весна и смерть. И память об утрате,
И чаемое воскресенье в духе.
Торжественность обряда векового.
То подлинное, что одно для всех.

All feelings will cool off, pass by, forgotten,
Joy will deceive, and pain itself will dull,

> The only things that will remain forever –
> Are spring and death. And memory of loss, and
> The longed-for resurrection of the spirit.
> The somberness of ancient ritual.
> That genuine, which is the same for all.

We have traversed an enormous distance in moving from Push-kin's ideal return (a personal immortality in a vision of his grandson) to Bulich's (a belief in resurrection that transcends the individual). The singing of hymns and lighting of candles she describes could not be further removed from the sense of continuity in nature that Pushkin conveys in ". . . Again I visited." Nonetheless, it is beyond question that Bulich expresses her convictions through Pushkinian forms, citations, and allusions. The three poems of "From [My] Diary" (the only blank verse in Bulich's entire book) indicate that, precisely a century after Pushkin's death, his work spoke clearly and influentially to a Russian woman poet in a vastly altered world.

In contrast to Knut's and Bulich's explicitly religious treatment of memory – but nonetheless with a distinct Pushkinian orientation – one finds Anna Akhmatova's "Severnye elegii" ("Northern Elegies"). This loosely knit cycle of poems, written over several decades of Soviet hardships, is connected primarily by the theme of lost time and by the form of blank verse. The fourth elegy, "Est' tri epokhi u vospominanii" ("There are three epochs to our recollec-tions"), "a veritable treatise on memory,"[66] can be understood as a pessimistic rewriting of ". . . Again I visited." In this meditation, Akhmatova describes memory in terms of place. In the first "epoch," joy and sadness are not yet forgotten and "piatno chernil ne sterto so stola" ("the ink stain is not yet removed from the table"). This period is brief, and it quickly turns into the second "epoch," which Akhmatova likens to a distant, secluded house, where "istlevaiut plamennye pis'ma" ("fervent letters decay"), where we are completely alone and no longer mind the solitude:

> И нет уже свидетелей событий,
> И не с кем плакать, не с кем вспоминать.
> И медленно от нас уходят тени,
> Которых мы уже не призываем,
> Возврат которых был бы страшен нам.[67]

> They are no more who witnessed the events,
> There's none with whom to cry or to remember.
> And slowly shadows move away from us,

Whom we no longer want to summon back, whose
Return would now be terrifying to us.

The final, "most bitter," epoch occurs when we realize that our
past no longer has any relevance to our present:

> Мы сознаем, что не могли б вместить
> То прошлое в границы нашей жизни,
> И нам оно почти что так же чуждо,
> Как нашему соседу по квартире,
> Что тех, кто умер, мы бы не узнали,
> А те, с кем нам разлуку бог послал,
> Прекрасно обошлись без нас – и даже
> Всё к лучшему . . .

> We understand, that we could not contain
> The past within the borders of our life,
> And that our past is now as strange to us,
> As to our neighbor in the next apartment,
> That those who died we'd recognize no longer,
> And those with whom God forced us to part ways,
> Have done quite splendidly without us – even
> That all is for the best . . .

With this shortened final line, recalling both the elliptical beginning and the truncated conclusion of ". . . Again I visited," Akhmatova depicts the full horror of time and memory. From the first stage,
when emotion is raw yet still meaningful, to the second stage, where
loneliness leads to apathy, to the final stage, which celebrates
oblivion, Akhmatova meditates on the very question that moved
Pushkin. Her poem replaces his active first-person singular protagonist with an eerie first-person plural (a disembodied version of
humanity). However, her constant emphasis on death and memory
combined with precise physical details (a table, a letter, a house),
when placed in the form of blank verse, leave little doubt that the
poem draws on the tradition we have been examining.

In Knut, Bulich, and Akhmatova, we see how Pushkin's combination of form, genre, and theme retains its attraction even when
these poets' conclusions depart quite radically from Pushkin's own.
Knut's specifically Jewish orientation has no basis in ". . . Again I
visited" (or, for that matter, in Pushkin's works in general), Bulich's
emphasis on religious community contrasts with Pushkin's personal
view of salvation, while Akhmatova's bleak conception of oblivion
thoroughly rewrites Pushkin's picture of the organic continuity of

memory. Yet these poets, like Blok, Gumilev, and Khodasevich before them – and Brodsky after them – took advantage of metrical semantics, voicing their own thoughts in a familiar, well-trodden form. For those who recognize these later poems as palimpsests, tradition becomes insistently dialogical. These poets revisit Pushkin, enriching their message through an immersion in poetic memory itself.

CHAPTER 3

The Onegin stanza: from poetic digression to poetic nostalgia

Зима!... Крестьянин, торжествуя,
На дровнях обновляет путь;
Его лошадка, снег почуя,
Плетется рысью как-нибудь;
Бразды пушистые взрывая,
Летит кибитка удалая;
Ямщик сидит на облучке
В тулупе, в красном кушаке.
Вот бегает дворовый мальчик,
В салазки *жучку* посадив,
Себя в коня преобразив;
Шалун уж заморозил пальчик:
Ему и больно и смешно,
А мать грозит ему в окно ...

Пушкин, Евгений Онегин, V, 2[1]

Ah, wintertime!... The peasant, cheerful,
Creates a passage with his sleigh;
Aware of snow, his nag is fearful,
But shambles somehow down the way.
A bold kibitka skips and burrows
And plows a trail of fluffy furrows;
The driver sits behind the dash
In sheepskin coat and scarlet sash.
And here's a household boy gone sleighing –
His Blackie seated on the sled,
While he plays horse and runs ahead;
The scamp's got frozen fingers playing
And laughs out loud between his howls,
While through the glass his mother scowls.[2]

Pushkin, Eugene Onegin V, 2

Зима! Пейзанин, экстазуя,
Ренувелирует шоссе,
И лошадь, снежность ренифлуя,

Ягуарный делает эссе.
Пропеллером лансуя в'али,
Снегомобиль рекордит дали,
Шофер рулит; он весь в бандо,
В люнетках, маске и манто.
Гарсонит мальчик в акведуке:
Он усалазил пса на ски,
Мотором ставши от тоски,
Уж отжелировал он руки.
Ему суфрантный амюзман,
Вдали ж фенетрится маман.
  Неиз., "Перевод Пушкина на язык эгофутуристов"[3]

Ah, Winter! . . . The paysan ecstatic
Now nouvellizes the chaussée
His horse renifs the neige erratic,
And makes a jaguarish essai.
Like a propeller through the valley
The snowmobile records a sally,
The chauffeur drives, with his bandeau,
Lorgnette and mask, and his manteau.
A boy, garçoning, aquaducing
Straps down his hound onto his ski
Becomes a motor – from ennui –
Just now his frozen hand producing.
How amusant for the young maître,
But Mama scowls from the fenêtre.
  Anon., "Translation of Pushkin into the Language of the Ego-Futurists"

ORIGINS

In the years 1823–31, Aleksandr Pushkin composed his "novel in verse" *Evgenii Onegin* (Eugene Onegin), a work commonly viewed as the single greatest literary achievement that Russia has ever produced. In terms of genre, Pushkin took his cue from Byron's verse narratives, yet he altered his model so freely and domesticated the form so successfully that his work has come to be considered quintessentially Russian.[4] The complexities of *Eugene Onegin* have attracted the attention of innumerable interpreters, and today's reader can benefit from a vast library of scholarship, which includes two of the most erudite *and* readable commentaries ever devoted to a work of literature.[5] For my present purposes, however, *Eugene Onegin* is less significant synchronically (as an individual creation of genius)

than diachronically (as a compelling, yet imposing model for subsequent Russian poets). I will investigate Pushkin's masterwork only
insofar as it affected the dynamics of poetic tradition.

I have already had occasion to note that Pushkin's poetic method
was primarily that of the borrower, not the inventor. However, for
this particular work, he devised a stanza unprecedented in literary
history. With very few exceptions, this so-called Onegin stanza
accompanies the reader through all of the novel's eight chapters,
providing a formal unity in the face of myriad unexpected changes
of time, place, character, and action. The uniqueness of the Onegin
stanza, combined with the immense popularity of *Onegin* itself,
produced an extraordinarily firm formal and semantic constellation
for Russian readers. Indeed, if one considers other European
national traditions, only Italian literature offers a parallel situation.
Dante created *terza rima* for the *Divine Comedy*, and the association of
this form with his thematics (in particular, epic visions of Hell)
subsequently became a given for both poets and readers.[6] Likewise,
Pushkin in a single stroke created a new form and the most
illustrious incarnation of it. For Russian poets, it proved to be a
model so powerful that relatively few would try to repeat it. Those
who did, however, fully expected their works to be understood (and
judged) against the background of Pushkin's prototype.

What was so special about the Onegin stanza? Its iambic tetrameter
lines would not have struck a contemporary as unusual: this meter
was already dominant in Pushkin's earlier work and firmly established
in the poetic repertoire of the period. Other formal elements gave the
stanza its distinctiveness. Its length (fourteen lines) was unusual and its
rhyme scheme unprecedented.[7] Simply put, the Onegin stanza
combined three distinct quatrains with a concluding couplet:

"Мой дядя самых честных правил,	A
Когда не в шутку занемог,	b
Он уважать себя заставил	A
И лучше выдумать не мог.	b
Его пример другим наука;	C
Но боже мой! какая скука	C
С больным сидеть и день и ночь,	d
Не отходя ни шагу прочь!	d
Какое низкое коварство	E
Полуживого забавлять,	f
Ему подушки поправлять,	f
Печально подносить лекарство,	E

Вздыхать и думать про себя:	g
Когда же черт возьмет тебя!"	g

"My uncle, man of firm convictions . . .	A
By falling gravely ill, he's won	b
A due respect for his afflictions –	A
The only clever thing he's done.	b
May his example profit others;	C
But God, what deadly boredom, brothers,	C
To tend a sick man night and day,	d
Not daring once to steal away!	d
And, oh, how base to pamper grossly	E
And entertain the nearly dead,	f
To fluff the pillows for his head,	f
And pass him medicines morosely –	E
While thinking under every sigh:	g
The devil take you, Uncle. Die!"	g

It will be noted that each of the three quatrains uses a different rhyme scheme, first alternating rhymes (a-b-a-b), then pair rhymes (c-c-d-d) and finally a "ring" construction (e-f-f-e).

It is always tempting to explain the unfamiliar in terms of the familiar. Several scholars (and poets) have argued that the Onegin stanza should be understood as a variant of a far more common fourteen-line form, the sonnet. Such a view is voiced frequently enough that a brief refutation is in order.[8] The most obvious counterargument is simply that Pushkin never showed much interest in the sonnet or its potential.[9] He wrote only three, and his first experiment in this form dates from 1830 (at which point the novel in verse was essentially *finished*).

Another historical detail should be emphasized: the sonnet played a distinctly minor role in the hierarchy of poetic forms and genres inherited by Pushkin's generation.[10] It did indeed come to prominence in Russia in the course of the 1820s, but its emergence as a significant poetic form occurred only after the work on *Onegin* had begun. The first hints of this impending "sonnet renaissance" were limited to four sonnets composed by Del'vig in 1822, which the exiled Pushkin appears to have come across only late in 1823.[11] However doubtful their influence on *Onegin*, there can be no question of their historical significance. Pushkin himself would later credit Del'vig with having brought the sonnet to Russia.[12] While various scholars have been eager to adduce parallels between the Onegin stanza and the sonnet *in abstracto*, few have thought to consider the problem in the context of the Russian sonnet writing (or lack thereof) of the early 1820s. For heuristic – rather than historical – reasons, we will briefly examine one of Del'vig's standard-setting sonnets and compare it to an Onegin stanza:[13]

Вдохновение
(Сонет)

1 Не часто к нам слетает вдохновенье,	A
И краткий миг в душе оно горит;	b
Но этот миг любимец муз ценит,	b
Как мученик с землею разлученье.	A
5 В друзьях обман, в любви разуверенье	A
И яд во всем, чем сердце дорожит,	b
Забыты им: восторженный пиит	b
Уж прочитал свое предназначенье.	A
9 И презренный, гонимый от людей,	c
Блуждающий один под небесами,	D
Он говорит с грядущими веками;	D
12 Он ставит честь превыше всех частей,	c
Он клевете мстит славою своей	c
И делится бессмертием с богами.[14]	D

Inspiration
(A sonnet)

1 We're seldom visited by inspiration,	A
It burns in us for but an instant, yet	b
That flash is treasured by the muses' pet,	b
As by the saint from Earth his separation.	A
5 Deceit in friendship, loss of love, frustration –	A
The venom of such hardships he'll forget.	b
The visionary poet's path is set,	b
And he already knows his destination.	A
9 A victim of societal curse and blame,	c
Lone under clouds he wanders and engages	D
In conversations with the future ages.	D
12 He cares but to preserve his honest name,	c
On slander he takes vengeance with his fame;	c
He shares with gods place on immortal pages.[15]	D

Like all of Del'vig's early sonnets, "Inspiration" is written in iambic pentameter with a caesura after the second foot. This type of line is far more structured than the caesura-free iambic tetrameter of *Onegin* and can in no way be confused with it. In terms of rhyme, differences stand out yet more clearly. Del'vig invariably bases his sonnets on four rhymes (two in the quatrains, two in the tercets), an extraordinary degree of organization even by sonnet standards.[16] This rhyme scheme makes far more exacting demands on the poet than does the rhyme scheme of an Onegin stanza. The Onegin stanza contains rhyme *pairs* (i.e., seven different rhymes in fourteen lines), while a Del'vig sonnet uses each rhyme a minimum of *three* times.[17]

Still more distinctive than meter and rhyme, however, are the structural and syntactic expectations of each form. Sonnets by definition require a carefully articulated poetic argument, which unfolds along predictable structural points. The octet presents the basic idea, with each quatrain generally offering a different perspective on it. The sestet marks a turn in the poetic logic, and it culminates in a synthesis. In "Inspiration," for example, the first quatrain considers the joyous moment of poetic insight, while the second functions as a contrast by describing the negative elements that the inspired poet leaves behind. In the sestet, these oppositions are resolved: the poet overcomes his temporary isolation and achieves immortality. The overall structure of Del'vig's sonnet is accentuated by the periods (after lines 4, 8, and 14) and even by the graphic layout.[18] Needless to say, sonnet writers can (and do) diverge in their observance of these rules. However, they are well aware that any deviation will be understood as a conscious departure from the canon.

The Onegin stanza, being the invention of Pushkin himself, allowed an extraordinary degree of creative freedom. While Pushkin set the rhyme scheme from the very beginning, he could determine the "rules" behind the syntactic structure of the individual stanza as he went along. If the first Onegin stanza could be neatly divided both syntactically and logically into subdivisions of 4-4-4-2, the following stanza indicates that Pushkin did not place much stock in such geometric regularity:

> Враги! Давно ли друг от друга
> Их жажда крови отвела?
> Давно ль они часы досуга,
> Трапезу, мысли и дела
> Делили дружно? Ныне злобно,
> Врагам наследственным подобно,
> Как в страшном, непонятном сне,
> Они друг другу в тишине
> Готовят гибель хладнокровно . . .
> Не засмеяться ль им, пока
> Не обагрилась их рука,

Не разойтиться ль полюбовно? . . .
Но дико светская вражда
Боится ложного стыда. (vi, 28)

The foes! How long has bloodlust parted
And so estranged these former friends?
How long ago did they, warmhearted,
Share meals and pastimes, thoughts and ends?
And now, malignant in intention,
Like ancient foes in mad dissension,
As in a dreadful senseless dream,
They glower coldly as they scheme
In silence to destroy each other . . .
Should they not laugh while yet there's time,
Before their hands are stained with crime?
Should each not part once more as brother? . . .
But enmity among their class
Holds shame in savage dread, alas.

   The logical pauses in this stanza come after lines 2, 9, and 12, and in the middle of line 5 (the English translation does not always mirror the syntactic breaks of the original). In short, with the exception of lines 12 and 14, the syntactic periods persistently sidestep the "logical" breaks implicit in the strophic design. Such liberties would be considered serious shortcomings in a sonnet, which is defined by its strictness of form. ("In der Begrenzung zeigt sich erst der Meister" ["The master shows himself in limitation"], as Goethe noted in a celebrated sonnet on the sonnet.)[19] Yet the Onegin stanza thrives on unpredictability. Pushkin clearly reveled in the freedom to play the semantics off *against* the form.[20] While certain tendencies have been noted (e.g., a stop after the fourth line), one suspects that they were established largely in order to be broken.[21] In extreme cases (always semantically motivated), Pushkin even used enjambment to connect the fourteenth line of one stanza with the first words of the next, thereby violating the basic *concept* of a stanza.

   In short, numerous formal features (meter, rhyme, syntax, and overall structure) distinguish the Onegin stanza from the Russian sonnet contemporary to it. Since Pushkin rarely devised a strophic form, one may safely assume that, when he did so, there was a compelling reason. A sonnet rhyme scheme would have been far too constricting for a lengthy and digressive novel in verse. Moreover, a sonnet would have brought with it the weight of previous practice (European, if not specifically Russian). By creating the Onegin stanza, Pushkin could define his own rules – and subsequently ignore them. He was beholden only to himself.

For poets after Pushkin, of course, the Onegin stanza took on new meaning. If Pushkin had devised his form as a sort of poetic *tabula rasa* (permitting him maximum creative freedom in a poetic culture dominated by borrowing), his successors turned to it for precisely the opposite reason – its rich associations. This fourteen-line stanza quickly became the most "marked" form in the entire Russian poetic repertoire. Subsequent poets had at their disposal a sure-fire means of recalling Pushkin's masterwork. It remains to be determined why they would wish to do so.

In a sense, Russian poets who write in Onegin stanzas commit an act of supreme arrogance, for they invite comparisons to a model generally acknowledged to be the cornerstone of the entire tradition. Yet a comparison is precisely what Pushkin's successors demanded. Virtually every poet who wrote in Onegin stanzas explicitly named his source, often in the very first lines of the new work.

While Pushkin was still alive, Lermontov was composing his "Tambovskaia kaznacheisha" ("The Tambov Treasurer's Wife"), which opens with the declaration:

> Пускай слыву я старовером,
> Мне все равно – я даже рад:
> Пишу Онегина размером;
> Пою, друзья, на старый лад.[22]

(Let me be considered an old believer, / I don't care – I'm even glad: / I write in the meter of Onegin, / I sing, my friends, in the old fashion.)

Several decades later, the Symbolist poet Maksimilian Voloshin would begin his "Pis'mo" ("Letter") in a similar way:

> Я соблюдаю обещанье
> И замыкаю в четкий стих
> Мое далекое посланье.
> Пусть будет он как вечер тих,
> Как стих "Онегина" прозрачен.[23]

(I am keeping my promise / And enclosing in precise verse / My distant epistle. / Let it be quiet as evening, / As transparent as the verse of "Onegin.")

Even the Futurist Igor' Severianin, writing his "Roial' Leandra" ("Leander's Grand Piano") after the Revolution, opens this "novel in stanzas" with an explanation of his formal choice:

Не из задора, не для славы
Пишу онегинской строфой
Непритязательные главы,
Где дух поэзии живой.

Мне просто нравится рисунок
Скользящей пушкинской строфы.
Он близок для душевных струнок
Поэта с берегов Невы . . .[24]

(Not out of passion, not for fame, / Do I write in the Onegin stanza / [My] unpretentious chapters, / Where the spirit of poetry is alive. // I simply like the outline / Of Pushkin's sliding stanza. / It is congenial to the spiritual strings / Of a poet from the banks of the Neva . . .)

These verses, it should be noted, are the only lines in the work *not* written in Onegin stanzas. However, the references to Pushkin continue as the work progresses. In the second part, Severianin includes an idiosyncratic homage to Pushkin in an Onegin stanza devoted to the cultural battles of prerevolutionary Russia:

Уже воюет Эго с Кубо,
И сонм *крученых бурлюков*
Идет войной на Сологуба
И символических божков.
Уж партитуры жечь Сен-Санса –
Задачи неодекаданса,
И с "современья корабля"
Швырять того, строфой чьей я
Веду роман, настала мода. (II, 9)

(Already Ego fights with Cubo, / And a host of *kruchenykh burliuks* / Comes to attack Sologub / And the little Symbolist gods. / Already it is the task of neodecadence / To burn Saint-Saëns' scores. / And it has become fashionable / To hurl from "modernity's steamship" / The one in whose stanza I am writing my novel .)

In this passage, Pushkin is brought in through the back door, so to speak, but nonetheless obviously enough that any of Severianin's contemporaries would have recognized him. We begin with a reference to the battle of the Ego-Futurists (Severianin's faction) with the Cubo-Futurists.[25] Severianin then alludes to the most famous Cubo-Futurist manifesto "Poshchechina obshchestvennomu vkusu" ("A Slap in the Face of Public Taste"), both in its attack on the Symbolist Sologub and, of course, in its most outrageous declaration: the necessity of throwing Pushkin off the steamship of modernity.[26]

This in turn provides the link to the Onegin stanza: "the one in whose stanza I am writing my novel."

Pereleshin, the last (chronologically speaking) in our series, repeatedly mentions the Onegin stanza in his *Poema bez predmeta* (Poem Without a Subject), completed in 1976. True to tradition, his first reference occurs in the opening stanza, when the muse addresses the poet:

> За ум берись, бросай лениться:
> талантик напрягая свой,
> пиши онегинской строфой –
> пора у Пушкина учиться.[27]

(Wise up, stop lazing about. / Pushing your little talent to its limits, / Write in Onegin stanzas – / It's time to learn from Pushkin.)

These examples should suffice to show the zeal with which poets proclaimed their formal debt to tradition. It may fairly be asked why they insisted on announcing that they were writing Onegin stanzas. After all, any literate Russian reader should recognize the form even without such metapoetic telegraphing. American critics (following Harold Bloom) commonly speak of the "anxiety of influence," whereby poets will do anything to avoid admitting their allegiance to their models. Here one can observe the opposite phenomenon: a virtual flaunting of influence. In the remainder of this chapter, I will attempt to explain why this is done and how it affects the reception of the new work.

Taking their cue from Pushkin's masterpiece, subsequent works in the Onegin stanza feature a more or less autobiographical first-person narrator who is quick to digress. However, given the variety of *Eugene Onegin* itself, it should come as no surprise that these works display an extraordinary heterogeneity of style, subject, and method. Each poet selects certain elements of *Onegin* and develops them, leaving others completely untouched. Very often, poets borrow not the plot or the genre, but "secondary" features: stylistic devices, intonation, syntax, rhymes, specific words or phrases. It should be recalled that the most famous passages of *Eugene Onegin* were committed to memory not only by literary scholars, but also by innumerable Pushkin admirers and generations of Russian (and later, Soviet) schoolchildren. These lines, with their familiar rhythms and rhymes, were so firmly implanted in the Russian cultural memory that the slightest allusion sufficed to recall the original Pushkinian context.

Eugene Onegin was published serially, over a period of several years, which meant that the work was widely known long before it was complete. One testimony to its immediate success can be found in a so-called novel in verse entitled *Evgenii Vel'skoi* (Eugene Velsky), which was published anonymously in 1828 (chapter I) and 1829 (chapters II and III). The work begins – not in Onegin stanzas, but in freely rhymed iambic tetrameter – with a discussion between an author and a bookseller. Pushkin himself, of course, had preceded the publication of the first chapter of *Onegin* (1825) with a dialogue in this same form between these very characters. In Pushkin's version, it was a poet's market: the conversation focused on the bookseller's attempts to procure for profit the work of the inspired poet. The dialogue in *Eugene Velsky* concerns the opposite problem: the author tries to convince his reluctant interlocutor that his new work is a potentially valuable investment. When the bookseller contends that poetry does not sell, the author responds by citing Pushkin's illustrious model:

Книгопродавец

Чего ж вам хочется, скажите?
Мне не понятна ваша цель –
И – кажется – не осудите!
Напрасно взяли вы – свирель.
Едва ли лавры вы пожнете;
Нет, мудрененько их достать –
В Жуковские не попадете
И Пушкиным вам не бывать!

Автор

А! вот о Пушкине – и кстати –
Ты знаешь у него в печати
Поэма есть . . .

Книгопродавец

Его Руслан?

Автор

О нет; тот маленький роман . . .

Книгопродавец

Евгений? Кто его не знает?
Роман нам этот доставляет
Такой порядочный доход,
И весь ученый ваш народ
Его как чудо выхваляет!

Автор

Согласен с ними и с тобой;
Как ни суди о нем кто строго –
Хорошего всё очень много:
Стихи прекрасны, слог живой,
И это-то стихотворенье
Я пародировать хочу . . .[28]

(Bookseller: "What do you want, tell me? / I don't understand your point, / And it seems to me – don't criticize me! – / That you have taken your reed pipe in vain. / It is very unlikely that you will reap laurels. / No, it would be rather strange were you to do so. / You don't reach the level of the Zhukovskys / And you're not going to be any Pushkin!" / Author: "Ah! You've mentioned Pushkin – and very opportunely – / You know that there is in print / A poem by him . . ." Bookseller: "His Ruslan [and Ludmila]?" / Author: "Oh no; that little novel . . . " / Bookseller: "Eugene? Who doesn't know it? / That novel gives us / Quite a decent income, / And all of your learned folk / Praise it as a miracle!" / Author: "I agree with you and them; / However strictly one may judge it – / There's still a lot of good stuff there: / The verses are splendid, the style lively. / And it's precisely this poem / That I would like to parody . . . ")

After this introduction, the tale itself begins. The author's claims notwithstanding, it is less a parody than an imitation – both on formal and thematic levels. The plot concerns the adventures of the youthful Eugene Velsky, a provincial lad with rakish inclinations, who leaves his native Tambov to come to Moscow. (This is an obvious reversal of Pushkin's text, where the eponymous hero is a sophisticated city dweller who relocates in the provinces.) Velsky's upbringing will be entrusted to a certain Count Znatov (old, jealous, rich) and his wife (young, beautiful, dissatisfied). The reader is led to expect a romance between the hero and Count Znatov's wife, yet myriad digressions prevent this overdetermined event from taking place. (The closest one gets is a voyeuristic scene in chapter II, where

Velsky unwittingly enters the countess's boudoir and observes her dressing for a masquerade.)

Not surprisingly, the poem proper is written in fourteen-line stanzas and, as the opening verses indicate, Pushkin's example looms large:

"Подвинь свой стул ко мне, Евгений,
Налюбоваться дай собой;
Ты мил, как солнца луч весенний,
В твоих чертах родитель твой –
О, будь душой ему подобен,
Будь так же тих всегда, не злобен,
И будешь счастлив ты – как он!
Желала б, сын мой, я душою
Не расставаться век с тобою:
Но грозный жребия закон
Непременим. Мой сын! кто знает,
Печаль, иль радость ожидает
Тебя на новом том пути,
В который хочешь ты идти?"
. . . .
Так говорила на прощанье
С Евгением старушка мать.
– А кто Евгений? восклицанье –
Готов сей час ответ вам дать:
Евгений мой, сын Дворянина,
Не очень хоть большого чина
Покойный был его отец,
Но впрочем нажил состоянье,
Кой-как дал сыну воспитанье
И после умер наконец,
Оставивши вдове и сыну
Две сотни душ. Но половину
Вдова давно уж продала,
Долги за мужа раздала.

("Move your chair closer, Eugene, / Let me admire you fully; / You're handsome as the spring sunlight, / Your features are those of your father. / Oh, if you'll be like him in your soul, / Just as quiet and not malicious, / You'll be happy – like him! / I would wish by my soul, my son, / To remain with you forever: / But the terrible law of fate / Cannot be altered. My son! Who knows / Whether sadness or happiness awaits / You on that new path / That you would like to take?" // Thus spoke at parting / With Eugene his old lady-mother. / But who is Eugene? you exclaim – / I'm ready to give you an answer immediately: / My Eugene was the son of a

Noble. / His deceased father, / Although not of very high rank, / Had nonetheless made a fortune, / Given his son some paltry education / And finally died, / Leaving to his widow and son / Two hundred souls. / But the widow had long ago sold half of them / To pay for her husband's debts.)

In terms of structure, these stanzas (the first and the third; I have omitted the second) depart slightly from Pushkin's model. The isolated couplet comes not at the end (as in Pushkin), but in lines 5 and 6. It is conceivable that this change results in a weakening of the stanza's closure; in any case, the author appears to have recognized a problem, for, as the novel progresses, the form becomes stricter, eventually turning into precise Onegin stanzas. Even in these first stanzas, however, the work's derivative nature is on display. Pushkin's novel begins with the interior monologue of the hero as he rushes off to attend to his sick uncle. The next few stanzas introduce the hero by discussing his parents and his upbringing. *Eugene Velsky* also commences with a monologue, but this time it is not imagined, but actually spoken – and not *by* the protagonist, but *to* the protagonist.[29] In these lines, the reader of 1828 would immediately have recognized similarities that extend beyond the level of plot. For example, the first line of stanza 3 is modeled on the intonation of the opening of stanza 2 of *Onegin*:

Так говорила на прощанье (*Velsky*)　　Thus spoke at parting (*Velsky*)
Так думал молодой повеса (*Onegin*)　　Thus thought a young rake (*Onegin*)

Moreover, the sudden turn to the reader is common to both novels (note the way even the punctuation [i.e., the colon] is borrowed!):

С героем моего романа
Без предисловий, сей же час
Позвольте познакомить вас: (*Onegin*)

(Allow me to introduce you to the hero of my novel, without a foreword, immediately:)

– А кто Евгений? восклицанье –
Готов сей час ответ вам дать: (*Velsky*, 1, 3)

(But who is Eugene? you exclaim – I'm ready to give you an answer immediately:)

Старушка рада. А Евгений?
Читатель! будь и с ним знаком: (*Velsky*, 1, 5)

(The old woman is happy. And Eugene? Reader! Be acquainted with him also:)

As the novel continues, the plot of *Eugene Velsky* gradually disintegrates into a series of digressions.[30] Thus, as the plot resemblances to *Onegin* fade, numerous details of content, style, construction, and form compensate, repeatedly reminding the reader of the subtext.

Eugene Velsky develops the provincial side of Pushkin's novel. These elements are particularly pronounced in the "journal" (several stanzas long) of the eponymous hero. Formally, these stanzas are remarkably free (note the e-f-f-f-e-e rhyme scheme of the last six lines in the passage quoted below). However, their lexicon and theme betray the enormous influence of Pushkin's example:

> "Пришла пора страстей жестоких;
> Мне минуло осмнадцать лет –
> И я, младый полу-поэт
> В кругу Тамбовок чернооких,
> Блистал не редко остротой
> И – даже иногда чужой . . .
> Но кто ж, любезный мой читатель,
> Кто в мире сем не подражатель?
> На гениев не урожай,
> А все кой-как да пролезают,
> Их остряками называют,
> Во всех журналах прославляют –
> Ну что ж? Хоть это подавай,
> Особенно в Тамбовский край!" (1, 18)

("The time of cruel passions arrived; / I became eighteen. / As a young half-poet / In a circle of dark-eyed Tambov girls, / I sparkled with my wit – / At times, with someone else's . . . / But who, my dear reader, / Who in this world is not an imitator? / There's no surplus of geniuses, / But everybody's getting by somehow / And they're called "wits" / [They] achieve fame in all the journals – / But what of it? Even this is sufficient, / Especially in the Tambov region!")

The first lines echo the famous opening stanzas of Pushkin's novel ("Когда же юности мятежной / Пришла Евгению пора" 1, 4 ["When the time of rebellious youth arrived for Eugene"]), while the theme of Tambov can be traced to the fifth chapter, where Pushkin introduced a certain "Monsieur Triquet," a guest at Tatiana's nameday party, as "остряк, недавно из Тамбова" ("a wit, not long ago from Tambov"). As it turns out, Triquet's cleverness consists in taking trite verses from old publications, altering them ever so slightly, and reciting them as his own. This detail carried considerable weight for the author of *Eugene Velsky*, who repeats the constellation of "Tambov" and "wit" (together with the motif of plagiarism) in the lines:

В кругу *Тамбовок* чернооких,
Блистал не редко *остротой*
И – даже иногда чужой . . .

(In the circle of dark-eyed *Tambov girls*, / I sparkled with my *wit* / At times, with someone else's . . .)[31]

Indeed, this minor moment in Pushkin's novel is essential to *Eugene Velsky*. The strategy here can be likened to Tom Stoppard's drama *Rosencrantz and Guildenstern Are Dead*, where minor figures of one work (Shakespeare's *Hamlet*) appear as the main characters of a subsequent one. Tambov, emblematizing everything that is backward, derivative, and laughable,[32] moves out of the shadows and into the limelight. Most curious, of course, is the way the Tambov theme supplies a link to Lermontov, whose "Tambov Treasurer's Wife" will be discussed presently.

LERMONTOV

"Who in this world is not an imitator?" asks the hero of *Eugene Velsky*. The question, more profound than it might seem on first glance, has direct relevance to the poetic apprenticeship of Mikhail Lermontov. As we have seen in chapter 1, the young Lermontov eagerly borrowed verse forms, plots, and techniques from Pushkin. Lermontov's interest in the Onegin stanza confirms his fanatic orientation toward Pushkin's example.[33] One of the earliest versions of "Demon" ("The Demon") dates from 1829 and begins with the following dedication:

Я буду петь, пока поется,
Пока, друзья, в груди моей
Еще высоким сердце бьется
И жалость не погибла в ней.
Но той веселости прекрасной
Не требуй от меня напрасно,
И юных гордых дней, поэт,
Ты не вернешь: их нет как нет;
Как солнце осени суровой,
Так пасмурна и жизнь моя;
Среди людей скучаю я:

Мне впечатление не ново . . .
И вот печальные мечты,
Плоды душевной пустоты! . . .[34]

(I will sing as long as I can sing, / As long – my friends – as my heart / Beats nobly in my chest / And pity has not died in it. / But do not demand from me / In vain that wonderful gaiety. / Oh poet! You will not return / Those proud days of youth: / They are no longer; / Like the bleak autumnal sun, / So too my life is gloomy; / I am bored among men, / Nothing is new to me . . . / And here are my sad thoughts, / The fruits of my spiritual emptiness! . . .)

Lermontov's work on "The Demon" spanned almost his entire creative lifetime, and the final product contains not a trace of this introduction. However, this early draft, a formally irreproachable Onegin stanza, clearly indicates the eagerness with which Lermontov sought a model in the work of Pushkin. In these verses, he assumes the persona of a man whose best days have passed and who is bored in the company of others. Such a "type" has its roots in Romantic literature and bears a certain resemblance both to the character of Onegin and that of the mysterious first-person narrator of Pushkin's work. If the introductory verses of *Onegin* offer the reader "the careless fruit of my amusements" ("nebrezhnyi plod moikh zabav"), then Lermontov's narrator gives the "fruits of my spiritual emptiness" ("plody dushevnoi pustoty"). However, as Dmitri Blagoi has noted, the most direct source of this phrase lies elsewhere.[35] In the 1821 lyric "Ia perezhil svoi zhelan'ia" ("I have outlived my desires"), Pushkin had written:

Я разлюбил свои мечты;
Остались мне одни страданья,
Плоды сердечной пустоты.

(I have ceased to love my dreams; / Only sufferings remain for me, / The fruits of my heart's emptiness.)

In the Russian text, we find the identical rhyme in a very similar semantic context. Such a conflation of sources (the lyric poetry as well as the novel in verse) suggests that Lermontov was seeking in as many ways as possible to claim himself as Pushkin's heir.

Nonetheless, Lermontov seems to have quickly realized the inappropriateness of the Onegin stanza for "The Demon." In Pushkin's novel in verse, the narrator plays a central role. Even when physically absent, his opinions are aggressively present. At times, he teases the reader by withholding crucial information or digressing in

the most suspenseful moments. In contrast, the guiding role of the
narrator in "The Demon" was to become negligible. With the
exception of this sole Onegin stanza, Lermontov's narrator belongs
to the background, a hidden yet omniscient observer (much like the
narrator of Pushkin's earlier – and less experimental – southern
poems). Indeed, in its exotic southern setting and tone of uninter-
rupted seriousness, "The Demon" is much closer to these poems
than to *Onegin*. Lermontov apparently associated the Onegin stanza
first and foremost with an intrusive narrator. When his conception of
"The Demon" became firm, this narrator proved superfluous.
Lermontov rejected the Onegin stanza after this lone attempt,
opting instead for a non-strophic iambic tetrameter (a model for
which can be found, not surprisingly, in Pushkin's less mediated
southern poems).

Yet Lermontov was not to be deterred in his attempts to find an
application for the Onegin stanza. He experimented with it again in
two works of 1832: a three-stanza meditation on mortality and an
eight-stanza "fragment" (in the Romantic sense of the word) entitled
"Moriak" ("The Sailor"). In the opening lines of the former, one
already finds a clear lexical echo of *Onegin*:

> Что толку жить! . . . Без приключений
> И с приключеньями – тоска
> Везде, как беспокойный гений,
> Как верная жена, близка.[36]

(What is the sense of living! . . . Whether without adventures / [Or] with
adventures – ennui / Is everywhere, like an agitated spirit, / Like a faithful
wife, [is] nearby.)

The comparison of ennui with "a faithful wife" has its origin in
the first chapter of *Onegin*, where Pushkin describes how his perpe-
tually dissatisfied protagonist is bothered by "spleen":

> Хандра ждала его на страже,
> И бегала за ним она,
> Как тень иль верная жена. (1, 54)

(Spleen stood watch over him / And ran after him, / Like a shadow or a
faithful wife.)

"Toska" ("ennui") and "khandra" ("spleen") were the twin
scourges of the age, and both figured prominently in *Eugene Onegin*.
Lermontov's simile of the faithful wife may appear striking, but an
awareness of his source greatly diminishes its effect. Both poets use a

similar technique (a double simile), yet Pushkin arranges the passage in such a way that the word "wife" falls on a rhyme – moreover, on the stanza's final rhyme. In Lermontov's poem, the phrase occurs in a less prominent position (the middle of the fourth line). As a result, it slips by, and the humorous quality of the comparison is all but lost. The image seems intended not so much to provide comic relief (otherwise entirely absent from Lermontov's pessimistic meditation) as to claim kinship. Indeed, the tone of the poem is relentlessly serious, thus distinguishing it from its formal model. A similar tone characterizes Lermontov's "The Sailor." This work has even less common ground with *Onegin*, being much closer in genre to Byron's Romantic verse tales (its epigraph comes from "The Corsair").[37] In short, while both of these relatively brief works revolve around the personality of a first-person narrator, they lack the ironic layering so central to *Onegin* and offer nothing to compensate for it except a traditional atmosphere of Romantic melancholy. Once again, it appears that Lermontov himself recognized the shortcomings of these experiments, breaking both off after a few stanzas.

Lermontov's final, most sustained, and most successful application of the Onegin stanza came in 1836–37, with "Tambovskaia kazna-cheisha" ("The Tambov Treasurer's Wife"). This work of fifty-three stanzas (roughly the equivalent of one chapter of *Eugene Onegin*) relates an anecdote from Russian provincial life. The plot may be summarized briefly: a visiting uhlan falls in love with the Tambov treasurer's wife and, after several failed attempts to woo her, "wins" her from her husband in a game of cards. In this work, the Pushkinian subtext provides much more than a formal model; it is a constant source of reference as well as a springboard for new ideas. Lermontov's allusions to *Onegin* are numerous and varied, ranging from the subtle to the extremely obvious. "The Tambov Treasurer's Wife" features a narrator who does not hesitate to interfere in his own narration. Like his counterpart in Pushkin, this narrator is an acquaintance of the hero and thus a minor character in the story that he tells. His own opinions, recollections, and digressions are woven into the fabric of that story, often impeding the narrative flow.[38]

In addition to the common narrative style, Lermontov develops many elements of plot from *Onegin*. In general, he expands on details provided by Pushkin. Lermontov scholars have repeatedly suggested biographical influences in the work's plot. (A soldier himself,

Lermontov had recently visited Tambov.) Yet literary precedents supply an equally plausible backdrop. It is surely not coincidental that Tambov is mentioned in Pushkin's novel as an emblem of provincialism.[39] More significantly, even the uhlan as hero may well be derived from *Eugene Onegin*. Not only does his name (Garin) rhyme with that of Pushkin's heroines (Tat'iana and Ol'ga Larin[a]), but an uhlan lover even appears in Pushkin's novel, sweeping Ol'ga off her feet after her intended husband Lensky has been killed (readers of Russian can appreciate how Pushkin prepares the very word "uhlan" phonetically through a series of "u," "l," and "n" sounds):

> Другой увлек ее вниманье,
> Другой успел ее страданье
> Любовной лестью усыпить,
> Улан умел ее пленить,
> Улан любим ее душою . . . (VIII, 10, emphasis added.)

(Another attracted her attention, / Another succeeded in lulling her suffering / With love's flattery. / An uhlan was able to captivate her, / An uhlan became the love of her soul . . .)

Here we observe another "Rosencrantz and Guildenstern" moment. The uhlan, a minor figure in *Onegin*, is "promoted" to romantic hero in Lermontov's poem. In this way, Lermontov sketches an entirely new "type," sanctioned – but never developed – by Pushkin.

Much of the effect of "The Tambov Treasurer's Wife" is based on a tacit assumption that the reader will constantly recognize the underlying Pushkinian model. Sometimes this is simply a matter of repeating old phrases in new contexts. For example, Pushkin says of his protagonist:

> Что было для него измлада
> И труд, и мука, и отрада,
> Что занимало целый день
> Его тоскующую лень, –
> Была наука *страсти нежной*. (I, 8, emphasis added.)

(What from his earliest youth / Was work, torment, and joy; / What all day occupied his yearning indolence, – / Was the science of *passion tender*.)

When introducing the treasurer's wife, Lermontov "transfers" this convenient epithet:

> Казалося, для *нежной страсти*
> Она родилась. (II, emphasis added.)

(It seemed for *tender passion* / She was born.)

In this instance, the reversal in word order appears to mirror the shift from Pushkin's hero to Lermontov's heroine.

Kirill Postoutenko, in a subtle study of the Onegin stanza, has convincingly demonstrated how Pushkin tended to use a given word or phrase in a fixed position of the line.[40] Certain words can be found almost exclusively in rhyming position; others tend to appear in the beginning or middle of the line. An examination of the interjection "akh!" ("oh!") confirms Postoutenko's findings and demonstrates to what extent Lermontov internalized the poetic technique of his predecessor. Pushkin displays a marked tendency to use this exclamation at the beginning of the line, usually on either the first or fourth syllable.[41] Both positions can be found in Tatiana's conversation with her nanny:

> – Ах! няня, сделай одолженье. –
> "Изволь, родная, прикажи."
> – Не думай . . . право . . . подозренье . . .
> Но видишь . . . ах! не откажи. – (III, 34)

> "Oh, nurse, a favor, please . . . and hurry!"
> "Why, sweetheart, anything you choose."
> "You mustn't think . . . and please don't worry . . .
> But see here, oh! just don't refuse!"[42]

In this passage, "akh" merely conveys heightened emotion. In the following examples, however, it signals both surprise and fear. Thus, when Eugene unexpectedly arrives at the Larins' estate, Pushkin combines the word with enjambment:

> Вот ближе! скачут . . . и на двор
> Евгений! "Ах!" и легче тени
> Татьяна прыг в другие сени. (III, 38)

> They're closer . . . coming here . . . it's he!
> Onegin! "Oh!" – And light as air,
> She's out the backway, down the stair.

Similarly, in the novel's famous dream sequence, Tatiana uses this interjection to express horror when a bear suddenly appears before her:

> Большой, взъерошенный медведь;
> Татьяна *Ах!* а он реветь,
> И лапу с острыми когтями
> Ей протянул. (V, 12)

A huge and matted bear appeared!
Tatyana Oh! He growled and reared,
Then stretched a paw . . . sharp claws abhorrent,
To Tanya.[43]

What is remarkable is that Lermontov employs precisely this technique in his own poem. The exclamation "akh" occurs several times, always on either the first or fourth syllable. The first time it is simply an exclamation on the part of the town's unmarried women, who hear of the imminent arrival of the uhlans:

Уланы, ах! такие хваты . . .
Полковник, верно неженатый – (3)

The Uhlans, oh! such manly fellows . . .
The colonel surely is unmarried–

In the emotional scene in which the uhlan pays an unexpected visit to the treasurer's wife, the word recurs three times. First, there is a knock at the door, which the heroine assumes to be that of her husband:

Вдруг дверью стукнули. "Кто там?
Андрюшка! Ах, тюлень ленивый!. . . . "
Вот чей-то шаг – и перед ней
Явился . . . только не Андрей. (34)

A sudden knock. "But who is there?
Andriushka! Oh, you lazy clod! . . . "
Here's someone's step – and in her way
Appeared . . . but it was not Andrei.

The uhlan makes his entrance and, a mere two stanzas later, includes an "akh" in his own declaration of love:

Я вижу, вы меня не ждали –
Прочесть легко из ваших глаз;
Ах, вы еще не испытали,
Что в страсти значит день, что час!

I see – you did not know I'd dash in
I understand from how you glower,
Oh, you have never felt such passion,
That knows not second, day nor hour.

Finally, in a turn of events unanticipated by the protagonist (but perhaps anticipated by the reader, who may recall the parallel situation in chapter VIII of *Onegin*), the husband enters. Lermontov records this moment with the classic fourth-syllable "akh" combined with enjambment:

Дверь настежь – и в дверях супруг.
Красотка: "Ах!" Они взглянули
Друг другу сумрачно в глаза; (38)

The door's ajar – the husband's there.
The beauty: "Oh!" And then they looked
Each other gloom'ly in the eye;

Here we encounter an indisputable stylistic allusion – in spite of the fact that these passages occur in scenes that have no direct equivalents in Pushkin's novel. An interjection is an example of language as pure expressivity, stripped down to its barest essentials. By handling this microcosmic element of speech in precisely the same way as Pushkin did, Lermontov goes beyond the level of semantics to that of pure sound, drawing extremely subtle parallels between his own work and that of his predecessor.

At times, the desire to align himself with Pushkin becomes so strong that Lermontov borrows wholly irrelevant elements of plot and narrative technique. For example, he begins stanza 13 with the claim:

Для бо́льшей ясности романа
Здесь объявить мне вам пора,
Что страстно влюблена в улана
Была одна ее сестра.

(For greater clarity of my novel, / Here it is time for me to announce to you / That her sister / Was passionately in love with the uhlan.)

Contrary to the narrator's assertion, this information adds no "clarity" whatsoever. In fact, the heroine's sister will never again be mentioned in the course of the work. Her presence can be explained only by the need to emulate both the pesky, irritating, and indulgent narrator of Pushkin's novel in verse, as well as its plot, for which the constellation of two sisters (in love with different suitors) is central. The most obvious oddity of this passage, however, is the very word "roman" ("novel"). Elsewhere, Lermontov calls his poem a "rasskaz" ("story") and even a "skazka" ("fairy tale"), yet only in this passage, where he pulls out all the stops to imitate his master, does he upgrade his anecdote to the level of a novel.

An equally improbable example can be found in stanza 40, when the love intrigue reaches its apogee:

Измучен тайною досадой,
Идет он дальше в кабинет . . .
Но здесь спешить нам нужды нет,
Притом спешить нигде не надо.
Итак, позвольте отдохнуть,
А там докончим как-нибудь.

(Worn out with secret anger, / He walks further into the study . . . / But here there's no need to hurry. / And besides, one should never hurry anywhere. / So, allow me to rest; / I'll finish up somehow.)

This sudden interruption on the part of the narrator is easily traced to *Onegin* (the final stanza of chapter III):

Но следствия нежданной встречи
Сегодня, милые друзья,
Пересказать не в силах я;
Мне должно после долгой речи
И погулять и отдохнуть:
Докончу после как-нибудь.

(But my dear friends, / I don't have the strength today to narrate / The results of this unexpected meeting; / After a long speech I need / To walk and rest: / I'll finish up later somehow.)

In this instance, Lermontov repeats the idea as well as the exact rhyme words of the final couplet. However, the difference is immense. *Onegin*, after all, was published serially. In a work that constantly and conscientiously meandered, Pushkin had created toward the end of the chapter in question a rare moment of suspense (Onegin's meeting with Tatiana after he receives her love letter). By cutting this scene off abruptly, he forced the reader to wait approximately one year – until the next chapter was published. In Lermontov's poem, which consists of a single chapter, the digression is limited to a mere two stanzas, after which the poet plunges into the denouement.

Were "The Tambov Treasurer's Wife" nothing more than a series of such echoes, it would have to be considered at best a clever imitation. However, Lermontov displays genuine originality in his ability to weave Pushkinian diction, poetic devices, and narrative technique into an altered plot. Because his subtext was so familiar to his readers, Lermontov could take advantage of their expectations. One of the linchpins of Pushkin's plot is the duel, set in motion when Onegin's neighbor Zaretsky appears with a "zapiska." Literally, this word means "note," but in the context of *Onegin*, it obtains a more specific meaning: a "challenge":

> Тот после первого привета . . .
> Вручил *записку* от поэта. (vi, 8, emphasis added.)

(He, after the first greeting . . . / Handed over the poet's *note*.)

Lermontov's poem has no duel, yet he carefully sets the poetic machinery in motion. After his declaration of love (modeled on Tatiana's letter to Onegin)[44] has been interrupted by the appearance of his rival (the treasurer himself), Lermontov's uhlan hero sets off for home:

> И Гарин вышел. Дома пули
> И пистолеты снарядил.
> Присел – и трубку закурил.

(And Garin left. At home / He prepared bullets and guns. / He sat down – and began to smoke his pipe.)

Thus concludes stanza 38. The reader assumes, of course, that a duel is afoot. Not only has the uhlan been caught in the act of trying to seduce a married man's wife, but, upon returning home, he prepares his pistols (cf. Onegin vi, 29, where references to pistols and bullets can be found, with the word "puli" [bullets] also occupying a rhyming position). The plural form ("pistols" rather than "pistol") strongly suggests that one is for Garin and the other for his opponent. The subsequent stanza begins by encouraging the reader in precisely these expectations:

> И через час ему приносит
> *Записку* грязную лакей. (Emphasis added.)

(And in an hour a lackey / Brings to him a soiled *note*.)

For the initiated reader, the familiar word "note" ("zapiska") immediately recalls the "challenge" that Pushkin's Zaretsky delivered. Even the fact that a "lackey" bears the note has a certain resonance with *Onegin*, for in Pushkin's duel scene Onegin insults his opponent by using a lackey as his second. However, all of these expectations are neatly dashed in the course of the next few lines:

> Что это? чудо! Нынче просит
> К себе на вистик казначей,
> Он именнниик – будут гости . . .
> От удивления и злости

Чуть не задохся наш герой.
Уж не обман ли тут какой?

(What's this? A miracle! Today / The treasurer is asking him to a little game of whist. / It's his nameday – there will be guests . . . / From amazement and anger / Our hero almost choked. / Is this not some sort of deception?)

The duel that seemed so inevitable, that in Pushkin occasions several stanzas of soul-searching, is thus transformed into a "little game of whist." Like the uhlan, the reader feels he has been deceived. Of course, the ultimate irony is that this card game proves to be similarly devastating. In Lermontov's variant, the challenger (i.e., the treasurer) loses his possessions, his honor, and his wife.

To summarize, in "The Tambov Treasurer's Wife" Lermontov uses Pushkin's Onegin stanza to create an idiosyncratic verse narrative highly indebted to *Eugene Onegin*. Virtually every stanza of Lermontov's poem can be traced in one way or another (from direct citation to subtle allusion, from elements of plot to narrative devices) to Pushkin's novel in verse. So laden is Lermontov's text with references that the reader must constantly read the work through the prism of its subtext. Yet Lermontov does not slavishly imitate; he reorganizes and adds to the material that Pushkin puts at his disposal. The achievement of "The Tambov Treasurer's Wife" is that, by repeating, reshaping, and creatively parodying, it gives new life to the Onegin stanza. Lermontov borrows, alters, and adds; yet he also *omits* entire layers of Pushkin's masterwork. In short, when Lermontov finally found an application for the Onegin stanza, it was for a work that could easily be categorized as a comic poem. *Onegin* itself, while containing indisputably comic elements, can in no way be reduced to such a designation. Curiously, this association of the Onegin stanza with humorous or satirical content represents the dominant trend of the nineteenth century.[45] In contrast, the writers of the early twentieth century were to develop the Onegin stanza in precisely the opposite direction – seriousness.[46]

SYMBOLIST AND FUTURIST ONEGIN STANZAS

In 1904, the Symbolist poet Maksimilian Voloshin wrote two letters in verse to his beloved, Margarita Sabashnikova. Sabashnikova had recently returned to her family in Moscow, while Voloshin remained in Paris, where the two had met and fallen in love. Voloshin had suggested to her, "Shall we write not in words, but only in pictures and verse?"[47] In the Russian poetic tradition, verse epistles are by no means an oddity, yet Voloshin's letters stand out through their form: Onegin stanzas.[48] The obvious irony here is that, while letters play a central role in the plot of *Eugene Onegin*, they belong to the extremely small number of verses in that work *not* written in the Onegin stanza. Mikhail Gasparov has suggested that Voloshin – and Russian readers in general – nonetheless associated the Onegin stanza with these famous interpolated letters. In other words, in the Russian cultural memory, these letters took on the formal coloration of their larger context.[49] Perhaps this is so, but there are stylistic as well as formal incongruities that must be considered. The reflective and retrospective quality of Voloshin's letter contrasts starkly with the impulsive rambling that characterizes the epistles of Pushkin's main characters. Moreover, any easy association of Voloshin's work with Pushkin's model epistles is made problematic by the fact that – as Voloshin and all Russian readers well knew – both letters in *Onegin* (if judged by traditional love plots) lead to disastrous results. Surely there must have been other reasons that contributed to Voloshin's formal choice.

It will be simplest to begin with the first stanza:

> Я соблюдаю обещанье
> И замыкаю в четкий стих
> Мое далекое посланье.
> Пусть будет он как вечер тих,
> Как стих "Онегина" прозрачен,
> Порою слаб, порой удачен,
> Пусть звук речей журчит ярчей,
> Чем быстро шепчущий ручей . . .
> Вот я опять один в Париже
> В кругу привычной старины . . .
> Кто видел вместе те же сны,
> Становится невольно ближе.
> В туманах памяти отсель
> Поет знакомый ритурнель.

> In this exacting form I'll fetter
> And thus my word to you I'll keep,
> This distant solitary letter.
> May it be like the evening deep,
> And like Onegin's verse transparent;

Its weaknesses and strengths apparent,
And let the speech ring out still clearer,
Than streams that sound when we are nearer . . .
Yes, now I am again in Paris
Among antiquities we've seen
Who'er has dreamt this very dream
Comes closer to me than she now is.
Amid the mists of memory's well
Sings a familiar ritournelle.

In addition to naming his source explicitly and praising its "transparence" (a concept we shall return to), Voloshin even appears to include in his sixth line a veiled reference to the introductory lines of *Onegin* itself. In a dedication, Pushkin had addressed his reader with the words:

> Прими собранье пестрых глав,
> Полусмешных, полупечальных.

(Accept this collection of motley verses, / Half-funny, half-sad.)

In Voloshin's expression "poroiu slab, poroi udachen" (literally: "at times weak, at times successful"), one may detect an echo of Pushkin's own phrase "polusmeshnykh, polupechal'nykh" ("half funny, half sad").[50] In terms of his larger strategy, however, the final couplet is the most revealing. Technically speaking, the term "ritournelle" designates a strict poetic form of Italian origin (never popular in Russia), but Voloshin uses it with deliberate imprecision. In this passage, Voloshin takes advantage of the word's latinate root ("to return"). In the following stanzas of the "Letter," he relives various events from the previous months. These scenes took place in Paris and its environs, yet they transcended their temporal and spatial boundaries, allowing the Russian visitors to "return" to earlier eras and places:

> Для нас Париж был ряд преддверий
> В просторы всех веков и стран,
> Легенд, историй и поверий.

(For us Paris was a row of thresholds / Into the expanses of all centuries and countries, / [All] legends, histories, and beliefs.)

In short, as the gateway to earlier civilizations, Paris serves as a type of Symbolist paradise, a place of cultural synthesis. Just as the scenes depicted in the "Letter" recall earlier times (first the recent past, then ancient history and mythology), so the Onegin stanza itself serves as the vehicle for another kind of return. Through this strongly marked form, the poet brings the reader back to the "Golden Age" of Russian poetry, indeed, to its most illustrious achievement. Voloshin's verses seek to be "transparent" in the sense that they create a seamless passage from contemporaneity to the timeless past. The Onegin stanza serves as the formal equivalent to this powerful love, which strives to draw the past happiness into the present.

As far as plot and textual echoes are concerned, Voloshin's poem is surprisingly lacking in references to *Eugene Onegin*. In Lermontov's "Tambov Treasurer's Wife," one could barely find a line without some connection to Pushkin's novel in verse. And while the plot was distinct from that of *Onegin*, there were nonetheless immediate and frequent points of contact. Yet aside from the fact that it is a love letter in verse, Voloshin's poem displays no clear parallels to Pushkin's model. (It is virtually plotless, skipping from one reminiscence to the next.) Direct intertextual allusions are few and by no means obvious. In the fourth stanza, for example, Voloshin's reveries are interrupted by steps:

> И аромат воспоминаний,
> Как запах тлеющих цветов,
> Меня пьянит. Чу! Шум шагов . . .

(And the aromat of memories, / Like the smell of wilting flowers, / Intoxicates me. Hark! The sound of steps . . .)

These last words (and the following ellipsis) vaguely recall a phrase in the scene in which Tatiana, attempting to practice sorcery by holding a mirror upwards, is interrupted by the appearance of a mysterious passerby:

> Но в темном зеркале одна
> Дрожит печальная луна . . .
> Чу . . . снег хрустит . . . прохожий; (v, 9)

(But in the dark mirror, / The sad moon trembles all alone . . . / Hark . . . the snow crunches . . . a passerby;)

Likewise, in the phrase "Какая темная Обида" of Voloshin's "second" letter ("What dark Insult"), the reader may recognize a play on the intonation of Pushkin's exclamatory "Какое низкое коварство" ("What low perfidiousness"), which Lermontov had imitated in "Какое адское мученье" ("What devilish torment") and Pereleshin would later incorporate into one of his own Onegin stanzas as "Какая горькая обида" ("What bitter insult"). All of these Russian phrases are comprised of three trisyllabic words, the first of which is an adjectival "what."

Curiously, Voloshin's clearest allusions recall not Pushkin, but other nineteenth-century Russian poets. The seventh stanza describes the poet's desire to seize the impressions of a moment for eternity and (in the closing couplet) his recognition of the impossibility of the task:

> Я б из себя все впечатленья
> Хотел по-Вашему понять,
> Певучей рифмой их связать
> И в стих вковать их отраженье.
> Но только нет . . . Продленный миг
> Есть ложь . . . И беден мой язык.

(I would want to understand all my impressions / In your way, / To bind them with a sonorous rhyme / And forge their reflection into verse. / But no . . . the extended moment / Is a lie . . . and my language is poor.)

In contrast to the Pushkin echoes (which may be more coincidence than allusion), these references are truly obvious. A reader familiar with Russian verse cannot help but hear in the concluding line a pastiche of two extremely well-known poems, Tiutchev's "Silentium" (the oft-quoted dictum "Мысль изреченная есть ложь" ["A thought expressed is a lie"] and the opening of Fet's "Как беден наш язык" ("How poor is our language").[51]

It is telling that Voloshin does not hesitate to include references to these poets. For him, it seems, the Onegin stanza is connected less to specific passages and themes in Pushkin's masterwork than to that work's position within the Russian literary tradition.[52] When Voloshin reviewed a joyous period of his own life (in which, not coincidentally, art played a central role), he chose a form that, in terms of Russian literature, was the quintessence of artistic accomplishment. This uniquely Russian form mediated between Paris and Moscow, between present and past, between "Silver Age" (to use a term that Voloshin would not have recognized) and "Golden Age." The celebratory, syncretic spirit of Voloshin's Onegin stanza contrasts markedly with the satiric tone and anecdotal plot that Lermontov had associated with it. In short, the same form had radically different generic and thematic associations for these two poets.

It may seem fanciful to suggest that the Onegin stanza could function as a formal expression of the desire to return to an earlier time. Yet precisely this association is found in the work of Voloshin's contemporaries. In 1912, the minor Symbolist Sergei Solov'ev wrote a lengthy poem in Onegin stanzas entitled "Italiia" ("Italy"). As in Voloshin's case, physical separation from Russia appears to have called forth a specifically Russian poetic form.[53] In these verses, Solov'ev draws a nostalgic image of Italy through recourse to his own childhood memories (e.g., the beginning of the "Sorrento" section: "Который раз, как пустомеля, / Я детство вывожу на свет" ["How many times, like a windbag, / I bring up the subject of childhood"]).[54] These autobiographical recollections merge with tourist observations and, more significantly, cultural ruminations. Solov'ev's vision of Italy is indebted not only to the great artists who either lived or worked in the cities he visits (e.g., Petronius, Gogol', Goethe), but also by Pushkin himself, whose cadences ring recognizably throughout.[55]

Solov'ev's "Italy," like most of his poetry, cannot be considered a major work, but it clearly reflects a trend. Shortly after Solov'ev, Vyacheslav Ivanov commenced work on a long autobiographical poem entitled "Mladenchestvo" ("Infancy"),[56] which consists of forty-nine Onegin stanzas. It was begun in 1913, when most of the text (forty-six stanzas) was written, and completed in 1918. Two aspects of its history of composition deserve emphasis. First, since Ivanov's wife had given birth to their son in the summer of 1912, one may assume that the subject of infancy was close to the poet's thoughts. Secondly, this was the only instance (since his triumphant return to Russia in 1905) when Ivanov was spending numerous months abroad. In short, like Voloshin's "Letter" and Solov'ev's "Italy," Ivanov's poem is a product of a double separation: spatial (from Russia) and temporal (from the period of life under consideration: earliest childhood).

Unlike Voloshin and to a greater extent than Solov'ev, Ivanov includes a number of scenes, characters, and phrases reminiscent of *Eugene Onegin*. For example, when confronted with the opening line of Ivanov's poem ("Отец мой был из нелюдимых"[57] – "My father was one of the unsociable type"), a Russian reader ineluctably recalls the first line of Pushkin's masterpiece: "Мой дядя самых честных правил" ("My uncle was of the most honest principles"). Not only does Ivanov begin by mentioning a family member, he even describes this person with a marked adjective. The word "neliudim" ("unsociable person"), absent from Pushkin's first stanza, appears elsewhere in the novel (Tatiana's letter), where it is used as an epithet of Onegin himself ("Но говорят, вы нелюдим" – "But it is said you are an unsociable person").[58] Through his lexical choices, Ivanov conflates two unrelated passages of *Eugene Onegin*, thereby creating a new, yet strangely familiar context.

This technique extends beyond the first line, for the connection of the uncle (in *Onegin*) to the father (in "Infancy") is subsequently developed. In Pushkin's opening stanza, the uncle is mentioned because he is dying. The protagonist (Onegin) imagines with displeasure and cynicism a protracted deathbed scene. In "Infancy," the father's passing is established in the first stanza, but the actual deathbed scene occurs toward the end of the poem. On the thematic level, Ivanov's depiction of his father's death contrasts sharply to the nonchalance and callousness that characterize the opening of Pushkin's novel. In "Infancy," the future poet, still young and largely uncomprehending, looks on as his father struggles both physically and spiritually. In this strikingly different atmosphere, Ivanov borrows just enough material to remind the reader of his poem's Pushkinian origins:

> Из комнаты – достать *лекарства* – (Ivanov, stanza 40)
> Печально подносить *лекарство*, (Pushkin)
> And from the room – get *medication* (Ivanov)
> To bring in sadly *medication* (Pushkin)
>
> *С больным* спокойно говорит (Ivanov, stanza 41)
> *С больным* сидеть и день и ночь, (Pushkin)
> *With the sick man* calmly have a talk (Ivanov)
> *With the sick man* day and night to sit (Pushkin)

The phrases "with the sick man" and "medication" are hardly unusual in the context of a deathbed scene. However, when these words recur in the very same *position* of the line, the reader cannot but perceive them as allusions. It is noteworthy that one can find the "missing" Pushkinian verbs "sidet'" ("to sit") and "podnosit'" ("to bring in") in the surrounding passages, albeit in conjugated forms:

Подносит Чашу и велит (Ivanov, stanza 43)
Согбен, все там же гость *сидит* (Ivanov, stanza 41)
Brings in the chalice and commands (Ivanov, stanza 43)
Bent over, the guest still *sits* there (Ivanov, stanza 41)

Scholars have detected additional echoes, from the Pushkinian topos of the theater (Ivanov, stanza 32) to the name "Tat'ianushka" (Ivanov, stanza 13), to the theme of "Romanticism" (Ivanov, stanza 4), from familiar words ("toska," "ugrium") to unusual ones ("Quaker," Ivanov, stanza 8).[59] But what is the motive behind such fleeting allusions? It should strike the reader as odd that Ivanov's *autobiography* takes both its form and, to a significant extent, motifs and lexicon from Pushkin's novel. To an extent, this is surely linked to the Symbolist belief in "zhiznetvorchestvo" ("life-creation"), the conviction that there were no strict boundaries between literature and life, that life itself could be creatively constituted according to the same principles as a work of art.[60] Yet the general concept of "zhiznetvorchestvo" cannot explain Ivanov's specific choice of subtext.

As a poet and scholar, Ivanov was fastidiously conscious of the connection of meter, theme, and tone. His comment on Blok's "Vozmezdie" ("Retribution," another Symbolist autobiography in verse, but one which emphasizes the harshness of the twentieth century) serves as an excellent example of his sensitivity to questions of metrical semantics: "Pushkinian form is inappropriate to contemporary complexity; it seems like a golden raiment on a corpse."[61] Indeed, it has been argued that "Infancy" is a direct response to "Retribution," a polemical attempt on Ivanov's part to demonstrate to a wayward fellow Symbolist the "correct" application of Pushkinian poetic technique.[62]

For Ivanov, Pushkinian form defined Russia's nineteenth century and was therefore the ideal medium for works that sought to recreate the spirit of that simpler, "golden" age. In "Infancy," Ivanov's primary themes are time and memory. With warmth and nostalgia, the poet describes his own childhood and – using a Symbolist's sense of memory – the time that preceded it. Relying on a familiar myth, Ivanov equates his earliest years with a paradise:

> . . . не умирай,
> Мой детский, первобытный рай! (stanza 17)

(. . . Do not die, / My childhood, primordial paradise!)

It is therefore appropriate that the work itself conclude with the disappearance of this paradise:

> Впервые солнечная сила,
> Какой не знал мой ранний рай,
> Мне грудь наполнила по край
> И в ней недвижно опочила . . .
> Пробился ключ; в живой родник
> Глядится новый мой двойник . . .

(For the first time the sun's power, / Which my early paradise had not known, / Filled my breast to the brim / And motionlessly fell asleep in it . . . / A spring sounded forth; in [this] vital spring, / My new double looks at himself . . .)

In these final lines (the poem closes with a suggestive ellipsis), the protagonist crosses the threshold that separates infancy from later childhood. (The "new double" should be understood as new phase of existence. The underlying conception is that, as a person grows older, he discards previous "doubles.")[63] It is curious that this final passage – about the loss of paradise – was penned in 1918 in Soviet Russia. In this case the poet had overcome the spatial separation that marked the first forty-six stanzas, yet he was facing the extraordinary dislocation caused by the recent Revolution.

Like Voloshin, Ivanov ignores the comic side of Pushkin's work and the hectoring, chattering narrator. On the level of plot, his poem could hardly be further removed from its metrical model. Nonetheless, Pushkin's presence haunts the work, as is evident already in the introductory stanza:

> Вот жизни длинная минея,
> Воспоминаний палимпсест,
> Ее единая идея –
> Аминь всех жизней – в розах крест.
> Стройна ли песнь и самобытна
> Или ничем не любопытна, –
> В том спросит некогда ответ
> С перелагателя Поэт.
> Размер заветных строф приятен;
> Герою были верен слог.
> Не так поэму слышит Бог;
> Но ритм его нам непонятен.
> Солгать и в малом не хочу;
> Мудрей иное умолчу.

(Here is a long menology of life, / The palimpsest of memories. / Its unifying idea / Is the Amen of all lives, the cross in roses. / Whether the song is harmonious and original / Or in no way curious – / That the Poet will someday ask / Of him who sets it down. / The meter of the cherished verses is pleasant; / The style is true to the story's hero. / God does not hear a poem in this way; / But [H]is rhythm is incomprehensible to us. / Even in little things I do not want to lie; / It's wiser to be silent about some things.)

In the ninth and tenth lines, Ivanov alludes to his source, yet the passage is admittedly obscure. Not everything described in *Onegin* (or, for that matter, in "Infancy") can be considered "pleasant," nor is it clear why the form should be "true" to Ivanov's autobiographical protagonist (who does not correspond in any obvious way to Pushkin's hero). Most remarkable is the way this stanza combines religious imagery ("menology," "palimpsest," "Amen," "God") with poetic terminology ("meter," "style," "poem," "rhythm"). Ivanov seems to suggest that these two spheres are ultimately linked. The very word "zavetnykh" (meaning both "cherished" and "inherited") has both religious and poetic connotations. Derived from "zavet" ("testament"), it emphasizes, in the most literal sense (i.e., when modifying the noun "stanzas"), the connection between Pushkin and the Symbolists. The Onegin stanzas have been bequeathed from one generation to the next in much the same way as a human life is itself an inheritance that a child receives from his parents (hence Ivanov's extraordinary emphasis on parents in a work which might logically be devoted only to the child). Yet "zavet" also has strong religious connotations, being the Russian word for the Old and New Testaments. In this way, the formal aspects of the verse are connected to larger religious and philosophical concerns: the place of the individual in the universal order. Ivanov's ultimate purpose is to affirm life. He does so not by disregarding suffering (the reference to the rose and the cross attests to this), but by stressing continuity in the passage of generations, be it literal (his parents' relationship to him) or figurative (the concept of palimpsest). In the absence of God's own poetic language ("ritm ego nam neponiaten" – "[H]is rhythm is incomprehensible to us"), the Onegin stanza becomes the best alternative. Differences of plot, tone, and character notwithstanding, the familiar cadences of Pushkin's novel in verse prove most suitable to Ivanov's own purposes: the affirmation – at times even idealization – of the past.

Among prerevolutionary poets, few were as opposed to Ivanov's aesthetic ideals as Igor' Severianin. The founder of Ego-Futurism, Severianin ridiculed Ivanov as "rozhdennyi mertvetsom" ("born a corpse"), a backward-looking poet who sought to "obresti byloe / Umershee" ("obtain the dead past") while "v zhivushchem vidia zloe" ("seeing evil in that which is alive").[64] Yet Severianin's appropriation and application of the Onegin stanza are based on principles strikingly similar to those of his Symbolist counterpart. Once again, Pushkin's stanzaic form accompanies a nostalgiac turn to the past.

Severianin occupies a curious position among the Futurists, for he took pains to write in traditional forms (e.g., his numerous sonnets) and genres.[65] "Leander's Grand Piano" (subtitled "Lugne," after the female protagonist) belongs to a series of idiosyncratic poetic memoirs that Severianin wrote in Estonia in the 1920s.[66] This "novel in stanzas" consists of a brief introduction (five quatrains employing a variety of rhyme schemes), followed by 121 Onegin stanzas, which are divided into three parts (of forty-one, thirty-nine, and forty stanzas respectively) and a one-stanza epilogue. The events in the novel are set a mere decade or two before the actual time of composition, yet in terms of atmosphere and subject matter, the work conjures up a world forever lost and therefore as distant as ancient myth.

The plot of "Leander's Grand Piano" concerns Elena (also called, at various times, "Lena," "Hélène" and "Lugne"), who is in certain obvious respects modeled on Pushkin's Tatiana.[67] She grows up in the provinces, marries a rich general whom she does not love, and vastly prefers the country to the city.[68] Into her bleak existence enters Leander, a mysterious, at times seemingly incorporeal composer and piano virtuoso. He first appears in the park outside Elena's country estate, while Kiriena (her "sister"[69] and sole confidante) plays a piano sonata in the background:

> И подошел к ней, скромный, стройный,
> Желанный и ее достойный,
> Из их родного далека
> Знакомый многие века . . .
> – Не узнаешь? – спросил. Хотела
> Ответить "да," сказалось "нет," –
> И омрачился лунный свет,

И в краску бросило все тело . . .
– Не узнаешь? Мечту свою? . . . –
И Lugne шепнула: "Узнаю . . . " (I, 26)

(And [Leander] approached her, modest, handsome, / Longed for and worthy of her, / Known to her for centuries / From their own distant [place/time] . . . / "Don't you recognize me?" he asked. She wanted / To say "yes," but "no" came out. / And the moonlight became dark, / And her whole body blushed . . . / "Don't you recognize your dream? . . . " / And Lugne whispered: "I recognize [it] . . . ")

Leander is an embodiment of a past world (as his name suggests), who throughout the novel appears suddenly from nowhere and recedes just as quickly into timelessness. Elena repeatedly refers to him as "my thought" (e.g., I, 28, 38) and associates him with a dream. Indeed, she invariably "wakes up" after his departure. However, Leander does indeed seem to be real, insofar as Kiriena also meets and speaks with him. Their meetings lead to an exchange of love letters (as in Pushkin, the letters are included in the text, but Severianin retains the Onegin stanza; III, 1–7) followed by a piano recital given by Leander. Elena ultimately acknowledges her love for Leander, but insists that she remain true to her husband. This familiar Pushkinian sequence of events is broken only in the brief epilogue, where Severianin informs the reader that Elena subsequently left her husband, Kiriena shot herself, and Leander "thunders forth throughout the universe" ("gremit vo vsei vselennoi").

In addition to elements of character (the female protagonist, her husband, her admirer) and plot (the star-crossed lovers, the letters in verse), Severianin returns to Pushkin's novel most noticeably through narrative technique. As in Pushkin's work, the plot often plays a secondary role to the narration. In both cases, the story is related with lengthy digressions by an incidental figure who possesses clearly autobiographical traits. Not only does Severianin interrupt the work's dramatic climax to pontificate on the subject of skiing (III, 32), he devotes most of the work's second part to a chronicle of cultural events in prerevolutionary St. Petersburg, offering lengthy reminiscences of his own former glory (surely the largest "ego" in the Ego-Futurist movement) as well as fleeting glimpses of a host of poets, writers, artists, composers, and actors. This 31-stanza (!) digression concludes with the explanation:

Все нарисованное было
В девятисотые года,

Когда так много в душах пыла,
В поступках – еще больше! – льда . . .
Прошу простить за утружденье
Вниманья эрой вырожденья, –
Не все в ней, мнится мне, мертво:
Искусства явно торжество,
И этого вполне довольно,
Дабы с отрадой помянуть
Свершенный нами с вами путь,
А если спутал я невольно
Событий ход, виднее вам:
Мой справочник в глуши – я сам! (II, 32)

(Everything that I have depicted occurred / In the first decade of 1900, / When there was so much ardor in our souls / And still more ice in our actions . . . / I ask forgiveness for troubling / The reader's attention with this degenerate era. / It seems to me that not everything in it has died: / It is clearly a triumph of art, / And this is [reason] enough / To recall with joy / The path that you and I have taken. / And if I unwittingly confused / The sequence of events – you know better than I: / I'm my own reference book out here in the backwoods.)

In this way, Severianin not only recalls the heyday of Russian modernist culture (in which he himself played a considerable role), but also draws attention to his isolated present condition. Two stanzas later, a half-hearted attempt to return to the story of Lugne and Leander is thwarted by another autobiographical reminiscence:

Наружной выдержки порою
Достаточно, чтоб в колею
Жизнь встала, и я сам, не скрою,
Тем способом чинить люблю
Прорехи собственных ненастий,
Рассудку подчиняя страсти.
Я мыслил в юности не так,
Затем, что был большой чудак.
Теперь же здесь, в стране нерусской,
И хорошенько постарев,
Давлю в себе и страсть, и гнев,
Вполне довольствуясь закуской,
Какую мне дает судьба:
Мудра эстонская изба! . . . (II, 35)

(At times external composure / Is sufficient for life / To return to its routine, and I must admit / That I myself like to fix the rips in my own foul moods / By subjecting the passions to reason. / In my youth I did not think this way / Because I was quite an eccentric. / But now, in this non-Russian country, / Having aged significantly, / I repress in myself both passion and wrath, / Satisfying myself fully with the little snack / That fate is giving me: / The Estonian hut is wise! . . .)

None of this has any bearing on the novel's plot, yet it unambiguously situates the speaker in Estonia and thus encourages the reader to identify him with the biographical Severianin. This type of garrulous narrator, geographically separated from his subject matter, is clearly derived from *Eugene Onegin*:

Там некогда гулял и я:	There I myself once had my spree
Но вреден север для меня. (I, 2)	But north is dangerous for me.

In a footnote to these verses, Pushkin had noted that he was in Bessarabia, which signaled to his contemporaries that he was in southern exile for political reasons. Severianin, in self-imposed northern emigration, omits any reference to why he is in Estonia, yet readers of 1925 would hardly have needed an explanation. Like Pushkin before him, Severianin emphasizes a spatial and temporal divide: a carefree past is contrasted to a wiser yet troubled present.

"Leander's Grand Piano" should be understood as an idiosyncratic homage to Pushkin. Style, structure, theme, and biography all root it in the world of *Eugene Onegin*. Indeed, even the work's lexicon is closer to that of Pushkin than to the Frenchified neologisms that made Severianin's initial reputation (and which are parodied in the epigraph to this chapter).[70] In places, Severianin goes so far as to borrow key words from Pushkin, such as a personified "Toska" ("boredom," III, 15) or the phrase "nezhnoi strasti" ("tender passion," II, 13; cf. Pushkin I, 8).[71] However, Severianin freely adapts Pushkin's model in numerous ways. Lugne may be transparently derived from Tatiana, but the enigmatic Leander can hardly be confused with Onegin. Leander is an elemental force, a magical personality, a brilliant, self-confident artist and performer, and thus an alter ego of Severianin himself. The depiction of Leander's piano recital (III, 23–24), one of the work's extraordinary passages, shows him to be a true artist, a vast amplification of Pushkin's Istomina (*Eugene Onegin*, I, 20).

Such freedoms notwithstanding, it is remarkable that, when writing a loosely autobiographical retrospective poem about the timeless power of art, set in a world temporally close yet completely irrecoverable, Severianin opted for Pushkin's formal model. The dispossessed Futurist responded to his present circumstances much like his former "enemies" in the Symbolist camp: he turned to Pushkin as a means of poetic compensation.[72]

Valery Pereleshin's *Poem Without a Subject*, written in the 1970s by a veteran émigré, consists of 400 pages of Onegin stanzas. Like Ivanov's "Infancy," this work can be classified as a poetic autobiography. However, Pereleshin is less interested in exploring his own mystical beginnings than he is in charting the peculiar zigzags of fate that led him from St. Petersburg to Kharbin to Shanghai to Rio de Janeiro – a type of vastly expanded "Onegin's Journey." Characteristic of Pereleshin is his fanatic and explicit Pushkinian orientation. In addition to borrowing the Onegin stanza itself, Pereleshin chooses to divide his work into eight parts ("chapters" in Pushkin's novel, "cantos" in Pereleshin's "poem").[73] Like his predecessor, Pereleshin intersperses comic and tragic passages. Moreover, Pereleshin recalls his predecessor through lexical echoes and narrative technique (e.g., frequent digressions). In ways similar to Pushkin, Pereleshin devotes considerable attention to questions of poetry and poetic craft. Pushkin, for example, had teased his readers in regard to the limited rhyming possibilities of certain Russian words:

> И вот уже трещат морозы
> И серебрятся средь полей . . .
> (Читатель ждет уж рифмы *розы*;
> На, вот возьми ее скорей!) iv, 42

> The frost already cracks and crunches;
> The fields are silver where they froze . . .
> (And you, good reader, with your hunches,
> Expect the rhyme, so take it – Rose!).

Likewise, Pereleshin comments in passing on his own rhymes, for example:

> и да простит меня поэт:
> на "аще" рифмы больше нет.[74]

> forgive me, poet, for this one;
> of rhymes on "ashche" there are none.

Indeed, Pereleshin uses the issue of rhyme (and poetic craft in general) to vent his anger at the official Soviet poets, in particular Evgenii Evtushenko and Andrei Voznesensky (whom he at times conflates into a single personage: "Voznesensko-Evtushensky"):

> Ведь их утешит и устроит
> любой чахоточный рифмоид:
> "любовь" и "ноги," "сон" и "нос,"
> "апаш" – "клопа," "масон" – "разнос."[75]

> For they are simply overjoyed
> by any sickly, frail rhymoid:
> like "love" and "puppy," "nose" and "son,"
> "pan" and "apache," "nugget" – "gun."

Pereleshin attacks these poets not simply as political hacks, but as untalented craftsmen. In rejecting them, he repeatedly casts his lot with Pushkin. He expresses this spiritual kinship in various ways, from direct citation to minute questions of poetic technique. For example, one of Pushkin's accomplishments (according to a Pereleshin footnote) is a line of poetry in which the vowel "i" occurs three times in a row (from "Poltava" – "Vragi Ross*ii i* Petra"). Pereleshin repeats this feat in a similar construction ("Mezh tem Ross*ii i* Evrope,"), then – with uncharacteristic hubris – produces a line with *four* consecutive "i"s ("On na roiale podbiral / melod*ii i i*kh igral").[76] In Soviet propaganda parlance, one might say that Pereleshin "caught up with and surpassed" Pushkin.

Yet Pushkin is merely the beginning. As the first stanza of the fifth canto indicates, Pereleshin consciously conceives of himself as the (unlikely) heir to a lengthy list of illustrious predecessors:

> Пегас обрюзг и обленился,
> овсом объелся и халвой,
> а я ничуть не научился
> владеть онегинской строфой,
> но, чтоб вести рассказ дальнейший,
> сверялся с милой "Казначейшей"
> и, как от зноя ни устал,
> "Младенчество" перелистал.
> Увы, конец моей свободе:
> использованы все "хода"
> и – величайшая беда –
> простые рифмы на исходе,
> истерты лучшие слова
> от недостатка мастерства.[77]

(Pegasus has become fat and lazy, / he's stuffed himself with oats and halvah, / but I haven't even slightly learned / to master the Onegin stanza. / But in order to tell the rest of the story, / I've checked it against the darling "Treasurer's Wife" / and, despite my exhaustion from the heat, / I've even glanced at "Infancy." / Alas, it's the end of my freedom: / all the "moves" are already taken / and – oh, great misfortune – / the simple rhymes are coming to an end, / the best words seem threadbare / because of a lack of poetic craft.)

This passage gives a good sense of Pereleshin's syncretic approach to tradition. For him, the Onegin stanza recalls more than simply *Onegin* itself. Pereleshin is not joking when he specifically mentions both Ivanov's and Lermontov's works in this form, for at various times he alludes to both. Yet this same stanza is linked to Pushkin as well. Simon Karlinsky, the editor of Pereleshin's poem and its fervent advocate, has recognized here the traditional "modesty topos." He suggests that the passage brings us back to *Eugene Onegin*, specifically, to the narrator's admission of his inability to translate satisfactorily Tatiana's letter and the authorial digression about Baratynsky's superiority.[78] To these one should add another Pushkinian source. In the lengthy metapoetic introduction to the long poem "Domik v Kolomne" ("The Little House in Kolomna"), Pushkin writes: "Но Пегас / Стар, зуб уж нет" ("But Pegasus / Is [now] old, he has no teeth"). Pereleshin surely derived his undignified depiction of the eternally young mythological horse from Pushkin. Pushkin's Pegasus is too old and cannot eat (having no teeth), while Pereleshin's has grown lazy from overeating.[79] What is significant is less the specific image in question than the general principle. Pereleshin expands his perspective to include *all* works in the Onegin stanza as well as *all* of Pushkin's works (whether in Onegin stanzas or not).

At times, Pereleshin's poem resembles a "cento," a work consisting exclusively of citations. For example, he concludes one stanza with the following verses:

> "Мне время тлеть, тебе цвести,"
> но и тебя столкнет с пути
> пришелец, подойдущий следом . . .
> Мудрец об этом говорил,
> а я чужое повторил.[80]

("It's time for me to decay, for you to bloom," / but the newcomer who follows in your tracks / will also knock you out of the way. . . / A wise man spoke about this / and I repeated another's words.)

The first line (in quotation marks) comes from Pushkin's famous lyric meditation on death "Brozhu li ia" ("Whether I wander," 1829). However, the final lines have a more complicated pedigree. In *Eugene Onegin*, a stanza ends with the lines:

> Тут бы можно
> Поспорить нам, но я молчу;
> Два века ссорить не хочу. (IV, 33)

(Here we could / Argue, but I will be silent; / I don't want to set two ages against each other.)

This closing couplet left an obvious mark on Vyacheslav Ivanov, who borrowed the rhyme pair for the final lines of the first stanza of "Infancy":

> Солгать и в малом не хочу;
> Мудрей иное умолчу.

(Even in little things I do not want to lie; / It's wiser to be silent about some things.)

It is from Ivanov's *revision* of Pushkin that Pereleshin derives his own verses. He dispenses with the rhyme pair "khochu/molchu" ("want/be silent"), but borrows enough of the words and the sense to make the connection clear. Instead of the verb "to be silent," he uses the antonym "to speak"; instead of the comparative "mudrei" ("wiser"), he uses the noun "mudrets" ("wise man"). Finally, substituting "chuzhoe" for the almost synonymous "inoe," Pereleshin cobbles together his own closing couplet, the theme of which, not surprisingly, is the repetition of another's words:

> Мудрец об этом говорил,
> а я чужое повторил.

(A wise man spoke about this / and I repeated another's words.)

The "wise man," it follows, is not merely the Pushkin of "Whether I wander," but also the Ivanov of "Infancy." The act of "repeating," while not unique to Pereleshin, is certainly a central element of his poetic technique.

The intricate system of echoes devised by Pereleshin underscores the fundamental orientation of his entire work. A displaced and aged Russian poet alone in South America, Pereleshin seeks most of all to connect himself with a tradition. His work, in one sense an "encyclopedia of émigré poets" (to adapt Belinsky's characterization of *Eugene Onegin*), attempts to preserve the Russian poetic tradition that in Pereleshin's view was sacrificed to the Soviets:

> Не у партийного витии –
> орденоносной мелкоты –
> я нахожу моей России
> неистребимые черты,
> а у ничем не знаменитых
> поэтов, часто полусытых,
> которым платят за строку.[81]

(I find the indestructible features / of my Russia / not with the party's orator, / the medal-bearing small fry, / but with the obscure, / half-starved poets, / who get paid by the line.)

Pereleshin's Russia, insofar as it continues to exist, can be found only among obscure émigrés. In the work's concluding stanzas, the poet describes sending his completed work to Slavists, fellow poets, friends, and archives all over the world for safekeeping. The irony, of course, is that it remains unknown in his native land:

> Добавлю с грустью – и немалой,
> что здесь я ведом, как поэт,
> и лишь в России одичалой
> ни у кого поэмы нет.[82]

(I add with sorrow – and not a little, / that here I am known as a poet, / and only in barbarized Russia / does no one have my poem.)

In some sense, this failed return at the end of the eighth book recalls the plot of book VIII of *Onegin*, where the hero himself returns to a scene of dismal failure after the passage of many years. Yet Pereleshin's tone of genuine sadness, combined with his theme of longing for a lost homeland, aligns his poem less with Pushkin's novel than with the works of his twentieth-century forebears. Once again the Onegin stanza functions as a bridge between generations, an attempt to overcome temporal and spatial dislocation (far more severe in Pereleshin's case than in those of his predecessors).

Aleksandr Khazin's "Onegin's Return" ("Vozvrashchenie Onegina," 1946), a parody written in the Soviet Union, provides an interesting companion piece to Pereleshin's much longer *Poem Without a Subject*. The conceit of this work is that Onegin pays a visit to contemporary Leningrad. The following two stanzas can be considered representative of the whole:

У друга нашего немало
Забот и неотложных дел,
Но, как положено, сначала
Идет Онегин в жилотдел.
О, здесь моя бессильна лира,
Здесь музы требуют Шекспира,
И я там был, и я страдал,
И я там горя похлебал.
Вот он стоит с надеждой зыбкой,
Наивный пушкинский чудак,
Его же вопрошают так,
С весьма сочувственной улыбкой:
– Где вызов ваш и где наряд,
Как вы попали в Ленинград?

Затем вопрос поставлен твердо:
– Где проживали раньше вы?
Онегин отвечает гордо:
– Родился на брегах Невы.
– В каком прописаны вы доме?
– Описан я в четвертом томе,
И, описав меня, поэт
Не дал мне справки . . . – Справки нет?! –
Спросил уныло голос женский, –
Тогда помочь не можем вам,
Сегодня вы явились к нам,
А там придет товарищ Ленский,
Приедет bell[e]-Татианá,
Вас много там, а я одна.[83]

(Our friend has numerous / Worries and urgent matters, / But, as is appropriate, first of all / He goes to the Housing Office. / Oh, here my lyre is powerless, / Here the muses demand a Shakespeare, / For I also was there, and I suffered, / And there I gulped my share of grief. / And here he stands, with shaky hope – / Pushkin's naive eccentric. / And they ask him thus, / With a highly sympathetic smile: / "Where is your summons and your order, / How did you end up in Leningrad?" // After this the question is put firmly: / "Where did you live before?" / Onegin answers proudly: / "I was born on the banks of the Neva." / "In what house were you assigned?" / "In the fourth volume I was designed, / And, having designed me, the poet / Did not give me a certificate . . ." "No certificate?!" / A female voice asked gloomily. / "Then we can't help you. / Today you showed up here, / And then comes comrade Lensky, / [And then] belle Tatiana will drive up: / There are a lot of you and only one of me!")

In the ingenious interplay of Pushkinian phraseology (the passage contains direct quotes from *Onegin* as well as obvious allusions)[84] and

Soviet bureaucratese and colloquialisms (specific terms and locu-
tions),[85] Khazin makes explicit precisely what was implicit in the
other twentieth-century works under consideration: the contrast
between an imperfect present and a nostalgically remembered age of
Pushkin. In Khazin's case, the dislocation was not spatial, but
temporal and political. However, as the change in setting from
"Petersburg" to "Leningrad" itself indicates, the spatial continuity
itself contained radical changes. Not only had a tsar's capital been
renamed to honor a Bolshevik, but Leningrad had recently achieved
a new designation as "hero-city" in recognition of the decisive role it
had played in the Second World War. Khazin's parody was thus
aimed both at Soviet society in general (the central socialist concept
of the collective), as well as at one of its most potent symbols.[86]

The reception history of "Onegin's Return" is revealing. Unfortunately for Khazin, his work became extremely popular. In 1946, it
attracted the discerning eye of the Party, and Khazin found himself
listed, along with Anna Akhmatova and the prose satirist Mikhail
Zoshchenko, as a *persona non grata* in the now famous attack on the
journals *Zvezda* and *Leningrad*. At a meeting of Soviet writers, the ever
vigilant cultural watchdog Andrei Zhdanov spoke at length about
Khazin's work:

> There is a parody on *Eugene Onegin* written by a certain Khazin. It is said
> that this work is frequently performed on the stages of Leningrad. It is
> incomprehensible why the people of Leningrad allow someone to mock
> Leningrad from a public tribune like Khazin does. After all, the sense of
> this so-called literary parody consists not simply in empty laughter at the
> adventures of an Onegin who has appeared in contemporary Leningrad.
> The sense of this burlesque is that Khazin attempts to compare our
> contemporary Leningrad with Petersburg of Pushkin's time and to prove
> that our epoch is worse than Pushkin's. This is how the vulgarian [poshliak]
> Khazin has portrayed Leningrad and its inhabitants. This is the evil,
> depraved, rotten sense of this slanderous parody.[87]

Zhdanov's reaction was surely excessive, but one must give him
his due; he certainly recognized the function of the twentieth-
century Onegin stanza.

THE ONEGIN STANZA IN ENGLISH

A survey of the Onegin stanza in English poetry would go beyond
the scope of this study. For the present purposes, it is essential to

recognize one feature that these works share. Anglophone writers who attempt to domesticate this quintessentially Russian form invariably point to their source through explicit naming and obvious textual echoes.[88] Even so readers unfamiliar with Pushkin's masterpiece (and most English speakers fall into this category) cannot possibly appreciate the richness of the formal allusion. The fact that some of these works have enjoyed a positive reception by the general public can be attributed neither to the broad influence of Western Slavists (desirable as this might be) nor to the widespread popularity of equimetrical translations of Pushkin's novel. Rather, it would seem that readers have entirely overlooked the Onegin stanza's unique historical associations.[89]

The problem of translating the Onegin stanza and retaining its distinctive aura was closely scrutinized by Vladimir Nabokov. Nabokov spent several years in the 1950s carefully creating an English rendering of Pushkin's novel in verse. As he proudly explained:

In transposing *Eugene Onegin* from Pushkin's Russian into my English I have sacrificed to completeness of meaning every formal element including the iambic rhythm, whenever its retention hindered fidelity. To my ideal of literalism I sacrificed everything (elegance, euphony, clarity, good taste, modern usage, and even grammar) that the dainty mimic prizes higher than truth.[90]

This passage – and one could easily find others – indicates that Nabokov considered the Onegin stanza to be fundamentally untranslatable, that the form would necessarily be lost on the English reader. Accordingly, the translator could serve the original best by concentrating wholly on the "sense."[91]

Such a belief runs contrary to the premise of this book. I have repeatedly claimed that, for Russian poets, meaning cannot be divorced from form. Does Nabokov therefore become the great exception, the irrefutable counterexample? I think not. As a poet himself, Nabokov well understood the significance of forms in general and of the Onegin stanza in particular. His last Russian novel, *The Gift* (1935–37), generally regarded as the masterpiece of his Russian fiction, ends with an original Onegin stanza. In a work teeming with connections to Pushkin and whose "heroine . . . is Russian Literature,"[92] such a conclusion is not merely a magnificent final flourish, but also the work's logical culmination. By allowing these verses to appear (graphically speaking) in the form of a paragraph, Nabokov responds to Pushkin's "novel in verse" with his own "poem in prose." To simplify the present discussion, however, I will cite the passage in verse form (Nabokov himself reconfigured it in this way when preparing it for inclusion in a volume of his collected poetry):[93]

Прощай же, книга! Для видений
отсрочки смертной тоже нет.
С колен поднимется Евгений,
но удаляется поэт.
И все же слух не может сразу
расстаться с музыкой, рассказу
дать замереть . . . судьба сама
еще звенит, и для ума
внимательного нет границы
там, где поставил точку я:
продленный призрак бытия
синеет за чертой страницы,
как завтрашние облака,
и не кончается строка.

(Goodbye, [my] book! There is no / Postponing death also for visions. / Evgenii will get up off his knees, / But the poet departs. / And nonetheless one's hearing cannot immediately / Part with the music, [cannot] let / The story die away . . . fate itself / Still rings, and for the attentive / Mind there is no border / Where I have placed the period: / The extended specter of being shows blue, / Like tomorrow's clouds, / Beyond the edge of the page, / And the line does not end.)

It should be emphasized that Nabokov's usage of this Onegin stanza is entirely consistent with the other Russian twentieth-century examples we have examined. First of all, it explicitly names its model (the "Evgenii" mentioned is not a character in *The Gift*, but rather Pushkin's hero, who in the novel's final scene is left, figuratively speaking, on his knees). Secondly, it conveys, through formal allusion, an émigré's sense of connectedness with (and longing for) the prerevolutionary Russian literary heritage. By emphasizing that, "for the attentive mind," the work does not end with the final period, Nabokov uses the Onegin stanza as a parable for the way a work of art can inspire future generations. Formally speaking, Nabokov's verses stand out through their insistent use of enjambment (lines 5–9, far more than is usual in an Onegin stanza). In enjambment, of course, "ne konchaetsia stroka" ("the line does not end"). The novel's closing phrase thus contains a metapoetic statement; just as the enjambed verse lines move ineluctably forward, so the final line of the novel itself coaxes the reader onward.

How could these subtle connotations be explained to the English reader? In 1961, Nabokov carefully revised the English translation of *The Gift* that had been prepared by his son and Michael Scammell. In addition to reworking the prose, Nabokov himself rendered the numerous interpolated poems into English. Given his years of work on the *Onegin* translation (which was itself being readied for publication at this time), one would expect that Nabokov would have dispensed with rhyme when rendering his closing Onegin stanza. Yet in the English translation of *The Gift*, the final paragraph retains the formal elements of the original, unambiguously sacrificing precision to this end. (To give but one example: "Dlia videnii – otsrochki smertnoi tozhe net" ["There is no postponing death also for visions"] is rendered as "Like mortal eyes, imagined ones must close some day.") Once again, to simplify comparison, I will cite the passage as a stanza, although it appears graphically as prose in the novel:

> Good-by, my book! Like mortal eyes,
> imagined ones must close some day.
> Onegin from his knees will rise –
> but his creator strolls away.
> And yet the ear cannot right now
> part with the music and allow
> the tale to fade; the chords of fate
> itself continue to vibrate;
> and no obstruction for the sage
> exists where I have put The End:
> the shadows of my world extend
> beyond the skyline of the page,
> blue as tomorrow's morning haze –
> nor does this terminate the phrase.

It is true that Nabokov, while retaining the rhyme scheme, subtly alters the form by using exclusively masculine rhymes.[94] This one formal freedom notwithstanding, his English version betrays a tacit admission that, in this particular case, a literal translation was incapable of conveying his ideal "completeness of meaning." On the contrary, we find here the very approach that Nabokov – in his translation of Pushkin – had so ferociously condemned.[95] In short,

when translating his own Onegin stanza, Nabokov flagrantly vio-
lated his own cardinal rule. While he could not possibly have
expected his English reader to grasp the associations of the Onegin
stanza,[96] he nonetheless felt the need to preserve its structure.
Fidelity to form triumphed over "completeness of meaning" or, I
would argue, fidelity to form was necessary to ensure a more
"complete" meaning.

   In short, Russia's most celebrated apologist for literal translation
was forced to reassess his position when the question arose in regard
to his own poetry. Nabokov's work on *The Gift* testifies to the primacy
of form and the extraordinary communicative value of the Onegin
stanza.

CONCLUSIONS

It is important to step back and survey the entire history of the
Onegin stanza. As its subtitle suggested, Pushkin's idiosyncratic
"novel in verse" defied simple categorization. It offered a strange
combination of possibilities: a tale "half funny and half sad" and a
mysterious semi-autobiographical narrator, whose minor role in the
plot was offset by the tremendous influence of his digressions and
commentaries. For subsequent poets, the Onegin stanza represented
the height of poetic achievement, yet its specific significance varied.
When used by Pushkin's contemporaries, the comic and digressive
elements dominated. The narrator remained, but as a stylized
presence rather than a recognizable autobiographical construct. In
contrast, the poets of the early twentieth century used the Onegin
stanza as a strict autobiographical genre and a vehicle for seriousness. For them, the form was linked less to the specific plot of
Pushkin's novel than to a nostalgic *recollection* of an earlier time. This
central role of memory – at times serious, at times parodic – also
informed the Onegin stanzas written by poets after the Revolution.
It served the émigré well in his desire to conjure up a lost, yet once
vital culture (Nabokov, Pereleshin) – but it was fraught with danger
for the Soviet poet (Khazin), who was expected, after all, to celebrate
the new at the expense of the old.

   If we consider the circumstances of composition of the twentieth-
century works, some striking parallels emerge. Voloshin's "Letter" is
an actual verse epistle that he sent from Paris to Moscow, where his
beloved was living. The poem is devoted almost entirely to reminis-

cences of the time the two had recently spent together in France. Through his poem, Voloshin attempted to remove the distance that separated them. Ivanov wrote "Infancy" during a year-long visit to Geneva and Rome. Not only was he facing a spatial distance (Western Europe as against Russia, the setting of his childhood), but also a temporal one (a fifty-year old poet writing about the first years of his own life). Moreover, he chose to complete the poem in Moscow in 1918, at a time when the last vestiges of Pushkin's age were crumbling around him. Severianin's "Leander's Grand Piano," is devoted to Russian cultural life in the early years of Futurism. Once again, spatial as well as temporal obstacles were involved: at the time of composition, Severianin had left the Soviet Union for the relative freedom of Estonia. The concept of separation is nowhere more central than in Pereleshin, whose poem charts his peregrinations through four continents. What connects these twentieth-century works is not simply their sense of temporal and spatial dislocation (which comes out both in the texts as well as in the history of their composition), but also their frankly nostalgic feelings about that which has been left behind. For Voloshin, this is love; for Ivanov, the golden age of earliest childhood; for Severianin, it is the longing for the vibrant prerevolutionary culture that marked his greatest successes; for Pereleshin, it is a homesickness for Russia itself and the poetic tradition destroyed by Soviet pretenders. What we find common to all of these works, then, is not simply the theme of separation, but also the longing to connect with a lost paradise, represented in the minds of these twentieth-century poets by Pushkin's novel in verse. One might say that the fixed form of the Onegin stanza ultimately functioned as a topos – a *locus amoenus* accessible only through the poetic imagination.

This function, common to virtually all twentieth-century Onegin stanzas, may appear to rest on a paradox. There is little in *Eugene Onegin* itself to encourage an association with the theme of paradise. The plot contains nothing but jagged edges, disappointed hopes, and interrupted actions – whether in the form of the death of idealism (Lensky) or unrequited love (Tatiana and Onegin). When Tatiana rejects Onegin in the book's final chapter (VIII, 47), she thinks back to their earlier meetings and exclaims: "А счастье было так возможно, / Так близко!" ("But happiness was so possible, / So close!"). Relying largely on the Onegin stanza itself to convey this yearning for lost happiness, twentieth-century poets seem to have taken Tatiana's lament as their motto. These poets found harmony less in the specifics of Pushkin's plot than in his work's undisputed position as a model of poetic craft and as a *cultural landmark*. Because the form itself came to symbolize all Russian cultural achievement, subsequent poets felt free to include in their Onegin stanzas allusions to any number of Pushkin's works, as well as to Fet, Tiutchev, and Lermontov. They equated Pushkin's form not only with the Golden Age as a term of literary periodization, but also with a Golden Age in the metaphorical sense, a time when things were perfect (be it early childhood, first love, former glory, or a romanticized prerevolutionary Russia). The history of the Onegin stanza thus exemplifies the way a poetic form can lose many of its original associations and, with time, gain new ones. Any attempt to repeat Pushkin's achievement would have resulted, at best, in the work of an epigone. By judicious borrowing and development, major poets found a way to invest Pushkin's form with new meaning, thereby enriching poetic tradition.

CHAPTER 4

Russian Arcadia: the elegiac distich and classical stylization

Слышу умолкнувший звук божественной эллинской речи;
Старца великого тень чую смущенной душой.[1]
Пушкин, "На перевод Илиады" (1830)

Hearing the speech of immortal Hellas long lapsed into silence,
Humbled of soul I now sense Homer's magnificent shade.
Pushkin, "On the Translation of the *Iliad*" (1830)

Крив был Гнедич поэт, преложитель слепого Гомера,
Боком одним с образцом схож и его перевод.[2]
Пушкин, "К переводу Илиады" (1830)

Gnedich, the poet, blind Homer's translator, had one eye only,
And his translation itself, mirrors no more than one side.
Pushkin, "About the Translation of the *Iliad*" (1830)

In virtually all European national literatures, one can point to periods in which the reception of antiquity became central to the artistic process. The ancients provided the "moderns" with both a source of exemplary forms and a challenge. To assimilate the literature of the Greeks and Romans, whether through translations or stylizations, was to lay claim to a tradition of immense authority. In Russia, where questions of literary tradition were frequently intertwined with a cultural inferiority complex, poets jumped at the opportunity to demonstrate that their language was capable of rejuvenating both the letter and the spirit of classical verse. Indeed, Russians noted with pride the pervasive influence of antiquity on their religion, society, and even language, at times suggesting that this made them uniquely qualified to be the standard bearers of that tradition.[3]

For all their talk of kinship, Russian poets – no less than their modern European counterparts – encountered a major stumbling block in the form of fundamental linguistic differences. Ancient Greek and Latin prosody was based on quantity (long and short

syllables), a concept not relevant to most modern European languages. Moreover, rhyme, which quickly became a fixture of European poetry, was foreign to the verse of antiquity. In seeking to
recreate classical verse in a modern language, the poet was faced
with two choices: either to replace ancient meters with familiar
modern ones (rhyme and all), or to imitate the ancient meters, using
stressed and unstressed syllables in lieu of long and short ones. Both
methods, it should be emphasized, entailed significant compromise.
In Russia, after decades of experimentation (often accompanied by
fierce literary polemics), imitation won out over substitution: poets
chose to maintain – with the requisite compromises – the ancient
system of meters.[4] In this regard, they followed, as was so often the
case, the lead of the Germans.

Not surprisingly, the Russians focused their attention first and
foremost on the hexameter, for this was the meter of the *Iliad* and the
Odyssey. The lengthy history of the Russian hexameter has been
traced and need not detain us here.[5] For present purposes, two
aspects should be briefly noted. The first is generic: the Russian
hexameter, in keeping with its Greek origins, was reserved for epic
verse and other large poetic forms. The second point concerns the
specifically Russian realization of the hexameter, which is significant
insofar as the hexameter line provided the first half of the elegiac
distich.

As noted above, the Russian hexameter replaced the concept of
length (quantity) with that of accent. However, in making ancient
meter suitable for modern verse, Russians encountered additional
difficulties. Poets of antiquity had allowed themselves certain metrical freedoms, to which the modern ear was unaccustomed. In
particular, Greek and Roman poets regularly used spondees (two
consecutive long syllables, $\acute{}\,\acute{}$) to substitute for a dactyl (one long
and two short syllables, $\acute{}\,\smile\,\smile$). In a system of versification based
on length, it was logical that one long syllable could "equal" two
short ones. In a system of versification based on accent, however, it is
far more difficult to explain why one stressed syllable should be the
equivalent of two unstressed ones. Yet even if one accepts this
convention unquestioningly, another problem arises. The spondee is
simply not well suited to the Russian language, in which two
consecutive stressed syllables rarely occur. As a result, would-be
hexameter writers were forced to compromise yet again. Either
poets had to eschew these rhythmical substitutions altogether or they

had to allow trochees (a stressed syllable followed by an unstressed one) to take the place of the traditionally sanctioned spondees (two consecutive stresses). Both of these solutions eventually became part of Russian prosody, although the first solution was generally preferred. In other words, most poets kept trochaic substitutions to a minimum.[6]

The elegiac distich combined one line of this hexameter with a line of so-called pentameter. The classical pentameter should not be confused with more recent conceptions of this term. Like the hexameter (from which it was derived), it contained *six* long syllables.[7] Unlike the hexameter, it was divided into two equal parts, each consisting of three feet, the final one truncated immediately after the first syllable (which also coincided with a word boundary). As a result, the pentameter featured a caesura (i.e., a mandatory word break) between two consecutive strong syllables in the middle of the line. The symmetry of the pentameter line encouraged a bipartite semantics, in which the first half consisted of one complete thought, and the second acted as a type of answer. According to a scheme without spondeic or trochaic substitutions, the basic form of the distich can be reproduced as follows:

‿ ⏑ ⏑ ‿ ⏑ ⏑ ‿ ⏑ ⏑ ‿ ⏑ ⏑ ‿ ⏑ ⏑ ‿ ⏑ (hexameter)
‿ ⏑ ⏑ ‿ ⏑ ⏑ ‿ | ‿ ⏑ ⏑ ‿ ⏑ ⏑ ‿ (pentameter)

In actual practice, Greek and Roman poets frequently used substitutions. However, even in antiquity, certain elements never varied. The last two feet (the cadence) of both the hexameter and pentameter remained as in the model. Moreover, the two consecutive long syllables in the middle of the pentameter line were a distinguishing feature of the form and thus not subject to alteration. It is worth emphasizing that, already in classical times, the pentameter line was indented, making the elegiac distich immediately identifiable graphically. This convention, usually maintained by modern European poets, serves to "announce" the distich's presence before a single word has been read.

Friedrich Schiller, a poet and theoretician of poetry with a pronounced nostalgia for antiquity, composed a metapoetic distich in which he described this classical form in terms of a fountain: in the hexameter it rises, in the pentameter it falls "melodiously":

> Im Hexameter steigt des Springquells flüssige Säule,
> Im Pentameter drauf fällt sie melodisch herab.[8]

It will be noted that Schiller – like the Germans in general – makes frequent use of trochaic substitutions: three times in the hexameter line (the first, third, and fourth feet) and once (in the first foot) of the pentameter line. One can also detect the traditional semantic pause at the caesura of the pentameter – before the melodic "Abgesang."

Other European traditions did not gladly tolerate so many trochaic substitutions. Schiller's distich made the rounds of European languages, and, while his translators faithfully maintained his form and content (including the semantic pause at the caesura), they never allowed themselves his degree of rhythmic freedom. Coleridge's rendering (which, according to Theodore Ziolkowski, "helps us to understand why the form never became popular in English")[9] uses only one substitution (indicated by italics):

> In the hexameter rises the *fountain's* silvery column;
> In the pentameter, aye, falling in melody back.

Coleridge could have come much closer to the rhythms of the original through a simple change that would not significantly alter the meaning:

> In hexameter rises the fountain's silvery column;
> In pentameter, aye, falling in melody back.

However, he presumably decided that, given the English reader's lack of familiarity with the distich, it was safer to produce the form according to its "textbook" scheme.[10] Coleridge – like most of his Russian counterparts – apparently preferred rhythmic monotony to more authentic (but potentially confusing) substitutions.

This same hesitation characterizes the approach of three generations of Russian translators of Schiller's distich (I have italicized the infrequent substitutions):

> Светлым потоком струится гекзаметра стих грациозный;
> *Сжат и* гибок, и смел – вот он, пентаметр мой.
> (Translation by A. Strugovshchikov.)[11]

> Струи фонтана встают *в гекзаметре* стройной колонной,
> *И в пентаметре* вновь мерным напевом падут.
> (Translation by E. Dunaevskii.)[12]

> Гордо в гекзаметре *вверх взмывает* колонна фонтана,
> Чтобы в пентаметре вновь звучно на землю упасть.
> (Translation by E. Etkind.)[13]

In general, the *Russian* elegiac distich developed as the "poor relation" of the hexameter. Battles raged for decades over the appropriate method of rendering the hexameter, yet no one gave much thought to the "lesser" forms of antiquity. Vasily Trediakovsky, for example, composed a lengthy epic in hexameters, but his production of elegiac distichs was extremely limited.[14] Nikolai Gnedich translated the entire *Iliad* into Russian hexameters, but composed only two brief poems in distichs. Zhukovsky used the hexameter for his *Odyssey* translation, for numerous translations from the German, and for several original works, yet wrote only a handful of distichs.

In the literature of antiquity, of course, the elegiac distich was hardly a minor form. To today's readers, the term "elegy" usually connotes death (or, more generally, loss), but the traditional elegiac distich had a far broader range of thematic and generic applications, including epitaphs and eulogies, but also love lyrics and philosophical poetry:

The elegiac distich was felt to combine the narrative objectivity of the hexameter with the more emotional quality of the pentameter. The elegiac distich can tell a story – a battle episode, an erotic encounter, a mythological tale, a political anecdote – but the story is not told for its own sake, as in the epic; it is adduced to illustrate a general idea or a subjective feeling, as in a lyric poem.[15]

In German literature, the elegiac distich came to play an enormous role, including such celebrated works as Goethe's "Römische Elegien" ("Roman Elegies," based in spirit and form on the love poetry of the Roman elegists) and an entire series of profound philosophical meditations that started with Schiller and extended to Hölderlin and Rilke.[16] In the Russian tradition, however, the distich served a more modest function. If the hexameter was the vehicle for the epic, then the distich was reserved primarily for poetic miniatures.[17] While remaining largely within this limited sphere, the distich carved out a special niche for itself, at times achieving a level of extraordinary expressivity.

For practical purposes, the history of the Russian distich can be said to begin with Pushkin's schoolfriends Anton Del'vig and Wilhelm Kiukhel'beker. It is important to consider their works in this form, because they determined to a large extent the direction that Russian distichs were to take. While still studying at the legendary lyceum, these two aspiring poets were experimenting with classical forms. Since Kiukhel'beker was a native speaker of

German, it is likely that his interest in distichs developed from his readings in German literature, rather than in Greek (which was not part of the curriculum), Latin (which was), or even the infrequent attempts of earlier Russian poets (e.g., Aleksandr Radishchev and Aleksandr Vostokov). Whatever the source, the view of antiquity common to the works of both Del'vig and Kiukhel'beker can be summarized by Johann Joachim Winckelmann's famous and influential formulation: "edle Einfalt und stille Größe" ("noble simplicity and silent grandeur").[18] Accordingly, antiquity was conceived of less as a specific time and place than as a generalized spirit of myth, poesy, harmony, and lofty *sententiae*.

One of the earliest Russian experiments in elegiac distichs can be found, appropriately enough, in Kiukhel'beker's "Elegiia k Del'vigu" ("Elegy to Del'vig"). Written in 1817, the work consists of twenty lines, but the first ten should give a sufficient sense of the whole:

> Цвет моей жизни, не вянь! О время сладостной скорби,
> Пылкой, волшебной мечты, время восторгов – постой!
> Чем удержать его, друг мой? о друг мой, могу ли привыкнуть
> К мысли убийственной жить с хладной, немою душой,
> Жить, переживши себя? Почто же, почто не угас я
> С утром моим золотым? Дельвиг, когда мы с тобой
> Тайными мыслями, верою сердца делились и смело
> В чистом слиянии душ пламенным летом неслись
> В даль за пределы земли, в минуту божественной жажды
> Было мне умереть, в небо к отцу воспарить.[19]

> Flower of my life, do not wither! O, time of delicate grieving
> Time of our magical dreams, time of our joys, do not end!
> How shall we stop it, O friend? Allow, O allow me to ponder
> How to adjust to that thought – life with a cold and mute soul;
> Life having lived past one's prime. Why should I not have passed on while
> Still in the morning of youth? Del'vig! The time when we both
> Shared all our innermost thoughts and our deepest beliefs whilst we
>   wandered,
> Forging together our souls, into the summer's great heat,
> Passing the ends of the earth at a moment both bless'd and enraptured
> O! Had I then passed away, rising to father above.

While the poem lacks explicit classical allusions, its neo-classical orientation is unmistakable. Taking the form of an apostrophe to a friend, this elegy concerns the inexorable passing of time. Conventional exclamations (at times even accompanied by the vocative

"O") and rhetorical questions abound, as the poet turns to his friend for advice on how best to confront his fate. The metaphors ("flower of my life, do not wither!," "in the morning of youth") and vocabulary are not chosen for novelty, but rather for their very traditionality. The only oddity in this passage is syntactic; Kiukhel′-beker relies heavily on enjambment, which is common neither to the traditional distich nor to Kiukhel′beker's ordinary usage of the form. In all other respects, the poem is constructed in such a way as to make the reader perceive the stylized speech of Kiukhel′beker to Del′vig as a re-creation of an address by some nameless Greek philosopher of antiquity to his fellow thinker.

Since stylization is a concept central to the concerns of this chapter, it is worth stepping back to consider the way it functions. Mikhail Bakhtin has offered a convenient means of looking at this phenomenon by contrasting it with parody.[20] In both cases, a speaker repeats an earlier speaker's words in such a way that both voices remain discernible. However, in stylization, the speaker takes these words in the same direction (that is, he agrees with them and uses them to further his own argument), whereas in parody he takes them in the opposite direction (thereby drawing attention to their inadequacy).

Because stylization and parody are opposite poles of the same dialogical impulse, there is always a danger of the former turning into the latter. In the case of Kiukhel′beker's "Elegy to Del′vig," there was inarguably an element of ridiculousness in so elevated a theme and poetic manner being brought to bear on the concerns of two schoolboys. In 1833, a much changed Kiukhel′beker (already spending his eighth year in prison as a result of his role in the Decembrist uprising) looked back at this very poem and commented: "I was ashamed and amused to read in 'Son of the Fatherland' my piece 'Elegy to Del′vig.' I was barely over twenty when I wrote it; I had just finished the lyceum and had not yet lived, but was merely preparing to live. And yet the theme of that rhapsody was *the fading of youth*, disappointment, etc."[21] Kiukhel′beker's mature response to his own elegy indicates how a poem originally intended as a serious stylization can suddenly obtain comic qualities when the distance between the speaker and the speech he seeks to emulate is perceived as incommensurate. In general, however, the distich's parodic potential was rarely utilized – at least not consciously – by Russian poets.[22]

In terms of theme and style, Kiukhel'beker's "Elegy to Del'vig" can be considered typical of his early work in that form. Other distichs of 1817 include poems addressed to specific people, "K Filonu" ("To Philones," eight lines, written to a geography teacher at the lyceum; it is telling that Kiukhel'beker substituted a conventional Greek name for the addressee's hardly mellifluous real name – Ivan Petrovich Shchul'gin) and "K Matiushkinu" ("To Matiushkin," sixteen lines, written to a fellow graduate of the lyceum who was about to embark on a journey around the world), as well as poems on general philosophical concepts, "Razluka" ("Parting," his first extant poem in distichs, eight lines), "Sokratizm" ("Socratism," twenty lines; the various spheres of influence are reflected by the Greek title and a reference to Eloa, the hero of Klopstock's then popular epic *The Messiah*), and "Otchizna" ("Homeland," twenty-two lines, the title referring not to a specific country, but to the celestial realm).[23]

In the next few years, Kiukhel'beker used the distich with frequency, usually in short poems of a conventional or mythical nature. On his European journey, for example, he met with Goethe and, under the spell of that visit, composed "K Promefeiu" ("To Prometheus"), a poem in elegiac distichs in which he expressed his admiration for the German master.[24] In this case, there can be little doubt that the Russian poet was using a form for its historical associations, to pay homage to the man who had canonized the distich in modern European poetry.

After two relatively long poems of 1823, the distich drops out of Kiukhel'beker's poetic repertoire altogether. This sudden renunciation of the form is revealing, for it coincides with Kiukhel'beker's turn from pseudo-classicism to a special brand of Romanticism, which based its conception of poetic language on old forms of Russian, rather than stylizations of classical antiquity. These two final poems in distichs offer a glimpse of Kiukhel'beker as he passed from one stylistic phase to another. The opening lines of "Zakup" (the name of Iu. K. Glinka's estate, where the poet spent time from 1822 to 1823) indicate how clearly Kiukhel'beker recognized the semantics of poetic form:

> Сладкий глагол элегической, нежно тужащей камены,
>   Ты, о Тибуллов размер, о вожделеннейший стих,
> Мною покинутый в час роковой, когда я впервые,
>   Зов Мельпомены познав, ямбом себя воружил! –

Снова к тебе обращаюсь теперь, утешитель в печалях:
  Я тишину воспою, счастье родимой семьи!²⁵

Sweetest word of the muse elegiac and tenderly plaintive,
  You, O Tibullus' form, O most desired of verse,
Which was deserted by me when I heard in an hour most fateful
  Tragedy's muse calling forth, iambs it offered to me!
Now once again do I turn to you – you who consoles me in sadness
  I wish to sing now of peace, quiet, and family joy.

The poem begins with a metapoetic statement. Kiukhel'beker addresses the form of the distich itself ("O, Tibullus' form" – Tibullus having been one of the most celebrated of the Roman elegists), which he admits having abandoned after hearing "Tragedy's muse calling forth" (in the Russian text, Kiukhel'beker names Melpomene). Beneath these overt references to classical literature and mythology lurks an autobiographical subtext. In the years 1822–23, Kiukhel'beker had been at work on his tragedy – in unrhymed iambs – "Argiviane" ("The Argives"). Now he was returning to the distich in order to sing different themes: tranquility and family happiness. The remainder of the poem (thirty-eight more lines) is devoted to lauding the Glinka family and excusing his own former conduct. However, even these personal elements are made impersonal through hyperbolic statements and conventional language:

Ах! с рождения я, обреченный мучитель любезных,
  Грозной судьбою гоним, грусть за собою веду:
Ваш благодатный покой возмутил я неистовым сердцем!
  Рощи, простите! луга, вы помяните меня!²⁶

O, from the day of my birth I was fated to torment my dear ones
  Chased by a terrible fate, carrying always my grief.
Now with my furious heart I have troubled your peace so abundant . . .
  Groves, I bid you farewell! Meadows, remember me well!

The combination of conventional exclamation ("Akh!" – "O!"), the clichéd image of the poet driven by a dark fate, and the apostrophe to the groves and meadows make clear the deeply literary sources of this autobiographical poem.

Kiukhel'beker's final poem in distichs, entitled "Poshchada pevtsa" ("Mercy for the Singer"), is set entirely in the world of Greek myth. It portrays Zeus as he is about to send a fierce storm down upon mankind and thereby interrupt a tryst between the poet and his beloved. Apollo intercedes, asking his father to take pity on man, particularly on this particular poet, his favorite. Zeus smiles, nature becomes bright again, and the singer continues to kiss his beloved. In keeping with the neo-classical expectations of the form, the poem is saturated with Greek mythological names. Yet it also contains some of the Russian archaisms so characteristic of Kiukhel'- beker's next (and final) stylistic phase. These include specific lexical choices ("Как он молнии *шуйцей* метал и *десною* занесся"; emphasis added)[27] as well as a virtually unpronounceable conso- nantal cluster, the quality of which cannot even be approximated in translation and is therefore cited in transliteration (*Дхн*ешь – и вселенна дрожит; "*Dkhn*esh' – i vselenna drozhit"; emphasis added).

In contrast to Kiukhel'beker, Del'vig wrote distichs throughout his relatively brief poetic career. While Kiukhel'beker's distichs could be lengthy, Del'vig's stand out by virtue of their extreme brevity. His seventeen poems in elegiac distichs contain a mere ninety-eight lines (an average of about six lines per poem).[28] Generically speaking, these distichs belong to the category called "anthological" poems: epigrams, epitaphs, and inscriptions. Del'vig himself defined this genre in a poem to his fellow poet F. N. Glinka, which bore the explanatory subtitle "while sending him the Greek Anthology":

> Вот певцу Антология, легких харит украшенье,
>   Греческих свежих цветов вечно пленяющий пух!
> Рви их, любимец богов, и сплетай из них русским Каменам
>   Неувядаемые, в Хроновом царстве, венки.[29]

> Singer! Take this Anthology, sign of the lightness of graces,
>   Feathery flowers of Greece, always eternally fresh.
> Pluck them, beloved of gods, and make wreaths for Russia's own Muses,
>   Wreaths for Chronos' realm, never to fade in that world.

This brief poem can fairly be considered a neo-classical manifesto. The basic metaphor is derived from the word "anthology" itself, which in Greek meant a garland of flowers and – in a secondary (but obviously related) sense – a collection of poems.[30] In the first couplet, Del'vig gives his fellow Russian poet a copy of what has come to be known as the Greek anthology (presumably in German, since a Russian version did not yet exist), describing it in terms of flowers that are "eternally fresh." In the second couplet, he urges his fellow poet to pluck these flowers and make "never-fading" wreaths

of them for the "Russian muses." In short, Del'vig expresses his hope
that the Russians, following the example of the ancients, will create
their own Anthology. Del'vig's four-line poem, of course, gives a very
clear sense of the sort of poetry he envisioned. In addition to the
Greek form of the distich (realized in this case with one striking
mistake!),[31] he includes a plethora of mythological names (the Greek
graces of the first couplet, the Russian muses of the second) and neo-
classical paraphrase ("beloved of gods" for "poet," "Chronos'
realm" for "eternity"). Del'vig anticipated a Russian Anthology
characterized by a high degree of stylization in language and theme,
but also by brevity and a sense of timeless beauty.

This ideal is perhaps best exemplified in his "Nadpis' na statuiu
florentinskogo Merkuriia" ("Inscription on a Statue of a Florentine
Mercury," 1819–20):

Перст указует на даль, на главе развилися крылья,
    Дышит свободою грудь; с легкостью дивною он,
В землю ударя крылатой ногой, кидается в воздух . . .
    Миг – и умчится! Таков полный восторга певец.[32]

Fingers that point far away and with wings growing out of his helmet,
    Breathing with freedom complete, lightness incarnate is he.
Stamping his feet on the earth and leaping out into the azure,
    Now he will leave us behind! Such is the singer inspired.

The fleet-footed god Mercury (Hermes), traditional mediator
between the gods and mankind, embodies a conception of antiquity
as youth, freedom, and lightness. As the title makes clear, this is a
vision of the Roman deity mediated by art: an Italian *statue* of the
god, rather than the god himself. (This is by no means the last time
we shall observe the distich linked to the genre traditionally known
as "ekphrasis" – an artistic depiction of a work of art.) Numerous
active verbs give a paradoxical sense of motion to what is, after all, a
stationary object. In fact, the final line even adumbrates the god's
departure. This sudden activity introduces yet another metapoetic
twist: the winged Hermes, speeding away, is compared to the
inspired poet. Del'vig's classical inscription, then, turns an ancient
statue into a metaphor for art itself.

This metapoetic element, which connects antiquity to modernity,
is a fixture in Del'vig's distichs. His poem to Gnedich (1821–22), a
typical example, clearly shows his conception of the Russians as the
inheritors of the classical tradition:

Муза вчера мне, певец, принесла закоцитную новость:
   В темный недавно Айдес тень славянина пришла;
Там, окруженная сонмом теней любопытных, пропела
   (Слушал и древний Омер) песнь Илиады твоей.
Старец наш, к персям вожатого-юноши сладко приникнув,
   Вскрикнул: "Вот слава моя, вот чего веки я ждал!"[33]

Singer! The muse just brought me some news from the realm of the
                                                              shadows:
   Down into Hades so dark, recently entered a Slav;
There in a circle of curious shadows this Slav then recited
   Iliad's Russianized song; Homer was listening, too –
Nestling up to the newcomer's bosom our old man, rejoicing, cried loudly:
   "Waiting of epochs is past! This is true glory for me!"

Using the expected elements (brevity, specific classical allusions),
Del'vig narrates a tale supposedly related to him by the muse. A
nameless Slav descended to Hades and recited a canto of Gnedich's
Iliad translation to a "host of curious shades" (the combination of
literary, even elevated style of the nouns with the almost conversa-
tional adjective would be unthinkable in hexameters, but in the
distich it adds a touch of lightness). "Ancient Homer's" reaction, we
learn, was one of undisguised delight. The notion that Homer
should have been waiting for centuries for a Russian translation of
his epic was surely intended to sound hyperbolic (if not tongue-in-
cheek – the parodic potential again surfaces), but the general idea of
Russia's destiny as a "second Greece" links this distich very clearly
with the earlier ones.[34] From the standpoint of metrical semantics, it
is noteworthy that Gnedich's *Iliad* translation was written in hexameters. Del'vig's modest commentary, rather than following the
mighty examples of Homer and Gnedich, relies on the distich,
thereby signaling an awareness of its own status as miniature.[35]

In previous chapters, we sought to identify a single work that
"defined" the tradition. In the case of the distich, however, the
contours of the form were established not by one outstanding
example, but by a body of similar texts. The experiments in distichs
of Kiukhel'beker and Del'vig are minor works, yet they warrant our
attention because they created a firm set of expectations for
subsequent Russian poets.[36] First and foremost among these was
Pushkin himself, who, as we have so frequently observed, began to
use a form only after others had laid the groundwork. Despite the

fact that Pushkin had gone to school with Del'vig and Kiukhel'beker and was intimately acquainted with their early work, he was to write his first distich only in 1829 – more than a decade after his school-friends had pioneered the form. Pushkin's very first example demonstrates the degree to which he recognized and incorporated the distich's associations:

> Кто на снегах возрастил Феокритовы нежные розы?
>   В веке железном, скажи, кто золотой угадал?
> Кто славянин молодой, грек духом, а родом германец?[37]
>   Вот загадка моя: хитрый Эдип, разреши![38]

> Who has grafted on snow Theocritus' tender roses?
>   Tell me, in our iron age, who has the skill to find gold?
> What youthful Slav is in spirit a Greek, yet by blood a German?
>   That is my riddle for you; Oedipus, solve it at once!

Numerous elements link this poem to those previously examined. It is light-hearted and extremely brief, contains explicit allusions to antiquity (the Greek poet Theocritus, the myth of Oedipus), and treats the larger theme of cultural continuity, that is, the connection of the classical world ("golden") to the contemporary one ("iron"). Indeed, the significance of myth already stands out in Pushkin's parenthetical introduction: "while sending a bronze sphinx." Presumably, the subject of the sphinx prompted Pushkin to write a "riddle" (line 4).[39] Who, Pushkin asks, grows tender roses (a reference to the Greek Anthology) on the snow (i.e., in northern countries)? The reference appears to be to *Severnye tsvety* (Northern Flowers), the almanac that Del'vig had founded in 1825. In case that hint is not sufficient, Pushkin elaborates in line 3: he is a young Slav, in spirit a Greek, but by birth a German. For Pushkin's readers, the "solution" was transparent: Del'vig himself. In short, Pushkin uses his very first poem in distichs to pay homage to his friend – in ways formal, stylistic, thematic, and even personal.[40]

In an essay on Pushkin's versification, Valery Briusov noted: "Pushkin borrowed the technique of the hexameter and distichs (the hexameter with pentameter) from Gnedich and Del'vig, in essence not adding anything of his own."[41] While it is true that Pushkin's use of these meters draws extensively on the practice of his predecessors, his distichs nevertheless reveal the ingenuity of a master poet. Nowhere is this clearer than in "Rhyme," a poem written in 1830 and first published, along with three other poems in distichs, in 1832 under the rubric "Anfologicheskie [*sic*] epigramy" ("Anthological Epigrams"). Significantly, these poems appeared in the 1832 issue of *Northern Flowers* – an issue that Pushkin himself had organized as a tribute to the recently deceased Del'vig.[42]

"Rhyme" develops a motif that Pushkin had already treated in verse in 1828. That earlier untitled poem, beginning "Rifma, zvuchnaia podruga" ("Rhyme, sonorous friend"), was written in six-line stanzas of trochaic tetrameter with rhyme scheme A-A-b-C-C-b. In the first four stanzas, Pushkin had personified rhyme, addressing her as a capricious lover, who constantly left him and then returned (a phenomenon mirrored in the rhyme scheme itself, in which the "b" rhyme seems to disappear, only to return in the final word of the stanza). In the final four stanzas, Pushkin had changed themes, shifting genre from a love poem to a mythopoetical history:

> О, когда бы ты явилась
> В дни, как на небе толпилась
> Олимпийская семья,
> Ты бы с нею обитала,
> И божественно б сияла
> Родословная твоя.
>
> Взяв божественную лиру,
> Так поведали бы миру
> Гезиод или Омир:
> Феб однажды у Адмета
> Близ тенистого Тайгета
> Стадо пас, угрюм и сир.
>
> Он бродил во мраке леса,
> И никто, страшась Зевеса,
> Из богинь иль из богов
> Навещать его не смели–
> Бога лиры и свирели,
> Бога света и стихов.
>
> Помня первые свиданья,
> Усладить его страданья
> Мнемозина притекла.
> И подруга Аполлона
> В темной роще Геликона
> Плод восторгов родила.[43]

(O, if you had appeared / In the days when the Olympian family / Crowded the heavens, / You would have lived with them / And your genealogy / Would have shone divinely. // Having seized the divine lyre, / Hesiod or Homer / Would have told the world [the following]: / Once Phoebus Apollo, when living in Admetus' realm, / Near the shady Taygetus, / Was tending his flock, sullen and alone. // He wandered in the forest's darkness, / And because they feared Zeus, / None of the goddesses or gods / Dared to visit him, / The god of the lyre and the reed pipe, / The god of light and poetry. // Remembering their first meetings, / Mnemosyne came / To sweeten his suffering. / And Apollo's girlfriend / In the dark grove of the Helicon, / Gave birth to the fruit of [his] raptures.)

Pushkin refers to specific Greek myths (e.g., when Zeus banished Apollo from Olympus and forced him to serve the mortal Admetus), but his genealogy of rhyme is pure poetic invention. As Pushkin was well aware, rhyme played no role whatsoever in classical versification (see the epigraph to chapter 2 of this study, p. 59). Taking advantage of the subjunctive mood, he defies poetic history, placing his myth of rhyme in an ancient setting. According to the Greeks, Zeus impregnated Mnemosyne (memory), thereby creating the muses. In Pushkin's variant, Apollo (a lesser god, but nonetheless god of light and art) couples with Mnemosyne, producing another magnificent offspring: Rhyme. As one might expect from a metapoetic theme such as this, Pushkin uses a number of internal rhymes to supplement the rhymes dictated by the stanzaic form itself. For example, in the first stanza quoted above, the verb "*tolpílas'*" in line 2 not only rhymes with "*iavilas'*" of line 1; it also echoes in the adjective "*olimpíiskaia*" that begins the third line. In the next stanza, the rhyme pair "*liru/miru*" overdetermines the next rhyme word: "O*mir.*" The birth of Rhyme, in short, is accompanied by a proliferation of rhymes.

It is characteristic that, having completed one poem, Pushkin continued to explore other possibilities for the same material. Among his papers from that same year, scholars have found the fragment:

> Грустен бродил Аполлон с Олимпа . . .[44]
> Sad Apollo went forth from Olympus . . .

The image of Apollo sadly wandering away from Olympus strongly recalls the portrait of him in "Rhyme, Sonorous Friend." Metrically speaking, however, this fragment moves in another direction entirely. According to the versification of Pushkin's time, these words could be scanned only as four feet of classical hexameter (the third foot exhibiting a trochaic substitution for a dactyl). Pushkin never completed this sketch, but he returned to the idea of setting his own "Greek myth" in an appropriately Greek verse form. The result, written two years later, was "Rhyme":

Эхо, бессонная нимфа, скиталась по брегу Пенея.
    Феб, увидев ее, страстию к ней воспылал.
Нимфа плод понесла восторгов влюбленного бога;
    Меж говорливых наяд, мучась, она родила
Милую дочь. Ее прияла сама Мнемозина.
    Резвая дева росла в хоре богинь-аонид,
Матери чуткой подобна, послушна памяти строгой,
    Музам мила; на земле Рифмой зовется она.[45]

Echo the sleepless nymph was wand'ring along the Penaios,
    Phoebus, seeing this nymph, burned with a passion for her.
Echo carried the fruit of the smitten deity's raptures;
    While all the naiads conversed, tortured, she gave birth to a
Wonderful daughter. And Mnemosyne herself was the midwife.
    Playful the maiden grew up, midst all the muses divine.
Much like her sensitive mother, obeying memory's strictness,
    Dear to the muses. On Earth, Rhyme she was called from that time.

In numerous ways, this poem fits neatly into the tradition of Russian distichs that we have already observed. It is brief, refers to numerous mythological places and personages, and its larger theme is poetry. Yet Pushkin, never satisfied merely to repeat, varies the form, bringing unexpected elements to this largely predictable "anthological" genre.

The poem rests on an obvious paradox. It celebrates rhyme, yet does so in a form which, by definition, eschews rhyme. In his earlier poem on the subject, Pushkin had made rhyme a central element in both the plot and the form. Distichs, by definition unrhymed, necessitated a different approach. One changed element of plot suggests Pushkin's solution. In the earlier poem, it will be remembered, Mnemosyne had given birth to Rhyme. In the distichs, however, nymph Echo is the mother; Mnemosyne merely acts as a midwife. Speaking in metapoetic terms, Pushkin does not remove the concept of memory, but subordinates it to another favorite concept: echo. Earlier in this book (introduction, pp. 8–12), I had occasion to examine Pushkin's poem "Echo," demonstrating how the title became the driving force behind its very structure. In the distichs of "Rhyme," echo functions in a similar way.[46]

In "Rhyme, sonorous friend," the birth of rhyme was the poem's final flourish and therefore took place only in the concluding line. In "Rhyme," it is the main event, a fact Pushkin underscores by placing the actual "birth" at precisely the central point – in the enjambment between the fourth and fifth lines. Because enjambment occurs so rarely in Russian distichs (this is the sole incidence in the poem in question), this syntactic freedom begs to be understood semantically. Just as the beginning of rhyme can be seen historically as the end of the poetics of antiquity, so its birth interrupts, as it were, the measured flow of classical versification. It is as if the physical act of giving birth (literally "falling" – from one line to the next) breaks the confines of the distich form itself. This is, however, not the only time in this poem that Pushkin sets formal expectation against formal innovation.

In Pushkin's realization, echo gives birth to rhyme on both the mythological level as well as on the level of poetic technique. The rules of classical versification insist that rhyme *per se* cannot exist in the distich, yet Pushkin subtly suggests its imminent appearance through frequent assonances, alliterations, and "off-rhymes." For example, the Russian word for "rhyme" ("rifma") is almost an anagram for "nymph" ("nimfa");[47] in this way, Pushkin stresses the resemblance between mother and daughter. Similar strings of sound and sense are created in the repeated "s," "p," and "l" sounds of the sequence "vospylal / plod / ponesla," the "v," "b," and "g" repetitions in "vostorgov vliublennogo boga," the "m," "z," and "l" in "Muzam mila; na zemle." Most interesting, however, are the cadences. In the overwhelming majority of lines in the poetry of Pushkin's time, the cadence (end of the line) coincides with rhyme. The peculiarity of the distich, of course, lies in its rejection of this otherwise almost obligatory feature. Close examination of Pushkin's poem reveals that each line concludes with what can only be understood as rhymes in "embryonic" form: Pe*neia*/M*ne*mozina, vospy*lal*/rodi*la*, *boga*/*strogo*i, *aon*id/*ona*. According to the rules of nineteenth-century versification, none of these rhymes would have been completely acceptable.[48] However, in this poem, Pushkin is clearly portraying the first attempts at rhyme (the young girl) rather than its canonized form (the mature woman). In the distichs of "Rhyme," then, Pushkin takes advantage of the formal and semantic associations created by his predecessors, yet simultaneously pushes these conventions to their limits.

Pushkin does not attempt such radical experiments in his other poems in elegiac distichs. Rather, he takes full advantage of the classical aura the form provides. In terms of metrical semantics, for example, it is revealing that he chose to write "Trud" ("Work," or "The Task," 1830), a poem commemorating the conclusion of his many years of labor on *Eugene Onegin*, not in the Onegin stanza, but rather in the lapidary style of the distich. Why, Pushkin asks, having finally reached the end, does he feel sadness rather than joy?:

> Или жаль мне труда, молчаливого спутника ночи,
> Друга Авроры златой, друга пенатов святых?[49]

> Or am I sorry to part with my work, night's silent companion,
> Golden Aurora's friend, friend of the household gods?[50]

Were these verses to be transposed into the iambs of an Onegin stanza, they would sound as maudlin as Lensky's "romantic" elegy (the cliché-ridden verses he pens on the night before his fateful duel in the novel's sixth chapter). Yet in the classical context created by the distich, these allusions to Aurora and the Penates are appropriate, even expected. By opting for the distich, Pushkin creates a pathos of distance from the poetics and themes of his "contemporary" novel in verse.

Pushkin's remaining distichs draw directly on Del'vig's models. These include his two epigrams on Gnedich's translation of the *Iliad* and several poems describing statues, of which the following can be considered representative:

На статую играющего в бабки

> Юноша трижды шагнул, наклонился, рукой о колено
> Бодро оперся, другой поднял меткую кость.
> Вот уж прицелился . . . прочь! раздайся, народ любопытный,
> Врозь расступись; не мешай русской удáлой игре.[51]

(On a Statue of a Youth Playing Knucklebones: The youth took three steps forward, bent over, with one hand against his knee / Leaned vigorously; with the other he raised the well-aimed bone. / Now he has already taken aim . . . away! make way, curious folk, / Step aside; do not disturb the daring Russian game.)

Like Del'vig's depiction of Mercury, this ekphrasis is characterized by action rather than stasis. However, instead of portraying a god, Pushkin selects as his hero a nameless Russian youth at play at a traditionally Russian game. The verse form itself endows the subject with a certain classical majesty and the activity with a sense of mythic timelessness. With the exception of the distichs, Pushkin here assiduously avoids allusions to antiquity. In this way, he conflates "Russianness" with the spirit of antiquity; his Russian youth becomes an emblem of *homo ludens*. Pushkin's verses seem to fulfill Del'vig's prophecy for the genre: they are a playful offering to the *Russian* muses.

The distich continues to appear in the poetic practice of Pushkin's contemporaries. With very few exceptions, however, it is reserved for highly predictable "anthological" poems, either direct translations or stylizations of antiquity. Rather than move the form into other genres, Russian poets were content to take advantage of the already existing associations. Perhaps the most remarkable development can be found in the verse of Zhukovsky. Zhukovsky had of course overseen Pushkin's entire career, introducing him and defending him (and his verse) whenever possible. It was Zhukovsky's fate to attend to his younger friend on his deathbed and, after his death, to act as literary executor. Among Pushkin's papers, Zhukovsky found a blank notebook. He took it and wrote nine brief poems in it, seven of them in the unmistakable form of distichs. As the titles themselves suggest (e.g., "Nadgrobie iunoshe" ["Epitaph for a Youth"], "Golos mladentsa iz groba" ["Voice of an Infant from the Grave"], "Sud'ba" ["Fate"]), these poems are primarily concerned with death. Entirely in the spirit of the Russian distich (most are translations from the Greek Anthology), they do not rail against fate, but merely comment with resignation on life's brevity. However, the final poem stands out for several reasons:

Он лежал без движенья, как будто по тяжкой работе
Руки свои опустив. Голову тихо склоня,
Долго стоял я над ним, один, смотря со вниманьем
Мертвому прямо в глаза; были закрыты глаза,
Было лицо его мне так знакомо, и было заметно,
Что выражалось на нем, – в жизни такого
Мы не видали на этом лице. Не горел вдохновенья
Пламень на нем; не сиял острый ум;
Нет! Но какою-то мыслью, глубокой, высокою мыслью
Было объято оно: мнилося мне, что ему
В этот миг предстояло как будто какое виденье,
Что-то сбывалось над ним . . . И спросить мне хотелось: что
видишь?[52]

Motionless he lay, as if difficult work were completed,
Hands that were fully relaxed. Silently bending my head,

Long did I stand over him, all alone and attentively looking
Into the eyes of the corpse: eyes that were closed to the world.
Well had I known these features, and now upon them I noticed
That their expression had changed – on that face never
Had there been such a look. Inspiration was no longer burning,
No longer shone his bright mind;
No! But his face was enveloped by something, some thought there above
                                                                    him
Grand and profound was this thought. Thus did it seem then to me:
Some sort of vision revealed itself to him at that very moment.
Something had happened . . . I wanted to ask him: what are you seeing?

As scholars have long noted, these verses bear a striking resemblance (in places verbatim) to a passage from an extremely lengthy letter Zhukovsky wrote to Pushkin's father on February 15, 1837, in which he reported the details of the great poet's death:[53]

Never had I seen on that face anything resembling what was there in that first minute of death. His head was slightly inclined; his hands, which a few minutes earlier had shown a certain convulsive motion, were calmly extended, as if fallen to rest after difficult work. But I am incapable of saying in words what was expressed on his face. It was for me so new and at the same time so familiar! It was not sleep and not peace! It was not the expression of the mind, which had previously been characteristic of that face; it was not even a poetic expression! No! A certain profound, astonishing thought developed on it, something akin to a vision, to a certain full, profound, satisfied knowledge. Scrutinizing it, I wanted to ask him: "What are you seeing, my friend?" And what would he have answered me, if he could have come to life for a moment? These are the minutes in our life which fully deserve to be called great. In that minute, one might say, I saw death itself, divinely mysterious, death without a veil.[54]

Even a reader without benefit of the Russian prose text can recognize the obvious overlap of motifs and impressions. The interpretive question that arises concerns not the fact of the generic leap from a personal letter to a poetic text, but rather its function. What was to be gained by rewriting these prose observations in verse? One might argue that, as Pushkin himself was a poet, it would seem appropriate to narrate his death in verse. But why should Zhukovsky have chosen this particular poetic form? "Motionless he lay" cannot be neatly categorized in terms of the versification of Pushkin's time, but it clearly tends toward distichs. With the exception of lines 6 and 8 (strangely truncated pentameters), and line 12 (in which a hexameter takes the place of what should be a pentameter), all of the lines fit the metrical requirements of that form. Moreover, the fact that seven of the eight poems that preceded it in this idiosyncratic "cycle" were written in strict distichs strongly suggests that this poem is linked to that very tradition. A consideration of the semantics allows us to reconstruct a poetic logic behind Zhukovsky's formal decision.

Zhukovsky depicts Pushkin's death not as a national or even personal tragedy, but as a glimpse into a mysterious world beyond. The emphasis is therefore less on grief than on wonder. (The poem ends, significantly, with a question.) In the poetic version, there is nothing specifically Russian about this death. All biographical detail recedes into the background; there is no hint of the poet's age or the cause of death. In fact, without knowledge of the larger (prose) context, it would be impossible to know the identity of the deceased. The sole comment that adds specificity to the description is the rather hackneyed "flame of inspiration" (as "vdokhnoven'ia plamen'" would be rendered literally; lines 7–8), from which one may legitimately infer that the dead man was a poet.

Elegies can, of course, be devoted to death and loss. Some of the poems in Zhukovsky's own cycle are epitaphs, a genre traditionally written in distichs. Yet neither in antiquity nor modernity does the elegiac distich *necessarily* convey this theme. As we have observed repeatedly, Russian poets used the distich primarily to establish a link with antiquity, to lend a subject (be it contemporary or ancient) a mythical status. When Pushkin, for example, described in distichs a statue of a Russian youth (1836), he transformed it into an eternal emblem of humanity. In a similar way, the connotations of the meter allow Zhukovsky (only one year later) to establish a sense of universality. In measured, even stylized tones (e.g., the sole exclamation, "No!"), he treats Pushkin's death as he would the death of some great yet nameless singer of antiquity. In contrast to other poems occasioned by the same event (e.g., Lermontov's indignant, almost hysterical "Smert' poeta" ["Death of a Poet"], in the iambs so common to Pushkinian poetics), Zhukovsky uses a form on the margins of contemporary poetic practice. This conventional form creates a somber, suprapersonal tone, in which worldly concerns give way to otherworldly ones. If his letter eulogizes Russia's greatest poet, then his verse revision is a requiem – less for a man than for the inevitable fate of mankind.

In his letter, Zhukovsky had narrated the last hours of Pushkin's life as a sequence of events; in his lyric recreation, he focused on a single moment, creating the impression that time had stopped. "Motionless he lay" indicates one possible direction for the Russian distich: a depiction of an epochal event *sub specie aeternitatis*. It should be emphasized that this was by no means a radical reinterpretation of the distich. Zhukovsky had simply taken a highly stylized form and applied it to a contemporary event. In this way, a specific, potentially tragic situation became mythic. For contemporary poets, this poem remained unpublished and unknown;[55] for most subsequent poets, it represented a path not taken.

A few years after Zhukovsky's poem was written, a very different reevaluation of the distich's potential began to take place in the early poetry of Afanasy Fet. In general, Fet's poetry stands out for its formal experimentation and variety, and it is therefore not surprising that he should have explored the distich. In the years 1842–47, one finds approximately fifteen such poems. Some of these, grouped by Fet under the rubric of "Anthological Poems," reflect the neoclassical stylizations familiar from the work of previous Russian poets. Others, however, represent a new tendency:

Друг мой, бессильны слова, – одни поцелуи всесильны . . .
   Правда, в записках твоих весело мне наблюдать,
Как прилив и отлив мыслей и чувства мешают
   Ручке твоей поверять то и другое листку;
Правда, и сам я пишу стихи, покоряясь богине, –
   Много и рифм у меня, много размеров живых . . .
Но меж ними люблю я рифмы взаимных лобзаний,
   С нежной цезурою уст, с вольным размером любви.[56]

Words have no strength, O my friend, for only kisses have power . . .
   True, in the notes that you write, joyously I do observe
How the ebbing and flowing of feeling and thoughts can disturb your
   Hand as it puts to the page one or the other of them.
True enough, I myself do write verses, I yield to the goddess,
   Many a rhyme that I have, many a meter that lives,
But among rhymes I do love most of all the reciprocal kisses
   Gentle caesura of lips, with the free meter of love.

While a stray reference to a "goddess" and various metapoetic motifs recall the distichs of Fet's Russian predecessors, this poem clearly belongs to another genre: love poetry. The scene has shifted from antiquity to modern times, with the poet himself in the role of lover. Such overt eroticism certainly sets Fet's poem apart from the distichs we have examined, yet it was not unprecedented. Rather than following in the footsteps of Kiukhel'beker, Del'vig, and Pushkin, Fet was simply exploring the far more diverse Western tradition, where love poetry in the form of distichs was extremely common. Fet's direct source was not the Roman elegists, but Goethe, whose celebrated (even notorious) "Roman Elegies" had canonized the form in modern Germany. In Goethe's fifth elegy, the poet complements daytime study of the works of antiquity with nocturnal pleasures of the flesh, freely conceding his preference for the latter.[57] In a much quoted passage, Goethe had described the way he combined artistic and sensual pleasure:

> Oftmals hab' ich auch schon in ihren Armen gedichtet
>   Und des Hexameters Mass leise mit fingernder Hand
> Ihr auf den Rücken gezählt.[58]

> Often I practiced my poetry in her loving embraces
>   Softly upon her young back, tapping hexameter beats
> With my fingers.

Fet, of course, takes this basic idea (physical love as an expression and extension of poetic form) from Goethe and even exaggerates it. He praises "the gentle caesura of lips" (a phrase which itself neatly falls at the caesura) and the "free meter of love." Most interesting, from a formal point of view, is his willful anachronism: twice he refers to rhyme in a poem that derives its form from a poetic culture devoid of rhyme. It seems probable, then, that Fet is reading Goethe with a sidelong glance at Pushkin's own distich "Rhyme," where this poetic concept was the fruit of an erotic encounter.

Fet's attempts to bring Goethe's salutory influence to the Russian tradition were recognized, even appreciated, by his contemporaries.[59] The 1840s witnessed numerous translations of Goethe's distichs and even some (decidedly minor) imitations of them.[60] Yet Fet himself obviously lost interest in the enterprise; after the year 1847 the distich virtually disappears from his poetic repertoire.[61] Likewise, Russian poets of the second half of the nineteenth century displayed virtually no creative interest in the distich.

Only with the rise of the Symbolist movement, with its renewed attention to the possibilities of poetic language, did Russian poets again turn to this form. Guided by a spirit of synthesis, the Symbolists looked for poetic inspiration in the work of any number of cultural predecessors. Valery Briusov's "Nachinaiushchemu" ("To the Beginner," 1906) – written in distichs – presents this artistic credo with characteristic insistence:

> Нет, мы не только творцы, мы все и хранители тайны!
>   В образах, в ритмах, в словах есть откровенья веков.
> Гимнов заветные звуки для слуха жрецов не случайны,
>   Праздный в них различит лишь сочетание слов.
> Пиндар, Вергилий и Данте, Гете и Пушкин – согласно
>   В явные знаки вплели скрытых намеков черты.
> Их угадав, задрожал ли ты дрожью предчувствий неясной?
>   Нет? так сними свой венок: чужд Полигимнии ты.[62]

> No, we are not just creators, we also are keepers of secrets!
>   Images, rhythms, and words hold revelations of old.
> Intimate sounds of the hymns have for priests a mysterious meaning,
>   Only an idler would hear nothing but groupings of words.
> Pindar and Virgil and Dante, Goethe and Pushkin – together
>   Bound all the subtlest of hints into the clearest of signs.
> Guessing them, did you shake with an uncertain sense of foreboding?
>   No? Polyhymnia's wreath does not belong on your head.

Briusov's poem is based on a largely clichéd image of the poet as the possessor of secret knowledge. This poet is contrasted to the "idler" and the "beginner," both of whom lack the ability to discern the hidden meanings of poetry. This is hardly the first time we have seen a metapoetic poem take the form of distichs. However, Briusov adds a typically Symbolist twist. While he includes the obligatory allusions to antiquity (most notably, the muse Polyhymnia), he extends the concept of the "classical" both temporally and spatially. Briusov quite consciously populates his lyric pantheon with a Greek, a Roman, an Italian, a German, and, finally, a Russian[63] – none of whom, historically speaking, could be classified as Symbolists. If the Russians had previously used the distich to show their own culture as the rightful heir to antiquity, Briusov suggests that *all* great poets share this lineage, thus promulgating the generous, inclusive Symbolist view of tradition. A formal feature (not preserved in the translation) underscores the way the Symbolists actively develop the tradition. In blatant disregard of the classical norm, Briusov's distichs rhyme. By grafting a distinctly "modern" element onto a classical form, he exemplifies the agglutinative ideal of Symbolist poetics.

In the Russian tradition, Vyacheslav Ivanov's work displays the most intensive and extensive exploration of the creative potential of the distich. Ivanov's fascination with this form was surely linked to his formidable philological training. Unlike previous Russian poets, Ivanov had a specialist's command of Greek and Latin language, history, and culture. His awareness of subtleties of comparative poetics allowed him to contribute to more authentic Russian realizations of Greek prosody.[64] Moreover, his fluency in German assured a familiarity with Goethe's and Schiller's exemplary modern adaptations of this form. Every book of Ivanov's poetry contains distichs; indeed, his experiments in this form include original poems in German, Latin, and ancient Greek.[65]

Before the late nineteenth century, Winckelmann's superficial and idealized image of the harmony of Greek civilization had enormously influenced the use of the distich – in the practice of both the Germans and, indirectly, the Russians. In contrast, Ivanov's view of the Greeks was substantially indebted to Nietzsche, who had so emphatically drawn attention to the warring impulses within the Greek soul. In Ivanov's work, the distich often signals a turn to antiquity, yet the meaning of antiquity itself had broadened immeasurably.

So great are the distich's frequency and breadth of applications in Ivanov's poetry that it would require a separate study to catalogue all of its functions.[66] For present purposes, it is sufficient to sketch the parameters, relying on the briefest examples. Ivanov's first book of poetry, *Kormchie zvezdy* (Pilot Stars), includes an entire section of poems grouped together under the rubric "Distikhi" ("Distichs"). The first of these poems is clearly intended as a programmatic statement:

Veste Detracta

Грации, вами клянусь: милей Красота без одежды!
Полный гармоний без рифм стих обнаженный милей![67]

Graces, I swear by your name that Beauty is best without garments.
    Naked verse, too, is the best: harmony, yet without rhyme.

The Latin title itself ("When the Clothes Are Removed") calls to mind the erotic tradition of the Roman elegists. In the hexameter line, the poet elaborates on this suggestion, placing his striking title in a mythological context. Addressing the Graces (a conventional neo-classical touch), he proclaims his preference for an unclothed Beauty (here personified as a female goddess). In the pentameter line, the mythological becomes metaphorical. The "garments" of the title are understood not as clothes, but as rhymes. As in Pushkin and Fet, then, Ivanov uses a rhymeless form to comment on rhyme. However, whereas the previous poets had treated rhyme as a positive and seemingly "natural" development, Ivanov prefers "naked" verse, stripped of rhyme. If Pushkin viewed rhyme as a direct descendant of the gods of Olympus, Ivanov relegates it to the status of an inessential, artificial covering.

After this manifesto-like introduction, Ivanov proceeds to apply the distich to an extraordinarily wide range of topics. In addition to subjects drawn directly from antiquity (e.g., "Laeta," a celebration of Rome, a "joyous" response to Ovid's "Tristia," or "sad" elegies), the section includes poems on a Russian civic theme ("Deviatnad-tsatoe fevralia" ["February 19"] – the day serfdom was abolished), a New Testament theme ("Lazare, griadi von!" ["Lazarus, Come Forth!"]), a Buddhist theme ("Tat Twam Asi" – a quote from the Upanishads). Most important, however, are the mystical and philo-sophical poems. These can in no way be considered mere styliza-tions, for they express fundamental questions that Ivanov was simultaneously exploring in other areas of his work, most notably in his essays on aesthetics and philosophy. The poem "Samoiskanie" ("Searching for Oneself") is representative:

Ищет себя, умирая, зерно – и находит, утратив:
  Вот твой, Природа, закон! вот твой завет, Человек! . . .
Музыке темной внемлет Поэт – и не знает покоя,
  Слыша ясней и ясней звук предреченных речей.[68]

Dying, the seed will search for itself – and losing, will find it:
  Nature, this is your law! This is your testament, man! . . .
Poets perceive the dark music and cannot find peace while they're hearing
  Clearer and clearer the words that have already been said.

In the first two lines, Ivanov considers the image of the seed that must die in order to "find" itself (i.e., to be reborn) – a motif common to the myth of Dionysus, New Testament parable, and – from there – Dostoevsky's novels. As Ivanov emphasizes, this principle governs both nature and mankind. The second two lines take this fundamental insight and extend it to the creative process. An analogous phenomenon, it appears, informs the work of the poet. The "dark" music that he perceives becomes clearer and clearer, as he gradually recognizes the words of his predecessors.

This second half of the poem expresses one of Ivanov's basic convictions about the nature of poetic truth: the poet's essentially receptive nature ensures that he discovers, rather than invents. In short, the principle of repetition, of dying to be reborn, applies to nature, to man, and – ultimately – to the poetic word. The poet "seeks himself" by discerning clarity in the dark murmurings of the past.

How can we explain Ivanov's decision to write a poem like "Searching for Oneself" in distichs? While such philosophical distichs were unprecedented in Russian poetry, several elements connect his poem to the work of his Russian predecessors: the lapidary style, the overt reference to a divinity (a personified Nature), the metapoetic theme. Even the underlying concept of death leading to life (a mystical "rebirth" within the poet of his distant predecessors) ties in closely with the form's classical associations. In this case, the distich itself exemplifies the "dark music" of the past that gives the poet no peace until he has comprehended and repeated it.

One of the most striking qualities of Ivanov's artistic method was his tendency to express the most profound personal experiences in the strictest poetic forms. Ivanov's poetics, like his philosophy, was predicated on overcoming individualism, on forging a sense of community between poet and audience and between past and present. From this perspective, a poem of personal mourning could only gain by containing formal and semantic echoes to earlier exemplary works on the same subject. In the book *Cor Ardens*, for example, Ivanov included a poetic cycle to the memory of his wife Lidiia Dmitrievna Zinov'eva-Annibal in the highly intricate form of a garland of sonnets. The entire collection can best be understood as a poetic requiem to her, and it begins with a distich:

> Той, что, сгорев на земле моим пламенеющим сердцем,
> Стала из пламени свет в храмине гостя земли.[69]

(To her, who, having burned up on the earth in my flaming heart, became light from flame in the temple of the guest of the earth.)

The imagery of this distich is drawn from several sources. The burning heart refers to the book's title ("cor ardens" – an allusion at once biblical and Homeric).[70] The phrase "guest of the earth" appears to allude to Goethe's "Selige Sehnsucht" ("Blessed Yearning"), a mystical poem on death and resurrection and one of the epigraphs to *Cor Ardens*. What deserves emphasis is the fact that Ivanov reflects on his wife's death by combining literary and biblical sources, but in a form hallowed by antiquity. In this way, the personal verses become suprapersonal – somewhat akin to Zhukovsky's technique in his poem on Pushkin's death.

Cor Ardens itself includes a book entitled "Rosarium," which is devoted to a wide-ranging exploration of the rose in various cultural traditions. One small section of this book is called "Antologiia rozy" ("Anthology of the Rose"), and it consists entirely of epigrammatic, two-line poems, all in the form of distichs. As so frequently in Ivanov, the sources vary widely: "Isis" is based on Novalis, "Paolo and Francesca" on Dante, "The Bush" on the burning bush of the Old Testament, "Lotos" on the convergence of Buddhist and Christian themes. In all cases, Ivanov elaborates on these mythical motifs, adding a rose (hence the title "Anthology of the Rose") and consciously extending their symbolic potential. Ivanov's creative adaptation of his predecessors may be demonstrated on the basis of the distich "Sub Rosa" (literally, "under the rose"; in other words: "in secret"):

> Тайна, о братья, нежна: знаменуйте же тайное – розой,
> Нежной печатью любви, милой улыбкой могил.[71]

> Brothers, the secret is tender: the rose is the name of this secret,
> Tender impression of love, smile so dear of the graves.

Despite its Latin title, the source of this mysterious poem is German. In a set of distichs entitled "Votivtafeln" ("Votive Tablets"), Schiller included the following two-line poem:

> Der Homeruskopf als Siegel

> Treuer alter Homer! Dir vertrau' ich das zarte Geheimnis,
> Um der Liebenden Glück wisse der Sänger allein.[72]

> The Seal in the Form of Homer's Head

> Loyal old Homer! To you I entrust the secret so tender,
> Only the singer should know all that the lovers enjoy.

From the German text, Ivanov takes not only the form of the two-line epigrammatic distich, but also the key phrase "tender secret," and even the motif of the seal (German "Siegel," Russian "pechat'"). Schiller's poem, of course, fits in neatly with the light-hearted spirit of many Latin epigrams. The "secret" he mentions is clearly of an amorous nature. By sealing his love letter, the writer ensures that no one will see it except his beloved (and Homer, the *blind* poet of antiquity – a gentle irony). Ivanov considerably complicates this rather simple poem. He adds the mystical rose and, along with it, the all-important theme of death. His distich no longer concerns a love intrigue, but, rather, the profound mystical relationship of love and death.

"Sub Rosa" is, naturally, a miniature, yet its importance transcends the boundaries of its two lines. The poem is one of the innumerable expressions of an invariant in Ivanov's thought after his wife's death. Not only is the part of *Cor Ardens* that precedes "Rosarium" called "Liubov' i smert'" ("Love and Death"), but the subsequent book of poetry, drawing quite obviously on the distich we have examined, is entitled "Nezhnaia taina" ("Tender Secret"). In the title poem of that new collection (twenty lines, in distichs), Ivanov develops yet further the mystical implications of "Sub Rosa," leaving Schiller far behind.

In prerevolutionary culture, Ivanov played a central role as poet, theoretician, and teacher. He influenced an entire generation of poets, some of whom developed remarkably similar poetic ideals. Iurii Verkhovsky (1878–1956) was one of these: a minor figure in literary history, but a prolific creator of distichs. Verkhovsky's tastes were determined not only by his admiration for Ivanov, but also by his university studies in German literature and his scholarly research preparing editions of Russia's "Golden Age" poets (among others, Del'vig).[73] In an age often remembered for its radical poetic experimentation and innovation, Verkhovsky chose to look unabashedly backwards. This combination of factors explains his predilection for the distich and his tendency to use it in much the same way as his nineteenth-century counterparts had.

In a poem entitled "Arcadia," Verkhovsky writes an extraordinarily stylized dialogue in distichs between a youth and the muse. The former asks to be brought back to an idyllic golden age, to "dobrym pastukham, veselym pastushkam, startsam premudroprostym" ("kind shepherds, gay shepherdesses, and simple yet most wise elders"). The muse consents:

> Сладко и ныне сказать мне отрокам нежным и чистым:
> Да, Аркадия есть. О полетим же туда![74]

> Even today it is pleasant for me to tell youths pure and tender:
> Yes, Arcadia lives. O, let us fly there at once!

These verses date from 1908, but in terms of style, theme, and genre, they could easily have been written by Del′vig. Indeed, the poem bears as an epigraph a line from Del′vig's hexameter idyll "Konets zolotogo veka" ("The End of the Golden Age"). This line provides metrical continuity (since the first line of a distich is a hexameter), yet it appears to be used by Verkhovsky with a slight polemical thrust. Del′vig's poem laments that the "golden age" has passed, while Verkhovsky seeks to recover it.

In 1908, Symbolism was at its apex, and these distichs, while anachronistic, can be understood as an extreme expression of a certain Romantic nostalgia not inconsistent with the Symbolists' larger outlook. Most remarkable, however, is the fact that Verkhovsky continued to write verses of this sort long after other movements had pushed Symbolism from center stage. In 1917, he published his "Sel′skie epigrammy" ("Village Epigrams"), a cycle of forty-one poems in distichs, with direct allusions to Goethe's cycle "Venetianische Epigramme" ("Venetian Epigrams," also in distichs) and to Catullus, the great Roman love elegist. In the cultural context of the period, these poems can be explained only as a deliberate form of escapism. And even in 1922 Verkhovsky continued to compose distichs, sometimes as a form of commentary on his own era:

> В майское утро улыбчивой жизни певцов простодушных
>   Бархатом юной земли, тканью ветвей и цветов
> Был возлелеян безвестный певец и бродил, как младенец;
>   Путь указуя, пред ним резвый порхал мотылек.
> Так принимал ты посох дорожный, о вечный скиталец,
>   Ныне на темной земле осени хмурый поэт.[75]

> In the May morning of smiling life of singers most artless,
>   Coddled by velvet of earth, covered by flowers and leaves,
> Wandered the singer unknown like an infant at play without worry.
>   Showing the way out in front, butterflies hovered above.
> Thus have you grasped your staff for the journey, o wand'rer eternal,
>   Now it is gloomy on earth, poet autumnal and dark.

In this poem, Verkhovsky uses a series of obvious contrasts (spring/autumn, smiling/gloomy) and implicit oppositions (youth/age, then/now) to depict what might be called the "poet's progress." In these and other verses of his 1922 collection, one often senses a qualification of the certainty, expressed in "Arcadia," of the possibility of returning to a golden age. However, it would be misleading to suggest that distichs become for Verkhovsky a means of expressing dissent. More probably, he used the distich in the same way his contemporaries used the Onegin stanza – as a way of looking nostalgically backwards. One of Verkhovsky's 1922 poems is called "Revnost'" ("Jealousy") and it consciously emulates Pushkin's "Rifma" ("Rhyme"). In Verkhovsky's variant, Jealousy is the daughter of the maenad "Zarnitsa" ("Lightning") and a personified "Vikhr'" ("Whirlwind"). Although lacking Pushkin's metapoetic subtleties, the poem is nonetheless a masterpiece of stylization. It fits in completely with the light tradition of "album poetry," so popular in the age of Pushkin and so distant from the ideals of most Russian post-revolutionary poets.[76]

With very few exceptions, the Revolution coincides with the end of the history of the Russian distich. Within the boundaries of Soviet Russia, poets could hardly be expected to continue to practice a stylized form imbued with the classical spirit.[77] And even those émigrés who looked wistfully backwards saw their poetic ideals embodied not by classical Greece and Rome, but by prerevolutionary Russia. In the work of Vladislav Khodasevich, one finds a rare exception: a poem in distichs written in emigration. Khodasevich had experimented with distichs earlier, but this poem is unquestionably his most significant in that form.[78] I quote the first, fourth, and sixth (final) stanzas:

Был мой отец шестипалым. По ткани, натянутой туго,
  Бруни его обучал мягкою кистью водить.
Там, где фиванские сфинксы друг другу в глаза загляделись,
  В летнем пальтишке зимой перебегал он Неву.
А на Литву возвратясь, веселый и нищий художник,
  Много он там расписал польских и русских церквей.

. . .

Был мой отец шестипалым. Как маленький лишний мизинец
  Прятать он ловко умел в левой зажатой руке,
Так и в душе навсегда затаил незаметно, подспудно
  Память о прошлом своем, скорбь о святом ремесле.
Ставши купцом по нужде – никогда ни намеком, ни словом.
  Не поминал, не роптал. Только любил помолчать.

. . .

Был мой отец шестипалым. А сын? Ни смиренного сердца,
  Ни многодетной семьи, ни шестипалой руки
Не унаследовал он. Как игрок на неверную карту,
  Ставит на слово, на звук – душу свою и судьбу . . .

Ныне, в январскую ночь, во хмелю, шестипалым размером
И шестипалой строфой сын поминает отца.[79]

Father's hand had six fingers. Along the tautly stretched canvas
   Bruni, his mentor in art, taught him to paint with soft strokes.
There where the sphinxes from Thebes would stare in the eyes of each
                                        other,
   He with his light summer coat, crossed the Neva in the cold.
To Lithuania returned, this happy yet destitute artist
   Painted there many a church, Russian and Polish alike.

                . . .

Father's hand had six fingers. He'd hide his superfluous pinky
   Cleverly, quickly away, under his left hand clenched tight.
Just as he hid in his soul 'neath the surface where no one could see it,
   Memory of his own past, grief for his lost, holy craft.
Need having forced him to change his profession, he worked as a
                                   merchant,
   Neither with word nor with hint did he discuss what had been.

                . . .

Father's hand had six fingers. But what did his son then inherit?
   Neither the meekness of heart, not father's six-fingered hand,
Not the family rich with children. Much like a gambler,
   Placing his luck on one card, placing his soul on a sound
Now in the January night, somewhat drunk, in a six-footed meter,
   Using a form of six lines, son recalls father again.

To the extent that this poem has attracted scholarly attention, it has served primarily as a source of biographical information about the Khodasevich family. The poet's father did indeed have a six-fingered hand, he was in fact trained as a painter, and he did leave that profession to do something more practical (not to become a merchant, as Khodasevich implies, but rather to become a professional photographer).

Yet beyond these superficial facts, the poem represents a poet's memorial to his father and, to a certain extent, an émigré's remembrance of an earlier life. Khodasevich, at a temporal, spatial, and existential remove from his subject, uses the distich to emphasize distance. The world he writes about is not that of antiquity, yet the distich lends it an almost mythical aura. This occurs on the level of poetic diction, where exclamations like "Trudnyi i sladkii udel!" ("Sweet and difficult lot!," stanza 5) and paraphrases such as "sviatoe remeslo" ("holy craft") for "art" (stanza 4) hark back to an earlier age.[80] It also explains why Khodasevich, rather than directly naming the Academy of Arts in St. Petersburg (stanza 1), mentions the landmark located across from it: the sphinxes. These sphinxes, like so much else in the poem, supply both a realistic detail and an enormous symbolic weight. In keeping with the tradition of the distich, they call to mind an entire mythological complex, including the riddle of man and its solver, Oedipus.[81] Moreover, as statues themselves, a relic of a past age in the present one, these sphinxes embody the mystery of art so central to the poem.

Khodasevich entitled the poem "Daktili" ("Dactyls"), a point that has puzzled commentators, who dutifully (and correctly) note that this is – strictly speaking – an incorrect name for the distich.[82] The obvious question arises: how could a poet as form-conscious as Khodasevich make such an elementary error? The answer, of course, is that he did not err. Khodasevich chose his title purposefully – not to indicate the form (which would be obvious to any educated reader), but for other, more subtle reasons. When Blok called a cycle of poems "Iambs," he was not offering assistance to readers who were incapable of determining his meter. Rather, he was playing on a secondary meaning of "iamb" – since antiquity, the form was associated with satire and therefore invective.[83] When Khodasevich uses the inexact term "dactyls" to describe a verse form that virtually screams out its links to antiquity, the reader should suspect that he is alluding to something beyond the obvious.

In "Dactyls," Khodasevich focuses on a detail both real and highly symbolic. The physical deformity of Khodasevich's father (a seemingly superfluous sixth finger) lends both formal and symbolic structure to the poem. There are six stanzas of six lines each, with six stresses in each line; all begin with the identical phrase ("Father's hand had six fingers"). In the context of a poem whose form insistently draws the reader into the sphere of antiquity, it is worth recalling the etymology of the "dactyl." Khodasevich himself was surely aware of the word's Greek origin: it means "finger." In this poem, then, every metrical foot is actually a finger; rarely is the metapoetic level so carefully inscribed in a poem's form.

On the thematic level, the sixth finger emblematizes memory and art. The father hides his sixth finger as he hides his memories of his life as an artist (stanza 4). And his sixth child (the poet Khodasevich), expressly identifying himself with that sixth finger (stanza 3), ultimately fulfills the ambition that his father was forced to renounce. In the penultimate stanza, Khodasevich offers a definition of the creative process. The artist studies the world and then, "derzkoiu

volei, demonskoi volei" ("with a daring and demonic will"), creates
his own, other world. In "Dactyls," Khodasevich takes on precisely
this task; from the modest circumstances of his family history, he
weaves a mythology, even cosmogony. His poem recreates and adds
order to a lost world, filling it with meaning. In this way, the details
that in "real life" were considered superfluous become in poetry
symbols of the utmost significance. The elegiac distich contributes to
this process in several ways. As the "inherited" form *par excellence*, it
aptly conveys the theme of inheritance. As a form traditionally
associated with metapoetic thematics, it serves as an appropriate
vehicle for a poem about the artist. Most important, as a consciously
stylized marker of antiquity, it treats the recent past as if it were
ancient history, giving a scope and power that the events recounted
could otherwise not possibly attain.

As in the preceding chapters, our study of the elegiac distich has
shown a conscious continuity of purpose among Russian poets that is
inextricably linked to their formal choices. Several factors, however,
differentiate the distich from the forms previously under consideration. Elsewhere, I have been at pains to identify a specific *Russian*
source – a single powerful example – that gave birth to an entire
tradition. "The Black Shawl" and ". . . Again I visited," for
example, had Western European precedents, yet their Russian
incarnation proved so influential that the pre-Russian ancestry was
largely forgotten by subsequent poets. In the present case, the
process of reception followed a different pattern. Before it found its
place in the repertoire of Russian poets, the elegiac distich had
enjoyed enormous popularity – in antiquity (Greece and Rome) and
even in modernity (Germany). Rather than taking a foreign form
and domesticating it to the point where its origins became irrelevant,
the Russians took the distich as a means of pointing toward these
very origins. There is no single Russian "distich of genius" that, for
practical purposes, eliminated prior tradition – nor was any attempt
ever made to create such a thing. On the contrary, Russian poets
appreciated the distich as a means of pointing to a non-Russian
tradition. The form became the vehicle for a highly stylized conception of antiquity which was, like any stylization, exaggerated and
oversimplified.

There can be no question that this process of stylization considerably limited the rich potential of the classical distich. It is not simply

that Russian poets curtailed the form's generic, thematic, stylistic, and even rhythmic potential. More significantly, they added to the form a level of distance. If the poets of antiquity could express a wide variety of feelings and ideas in the distich, the Russians used the form to filter all feelings and ideas through a screen of antiquity. In short, this was poetry that insisted on communicating in mediated fashion. The history of the Russian distich thus provides an instructive lesson on the value of metrical stylization. As in any other type of poetic evolution, pure repetition quickly becomes uninteresting. However, even within the restricted sphere of the Russian distich, there was room for creative application. The works of Pushkin, Zhukovsky, Ivanov, and Khodasevich indicate how, by accepting an inherited and largely predetermined form, a poet can add new dimensions and depth to his work. The "minor masterpieces" we have examined in this chapter draw so insistently on associations of the distich that they simply could not exist in any other form.

CHAPTER 5

Heirs of Mayakovsky: the poet and the citizen

Уважаемые
                    товарищи потомки!
Роясь
         в сегодняшнем
                         окаменевшем г—,
наших дней изучая потемки,
вы,
     возможно,
           спросите и обо мне.
      . . .
Профессор,
              снимите очки-велосипед!
Я сам расскажу
              о времени
                    и о себе.
                    Маяковский, "Во весь голос"[1]

Respected / comrade descendants! // Rummaging / in today's
/ petrified sh—t, // Studying the darkness of our days // You,
/ possibly, / will also ask about me. // . . . Professor, / take off
your bicycle-eyeglasses! // I myself will tell / about [my] time /
and about myself.

Mayakovsky, "In Full Voice"

For a Western reader, one of the most striking innovations of
twentieth-century Russian poetry is *lesenka*, the so-called stepladder
construction, in which a single verse is split over a number of lines
(generally two, three, or four), with each respective segment beginning spatially where the previous one left off. This technique is
associated first and foremost with Vladimir Mayakovsky, who introduced it in 1923 and then used it in every poem until his death seven
years later.[2] Already in Mayakovsky's lifetime, the form began to
appear in the work of other poets. After his death, it achieved

widespread popularity, ultimately becoming a staple of the Soviet poet's repertoire.

Mayakovsky was not only the originator of *lesenka*; he was also the preeminent poet of his time. It is therefore hardly surprising that *lesenka* has attracted critical attention primarily within the context of Mayakovsky's own poetic practice.[3] My interest, however, lies in the evolution of *lesenka* beyond Mayakovsky, in establishing why subsequent poets chose to incorporate his innovation into their own work. For my purposes, then, Mayakovsky is important as a starting point, an invitation and model for others.

Lesenka differs significantly from the forms previously examined in this book, for it is a graphic construction and *not* a meter. In Mayakovsky's works, virtually all meters (from the strictest syllabo-tonic to the loosest accentual) fit neatly into the Procrustean *lesenka*, sometimes coexisting within a single poem. So easy to recognize, *lesenka* eludes simple definition, for – besides its unmistakable outline on the page – it contains few predictable elements. It is true that more words tend to appear in the final step than in the earlier ones,[4] but this fact contributes little toward explaining its function – or its attraction to Mayakovsky and his followers. Scholars have invested considerable effort in attempting to determine the precise significance of the elusive *lesenka*.[5] The form's obvious invariant is rhyme, which occurs consistently on the final word of each line's final step. As Mayakovsky stated in "Kak delat' stikhi" ("How to Make Verses"), his lengthiest and most sustained essay on poetics, "I always place the most characteristic word at the end of the line and find a rhyme for it at any cost."[6] Of course, rhyme was by no means unique to Mayakovsky's *lesenka* verse; it had been a central element in his earliest poetry and, in fact, in most Russian poetry since the eighteenth century. However, by tirelessly seeking out the untried and unexpected, Mayakovsky made rhyme one of the most noticeable aspects of his poetry.[7]

This emphasis on rhyme reflects a fundamental belief in sound as the dominant element of verse. For Mayakovsky, verse was meant to be recited, and the good poet was necessarily a good performer:

The majority of my poems are built on colloquial intonation. Yet, careful planning notwithstanding, even these intonations are not so strictly established. Indeed, I constantly vary my delivery when I read, depending on the makeup of the audience. Thus, for example, a printed text speaks somewhat indifferently, in that it assumes a qualified reader:

> Надо вырвать радость у грядущих дней.
> One must tear the joy away from future days.

Sometimes when reading on stage, I strengthen this line to a scream:

> Лозунг:
>   вырви радость у грядущих дней!

> Slogan:
>   Tear the joy away from future days![8]

While not devoted to *lesenka per se*, this passage is revealing because *lesenka* arises "naturally," as it were, in the course of the discussion. In an effort to describe his performance practice, Mayakovsky offers the reader two versions of the same line. Both scan as trochaic hexameter, but their effect is nonetheless quite different, the second being by far the more exclamatory. In order to create the intonation of a "scream," the poet alters words, grammar (an impersonal construction becomes an imperative), punctuation, *and* visual layout. The tiered graphic presentation accentuates the punctuation (a colon), breaking the line's rhythm by forcing a substantial pause before the main idea. In this way, the word "slogan" (which comes directly from the public genre of agitation propaganda)[9] becomes an independent entity and gains in importance. Simultaneously, its isolation serves to highlight that which follows (i.e., the slogan itself, rather than the word "slogan"). The stepladder construction thus creates an opposition that adds emphasis to both parts of the phrase. This sort of dynamism enhances the performative aspect of verse. In short, according to Mayakovsky's own claims, the seemingly visual element of *lesenka* contributes directly to the aural effect of verse.

A brief glance at a war poem by Semen Kirsanov (Mayakovsky's younger contemporary, friend, and admirer) indicates the extent to which Mayakovsky's ideas were internalized by his fellow poets. Written approximately fifteen years after "How to Make Verses," Kirsanov's "Sevastopol" describes the Soviet defense of the Crimea against the Nazis. The poem concludes with the lines:

> Лозунг:
>   "Смерть фашистским оккупантам!"
> значит:
>   жизнь
>   народу моему![10]

> (Slogan:
>   "Death to the fascist occupiers!"

Means:
   Life
      to my people!)

Mayakovsky's specific example is reflected in the lexical choice (the word "slogan"), the metrical foot (trochaic), the punctuation (colon and exclamation point), and, most obviously, the graphics (*lesenka*). As in Mayakovsky, a step in the stepladder separates the word "slogan" from the slogan itself. In the next line, Kirsanov develops his model by using a three-step construction. "Znachit" ("means") is set off as an exordium (just as "slogan" was in the previous verse). By placing "life" and "to my people" on separate lines, Kirsanov gives weight to each of them, thus accentuating his fundamental contrasts: "life" stands in apposition to "death" and "my people" in apposition to "fascist occupiers." (The statement appears to draw on an old Russian proverb: "what is healthy for a Russian is death for a German.")[11] It may justifiably be argued that Kirsanov's imitation is less interesting than his source, yet this is for present purposes secondary.[12] Most important is the obvious way in which Mayakovsky provided his successor with a formal and semantic model.

Like punctuation, the "step" cannot be seen by the audience, but it can presumably be felt. According to Mayakovsky, *lesenka* complements and improves on traditional punctuation. Readers tend to overlook periods and commas, he argues, but graphic design cannot be ignored. For example, a mediocre reader unwittingly travesties Pushkin's "Dovol'no, stydno mne / Pred gordoiu poliachkoi unizhat'sia" ("Enough! I am ashamed / To be humiliated before a proud Polish woman") by not pausing sufficiently after the comma, thus creating the completely inappropriate "Dovol'no stydno mne" ("I'm rather ashamed"). Mayakovsky explains:

So that it be read as Pushkin intended, it is necessary to split up the line as I do:

Довольно,   Enough,
    стыдно мне . . .   I am ashamed . . .

With this separation into half lines there will be neither semantic nor rhythmic confusion. The line division often is also dictated by the necessity of breaking the rhythm unmistakably, since our condensed economic verse formation often forces [one] to toss out little words and syllables, and if one doesn't make a pause after these syllables – often a bigger pause than between lines – then the rhythm stops short.

That's why I write:

Пустота . . .
        Летите,
            в звезды врезываясь.

Emptiness . . .
        [You] fly,
            cutting your way into the stars.

"Emptiness" stands apart, as the only word that characterizes the heavenly landscape. "Fly" stands apart, in order that it not be understood as an imperative: "Fly into the stars," etc.[13]

Just as a composer indicates phrasing in a musical score, so Mayakovsky hoped to show his reader how a given line should be pronounced. Strategic placement of words on a page, he argued, could contribute to producing a stage "performance" true to the author's intentions.

This appraisal may be have been overly optimistic, for *lesenka* had obvious limitations. On the one hand, it was primarily a defense against an unqualified reader. (A "good" reader would presumably read poetry correctly even without it.) On the other hand, as Mayakovsky himself admitted, an individual poet's reading was unique, and even *lesenka* was incapable of reproducing its complexities: "In every verse there are hundreds of the most subtle rhythmic, metrical, and other particularities at work, which no one except the author can get across – and through no means except his voice."[14] Indeed, the few extant recordings of his recitations indicate that Mayakovsky himself did not declaim his verses the way he set them out on the page.[15]

Regardless of its imperfections, *lesenka* indisputably held an attraction for Mayakovsky. Like rhyme, it was a device he employed to foreground the aural element in poetry. Yet rhyme – even when inexact and unexpected – was a part of traditional Russian verse. In contrast, *lesenka* was a virtually unprecedented means of graphic presentation.[16] Its very presence seemed to challenge conventional notions of poetry. This element of novelty was vital, for Mayakovsky saw his program as a genuine revolution (in poetics no less than in politics) and thus a complete and irreconcilable break with the past. In this sense, *lesenka* may well have been more significant symbolically (as a signal of "the new") than functionally. Aleksandr Arkhangel'sky, a contemporary of Mayakovsky and his most talented parodist, seems to suggest precisely this in his rewriting of Mayakovsky's discussion with Pushkin ("Anniversary Poem"):

Вы – чудак:

       насочиняли

           ямбы,

Только

    вот –

       печатали

          не впрок.

Были б живы,

       показал я

          вам бы,

Как

   из строчки

      сделать

         десять строк.

Например:

– Мой дядя

     самых

       честных

         правил . . .

Как это?

    – Когда

       не в шутку занемог,

Уважать,

    стервец,

       себя

         заставил,

Словно

   лучше

     выдумать

       не мог . . .[17]

(You're an eccentric: / you dreamed up / iambs // But / see – / you printed them / incorrectly. // If you were alive, / I would show / you, // How / out of one little line / you could make / ten lines. // For example: // My uncle / is of the most / strict / principles . . . // How's that go? / When / he got good and sick, / He / (the bastard) / forced others / to respect / him, // As if / he couldn't / think up / anything better . . .)

In Arkhangel'sky's version, Mayakovsky takes the most famous lines of Russian poetry (the opening stanza of *Eugene Onegin*), and reproduces them in *lesenka* – adding only a few jarring colloquialisms.[18] The great innovation of *lesenka* is thus reduced to making several lines out of one.

Ironically, even Mayakovsky's fascination with declamation (which for him justified *lesenka*) was not novel, for it developed the ideas of the most venerable and canonic of Russian poets – the eighteenth-century odists. As Mayakovsky's contemporary Iurii Tynianov demonstrated, the work of these poets had a marked oratorical orientation. Lomonosov, for example, put such emphasis on the act of recitation that he even developed a series of conventional gestures that the poet was to employ as an accompaniment to his verses.[19] It is noteworthy that stylized hand gestures were an integral part of Mayakovsky's own performance practice.[20] Most importantly, like most eighteenth-century odes, Mayakovsky's *lesenka* verse was written with a "tendency" – either to glorify, to commemorate, or to excoriate.[21]

Western readers often think of poetry as a lyrical expression of intimate feelings or subtle moods and relationships. Public readings tend to be fairly unemotional affairs, and poets themselves seldom consider such "performances" central to their poetic production. However, from his very first poems, Mayakovsky wrote for the stage, fully intending his verses to be read – and read loudly, "in full voice" (as he called his final, unfinished long poem). This emphasis on declamation became even more pronounced in the Soviet period: "Poetry has stopped being only that which is seen by the eyes. The revolution has given us the word that one hears, poetry that is heard."[22] Whereas his prerevolutionary verse tended to be mocking, blasphemous, and intentionally outrageous, the post-revolutionary poems (and it should be recalled that the work with *lesenka* belongs exclusively to this period) had another goal entirely. They were intended to strengthen the Russian people as they worked to build socialism. The later Mayakovsky believed that genuine poetry should originate in a "sotsial'nyi zakaz," that is, in response to a societal need, be it practical (e.g., the campaign against smoking, the need to expose hypocritical bureaucrats), political (e.g., the life and fate of the working class), or philosophical (i.e., the ideals of Marxism-Leninism).[23]

Like the great odic poets before him, Mayakovsky employed language in order to sway his audience by eloquence rather than convince them through rational argument. At times, his poem's "moral" may seem like an afterthought (as it in fact was in the famous "Bruklinskii most" ["Brooklyn Bridge"], which – up until a digression at the end – appears to be a panegyric to capitalist society). In certain cases, it may be difficult to determine what direct benefit Soviet society was expected to derive from a given poem.

Without the poet's own explanation, for example, readers might not guess the immense social significance that Mayakovsky attributed to his lengthy personal attacks on a recently deceased fellow poet in "Sergeiu Eseninu" ("To Sergei Esenin"). Nonetheless, the concept of the poet as teacher – and political agitator – was one of Mayakovsky's main bequests to posterity.

Western critics generally consider Mayakovsky's later verse (i.e., from the *lesenka* period) as artistically inferior to his earlier work. This evaluation has nothing to do with *lesenka* itself, but rather stems from the fact that, with the passage of time, Mayakovsky toned down his stylistic experimentation and became less adventurous and irreverent in his choice and treatment of topics.[24] The propagandistic and political element, already present in Mayakovsky's early post-revolutionary poems, becomes overwhelming in much of the *lesenka* verse. Innumerable poems praise the leading Bolsheviks or the Bolshevik cause. So, for example, one finds a 1923 poem on the assassination of the Soviet ambassador Vatslav Vorovsky, where Mayakovsky urges a mass demonstration (common at the time) to send a message to the foes of communism. The poem concludes with a series of imperatives:

> Ответ
>> в мильон шагов
>>> пошли
>>>> на наглость нот.
> Мильонную толпу
>> у стен кремлевских вызмей.
> Пусть
>> смерть товарища
>>> сегодня
>>>> подчеркнет
> бессмертье
>> дела коммунизма.[25]

(Send / an answer / of a million footsteps / to the insolence of diplomatic notes. // Snake around the Kremlin walls / a crowd of a million people. // Let / the death of a comrade / today / emphasize // the immortality / of the communist cause.)

In this passage one finds stylistic complexity (alliteration, unexpected rhymes, neologism) wedded to a purely propagandistic thematics. In the final sentence, the complexity virtually disappears, allowing the political point to stand out all the more clearly.

The refrain of "Komsomol'skaia" ("Komsomol Song," 1924) offers perhaps the clearest example of Mayakovsky's socialist simplicity:

Ленин
    жил
Ленин
    жив.
Ленин
    будет жить.[26]

(Lenin / lived. // Lenin / lives. // Lenin / will live.)

Today, lines such as these do little to enhance Mayakovsky's reputation. However, it must be admitted that they represent a significant portion of his later poetry. Without these poems, Stalin would never have made his famous 1935 proclamation, unthinkable outside a totalitarian context, that "Mayakovsky was the greatest and most talented Soviet poet. Indifference to his memory and his works is a crime."[27] This pronouncement had a predictable effect: the Soviet cultural watchdogs did everything possible to see that Mayakovsky was remembered not as an iconoclast, but as a faithful adherent of the Party line. Soviet scholarship dismissed Mayakovsky's early Futurist experiments as insignificant and short-lived, played down his clashes with the Soviet literary establishment in the 1920s, and obscured the circumstances of his suicide in 1930. In Soviet schools, teachers explicated a carefully selected canon of Mayakovsky's works in such a way to ensure that students appreciated his unquestioning patriotism. Even the populace at large was not spared this particular Mayakovsky, whose most obsequious passages (e.g., the above-quoted lines from the "Komsomol Song"), achieved socialist immortality by being converted into posters and displayed in prominent places throughout the USSR. Insofar as one dare speak of a "Soviet cultural memory," the firm association of Mayakovsky, *lesenka*, and political propaganda lay at its foundation.

For aspiring Soviet poets, Mayakovsky was necessarily a towering influence. To write like Mayakovsky became the highest possible aspiration. And because it represented Mayakovsky at his most Soviet, *lesenka* offered a particularly attractive model. No Soviet poet after Mayakovsky wrote exclusively in *lesenka*, yet many turned to this distinctive form in a significant percentage of their verses. In short, what for Mayakovsky (in his later period) had been an invariant became for his successors an option. What for Mayakovsky had been an innovation became for his followers a pledge of allegiance.

For the present investigation, the central question concerns the circumstances that inspired Soviet poets to take advantage of this technique. Observations of the work of several highly regarded Soviet poets reveal a number of insistent generic, thematic, and stylistic associations.[28] The Soviet poet could (and did) use *lesenka* for virtually any subject matter. However, one finds it insistently linked to three – by no means mutually exclusive – verse types: civic, odic, and didactic.

As a fixed form (with strict formal characteristics), the ode had more or less disappeared from Russian poetic practice by the early nineteenth century. It has been suggested that its sudden disfavor had much to do with the decline of the patronage system.[29] In short, when poets' livelihoods depended on the favor of wealthy and powerful individuals, one could count on a significant body of literature being produced in which those individuals were praised. A poet employed by a sovereign was expected to produce a steady supply of verse extolling that sovereign or his most recent military and diplomatic accomplishments. In the peculiar literary establishment created in the Soviet Union, the writer was employed by the state, which itself was inextricably linked to the Party. One cannot be surprised, then, at the immense amount of energy and verse devoted to the task of praising the Soviet system. With remarkable frequency, such verse took the form of *lesenka*.

Not only did Soviet poets produce a considerable number of doxologies to their society, to a certain extent they even reclaimed the term "ode." Mayakovsky himself, it should be noted, penned an "Ode to the Revolution" in 1918. However, this poem belongs to his pre-*lesenka* phase. In this particular regard, Mayakovsky remained true to his Futurist orientation: he was more interested in developing new revolutionary genres (e.g., the march, the order ["prikaz"]) than in revivifying older ones. In the *lesenka* period, he was skeptical of the term "ode." A poem of 1927 entitled "Vmesto ody" ("Instead of an Ode") begins with the lines:

> Мне б хотелось
> вас
> воспеть
> во вдохновенной оде.

только ода

что-то не выходит.[30]

(I would like / to sing / of you / in an inspired ode. // But an ode / somehow just isn't coming out.)

The first line, with its elevated theme and alliterations (repeated "vos" and "vo" sounds in the second, third, and fourth steps) creates an illusion of high style. The second line immediately destroys this illusion with its colloquial negation. As it turns out, the poem concentrates on the life of a simple Soviet woman ("baba sovets-kaia"), who is married to a careerist mailman, who beats her and then sends flowers and love notes to keep her from running to the authorities and thus compromising him. Most of the poem is dedicated to "unmasking" the husband. (Even in his later work, Mayakovsky was not simply a singer of praise. He felt that criticism was legitimate if it was directed at compromise, pretense, and opportunism in his fellow citizens.) At the poem's conclusion, Maya-kovsky states his own position by returning to the theme of the ode:

Я

    напыщенным словам

                всегдашний враг,

  и, не растекаясь одами

             к Восьмому марта,

 я хочу,

     чтоб кончилась

            такая помесь драк,

  пьянства,

      лжи,

        романтики

          и мата.

(I am / the permanent enemy / of high-flown words, // And, not spilling forth odes / for the eighth of March,[31] / I want / an end / to this mixture of fights, / drinking, / lying, / romance, / and cussing.)

The implication is that odes are inappropriate for the contemporary poet, "the permanent enemy of high-flown words." High style is the province of hypocrisy, represented in this poem by the husband. Such language distracts from reality, from the issues of Soviet society that genuinely need to be addressed.

In the very same year, perhaps not coincidentally, the theme of the ode appeared in the work of Nikolai Aseev, Mayakovsky's close friend and comrade-in-arms. Aseev, while revisiting Kharkov (where he had spent several years as a student), wrote "Novaia Ukraina" ("The New Ukraine"), a poem in which he hailed the changes that had occurred since the Revolution. Unlike Mayakovsky, whose close inspection of Soviet man revealed numerous flaws, Aseev looked on a grander scale and expressed unqualified admiration at the new trams, buildings, and houses. Having given voice to his enthusiasm, he included a passage in which he anticipated the comments of his detractors:

> Скажут и так:
> Борзописец од.
> Но как же
> к тебе,
> эпоха новая,
> кроме как в оде,
> отыщешь вход?[32]

(As it is they'll say: / He's a hack writer of odes. // But how then / to you / O new epoch, // can one find an entry / Except in an ode?)

A similar passage can be found in a poem Aseev wrote approximately thirty years later, "Piatoe desiatiletie" ("The Fifth Decade [of the USSR]"):

> Я
> не слагатель
> од благолепных
> и в одописцы
> не тщился попасть . . .
> Но как обойтись
> без светлых,
> хвалебных
> слов
> про родную
> советскую власть![33]

(I / am not a creator / of glorious odes // and I never attempted to join / the ranks of odists . . . // But how can I avoid / radiant / laudatory // words / for my native / Soviet power!)

Both of these passages display a curious ambivalence toward the ode. Mayakovsky had deemed the ode inappropriate because it glossed over problems. Aseev's unease stems from a different source: its very traditionality. As a Futurist, Aseev apparently recognized that an ode entailed a compromise with former principles. On the other hand, as a political poet wishing to celebrate the achievements of his country, he recognized the appropriateness of the ode. (Indeed, one could easily imagine an eighteenth-century poet writing an ode to commemorate an important historical event or anniversary.) In both passages, Aseev thematizes his uncertainty, initially distancing himself from the odic tradition, but ultimately accepting it (with, respectively, a rhetorical question and an exclamation). It is noteworthy that, in both cases, he borrows Mayakovsky's *lesenka* as if to demonstrate that his work has the master's sanction. However, the critical element of Mayakovsky's "Instead of an Ode" is wholly absent; what remains is *lesenka*'s larger semantic association: Soviet patriotism.

In the work of Margarita Aliger, the connection of the patriotic ode and Mayakovskian form becomes unmistakable. Born in 1915, Aliger belonged to a generation of poets raised in strict conformity with Soviet norms. While she never met Mayakovsky (as an impecunious student, she could not afford to attend poetry readings and thus passed up her single opportunity to hear him recite), her admiration for him was immense.[34] In contrast to the members of LEF (Mayakovsky, Aseev), she was untouched by Futurist attitudes toward tradition. She thus had no difficulty reconciling contemporary and odic poetry. Moreover, unlike Mayakovsky, she apparently had no complaints whatsoever about Soviet life. Her "Oda" ("Ode," written in 1934, when the poet was only eighteen years old) clearly reflects the optimism of the Stalinist poet:

> Страна моя,
> верная муза моя,
> помоги мне, –
> дерзну ли одна,
> подыму ли
> неслыханный труд –
> единым дыханьем
> воспеть в утверждающем гимне
> горячие чувства,
> которые в сердце живут?
> Когда я иду
> под сводом трудящейся ночи,
> когда я иду
> под сводом рабочего дня,
> тревога, как счастье,
> большая и легкая очень,
> крутою волною
> до звезд подымает меня.

Прости меня, жизнь моя.
                    Что мне простыми словами
сказать о тебе,
              если путь моей мысли далек?[35]

(My country, / my loyal muse, / help me, – // Do I dare all alone / to
attempt / the unprecedented task – // with my single breath, / to sing in
an affirmative hymn // the fervent feelings / that live in my heart? //
When I walk / under the firmament of the laborers' night, // when I walk
/ under the firmament of the workers' day, // a concern, like happiness, /
great and very light, // like a steep wave / raises me up to the stars. //
Forgive me, O my life. / What am I with my simple words // to say about
you, / if the path of my thought goes so far?)

These opening lines deserve attention for a number of reasons.
Whereas her predecessors had displayed a certain discomfort with
the term "ode," Aliger proclaims her pride in the genre. She not
only uses it as her title (stating *only* the genre, not even the subject),
she also genuinely draws on the conventions of odic poetry,
beginning with an invocation to the muse (who, significantly, is not
a deity, but rather her own country) and continuing with the
traditional "modesty topos" (in which the poet declares his/her
unworthiness for the important task ahead). Aliger states her
purpose explicitly – to affirm ("vospet' v utverzhdaiushchem
gimne") the patriotic feelings that stir within her. Mayakovsky, it
should be remembered, was completely convinced in the principles
of socialism, but he did not hesitate to condemn individual aspects
of its implementation. In short, his works display unwavering
loyalty to the system, but undisguised animosity toward the elements of contemporary society that impede progress. For Aliger
(and, in general, for Stalinist poets), enthusiasm leaves no room for
doubt. Aliger's "Ode" depicts a state of satisfaction and joy that,
for Mayakovsky, could have been achieved only under true communism. For our purposes, it is not necessary to investigate the
remainder of Aliger's ode. More significant is the question of why
she chooses the *lesenka* form. For reasons not difficult to imagine,
women poets tended to avoid *lesenka*. This technique was so closely
associated with the combative stance, aggressive delivery, and
"masculine" personality of Mayakovsky that – given the sexism
that prevailed in the Soviet Union – it would have appeared
somewhat incongruous for a woman to assume this role.[36] Even in
Aliger's poetry, the form appears rarely. However, it seems that, in

works of extreme patriotic pathos, Aliger turned to *lesenka* to express those ideals which her society held highest.[37]

While poems entitled "ode" remained infrequent in the Soviet period, there can be no doubt that the Soviet Union gave its poets numerous occasions for odic (celebratory) verse: holidays, anniversaries (particularly of the Revolution), deaths (of famous leaders), and abstract concepts (the Party, communism). In all of these areas, Mayakovsky created the standard against which subsequent poets measured themselves, and Mayakovsky's *lesenka* became the preferred form of expression.[38]

For the Soviet poet, Lenin was the greatest of all possible subjects. He was George Washington, Moses, and Jesus Christ in one: the father of a country, the moral lawgiver, the god in the form of man. In a country that forbade religion, the image of Lenin offered an acceptable outlet for the vestiges of spirituality. It has long been noted that Soviet depictions of Lenin borrow from the Russian religious tradition. Lenin's life became the subject of modern-day hagiography, his premature death a source of inspiration for future generations. For Soviet poets, Mayakovsky paved the way, creating numerous and lengthy paeans to the great man.[39] A few examples should suffice. The first comes from the seventy-page poem "Vladimir Il'ich Lenin":

> Партия и Ленин –
> > близнецы-братья –
> кто более
> > матери-истории ценен?
> Мы говорим – Ленин,
> > подразумеваем –
> > > партия,
> мы говорим –
> > партия,
> > подразумеваем –
> > > Ленин.[40]

(The party and Lenin / are twin brothers – // who is more valuable / to mother history? // We say "Lenin," / we mean / "Party," // we say / "Party," / we mean / "Lenin.")

Mayakovsky creates a mythology: History (the mother) gave birth to twins: Lenin and the Party. The two are virtually identical and even interchangeable; in naming one, the other also comes immediately to mind. In another of Mayakovsky's poems (one of his last),

Lenin is quite obviously portrayed as a god; the refrain reads: "tak velel . . . Il'ich" ("thus Lenin commanded").[41] Indeed, a central element of Mayakovsky's presentation of Lenin is the motif of immortality. Over and over, the deceased Lenin is shown to live on in spirit – "Lenin / i teper' / zhivee vsekh zhivykh" ("Lenin / even now / is more alive than all living [people]").[42]

This image of the immortal and omniscient Lenin can be found in the work of any number of subsequent poets. In a 1940 poem called, appropriately enough, "Lenin," Kirsanov describes the continuing benevolence of the departed leader:

> С дороги сбившись,
> > лётчик ищет
> маяк Москвы
> > в туманной каше,
> И Ленин
> > ласковой ручищей
> аэродром
> > ему покажет.
> Гроза решит
> > раскатом грома:
> – Паду на дом,
> > огонь раздую! . . .
> Но Ленин
> > отведет
> > > от дома
> огонь
> > и бомбу грозовую.[43]

(Having lost his way, / the pilot seeks // the beacon of Moscow / in the foggy kasha, // And Lenin / with his huge caressing hand // Shows him / the airport. // The storm decides / with a peal of thunder: / "I'll fall on the house, / I'll make a fire! . . ." // But Lenin / leads away / from the house // the fire / and the storm's bomb.)

Where human abilities fail, the superhuman Lenin takes over, directing the lost pilot back to the Soviet capital or protecting the Soviet houses from the elements. Kirsanov offers a bizarre mix of hoary superstition and modern technology. On the one hand, his depiction of Lenin draws on folk belief. The thunderstorm is personified as a force with evil intentions (one thinks of the ancient Slavic deity Perun), while Lenin takes on the role of the traditional Russian house spirit ("domovoi"), whose purpose was to guard the peasant's dwelling from evildoers. These folkloric elements are combined with references to twentieth-century military innovations (airplanes, bombs). In the figure of a ubiquitous Lenin (Kirsanov uses the augmentative form of hand ["ruchishcha"] to emphasize his enormous grasp), Soviet man finds his protector.

Other supernatural attributes of Lenin come across in Evgeny Evtushenko's "V minutu slabosti" ("In a Minute of Weakness," part of his long poem of 1964 "Bratskaia GES" ["The Hydroelectric Station in Bratsk"]):

> В минуты
> самые страшные
> верую,
> как в искупленье:
> все человечество страждущее
> объединит
> Ленин.
> Сквозь войны,
> сквозь преступления,
> но все-таки без отступления,
> идет человечество
> к Ленину,
> идет человечество
> к Ленину . . .[44]

(In minutes / most terrifying // I believe / as [I believe] in redemption: // all of suffering humanity / will be united / by Lenin. // Through wars, / through crimes, // but all the same without deviation, // humanity moves / toward Lenin, // humanity moves / toward Lenin . . .)

In this passage, the poet unabashedly takes words with strong religious connotations ("veruiu," "strazhdushchee," "iskuplen'e" ["I believe," "suffering," "redemption"] – the first two are distinctly archaic, Church Slavonic forms) to describe his unwavering faith. Through repetition of the final lines, he creates an atmosphere of religious ritual. It is hard not to recognize a latter-day Christ in Lenin's "uniting suffering humanity." Especially noteworthy is the teleological principle on which the final lines are based. The poem concludes with a picture of the whole of humanity ultimately joined together in its striving toward Lenin.

The conclusion of Andrei Voznesensky's long poem "Longjumeau" (1962–63) takes place in the Lenin Mausoleum, where a group of young communists turns to their leader to ask whether they are worthy of his legacy:

"Скажите, Ленин, мы – каких Вы ждали, Ленин?!
Скажите, Ленин, где
                победы и пробелы?
Скажите – в суете мы суть не проглядели? . . ."
"Скажите, Ленин, в нас идея не ветшает?"
И Ленин
        отвечает.
На все вопросы отвечает Ленин.[45]

("Tell us, Lenin, are we the ones you awaited, Lenin?! // Tell us, Lenin
where / are the victories and the gaps? // Tell us – did we miss the central
point in our vanity? . . ." // "Tell us, Lenin, is your idea aging in us?" //
And Lenin / answers. // Lenin answers all questions.)

Using a type of paronomasia reminiscent of Mayakovsky (e.g.,
"*pobedy*," "*probely*," or "*suete*," "*sut'*"), Voznesensky presents an
image of the youthful worshiper(s) before the shrine of their all-
knowing god. These pilgrims, recognizing their imperfections
("probely" – "gaps") and sins ("sueta" – "vanity"), ask for forgiveness and are rewarded when their long-dead idol responds.

In all these passages (and it would not be difficult to find
additional examples), we are dealing not simply with a highly
spiritualized portrayal of Lenin, but – on a formal level – with
lesenka. While it would be inaccurate to suggest that *all* verse on the
subject of Lenin was written in *lesenka*, there can be no doubt that
lesenka clearly attracted this type of poetry. This connection is even
thematized in Robert Rozhdestvensky's "Pis'mo v tridtsatyi vek"
("Letter to the Thirtieth Century"):

Житель Праг,
Берлинов,
Гаван.
По широким
                ступеням
                        столетий
поднимается ЛЕНИН
к вам![46]

(Inhabitant of Pragues, // Berlins, // Havanas. // Along the wide / steps
/ of centuries // LENIN ascends // to you!)

According to Rozhdestvensky, Lenin moves step by step (along a
metaphorical *and* graphic ladder)[47] to the inhabitants of the thirtieth
century. Ultimately (in the continuation of the same passage), he
leads them forward. No matter how many centuries forward we may

travel, it seems, Lenin will always be ahead of us. Unfortunately, a citation cannot do justice to the rich design features that Rozhdestvensky employs. Not only does he use *lesenka* to signal those steps into the future, not only does he write Lenin's name in all capital letters (using a larger type size). Lenin's name and all words derived from it are printed in *red* ink (signifying, of course, the color of revolution, but also recalling editions of the Bible in which Jesus' words are highlighted in this same way). In a final stroke of the sledgehammer, Rozhdestvensky includes on the facing page a classic picture of an avuncular Lenin.

One is tempted to ask whether this cult of Lenin reflected Soviet poets' genuine convictions or the pressure of propaganda. This complicated question, crucial for the social scientist, historian, or literary biographer, is only a secondary consideration for the student of poetics. After all, the painters of the Italian Renaissance did not necessarily choose religious subjects to express their approval of Christianity. Rather, they created the art that their patrons expected of them. The religious theme was a given; its execution was the responsibility of the individual. Similarly, Soviet poets responded – whether out of sincerity or servility – to the dictates of their "patron." For the present investigation, the central concern is the treatment of a given subject, not the reason why that subject is chosen. In this regard, the evolution of Soviet poetry is consistent with artistic traditions that arise in less restrictive political climates. A powerful model (formal, generic, and semantic) served as the touchstone for future creation. In this particular case, the model was doubly effective, for it resulted from both the boldness of Mayakovsky's poetic innovations and their subsequent canonization by Stalin, the supreme arbiter in all cultural questions.

The rich tradition of poems about Mayakovsky himself indicates how the mere mention of the poet's name was sufficient to trigger the *lesenka* form. Indeed, nowhere in Soviet poetry is the connection of form and content so predictable as in this subgenre.[48] As usual, the first models can be found in Mayakovsky's own verse. The closing passage of "Brooklyn Bridge" offers a famous example of unabashed self-aggrandizement when Mayakovsky envisions a geologist of the future who will look back on the scene:

И дальше
          картина моя
                    без загвоздки
по струнам-канатам,
                  аж звездам к ногам.
Я вижу –
          здесь
                стоял Маяковский,
стоял
          и стихи слагал по слогам.[49]

(And further / my picture [continues] / without a hitch // Along the string cables, / all the way to the foot of the stars. // I see / here / stood Mayakovsky, // stood / and composed verses by the syllable.)

This future scholar, we are assured, will marvel at the architectural achievement of capitalism and recall the great Soviet poet (its conqueror) astride it. The immodesty of this passage is characteristic: Mayakovsky raises himself to the level of the superhuman, just as he does with Lenin and the other leading Bolsheviks.

It may still be premature to say whether the archeologist of the future will remember this classic pose, but there can be no doubt that Soviet poets did. In a poem written shortly after Mayakovsky's suicide, Kirsanov wrote:

Поднимает город
                грандиозный остов,

по Гудзону
          круглый
                приплывет буёк . . .

Вижу –
          Маяковский
                с Бруклинского моста

строгими глазами
                смотрит на Нью-Йорк.[50]

(The city raises / its grandiose skeleton, // along the Hudson / a round / buoy swims up . . . // I see – / Mayakovsky / from the Brooklyn bridge // with his strict eyes / looks at New York.)

In short, Kirsanov recalls his friend and teacher in precisely the way Mayakovsky had predicted. Kirsanov's sole departure from the original (the "strict" eyes) is fully in the Soviet spirit, emphasizing, as it does, Mayakovsky's critical attitude toward the capitalist world. (Mayakovsky did in fact disapprove of New York, yet the tone of "Brooklyn Bridge" hardly reflects this. On the contrary, Mayakovsky expresses awe and even delight, likening himself looking at New York to an artist gazing "lovingly" at a Madonna.)

With slight variations, the larger-than-life image of Mayakovsky appears repeatedly in the *lesenka* of subsequent poets. Kirsanov's work contains numerous poems in which the great poet appears. Except for a poem of 1925 (when *lesenka* was quite new and apparently not yet in Kirsanov's own repertoire), the character and theme of Mayakovsky is *always* accompanied by *lesenka*. For example, in one poem, a brand of tank called "Mayakovsky" calls out patriotically to his comrades:

> Рев
>   сложился в речь:
>   "Товарищи! Я с вами!
> Жив
>   и горд –
>   Советской родины поэт,
> что, неся на башне
>   боевое знамя,
> двигаюсь,
>   как танк,
>   по улицам побед."[51]

(The roar / turned into speech: / "Comrades! I am with you! // Alive / and proud / is the poet of the Soviet motherland, / in that, carrying on the tower / the battle flag, // I move, / in the form of a tank, / along the streets of victories.")

This image of Mayakovsky is based on several familiar, almost clichéd characteristics: his mighty voice (the speech develops out of the roar of the motor – in Russian "rev" becomes "rech'"), his patriotism, his fighting spirit. At the poem's basis is a metamorphosis (the deceased poet returning as a form of technological innovation), which is itself derived from Mayakovsky. In the famous "Tovarishchu Nette parokhodu i cheloveku" ("To Comrade Nette, the Steamship and the Man"), Mayakovsky had described how the assassinated Nette comes back to life, as it were, in the form of a steamship.

Indeed, "To Comrade Nette" appears to have been a central poem for Kirsanov. He refers to it explicitly in "Piatiletka" ("The

Five-Year Plan'') and bases his "Metro Station Mayakovsky" on the same conceit. Kirsanov's "Odessa" begins with the words:

Город-воля,
штормовое лето,
порт,
где бочек
крупное лото,
где встречался
с "Теодором Нетте"
Маяковский
в рейде золотом.[52]

(The city of freedom, / a windy summer, // the port, / where there is an enormous bingo game / of barrels, // where in the golden roadstead / Mayakovsky // met / with the "Theodore Nette.")

In this case, even the rhyme "leto/Nette" [summer/Nette] comes directly from the opening passage of Mayakovsky's poem. Mayakovsky's "Nette" apparently loomed so large that Kirsanov proved incapable of writing about Odessa without referring to it. The city itself became a topos, which demanded certain references (Mayakovsky, Nette) and a specific form (*lesenka*).

The Mayakovsky theme plays an equally visible role in the work of Nikolai Aseev. As early as 1927 (with Mayakovsky still alive) he appears as a symbol of youth in the *lesenka* of "Moskvichi" ("Muscovites"):

В ответ на язвительный
старческий смех
мы нянькам ответили:
"Наш – Маяковский,
с бульвара
плечьми
протолкавшийся в век.
Мы с ним
не потупимся
прищурью зоркой,
и мы не сгорим
от грошовой свечи,
с обношенной шапкой,
с обглоданной коркой,
мы,
новой формации москвичи!"[53]

(In answer to the vicious / laughter of the old folk // we answered the nannies: / "Mayakovsky is ours // From the boulevard / with his shoulders

/ pushing into the age. // We / will not cast down / our sharp squint-eyed glance, // and we won't burn / from a cheap candle. / With a worn-out cap, / with a gnawed crust, // we / are Muscovites of the new formation!")

Here Aseev uses Mayakovsky to symbolize novelty and youth, which he offers as a response to the dismissal of the older generations.

Most interestingly, this connection of an energetic, youthful Mayakovsky and *lesenka* recurs in two poems written in the early 1960s, at the very end of Aseev's life ("Bessonnye stikhi" ["Sleepless Verses"] and "Zhivoi" ["Alive"]). At this time, Aseev had more or less stopped using *lesenka*, and against this background of traditional graphic layout, the poems stand out all the more starkly. In the second, Aseev reminisces about how Mayakovsky used to walk around Moscow:

> Как по улице
> по московской,
> еще веющей
> стариной,
> шел – вышагивал
> Маяковский,
> этот самый.
> Никто иной!⁵⁴

(As along the street, / the Moscow street, // which still wafted / antiquity, // walked – stepped out / Mayakovsky, // he himself. / Nobody else!)

The poem concludes in the present, with Mayakovsky (now in the form of a monument) stepping off his pedestal:

> Вот идет он,
> мой друг сердечный,
> оттолкнув
> ногой пьедестал, –
> неизменный
> и бесконечный,
> тот,
> кто бронзовым
> так и не стал.

(There he goes, / my bosom buddy, // having kicked away / with his foot the pedestal, // unchanged / and infinite / he, / who never did become / bronze.)

Despite the passage of several decades, Mayakovsky remains unchanged. He kicks away the pedestal to his own statue, refusing to accept his immobile iconic status. These final lines are clearly based on Mayakovsky's own "Anniversary Poem," in which the poet, addressing Pushkin's statue, affirms life and rejects death (even in the form of a monument). In fact, the very title "Alive" probably refers to "Anniversary Poem," where Mayakovsky says to Pushkin: "Ia liubliu vas, / no zhivogo, / a ne mumiiu" ("I love you, but alive, not as a mummy").[55] In short, Aseev (like Kirsanov before him) recalls his friend through the prism of his *lesenka* form as well as through a specific master-text.

Vladimir Lugovskoi was not close to Mayakovsky personally, but he came to recognize him as the great poet of the age. In his *lesenka* poem "Olimpiada" ("The Olympics"), he introduces Mayakovsky indirectly:

> Стихи Маяковского
> > грозно читает
> Колхозный
> > прославленный бригадир.
> И это для нас
> > торжество такое,
> Такой всенародный
> > творческий взлет,
> Что слышно,
> > как Партия доброй рукою
> Вперед,
> > в коммунизм
> > > Украину ведет.[56]

(The glorious brigadier / from the collective farm // Sternly reads / the verses of Mayakovsky. // And for us this is / such a celebration, // Such a nationwide / creative flight, // That one hears / how the Party, with its kind hand, / Leads Ukraine / forward / to communism.)

This passage offers a classic example of a text inside a text: the head of a collective farm reads Mayakovsky's verses aloud. His reading is apparently so moving that the audience can actually hear how the Party (presumably in sympathetic vibration with the patriotic verse) gently leads Ukraine to its utopian future. If Mayakovsky had equated Lenin with the Party, Lugovskoi goes one step further by equating Mayakovsky himself with the Party (and thus, by extension, with Lenin).[57] He thus not only emphasizes the inspirational qualities of Mayakovsky's poetry in general, he also envisions poetry as a direct means to a political end. The fact that the imagined audience is composed of all segments of society suggests the inclusivity of Mayakovsky's verse (its "vsenarodnyi vzlet").

Evgeny Evtushenko's work demonstrates how this tradition continued smoothly into the post-Stalin period. Evtushenko gave Mayakovsky an exalted place among Russian poets, writing poems not only about the poet himself, but even about his mother.[58] One of Evtushenko's more ambitious works is a long poem entitled "The Hydroelectric Station in Bratsk." Numerous aspects of this work are derived from Mayakovsky. To begin with, the very idea of combining poetry with technological achievement can be traced back to Mayakovsky. Following his lead (again with the gentle encouragement of the Party), numerous Soviet poets sang the praises of heavy machinery, factories, dams, etc. Evtushenko's work, however, has a different focus: the Siberian hydroelectric station serves as the backdrop for a series of meditations on Russian (and Soviet) history. In the introductory section, "Molitva pered poemoi" ("A Prayer Before the Poem"), Evtushenko appeals for guidance to his poetic forebears (Pushkin, Lermontov, Nekrasov, Blok, Pasternak, Esenin, and – finally – Mayakovsky). This "Prayer" is written in stanzas of varying length and traditional graphic form. However, at the very conclusion, in an apostrophe to Mayakovsky, the verse suddenly takes the shape of *lesenka*:

> Дай, Маяковский, мне
> глыбастость,
> буйство,
> бас,
> непримиримость грозную к подонкам,
> чтоб смог и я,
> сквозь время прорубясь
> сказать о нем
> товарищам потомкам.[59]

(Give me, O Mayakovsky / the bulk, the wildness, the bass voice, // the stern irreconcilability with scum, // that I might also, / tearing through time, / speak about it / to my comrade-descendants.)

In these verses, Evtushenko unambiguously expresses his desire to take on the mantle of the great Soviet poet. Appearing as it does against the background of traditional graphic layout, *lesenka* could hardly be a more transparent symbol for Mayakovskian poetics. It is telling that Evtushenko refers to Mayakovsky's bass voice (i.e., his oratorical prowess) as one of his central attributes. Indeed, the final lines directly allude to the opening of Mayakovsky's "In Full Voice" (quoted as the epigraph to this chapter), a passage in which the poet conceives of his voice as a means to achieve direct contact with future generations. Evtushenko himself was at this point primarily known for his declamation of his own verses.[60]

Approximately sixty pages later, these brief references to Mayakovsky are developed. One of the last sections of "The Hydroelectric Station in Bratsk" is called "Mayakovsky":[61]

> . . . И, вставши у подножья Братской ГЭС,
> подумал я о Маяковском сразу,
> как будто он костисто,
>   крупноглазо
> в ее могучем облике воскрес.
>
> Громадный,
>   угловатый,
>   как плотина,
> стоит он поперек любых неправд,
> натруженно,
>   клокочуще,
>   партийно,
> попискиванья
>   грохотом поправ.
> Я представляю,
>   как бы он дубасил
> всех прохиндеев
>   тяжестью строки
> и как бы здесь,
>   тайгу шатая басом,
> читал бы он строителям стихи.
> К нему не подступиться
>   с меркой собственной
> но, ощущая боль и немоту,
> могу представить все,
>   но Маяковского
> в тридцать седьмом
>   представить не могу.

(. . . And, having taken my place at the foot of the Hydroelectric Station of Bratsk, // I immediately began to think about Mayakovsky, // as if he in his bony, / huge-eyed way // had been resurrected in its powerful form. // Enormous, / angular, / like a dam // he stands apart from all falsehoods, // tired from work, / boiling over, / in accordance with the Party, / having stamped on the squeals / with his rumbling. // I imagine, / how he would

have drubbed // all the scoundrels / with the weight of his line // and
how here, / shaking the taiga with his bass voice // he would have read his
lines to the construction workers. // One shouldn't approach him / with
one's own measure // but, feeling pain and numbness, // I can imagine
everything, / yet Mayakovsky // in the year 1937 / that I cannot imagine.)

While standing at the foot of the latest Soviet technological
marvel (a hydroelectric plant in Siberia), Evtushenko "immediately
began to think of Mayakovsky." As in the "Prayer," the very
mention of Mayakovsky's name is sufficient to set *lesenka* verse in
motion (line 3). This construction is accompanied by familiar
associations. Evtushenko thinks of Mayakovsky's enormous bass
voice, capable of shaking the taiga (i.e., a hyperbolic variation on
the theme of declamation), as well as his moral authority (how
Mayakovsky would have "drubbed all the scoundrels with the
weight of his line"). The Russian adjectival form of "Bratsk" is
identical with the word "brotherly," and Evtushenko, as we shall
see, takes advantage of these associations. Since the noun "pod-
nozh'e" often means "pedestal," one envisions Evtushenko standing
at the foot of a monument to Mayakovsky. (The fact that Mayakovsky is replaced not by a statue, but by a hydroelectric plant,
reflects Mayakovsky's own awe of modernization and industrial-
ization.) The setting should by now be familiar: it recalls Mayakovsky's own "Anniversary Poem," where the poet depicted himself
standing at the foot of Pushkin's statue. Evtushenko's poem, true to
Mayakovsky's model, is devoted to a contemporary poet's reflections
on his mighty predecessor. In a manner reminiscent of Lugovskoi,
Evtushenko draws on the (false) association of Mayakovsky and the
Party (he stands "partiino" – in accordance with the Party).
Historically accurate or not, this detail is essential, for Evtushenko's
poem rapidly enters the sphere of politics. Having emphasized
Mayakovsky's unwavering loyalty to the cause and his tremendous
talent, Evtushenko shifts direction. He can imagine almost everything, he says, but he cannot imagine Mayakovsky in the year 1937
(i.e., at the height of Stalin's purges):

> Что было б с ним,
>   когда б тот револьвер
> не выстрелил?
>   Когда б он жив остался?
> Быть может, поразумнел!
>   Поправел?

Тому, что ненавидел,
                все же сдался?
А может,
        он ушел бы мрачно в сторону,
молчал,
        зубами скрежеща,
                        вдали,
когда ночами где-то
                в "черных воронах"
большевиков расстреливать везли?
Не верю!
        Несгибаемо,
                тараняще
он встал бы и обрушил
                вещий гром,
и, в мертвых ставший
                "лучшим и талантливейшим,"
в живых —
        он был объявлен бы врагом.
А если бы тот выстрел не
                раздался, —
себе наград и славы не ища,
как многие,
        он честен бы остался,
эпоху на плечах своих таща.[62]

(What would have happened to him, / if that revolver // had not fired? / If he had remained alive? // Perhaps he would have wisened up! / Shifted to the right? // In spite of everything, [would he have] given in to that which he hated? // Or, maybe, / he would have stepped gloomily to the side, // been silent, / gnashing his teeth, / afar, / while during the nights somewhere // in the NKVD vehicles / they led the Bolsheviks away to the firing squad? // I don't believe it! / Unbending, / like a battering ram // he would have stood up and let loose / with prophetic thunder, // and he who in death had become / "the greatest and most talented [Soviet poet]" // in life / would have been declared an enemy [of the people]. // And if that shot had not / rung out, // not seeking rewards or glory for himself, // as many people [do], / he would have remained honest, // bearing the epoch on his shoulders.)

Evtushenko thus brings up two formerly unmentionable themes: Mayakovsky's suicide and Stalin's purges. The revolver he refers to is the gun with which Mayakovsky killed himself in 1930. Using Stalinist terminology from the mid-1930s and beyond (recognizable to any Soviet reader), Evtushenko notes that, had Mayakovsky remained alive, this "best and most talented Soviet poet" would have been declared an "enemy of the people." In contrast to opportunists, Evtushenko insists, Mayakovsky would have "remained honest." Comparing Mayakovsky to Atlas ("bearing the epoch on his shoulders"), Evtushenko again grants the Soviet poet super-human powers and status.

The poem's conclusion reveals an optimism that puts it firmly within the recently expanded boundaries of Soviet literature:

> Пусть до конца тот выстрел не разгадан,
> в себя ли он стрелять нам дал пример?
> Стреляет снова,
>   рокоча раскатом,
> над веком
>   вознесенный
>   револьвер –
> тот револьвер,
>   испытанный на прочность,
> из прошлого,
>   как будто с двух шагов,
> стреляет в тупость,
>   в лицемерье,
>   в пошлость:
> в невыдуманных –
>   подлинных врагов.
> Он учит против лжи,
>   все так же косной,
> за дело революции стоять.
> В нем нам оставил пули Маяковский,
> чтобы стрелять,
>   стрелять,
>   стрелять,
>   стрелять.

(Even if that shot is not entirely explained, // did he give us an example to shoot ourselves? // The revolver, / raised / above the age, / shoots again, / letting out a peal of thunder – // that revolver, / practiced on firm targets // from the past, / as if from a distance of two steps, // shoots at stupidity, / hypocrisy, / vulgarity: // not at invented / but at genuine enemies. // It teaches against lies, / always stubborn, // [it teaches] to stand up for the revolutionary cause. // Mayakovsky left bullets in it for us, // To shoot, / shoot, / shoot, / shoot.)

Evtushenko ultimately sidesteps the politically slippery question of Mayakovsky's suicide. He transforms the physical gun that Mayakovsky used to kill himself into a metaphorical weapon, capable of slaying the traditional foes of Soviet society: stupidity, hypocrisy, and vulgarity. Mayakovsky's gun thus becomes didactic. Rather than serving as an example for people to commit suicide (hardly an appropriate lesson for Soviet citizens), it teaches against falsehood and inspires confidence in the revolutionary cause. The poem's "moral" becomes clear and unmistakable: Stalin corrupted the Soviet Union, and Mayakovsky, as a true poet of the Revolution and citizen *par excellence*, would never have stood by silently when evil was taking place (the only crime explicitly mentioned is the purge of Bolsheviks). The poem thus neatly combines the traditional image of Mayakovsky with the new political mood of destalinization. In terms of the interests of this chapter, it should be emphasized that the "new" image of Mayakovsky offered by Evtushenko does not differ greatly from that found in the works of earlier poets. As a representative of the Khrushchev era, Evtushenko was allowed to incorporate elements that were taboo in the Stalin period. However, his portrait of Mayakovsky follows most of the decade-old clichés (the poet as teacher of civic virtue), imagery (martial), tropes (hyperbole), and, of course, graphic construction (*lesenka*). The principle innovation lies in Evtushenko's explicit attempt to fill the void left by Mayakovsky, thus adding a hyperbolic view of himself to the already inflated image of Mayakovsky.

It was not uncommon for poets of the post-Stalin period to claim for themselves the role of Mayakovsky's heir.[63] Robert Rozhdestvensky begins his already cited "Letter to the Thirtieth Century" with an address to future inhabitants of the planet:

> Эй,
> родившиеся
>   в 3000-м
> удивительные умы!
> Археологи ваши
>   отыщут,
> где мы жили,
> что строили
>   мы.

(Hey, / you, born / in the 3000th year// Extraordinary minds! // Your archeologists / will seek out // where we lived, / what we / built.)

This passage should be understood as a pastiche of at least two famous Mayakovsky poems. The idea of the "archeologist born in the year 3000" is transparently derived from Mayakovsky's poetry, where the motif of a future scientist looking back on the twentieth century recurs insistently: e.g., the "geologist of the centuries" in "Brooklyn Bridge," and, yet more obviously the source of Rozhdestvensky's poem, the "chemist of the thirtieth century" at the conclusion of the 1923 "Pro eto" ("About That"), Mayakovsky's first long poem in *lesenka*. These scientists, from their temporally distant vantage points, seek to reconstruct twentieth-century society based on architectural evidence (in the case of "About that," the chemist is asked to resurrect Mayakovsky himself). However, Rozhdestvensky takes the idea of directly addressing his future audience (apostrophe) from another source: the opening of Mayakovsky's "In Full Voice" (quoted as the epigraph to this chapter). Both poets use exclamatory intonation and colloquial diction, as if addressing an enormous crowd.[64] Both suggest that their own works belong to the future and, if only indirectly, both express confidence that the future – poetically speaking – is *lesenka*.

But what *was* the fate of *lesenka*? The work of Naum Korzhavin provides an interesting postscript to our discussion. Born in 1925, Korzhavin was inculcated into the spirit of Stalinism at a young age. As a youth, he idolized Mayakovsky and his "anti-bourgeois pathos" and was attracted by the "Romanticism" of the Revolution.[65] Korzhavin wrote a number of poems on civic subjects and, not surprisingly, used *lesenka*. However, he believed in speaking his mind rather than formulaically repeating Party dictates. This led to a checkered career. In 1947, although widely recognized as one of the most talented students at Moscow's Gorky Literary Institute, he was arrested. "Rehabilitated" after Stalin's death, he was able to finish his studies and enjoy a relatively successful, if brief, career in official Soviet literature. By 1970, his uncompromising positions led to forced emigration in the United States.

Korzhavin's poem "Na smert' Stalina" ("On the Death of Stalin," 1953) is remarkable for the Soviet poetry of that time. In general, poems written to commemorate the death of major Soviet political figures were encomiums. Korzhavin takes the appropriate form (*lesenka*) and tone (patriotic), but invests it with an unexpected pathos. His poem unambiguously conveys the spirit of terror and lawlessness that thrived under Stalin. The poem concludes with an apostrophe to the homeland, which contrasts markedly with the expected treatment of this subject (cf. Aliger's "Ode"):

> Моя страна!
>   Неужто бестолково
> Ушла, пропала вся твоя борьба?
> В тяжелом, мутном взгляде Маленкова
> Неужто нынче
>   вся твоя судьба?
> А может, ты поймешь
>   сквозь муки ада,
> Сквозь все свои кровавые пути,
> Что слепо верить
>   никому не надо,
> И к правде ложь
>   не может привести.[66]

(My country! / Is it possible that, in this senseless way, // All of your struggle has passed and disappeared? // Is it possible today / that all your fate // [Lies] in the dull and heavy glance of Malenkov? // But maybe you will understand / through the tortures of hell, // Through all of your bloody paths, // That to believe blindly / is useless, // And that falsehood / cannot lead to truth.)

In these verses, a fundamental belief in the aims of the October Revolution coexists with an awareness of the atrocities to which they have led. Such thoughts would become official policy several years later under Khrushchev's "destalinization" policies. In fact, Evtushenko would voice remarkably similar sentiments (see the above-quoted "Mayakovsky" or his once famous "Heirs of Stalin," also in *lesenka*). Yet Korzhavin's poem, as opposed to Evtushenko's work, indicates that *lesenka* was not *necessarily* a mouthpiece for party policy.[67] For Korzhavin, it was associated with civic content and therefore could be used not simply for propaganda purposes, but also to express an anti-Soviet political stance.

This chapter has shown how a fundamentally non-semantic element of verse (graphic layout) can obtain thematic and generic significance. In the context of Soviet poetry, Mayakovsky's innovation (*lesenka*) became the preferred and, ultimately, expected vehicle for conveying patriotic pathos, whether in depictions of historical figures or in commemorations of historical events. Though initially devised as a means of ensuring the correct declamation of verse, it achieved success less through any inherent qualities than through Maya-kovsky's unquestioned status as leader of the new poetry and the new society. To a remarkable extent, therefore, *lesenka*'s influence can be measured ideologically. Its popularity seems to have been limited to the poets (whether contemporaneous or of subsequent generations) who shared – or pretended to share – a belief in Lenin's legacy and the Soviet Union's bright future. While aspects of Mayakovsky's poetics drew admiration (at times grudging) from authorities as varied as Andrei Bely, Anna Akhmatova, Boris Pasternak, and Vladimir Nabokov, none of these poets ever used *lesenka*. Even Korzhavin, upon emigrating, ceased writing in this form. Obviously sensitive about any connections to official Soviet literature, he has recently suggested that his *lesenka* poems be reprinted in traditional graphic patterns (i.e., without steps).[68] In the later period of Soviet history, Russian poets who wished to set themselves off from the official mainstream eschewed *lesenka*. Indeed, the demise of the Soviet Union appears to have spelled the end of *lesenka* as a vital technique. This fact is in itself significant, for it indicates the extent to which factors not intrinsically poetic affect poetic form. *Lesenka* as such is presumably as effective today as it ever was. However, its associations have become so inextricably linked to a discredited ideology as to make it unacceptable to the present generation of Russian poets.

Afterword: the meaning of form

Стихи писать – не плод единыя охоты,
Но прилежания и тяжкия работы.
        Александр Сумароков, "Наставление хотящим быти
                        писателями (1774)[1]

Writing poetry is not the fruit of pleasure alone,
But of diligence and hard work.
        Aleksandr Sumarokov, "Instruction for Those Wishing
                        to Be Writers" (1774)

In his celebrated *Pis'ma russkogo puteshestvennika* (Letters of a Russian Traveler), Russia's young man of letters and unofficial cultural ambassador Nikolai Karamzin describes his meeting of 1791 with the Danish poet Jens Baggesen (1764–1826). Baggesen had recently become engaged and, under the spell of love, was in the process of reevaluating his views on life and art. As Karamzin recalls: "We began to speak about poetry. Baggesen insisted that he would never again write in verse, because this type of work is completely unnatural and prevents one's feelings from pouring out in all of their fullness and freedom."[2] Baggesen may not have been one of the towering figures of his age, but his argument possesses an indisputable logic. If one wishes to speak naturally and give free rein to feelings, poetry is probably *not* the most appropriate means of expression.

But to what extent can such "natural" expressivity be achieved? The following anecdote, as related by Sigmund Freud, is instructive:

A doctor who is requested to attend to a baroness as she gives birth explains that the moment has not yet come. He suggests to the baron that they play a game of cards in the next room. In a short while the baroness' screams of pain penetrate the ears of both men: "Ah mon Dieu, que je souffre!" The husband jumps up, but the doctor delays: "It's nothing, let's keep playing." A while later they again hear her scream, "Mein Gott, mein Gott, was für Schmerzen!" The baron asks, "Don't you want to go in, Herr Doctor?" He

239

replies, "No, no, it's not time yet." Finally they hear an unmistakable "Ouch, oww, oww!" – Thereupon the doctor casts the cards aside and says: "It's time."[3]

Among other things, this passage makes clear the enormous gap between nature and culture. Like any good German aristocrat, the baroness voices her initial discomfort in French. As the pain becomes worse, she makes the same statement, but this time in her native language. Finally, when the pain becomes intolerable, language ceases: her exclamations become nonverbal interjections. In this final stage, the niceties of civilization are stripped away, and true emotion surfaces from behind the veneer of civilization. The doctor leaves his own cultural ritual (the card game) and moves to assist the woman. Freud's anecdote thus takes Baggesen's lament one step further. While the Danish poet insisted that poetry is an unnatural form of communication, the Viennese doctor points out the artificiality of language itself. Nature speaks not through French or German, he implies, but through grunts and screams.

It is worth considering these two passages as we conclude our study of poetic form. If language is mediated emotion (Freud), then poetry – as a highly mediated form of language (Baggesen) – is located at an additional remove from genuine experience. Accordingly, much-quoted claims like "all good poetry is the spontaneous overflow of powerful feelings" must be understood as a Romantic's dream rather than an adequate description of the poetic process.[4] To put the matter most bluntly, it is difficult to imagine a poet – even in the heat of inspiration – *spontaneously* composing a sonnet.[5] Rather than expressing life as it is experienced, all poetry (good *or* bad) offers a self-conscious, inevitably conventionalized, and often highly stylized condensation of experience. Indeed, the very concept of artistic form is diametrically opposed to "real life." Life itself tends toward maximum entropy and thus functions as a centrifugal force; form, a centripetal force, demands order.

At certain (usually early) periods in the development of a national literature, form is imposed on poets from without. In Russia, this occurred in the eighteenth century. Poet-theoreticians such as Trediakovsky and Lomonosov, drawing more or less explicitly on earlier Western European models – Boileau in France, Opitz in Germany – wrote treatises in which they explained the rules of verse for would-be Russian poets. An ode, according to Lomonosov, should treat a heroic theme, use elevated diction, and be written in ten-line stanzas of iambic tetrameter. Other genres were defined along similar lines.[6] In Russia (as in Boileau's France and Opitz's Germany), this method of "poetics by decree" established a certain level of competence, yet ultimately proved too restrictive to be of lasting value. According to a truism of literary history, virtually all periods of normative poetics lead inevitably to a breakdown of the very rules they champion.

The poems analyzed in the previous chapters lead me to argue that this breakdown is not so dramatic as is commonly supposed. While subsequent generations of poets did not generally consult a manual to compose their verse, they nonetheless had a very precise understanding of the way a given subject had been handled in the past. From prior works, they derived their own approach – formal, thematic, and generic. Poetic memory, more subtle than a written compendium of rules, essentially fulfilled that very purpose. In short, once poets could find numerous successful models in the work of their predecessors and contemporaries, there was no longer any necessity for them to study an academic treatise. The process I am describing may not occur along strictly intellectual lines: it is impossible to determine the degree to which poets *consciously* pattern their verse on earlier practice. However, the preceding chapters all corroborate a certain basic principle: Russian poets relate a specific poetic form to a specific content (whether generic or thematic), and their own usage of inherited forms reflects this awareness. My work begins with an empirical observation: once a metrico-semantic connection is set (in an exemplary poem or series of poems), it creates a firm association for future poets.

This basic insight has profound interpretive implications. A poet's attitude to the larger literary tradition is revealed with striking clarity when his work is placed in the formal and semantic context established by his predecessors. A critical approach of this type, while not claiming to determine poetic quality with mathematical precision, can at least offer criteria for distinguishing a major poet from a minor one. First and foremost, it becomes evident that "originality" – understood in the sense of creation *ex nihilo* – does not necessarily lead to magnificent art. The finest poets are capable of adapting what others have bequeathed to them, taking this pre-formed material in new and unexpected directions. It is often a careful balance of familiarity and novelty that creates masterpieces.

In the first three chapters, the most influential exemplar was found in Pushkin's work, yet in only one case did Pushkin actually invent the form in question. Although not conceived as a tribute to Pushkin, the present study contains much that would support his reputation as Russia's greatest poet. It also helps to explain why, when removed from his national linguistic and poetic context, Pushkin has failed to win admirers. Discerning readers outside Russia have generally been baffled by his canonic status.[7] Poetic genius, it would appear, is not simply active, but fundamentally *reactive*: it locates and develops potentially rewarding models. Those models, when rescued by the scholar from the oblivion to which they are often deservedly consigned, can reveal a surprising degree of similarity to the far better works they spawned.

The underlying claim that poetic form and meaning are related is, in and of itself, neither startlingly new nor particularly useful. It has been my purpose to show how this generalization can be turned into a precise and practical interpretive tool. In each of the preceding chapters, I examined a series of poems that were linked by both form and semantics (understood either thematically, motivically, generically, ideologically, or any combination thereof). My conception of form has allowed a considerable degree of flexibility, being by turns metrical (blank verse), metrical and strophic (ballad, Onegin stanza), metrical and graphic (elegiac distich), and solely graphic (*lesenka*). Throughout, a specific form could be linked to a specific content, but in each case it functioned *differently*.

I began with the ballad, because it offered a test case with relatively few variables. Since the combination of meter and stanza found in Pushkin's "Black Shawl" occurs in only a limited number of Russian poems, I was able to examine most of the corpus of relevant texts. Moreover, in keeping with the genre of the ballad, the poems in question were all plot-oriented and relatively simple. On the basis of the nineteenth-century material, it could be shown that Pushkin's poem accounted for almost all subsequent generic realizations of the form and a large number of thematic (or motivic) ones. Interestingly enough, few of these poems were actually designated as "ballads" by their authors. This attribution was made on the basis of Pushkin's source (Uhland, whom Pushkin himself knew only indirectly, through Zhukovsky's translation) and through various features long associated with the ballad in its modern European incarnation. The reception of "The Black Shawl" by twentieth-century poets revealed considerably greater freedoms. The connection between amphibrachic tetrameter couplets with masculine rhyme and balladic content was no longer binding, yet – when altered slightly – it continued to operate in a remarkably wide range of poetic texts.

In the case of blank verse, I chose to examine a single extremely productive line of development. Beginning with Pushkin's poetic practice (a very gradual acceptance, culminating in the masterpiece ". . . Again I visited"), I traced a series of major poems which drew on Pushkin's model. In that chapter, there was no attempt to trace the *entire* trajectory of this form. Such a task – a book-length project in itself – would have entailed analyses of several significant poems clearly indebted to those I did consider (e.g., Mikhail Kuzmin's "Konets vtorogo toma" ["End of the Second Volume,"][8] Pasternak's "Belye stikhi" ["Blank Verse"]), as well as numerous poems where the connection is less evident (Vyacheslav Ivanov's "Poslanie na Kavkaz" ["Epistle to the Caucasus"], Voloshin's cycle of poems on Russia, Lugovskoi's book *Seredina veka* [The Middle of the Century]). Mikhail Gasparov has argued that virtually all of these poems derive from a single generic source: the dramatic monologue, familiar to Russians already in Pushkin's day through European drama (e.g., Shakespeare).[9] If this is in fact the case – and much suggests that it is – then it would be fair to say that my own chapter deals with a subset of a larger phenomenon. In short, while Pushkin's ". . . Again I visited" did not inform *all* subsequent Russian lyric poems in blank verse, its combination of form, theme, and genre clearly provided an impulse for several first-rate poets (and poems). If, in the first chapter, the reception of twentieth-century poets revealed a degree of formal adaptation, the blank verse examples are remarkably true to Pushkin's form. This perhaps reflects the fact that the blank verse lyric was still largely a *terra incognita* in the twentieth century, whereas the possibilities of amphibrachic tetrameter couplets had been virtually exhausted by numerous nineteenth-century imitations, adaptations, and parodies. Whatever the reason, the blank verse of Blok, Gumilev, Khodasevich, Akhmatova, and Brodsky indicates that major Russian poets consider their predecessors' choices of form and content to be highly meaningful. Indeed, a reading of these twentieth-century poems that does not consider their Pushkinian origin inevitably misses an essential part of their impact. It is one thing for a poet to use the motif of repeated visits to introduce a meditation on time and death; it is quite another to do so in the same metrical form as an earlier meditation on these very themes.

The third chapter concerned the Onegin stanza, a perhaps unique instance in the Russian tradition of a strongly marked form where the initial usage coincides with the most famous exemplar. To the Russian reader, this form screams out its Pushkinian origins. Any new work in Onegin stanzas insists upon a comparison with Pushkin's novel in verse. In such a case, it seems, subsequent poets either sidestep the form altogether or use it to take advantage of these "automatic" associations. The relative dearth of Russian poems in Onegin stanzas indicates a general reluctance to compete with Pushkin on his own sacred ground.[10] It is thus highly significant that those poets who dared to accept the challenge did so with an extraordinary degree of generic and thematic freedom. In the twentieth century, the "meaning" of this form began to change, but in directions that can be logically reconstructed. Silver Age poets found in the Onegin stanza a nostalgiac backdrop rather than a specific source of plot.[11] In short, a form became associated less with its original content than with its status within the larger tradition as both a creation of genius and a symbol of the artistic achievement of a bygone age.

In distinct contrast, the fourth chapter – the history of the Russian elegiac distich – revealed an extraordinary degree of stasis (considerably greater than in the classical tradition that gave birth to the form). The semantic associations of the Russian distich were derived not from a single influential poem (as in the earlier chapters), but from an entire corpus of poems. Despite the impossibility of locating a specific source, the distich proved more predictable than any of the other forms under consideration. The same type of lapidary, classically tinged generic and thematic realizations that characterized Russia's Golden Age models also accounted for the vast majority of later poems in this form. Moreover, the relatively few attempts to alter these associations (e.g., Ivanov and, to a lesser extent, Fet) did not move in random directions. No one tried to write a ballad in elegiac distichs and, indeed, so strong is the form's neo-classical aura that an intelligent reader could view such an attempt only as a parody or otherwise deliberate distortion. Fet tried to shift the genre in the direction of the love poem (clearly using Goethe's "Roman Elegies" as his model), while Ivanov took his thematics and even certain subtle prosodic elements directly from the classical tradition with which, as a scholar of antiquity, he was extremely familiar. In short, while departing from conventional *Russian* realizations of the distich, these poets followed the conventions created by Greek, Latin, and German elegists. One might say, borrowing a generational metaphor, that this was a case of ignoring the parents in order to follow the grandparents.

In the final chapter, I explored the possibility of treating form in an extraordinarily broad sense. *Lesenka* cannot be described in terms of meter, stanza, or even genre. It accounts for all of the poems completed by Mayakovsky in the last seven years of his life and a significant percentage of the Soviet poetry written over the next six decades. The sheer volume of verse guarantees that any study of the phenomenon will be incomplete. Moreover, even a cursory glance at the material indicates its semantic unpredictability. While poems on certain subjects (e.g., patriotic) and in certain styles (e.g., odic) seem particularly well suited to the form, one finds love lyrics as well. This breadth of applications notwithstanding, one need not conclude that *lesenka* is formal element devoid of meaning. In this instance, form acts as a crucial ideological marker. *Lesenka* conferred upon a poet the Soviet seal of approval, the officially sanctioned Mayakovskian blessing. For this reason, it appears frequently in poems extolling socialist heroes and almost without exception in works about the canonized founder of Soviet poetry: Mayakovsky. In the case of *lesenka* verse not devoted to civic themes, it would seem that the *specific* content of these poems became subordinate to their larger, implicit (yet transparent) theme of Party loyalty ["partiinost'"].

The case studies of the earlier chapters lead naturally to a larger methodological question: to what extent can this approach be applied to other material? Already in regard to Taranovsky's pioneering work in the area of metrical semantics, scholars voiced reservations. Taranovsky, it was pointed out, claimed a connection between the journey and the Russian trochaic pentameter line, yet not all poems about the journey were written in trochaic pentameter and not all trochaic pentameter poems described a journey.[12] In my view, this criticism is correct yet misguided. Were poetic scholarship striving to become predictive, such an argument would indeed be devastating. However, any attempt to trace the meaning of meter seeks only to delineate certain tendencies, not to create or insist on norms. Taranovsky did not prove an *obligatory* connection of the trochaic pentameter with the journey; he simply demonstrated that an astonishing number of poets had sensed this connection and made use of it in their own work – long before any critic had brought this phenomenon to their attention.[13] The fact that other poets chose not to develop this aspect of the trochaic pentameter does not invalidate Taranovsky's findings. Indeed, even the "rhythmical-syntactic figure" that Taranovsky adduced (and which has subsequently been disputed by such an authority as M. L. Gasparov) seems to me potentially valuable.[14] The shortcoming of Taranovsky's essay – and the danger of this sort of scholarship as a whole – lies in its one-sidedness. In his efforts to convince through the sheer number of his examples, Taranovsky rarely stopped to ask interpretive questions about individual poems.[15] In other words, while it is certainly noteworthy that so many poets responded to Lermontov's model, the truly interesting questions concern the *variety* of their responses.

For the serious poet, of course, form is never an artistic straitjacket. Its apparent constraints offer immense potential for continuity, development, and variation. By using an inherited form, the poet grounds his own creative impulses in authoritative prior texts. However, to demand at all times from all poets a strict fidelity to the formal and semantic choices of their predecessors would be to condemn art to banality and predictability. After all, meter, rhyme, stanza, and graphic layout are not the only factors involved. Rhetoric, tropes, topoi, imagery, and genre also have lengthy traditions that inform a poet's work. Formal questions are paramount for poets, yet this does not mean that they always focus their primary attention on meter.

A more complicated methodological question concerns forms that occur with particularly high frequency. For obvious reasons, unusual forms will stand out more than common ones. When a metrical and stanzaic model occurs in only a handful of poems, it should come as no surprise that these few poems are related. But what is the would-be interpreter to do when confronted with Russian poems in iambic tetrameter? Even if one attempts to narrow the corpus of texts by concentrating on specific strophic forms and rhyme schemes, the meter still appears so commonly that it would be absurd to try to limit it to a genre, let alone to delineate its thematic range. However, from this indisputable fact one should not infer that iambic tetrameter has no formal significance. Within the enormous corpus of verse in this meter, one finds subgroups of individual poems that are most definitely connected. For example, Pushkin's "Stansy" ("Stanzas"), a political poem in iambic tetrameter quatrains, unquestionably inspired later political statements in the identical form by Vyacheslav Ivanov and Boris Pasternak.[16] Likewise, Andrei Bely's experiments in thematizing particularly rare rhythmic variants of iambic tetrameter left their mark on the work of certain contemporaries as well as some subsequent poets.[17]

When considered in general terms of literary history, even the most common meters have strong semantic associations. The predilection for iambic tetrameter in the repertoire of the poets of Russia's "Golden Age" gives that meter a "traditional" (even conservative) aura that was strongly felt by poets of the twentieth century. Somewhat akin to the Onegin stanza, the iambic tetrameter took on an "emblematic function"[18] – it served as a marker of Pushkinian poetics. And just as poems about Mayakovsky almost inevitably appeared in the form of *lesenka*, so one finds a distinct tendency for poems about Pushkin to be written in iambic tetrameter. It is typical – and interpretively significant – that Mikhail Kuzmin selected an iambic tetrameter meter for the poem "Pushkin," with which he opened various Pushkin festivities of 1921.[19] The final lines of that poem clearly reflect the emblematic function of the meter, recalling Pushkin's poetic voice through the iambic tetrameter (with alternating rhymes) so characteristic of his verse:

> Так полон голос милой жизни,
> Такою прелестью живим,
> Что слышим мы в печальной тризне
> Дыханье светлых именин.[20]

([Pushkin's] voice is so full of dear life, / Animated by such charm, / That we hear at the sad funeral, / The breath of a luminous saint's day [celebration].)

Sergei Esenin's 1924 poem "Pushkinu" ("To Pushkin"), set at the Pushkin monument in the center of Moscow, uses meter in this same way:

> Мечтая о могучем даре
> Того, кто русской стал судьбой,
> Стою я на Тверском бульваре,
> Стою и говорю с собой.

Блондинистый, почти белесый,
В легендах ставший как туман,
О Александр! Ты был повеса,
Как я сегодня хулиган.

Но эти милые забавы
Не затемнили образ твой,
И в бронзе выкованной славы
Трясешь ты гордой головой.[21]

(Dreaming about the powerful gift / Of him, who became Russia's fate, / I stand on Tverskoi boulevard, / I stand and speak with myself. // Blondish, almost whitish, / Having become like fog in legends, / O Aleksandr! You were a rake [then], / Like I am a hooligan today. // But these dear amusements / Did not darken your image, / And in the bronze of forged glory / You shake your proud head.)

In this passage (the first three of five quatrains), the autobiographical speaker confronts the "classic," using the latter's beloved form and, to a large extent, his lexicon (e.g., the adjective "milyi" ["dear"], so common in Pushkin's verse and which – not coincidentally – also finds its way into the Kuzmin excerpt cited above). The twentieth-century poet consciously sets himself parallel to his precursor, yesterday's "rake" (the word "povesa" is of course sanctioned by its use in the second stanza of *Eugene Onegin*) being today's "hooligan" (a word with distinctly twentieth-century overtones and in any case outside the sphere of traditional poetic vocabulary).

Yet the iambic tetrameter need not be so closely linked to Pushkin himself, but more generally to his entire epoch. When Zinaida Gippius – one of the great experimenters in the history of Russian versification – attacked contemporary attempts at free verse (in a 1915 poem called "Svobodnyi stikh" ["Free Verse"]), she chose to do so in iambic tetrameter quatrains with alternating rhyme.[22]

For similar reasons, Vladimir Khodasevich wrote a number of programmatic and metapoetic poems in iambic tetrameter quatrains.[23] His polemic against the Futurists and their "trans-rational language" ("Zhiv Bog! Umen, a ne zaumen" ["God lives! Wise, but not trans-rational"]) combines this same meter with a peculiar rhyme scheme that encourages a number of associations, both general and specific:

Жив Бог! Умен, а не заумен,
Хожу среди своих стихов,

Как непоблажливый игумен
Среди смиренных чернецов.
Пасу послушливое стадо
Я процветающим жезлом.
Ключи таинственного сада
Звенят на поясе моем.
Я – чающий и говорящий.
Заумно, может быть, поет
Лишь ангел, Богу предстоящий, –
Да Бога не узревший скот
Мычит заумно и ревет.
А я – не ангел осиянный,
Не лютый змий, не глупый бык.
Люблю из рода в род мне данный
Мой человеческий язык:
Его суровую свободу,
Его извилистый закон . . .
О, если б мой предсмертный стон
Облечь в отчетливую оду![24]

(God lives! Wise, but not trans-rational, / I walk among my verses, / Like a
Father Superior who offers no indulgences / [Walks] among [his] humble
monks. / I tend the obedient flock / With a blooming staff. / The keys to a
mysterious garden / Ring on my belt. / I am a thinking and speaking
[person]. / Only an angel standing before God / Perhaps sings trans-
rationally. / And cattle that have not seen God / Low and roar trans-
rationally. / But I am not a radiant angel, / Not a cruel serpent, not a
stupid ox. / I love my human language / Given to me from generation to
generation: / Its stern freedom, / Its sinuous law . . . / O, if only my death
rattle / Could be clothed in a precise ode!)

The poem's first twelve lines are rhymed in the canonic alternating A-b-A-b form, the same arrangement found in the quatrains
of Esenin's "To Pushkin" and Gippius' "Free Verse." However, this
pattern suddenly shifts: the thirteenth line ("Lows and roars trans-
rationally") presents a wholly unexpected turn, since it rhymes with
the line that precedes it.[25] The following four lines then revert to the
familiar alternating pattern (A-b-A-b), only to shift in the final four
lines to an unprecedented – but hardly unusual in terms of the
Russian verse tradition – "embracing" (A-b-b-A) rhyme scheme. As
always when a strict pattern is broken (and particularly when this
occurs in the work of a craftsman as careful as Khodasevich), one
wonders why. After all, it seems inappropriate that the closing

passage of a poem that celebrates formal exactitude should contain formal "imperfections."

This shift from a regular rhyme pattern to a highly irregular one serves a precise function. In the closing lines, Khodasevich expresses the wish that his "death rattle be clothed in a precise ode." The dominant poetic genre of the eighteenth century, the Russian ode, was written – like Khodasevich's metapoetic poem – in iambic tetrameter. The canonic ode contained two differently rhymed quatrains (alternating [a-b-a-b] and "embracing" [a-b-b-a]) separated by a rhymed couplet – in schematic terms: a-b-a-b-c-c-d-e-e-d. However, in actual eighteenth-century practice the odic stanza varied.[26] In certain cases – Derzhavin's "Na schastie" ("On [Good] Fortune"), to name an ode by a poet whom Khodasevich particularly admired – one finds the rare rhyme scheme of a-a-b-c-b-c-d-e-e-d.[27] Curiously, this pattern coincides with that of Khodasevich's ten final lines (albeit with masculine and feminine rhymes reversed). In short, by adding a seemingly superfluous line that appears to break the poem's symmetry, Khodasevich actually creates a greater structural unity. In "God lives," the iambic tetrameter ultimately serves a double function. In the opening quatrains, it must be understood in broad terms, as an emblem of the verse of Russia's "Golden Age."[28] In the final ten lines, the metrical allusion becomes more specific, reaching back beyond Pushkin's age to the odic practice of the eighteenth century. The iambic tetrameter line itself represents the "human language" that Khodasevich so loves, which was "given to [him] from generation to generation."

By bringing up these examples, I by no means wish to suggest that all twentieth-century poems in iambic tetrameter are ineluctably linked to Pushkin or his time. Nor do I claim that twentieth-century poems to Pushkin were *necessarily* written in iambic tetrameter.[29] However, the meter itself provided a convenient backdrop or "horizon of expectations," which could be accepted, rejected, or ignored. If Kuzmin, Esenin, Gippius, and Khodasevich took advantage of this meter to create a strong sense of continuity, Mayakovsky used iambic tetrameter quatrains in his early verse to emphasize rupture (e.g., "Port," 1912). This is a typical modernist stance – taking the "classical" forms and making them new. In such poems, Mayakovsky's innovations are found in lexicon and theme, but also in his conscious deformation of rhyme and even stanzaic structure. For example, the programmatic poem "A vy mogli by?" ("But Could

You?," 1913), its somewhat unusual graphic layout and extremely novel imagery notwithstanding, is transparently derived from an iambic tetrameter base.

Throughout this book, I have emphasized how poets readily follow the models set out by their predecessors. As a rule, this is done by using the same form. However, there are times when a response occurs in a different form – not because the later poet was insensitive to metrical semantics, but precisely because he wished to bring out a different aspect of the earlier work. This is an area of scholarship that does not readily lend itself to generalizations. However, a brief examination of a single Pushkin poem and the responses it elicited should give a sense of the rich possibilities involved. The series of poems that I wish to discuss has not lacked scholarly attention. My emphasis, however, will be on the formal manipulations, which have played a subordinate role in previous interpretations.

Perhaps the most famous of Pushkin's distichs is called "Tsarsko-sel'skaia statuia" ("The Statue at Tsarskoe Selo," 1830). In Russian cultural history, the small town of Tsarskoe Selo ("The Tsar's Village") takes on almost mythical proportions.[30] Pushkin had spent extremely happy student years at the lyceum there, and his love of the *genius loci* is reflected in poems from various periods of his life. "The Statue at Tsarskoe Selo" describes a work of art located in the spacious gardens of the tsars' summer residence:

Урну с водой уронив, об утес ее дева разбила.
    Дева печально сидит, праздный держа черепок.
Чудо! не сякнет вода, изливаясь из урны разбитой;
    Дева, над вечной струей, вечно печальна сидит.[31]

Dropping her water-filled jar on the rock, the maiden has smashed it.
    Sadly the maiden there sits, holding the now useless shard.
Wondrous! not stopping, the water still flows from the jar that was broken;
    O'er the eternal spray sits, maiden eternally sad.

This poem fits neatly into the larger tradition of distichs examined in chapter 4. It is an ekphrasis, in this case a depiction of a statue (see the earlier discussion of Pushkin's "On a Statue of a Youth Playing Knucklebones," pp. 188–89). In terms of Pushkin's works as a whole, the statue brings to mind an entire complex of motifs, especially of statues coming to life.[32] However, in this particular instance, it is the opposite phenomenon that astonishes the poet: an action is frozen in time. Lev Loseff has pointed out how Pushkin "reads a completely new meaning into Sokolov's famous sculpture, a notion which differs entirely from that of the artist."[33] Passing over several potential interpretations (e.g., prosaic, didactic, sexual), Pushkin concentrates on creating an atmosphere of timelessness. While the poem contains no explicit allusions to antiquity, one easily recognizes stylized elements (e.g., the nameless "deva" ["maiden"], the exclamation). In this brief a poem, the repetition of individual words (e.g., "maiden," "sad") is particularly striking and seems to reflect the crucial concept at the basis of the poem: permanent repetition. Fundamental to this concept is the very word "eternal," which appears in each of the final line's hemistichs.

These preliminary words should suffice to introduce three poetic responses. The first of them, written by Aleksei Tolstoi in the margins of a volume of Pushkin's poetry (next to the text of "The Statue at Tsarskoe Selo"), is what the previous chapters have led us to expect:

> Чуда не вижу я тут. Генерал-лейтенант Захаржевский
> В урне той дно просверлив, воду провел чрез нее.[34]

> I see no miracle here. The lieutenant, esteemed Zakharzhevsky
> Drilling a hole in the base, caused all that water to flow.

Using the identical verse form and certain easily recognizable vocabulary to draw attention to his source, the new poet produces a parody. In the stylized tones of the distich, he "explains" the paradox that had so intrigued Pushkin. In Tolstoi's verses, one is immediately struck by the appearance of a distinctly Slavic – and hardly mellifluous – proper name. With the exception of gods and conventional mythical figures, proper names are generally avoided in the distich, as this would lend a specificity inappropriate to antiquity. Yet Zakharzhevsky, who has replaced the nameless maiden of Pushkin's verses, proves to be the solution to Pushkin's "riddle." As the director of the palace administration at Tsarskoe Selo, he was responsible for the water's continuous flow. Where Pushkin had offered a paean to art itself (its ability to "freeze" a moment into eternity), Tolstoi pretends to elucidate this apparent paradox through recourse to engineering know-how.

A considerably more subtle reception of Pushkin's "Statue" can be found in the work of Innokenty Annensky. An outsider to the leading literary circles of his day, Annensky spent most of his life working as an inspector of schools. His poetic output was small and his fame largely posthumous. However, both the Symbolists and the Acmeists came to recognize him as a major figure in the development of twentieth-century Russian verse. Annensky lived many years in Tsarskoe Selo, and it was only logical that he became "infected" by the Pushkinian spirit of the place. One of the so-called trefoils (i.e., three poems on a single subject) of Annensky's book *Kiparisovyi larets* (The Cypress Chest) is devoted to various statues in Tsarskoe Selo and, inevitably, to Pushkin himself.[35] Though the second poem of the trefoil describes a statue of Pushkin (and even concludes with the very Pushkinian motif of the statue coming to life), the third poem "Pace: The Statue of Peace" is more relevant to the present interests:

Pace

Статуя мира

Меж золоченых бань и обелисков славы
Есть дева белая, а вкруг густые травы.

Не тешит тирс ее, она не бьет в тимпан,
И беломраморный ее не любит Пан,

Одни туманы к ней холодные ласкались,
И раны черные от влажных губ остались.

Но дева красотой по-прежнему горда,
И трав вокруг нее не косят никогда.

Не знаю почему – богини изваянье
Над сердцем сладкое имеет обаянье . . .

Люблю обиду в ней, ее ужасный нос,
И ноги сжатые, и грубый узел кос.

Особенно, когда холодный дождик сеет,
И нагота ее беспомощно белеет . . .

О, дайте вечность мне, – и вечность я отдам
За равнодушие к обидам и годам.[36]

("Pace": The Statue of Peace: / Among the gilded baths and obelisks of glory / There is a white maiden, and around her [is] thick grass. // Her thyrsus does not please her, she does not beat on her timbrel, / And the Pan of white marble does not love her. // Only the cold fogs have caressed her, / And black wounds remain from their moist lips. // But as before, the maiden is proud of her beauty, / And the grass around her is never cut. // I do not know why the statue of this goddess / Has a sweet charm over my heart . . . // I love the insult in her, her terrible nose, / And her legs pressed together, and the coarse knot of her braids. // Especially when a cold light rain comes, / And her nakedness helplessly shows white . . . // O, give me eternity – and I'll give up eternity / For indifference to insults and years.

As the title itself makes clear, Annensky's poem is devoted to a different statue. However, much suggests that he views this statue through the prism of Pushkin's earlier poem. In both cases, the speaker expresses his admiration for a solitary female figure (a "deva" – "maiden") who is suffering. When the final passages of these poems are compared, a striking resemblance comes to the fore. In the space of a single line, each poet twice uses the essential word "eternity." Pushkin writes: "Deva nad *vechnoi* struei *vechno* pechal'na sidit" ("O'er the *eternal* spray sits, maiden *eternally* sad"), while Annensky answers: "O, daite *vechnost'* mne, – i *vechnost'* ia otdam" ("O, give me *eternity*, – and I'll give up *eternity*"). If one accepts that such repetitions are not coincidental, the question naturally arises as to why Annensky responds to Pushkin's poem yet ignores his form.

Once again, it is essential to consider the historical associations of a meter. Instead of using a distich, Annensky writes in couplets of iambic hexameter, with a caesura after the third foot and pair-rhymes alternating between feminine and masculine. This form, the Russian alexandrine, has a long and distinguished tradition. It first became popular among Russia's eighteenth-century poets, where it was the meter of choice for any number of genres.[37] However, it lost its privileged position in Pushkin's time, when the iambic tetrameter became dominant. Pushkin continued to use the alexandrine throughout his career, but never did he favor it until his very last years, when he suddenly turned to it in a series of major philosophical poems. One of them, "Kogda za gorodom" ("When beyond the city"), begins with a visit to a city graveyard (with its hideous statues and disfigured monuments) and leads to questions of eternity. However, the poem most relevant to "Pace" is written in a variation of the alexandrine line: Pushkin's version of Horace's "Exegi monumentum." The theme of this poem is, once again, a monument, albeit an incorporeal one. And it is the lexicon of this poem (in particular, that of the hexameter lines) that Annensky seems to borrow. Pushkin writes of his monument: "K nemu ne zarastet narodnaia tropa" ("The people's path to it will not be overgrown"), while Annensky "answers" with: "I trav vokrug nee ne kosiat nikogda" ("And the grass around her is never cut"). Beyond the oppositions of a clear and overgrown path to a monument, these lines echo each other phonologically (the recurrence of four consecutive stressed vowel sounds (u-o-o-a); the negated verb, the echo of "*trav*" in "*tropa*," etc.) The most striking repetition, however, occurs in the phrase "ravnodushie k obidam" ("indifference to insults") in Annensky's final couplet (where the repeated "eternity" had already pointed toward the first Pushkinian source). In the final hexameter lines of "Exegi monumentum," both of these words appear: "*Obidy* ne strashas', ne trebuia ventsa; / Khvalu i klevetu priemli *ravnodushno*" ("Not fearing *insult*, not demanding a crown; / Accept praise and slander *indifferently*").[38] In short, Annensky's poem to a statue in "Pushkin's" park brings together any number of Pushkinian subtexts. But beyond these precise allusions, Annensky's meter indisputably serves an emblematic function: in the early twentieth century, alexandrine lines were used infrequently and thus sound almost as stylized as the distich in Pushkin's time.[39] Annensky's shift away from the distich can thus be logically explained through metrical semantics, both general (the practice of an earlier age) and specific (individual alexandrine lines in Pushkin).

Anna Akhmatova, another long-time resident of Tsarskoe Selo and a fanatic admirer of both Pushkin and Annensky, contributed in an important way to the tradition under consideration. Akhmatova dedicated a poem to the precise statue that Pushkin had singled out in his distich, even going so far as to give her poem the identical name: "Tsarskosel'skaia statuia" ("The Statue at Tsarskoe Selo"):

> Уже кленовые листы
> На пруд слетают лебединый,
> И окровавлены кусты
> Неспешно зреющей рябины.
>
> И, ослепительно стройна,
> Поджав незябнущие ноги,
> На камне северном она
> Сидит и смотрит на дороги.
>
> Я чувствовала смутный страх
> Пред этой девушкой воспетой.
> Играли на ее плечах
> Лучи скудеющего света.

И как могла я ей простить
Восторг твоей хвалы влюбленной . . .
Смотри, ей весело грустить,
Такой нарядно обнаженной.[40]

(The maple leaves are already / Falling onto the swan pond, / And the bushes are blood-colored / Of the unhurriedly ripening rowan tree. // And blindingly beautiful, / Pressing together legs that do not freeze, / On the northern stone she / Sits and looks at the roads. // I felt a vague fear / Before this girl who has been sung. / On her shoulders played / The beams of the diminishing [day]light. // And how could I forgive her / The rapture of your infatuated praise . . . / Look, she's happy to grieve, / In such well-dressed nakedness.)

Akhmatova's poem, while markedly different in tone and emphasis, nonetheless looks back to Pushkin's. Pushkin had seen the statue as being fundamentally paradoxical. Akhmatova relies on a series of oppositions, both motivic (e.g., the dying maple leaves and the ripening rowan tree, the statue's "blinding" beauty against the background of diminishing daylight) and rhetorical (the closing oxymorons "happy to grieve" and "well-dressed nakedness"), to convey a no less paradoxical impression. If Pushkin had overlooked the sculptor's didactic intention, Akhmatova goes still further, ignoring the statue's most obvious features. (Even a cursory glance indicates that the statue is contemplating the broken jug rather than looking "at the roads.") However, Akhmatova's most radical change is in genre: she takes Pushkin's metapoetic meditation (on permanence and art) and, by viewing the statue as her rival, transforms it into a love poem. In doing so, she converts Pushkin's stately distichs (the stylization of antiquity) into iambic tetrameter quatrains. In her essay on these poems, Wendy Rosslyn has suggested that this new meter is selected because it is the form of many of Akhmatova's own early love poems.[41] This is certainly relevant, yet, as I have noted, the more significant association of iambic· tetrameter is as an emblem of Pushkinian poetics (attested to, incidentally, by Akhmatova's own early work in this form). In short, Akhmatova responds to Pushkin's poem by using Pushkinian means, shifting from the meter of distanced pathos and antiquity to a form that traditionally conveys the highly personal emotions of love poetry.

These few examples should suffice to show that poets can respond to their predecessors not only by retaining a form, but also by altering it in order to take advantage of different metrical-semantic associations. As far as iambic tetrameter is concerned, while it is impossible to trace every instance of this common form to a specific model, one can often come to useful interpretive conclusions by considering its more general implications. Particularly in connection with frequent meters, it is essential to consider the era and even the poetic school involved. Iambic tetrameter may indeed be unmarked in the age of Pushkin, but it becomes increasingly marked in the twentieth century, notwithstanding the fact that it remains common in terms of percentages.[42]

Throughout this book, I have insisted that poets think diachronically, not simply in drawing on the themes and images of their predecessors (an idea that few scholars would dispute), but also in regard to basic questions of form. To demonstrate this point, I have deliberately focused my attention on the poetic "producer" rather than the "consumer." Comparing text with subtext(s) has allowed me to approximate – speculatively, of course – what goes on within the mind of the poet, to reconstruct what might be termed a "poetic logic" behind formal decisions. Clearly, this process varies depending on the poet in question, and it would be useful to apply and refine this approach through detailed study of a few exemplary poets. Yet the differences, I would argue, are of degree rather than kind. In this book, I have consciously avoided concentrating on any single movement or period in order to emphasize that general principles are involved. Without pretending to quantify the creative process, my approach accounts for an otherwise inscrutable and inexplicable element of poetic tradition – the continuity of form (understood primarily as a combination of meter, stanza, and rhyme scheme) in the work of poets belonging to different generations and subscribing to a wide range of aesthetic and ideological views.

In focusing on specific poets and poems, I have largely avoided issues of general reader reception. However, it may fairly be asked to what extent an audience need be aware of the questions central to this book. More precisely, is it essential – or even desirable – for a reader to know the pedigree of a given poem's meter? Before answering this question, it is important to recognize that there exists for any poet no single reader, but always a multiplicity of possible readers, who bring to a work their own knowledge, experience, expectations, and prejudices. A scholarly and a popular audience will not necessarily concur in their critical judgments, nor should they. Naum Korzhavin's characteristically blunt statement – "I don't write [poetry] for Slavists; I write for normal people"[43] – is entirely justified. Ideally, a poet writes for an audience whose emotional responses are immediate; a scholar or critic functions as a mediator between a poet and the audience he would prefer to address directly. As an immensely popular Russian poet who lost a generation of readers through forced emigration, Korzhavin looks on this problem with understandable annoyance. Yet his situation ultimately reflects the fate of any writer, for reception inevitably has a historical component: a poet's contemporaries will respond differently from readers several decades (or centuries) later. Poets may lament their contemporaries' lack of comprehension and idealize their future audience (as in Mandel'shtam's celebration of a poem as a message in a bottle, tossed out to sea in order to reach its reader),[44] but the unfortunate fact is that these contemporaries are generally far more likely to understand them than are subsequent generations. Time and distance may bring greater experience, a broader sensibility, and a more dispassionate evaluation, but these valuable gains are offset by equally significant distortions. To return to an example from the previous chapters: both blank verse and the elegiac distich stood out in Pushkin's day by virtue of their rejection of rhyme. These forms were marked by a conspicuous absence, a poetic nakedness, which was clearly perceived by both the poet and his audience. Many of today's Western readers, in contrast, consider rhymeless poetry the norm and thus – unless educated otherwise – bring a fundamental misconception to their reading of these forms. Not only do they overlook these poems' most salient feature; they are most comfortable with precisely the aspect that made earlier readers uneasy.

In Russian culture, memory has historically played a crucial role in the creation and the dissemination of verse and even in the still powerful myth of the poet. I have in mind not simply the period of high Stalinism, when the act of writing was sufficiently dangerous to force poets to confide their verses to the memory of a few trusted friends. Nor do I mean only the impressive, if anecdotal evidence of the ability of certain Russian poets and poetry enthusiasts to recite page after page of verse without so much as glancing at a text. What deserves emphasis is not the talents of a few extraordinary individuals but rather the fact that, in the Russian context, memorization is considered the ideal means of appreciation (much more so than, for example, close reading). It was by no means an empty or idiosyncratic gesture that Joseph Brodsky, when asked for advice about American curriculum reform, challenged decades of educational philosophy by insisting: "What level are you talking about – college, high school? – nevertheless, it's all the same. I would suggest, I would urge you, and if I had the semblance of power, I would *legislate* that teachers make your students memorize poetry."[45] Memorization, of course, expressly draws emphasis to rhythm and sound. And it is by *hearing* and repeating verse that the average Russian comes to recognize meters and – given sufficient time and interest – to associate certain ones with certain genres or themes. Such knowledge generally has no connection to nomenclature; one can recognize amphibrachs without knowing the traditional designation for them, just as one can sing a melody correctly without knowing musical notation. The analytically minded scholar, of course, tends to read, reread, and scan rather than simply to listen, but the ultimate result should be similar: an awareness of a poem as part of a larger aural and semantic tradition. In short, the approach I am advocating for the Western reader parallels the way generations of Russians have learned about poetry.

But there is a further motivation behind this study. Rather than dismissing the past as fundamentally irrecoverable and reinventing an artwork in accordance with the tastes of our own era, it behooves the literary scholar to reconstruct the artistic environment in (and *from*) which a given work arose. A poet's original creative impulse will necessarily elude us, yet a poem's formal background can be traced to a remarkable degree. In the case of Russian poetry, the elements of meter, rhyme, and stanza have never been neutral. In each individual poem, they must be conceptualized: that is to say, the form, together with its generic and semantic realization, must be placed in a diachronic context. When this is done, an extraordinarily detailed picture emerges: of likes and dislikes, continuation and rupture, parody and stylization. According to Brodsky, "the only way you can follow a poet's evolution is by his prosody, by his meters."[46] Russian poets have always been provoked and enticed by questions of form, and the interpreter who ignores such "traditional" elements may fail to grasp the significance of tradition itself.

Notes

1 Boris Pasternak, *Sobranie sochinenii v piati tomakh*, 5 vols. (Moscow: Khudozhestvennaia literatura, 1989–92), vol. III, p. 281.
2 Laurent LeSage, *The Rhumb Line of Symbolism: French Poets from Sainte-Beuve to Valéry* (University Park: Pennsylvania State University Press, 1978), p. 86.
3 Roman Jakobson, *Language in Literature* (Cambridge, MA: Harvard University Press, 1987), p. 71.
4 Russian proponents of free verse argue that it was actively discouraged and thus artificially rooted out by vigilant Soviet censors who could not countenance the presence of a Western-influenced "countertradition." See Karen Dzhangirov (ed.), *Antologiia russkogo verlibra* (Moscow: Prometei, 1991), p. 8. The issue is surely more complicated than this, however, since a powerful sense of form and tradition informs not only the work of official Soviet poets, but also the verse of dissidents and émigrés. For a skeptical view of Russian free verse that cannot be attributed to a representative of the official Soviet establishment, see M. L. Gasparov, "V poiskakh 'nastoiashchego verlibra,'" *Literaturnaia ucheba* 6 (1980), 208–11.
5 Boris Unbegaun, *Russian Versification* (Oxford University Press, 1956); Barry P. Scherr, *Russian Poetry: Meter, Rhythm, and Rhyme* (Berkeley: University of California Press, 1986).
6 Scherr devotes nine pages to "the semantics of verse forms" (*Russian Poetry*, pp. 277–85), while Unbegaun discusses the issue only in passing (e.g., "The two-foot anapaestic [*sic*] line is suited perfectly to romances," *Russian Versification*, p. 50).
7 In the Russian tradition, Nekrasov consciously revised the metrical-generic system of his predecessors, leading puzzled contemporaries to conclude that he had made "mistakes." See Boris Eikhenbaum, *O poezii* (Leningrad: Sovetskii pisatel', 1969), pp. 63–65. In Latin poetry, Catullus played a similar role, reinterpreting the meters bequeathed to him by the Greeks. See M. L. Gasparov, *Izbrannye stat'i* (Moscow: Novoe literaturnoe obozrenie, 1995), p. 382.

8 Among Russian poets, the idea that specific qualities are inherent to various meters dates back to the beginnings of syllabo-tonic poetry, in Lomonosov's arguments for the iamb as being particularly appropriate for elevated themes. See M. L. Gasparov, *Ocherk istorii russkogo stikha* (Moscow: Nauka, 1984), pp. 55–56. Among twentieth-century poets, Nikolai Gumilev's fanciful descriptions of the semantic associations of each meter continue this tradition: Nikolai Gumilev, *Sochineniia v trekh tomakh*, 3 vols. (Moscow: Khudozhestvennaia literatura, 1991), vol. III, pp. 31–32.

9 I have in mind, of course, readers unfamiliar with this Western tradition. To my knowledge, the first attempt to bring the limerick to Russia appeared anonymously under the misleading title "Novye perevody" ("New Translations") in *Novoe literaturnoe obozrenie* 6 (1994), 278–79. Alexander Zholkovsky, in a private communication of April 1997, has noted that – presumably because of the novelty of the genre – this poet confuses the limerick with the epigram (i.e., a brief poem targeted at a specific individual). See, for example, "Mastityi slavist Kalifornii" ("A venerable Slavist from California"), a "limerick" directed at Zholkovsky himself.

10 Leonard Stein (ed.), *Style and Idea: Selected Writings of Arnold Schoenberg* (Berkeley: University of California Press, 1984), p. 76.

11 From the 1958 essay "Strofika Pushkina," reprinted in B. V. Tomashevskii, *Pushkin: raboty raznykh let* (Moscow: Kniga, 1990), p. 357.

12 N. Iakovlev, "Poslednii literaturnyi sobesednik Pushkina," *Pushkin i ego sovremenniki* 28 (1917), 5–28.

13 The year was apparently 1828. See Mstislav Tsiavlovskii, "Pushkin i angliiskii iazyk," *Pushkin i ego sovremenniki* 17 (1913), 70–71. According to a contemporary, Pushkin taught himself to read the English of Byron and Shakespeare "as if it were his native language" in a period of four months. This time frame may well be accurate, but the estimation of Pushkin's command of English is clearly exaggerated (see my discussion of his translation from Robert Southey's "Hymn to the Penates" in chapter 2, pp. 67–68).

14 *The Poetical Works of Milman, Bowles, Wilson, and Barry Cornwall* (Paris: A. and W. Galignani, 1829), part 4, pp. 176–77.

15 A. S. Pushkin, *Polnoe sobranie sochinenii*, 10 vols. (Leningrad: Nauka, 1977–79), vol. III, p. 214.

16 A. S. Pushkin, *Pushkin Threefold*, Walter Arndt (trans.) (New York: E. P. Dutton, 1972), p. 46. I have slightly adjusted a few lines of the translation to bring them closer to the semantics of the original.

17 Pushkin was obviously intrigued by the possibilities of Nymph Echo, but he explored them in another poem. See my discussion of "Rifma" ("Rhyme," 1830) in chapter 4, pp. 186–87.

18 These verses come from a long poem in Onegin stanzas conventionally called "Ezersky," which Pushkin worked on in 1832–33, but never

completed. The lines quoted are the final couplet of stanza 13: Pushkin, *Polnoe sobranie sochinenii* (Leningrad), vol. IV, p. 250.

19 Strictly speaking, Cornwall's verses do not really display enjambment at all, since they lack a syntactic break preceding the end of the line (the *contre-rejet*) or immediately following the beginning of the next (the *rejet*). See Kiril Taranovski, "Some Problems of Enjambement in Slavic and Western European Verse," *International Journal of Slavic Linguistics and Poetics* 7 (1963), 80–84.

20 For an attempt to quantify the relative degrees of enjambment, see S. A. Matiash, "Stikhotvornyi perenos: k probleme vzaimodeistviia ritma i sintaksisa," in Dmitrii Bak, James Bailey, Iurii Orlitskii, and Kirill Postoutenko (eds.), *Russkii stikh: metrika, ritmika, rifma, strofika* (Moscow: Rossiiskii gosudarstvennyi gumanitarnyi universitet, 1996), pp. 189–202.

21 Pushkin used Cornwall's form in one other poem, "Obval" ("The Avalanche"), which depicts untamed nature in a way that clearly recalls "A Sea-Shore Echo." See Iakovlev, "Poslednii sobesednik," 25–27.

22 Vladimir Maiakovskii, *Polnoe sobranie sochinenii v trinadtsati tomakh*, 13 vols. (Moscow: Khudozhestvennaia literatura, 1955–61), vol. I, p. 181.

23 *Ibid.*, vol. XII, p. 86.

24 *Ibid.*, vol. VI, p. 54.

25 For a reading quite different from my own, but also based on Pushkinian echoes, see M. Shapir, "Iz istorii 'parodicheskogo balladnogo stikha,'" in N. Bogomolov (ed.), *Anti-mir russkoi kul'tury* (Moscow: Ladomir, 1996), pp. 356–63.

26 This was first noted, to my knowledge, in Aleksandr Zholkovskii, *Inventsii* (Moscow: Gendal'f, 1995), p. 128.

27 For numerous examples of Mayakovsky's metrical borrowings, see V. M. Zhirmunskii, *Teoriia stikha* (Leningrad: Sovetskii pisatel', 1975), pp. 562–64. For another revealing instance, see Richard Burgi, *A History of the Russian Hexameter* (Hamden, CT: Shoe String Press, 1954), p. 173.

28 See the essay "Dostoevskii i Gogol': k teorii parodii," in Iu. N. Tynianov, *Arkhaisty i novatory* ([Leningrad]: Priboi, 1929), pp. 412–55.

29 S. A. Reiser (ed.), *Vol'naia russkaia poeziia XVIII–XIX vekov*, 2 vols. (Leningrad: Sovetskii pisatel', 1988), vol. II, p. 321.

30 A. A. Fet, *Stikhotvoreniia i poemy* (Leningrad: Sovetskii pisatel', 1986), p. 192.

31 This particular Fet poem attracted numerous parodies, all of which took aim at aspects of Fet's life that seemed inconsistent with his impressionistic and sensitive love lyrics. It was widely known that Fet, in order to secure the title of nobleman, had served in the army for several years. Thus, one parody combines the easily recognizable metrical and stanzaic form of his "signature" poem with military thematics ("Topot, radostnoe rzhan'e" ["Clank of hoofs and joyous neighing"]). Another

places the landowner Fet in a less than idyllic provincial backwater ("Kholod, griaznye selen'ia" ["Cold and villages all dirty"]). Both of these parodies were written by Dmitri Minaev in 1863. For the complete texts, see A. A. Morozov (ed.), *Russkaia stikhotvornaia parodiia* (Leningrad: Sovetskii pisatel', 1960), pp. 507, 510.

32 Gr. Gukovskii, "Iz istorii russkoi ody XVIII veka," *Poetika* 3 (1927), 129–47.

33 That is to say, it fails as parody. Unrecognized parodies have been known to take on a life of their own. As Iurii Tynianov has demonstrated, early Dostoevsky had considerable success even though his readers did not recognize his fundamentally parodic stance vis-à-vis Gogol': Tynianov, *Arkhaisty i novatory*, pp. 412–55.

34 The scholarship on Russian verse is too vast to be surveyed or evaluated here. Interested readers should consult the invaluable annotated bibliographies devoted to this subject: Ian K. Lilly and Barry P. Scherr, "Russian Verse Theory, 1982–1988: A Commentary and Bibliography," *International Journal of Slavic Linguistics and Poetics* 41 (1997), 161–62. For these authors' earlier installments, see the 22 (1976) and 27 (1983) issues of the same journal.

35 Kirill Taranovskii, "O vzaimootnoshenii stikhotvornogo ritma i tematiki," in *American Contributions to the Fifth International Congress of Slavists*, 2 vols. (The Hague: Mouton, 1963), vol. I, pp. 287–322.

36 M. L. Gasparov, "The Semantic Halo of the Russian Trochaic Pentameter: Thirty Years of the Problem," *Elementa* 2, 3–4 (1996), 191–214. This essay includes a bibliography of Gasparov's own work on specific meters.

37 For a thorough examination of this term, see M. I. Shapir, "'Semanticheskii oreol metra': termin i poniatie," *Literaturnoe obozrenie* 12 (1991), 36–40.

I THE RUSSIAN BALLAD: PASSION, BETRAYAL, REVENGE, AND THE AMPHIBRACHIC TETRAMETER LINE

1 A. S. Pushkin, *Polnoe sobranie sochinenii*, 10 vols. (Leningrad: Nauka, 1977–79), vol. IV, p. 380.

2 See Michael R. Katz, *The Literary Ballad in Early Nineteenth-Century Russian Literature* (London: Oxford University Press, 1976), p. 4. "The 'narrative attitude' of the ballad is one of absolute impersonality. There are no lyrical digressions, no moralization, no emotionalism, no physical or psychological description – in short, no interference in or interpretation of the action." See also Friedrich Wilhelm Neumann, *Geschichte der russischen Ballade* (Königsberg: Ost-Europa-Verlag, 1937), pp. 6–7.

3 Wolfgang Kayser, *Geschichte der deutschen Ballade* (Berlin: Junker und Dünnhaupt Verlag, 1936), pp. 148–49, 218.

4 In other words, literary and popular ballads inevitably became intertwined. For numerous examples, see Natascha Würzbach, "Tradition

and Innovation: The Influence of Child Ballads on the Anglo-American Literary Ballad," in Joseph Harris (ed.), *The Ballad and Oral Literature* (Cambridge, MA: Harvard University Press, 1991), pp. 171–92.

5 See Wolfgang Kayser, *Geschichte des deutschen Verses* (Munich: Francke Verlag, 1981), pp. 20–24, and Christian Wagenknecht, *Deutsche Metrik: eine historische Einführung* (Munich: Verlag C. H. Beck, 1981), p. 48.

6 Some of these texts are discussed (though with different emphasis) in K. D. Seemann's pioneering essay, "Studien zum russischen Balladenvers I," *Zeitschrift für slavische Philologie* 46 (1986), 318–35.

7 V. A. Zhukovskii, *Zarubezhnaia poeziia v perevodakh V. A. Zhukovskogo*, 2 vols., K. N. Atarova and N. T. Beliaeva (eds.) (Moscow: Raduga, 1985), vol. II, p. 329.

8 M. L. Gasparov, *Ocherk istorii russkogo stikha* (Moscow: Nauka, 1984), pp. 121–22, 146–47.

9 There are minor differences (e.g., Uhland's Rhine becomes a nameless river in the Russian translation), but these are not essential to the present concerns. For a detailed comparative analysis, see Matthew Volm, *W. A. Zhukovskii als Uebersetzer*, 4 vols. (Ann Arbor: Edwards Brothers, 1945–47), vol. III, pp. 21–25. Both the Uhland original and Zhukovsky's translation can be found in Zhukovskii, *Zarubezhnaia poeziia*, vol. II, pp. 328–29.

10 Pushkin, *Polnoe sobranie sochinenii* (Leningrad), vol. II, p. 16.

11 B. V. Tomashevskii, *Pushkin: raboty raznykh let* (Moscow: Kniga, 1990), pp. 298–99.

12 Pushkin experimented with this meter in an early sketch (presumably in 1821) for his narrative poem "Brat'ia razboiniki" ("Brigand Brothers"), which serves as the epigraph to this chapter. This sketch, while only ten lines long, is clearly connected to "The Black Shawl" both generically (it is even subtitled a "Moldavian Song") and phonologically (cf. "zhalkuiu mladost'" ["Brigand Brothers"] and "krotkaia zhalost'" ["Black Shawl"]) as well as the repeated phrase "my vyshli"). The meter recurs in another poem on a criminal theme, the twelve-line "Uznik" ("The Prisoner," 1822). However, in neither of these roughly contemporaneous works did Pushkin repeat the visually distinctive two-line couplets of "The Black Shawl." See V. V. Vinogradov, *Stil' Pushkina* (Moscow: Goslitizdat, 1941), p. 355.

13 To my knowledge, this point was first made by Annette Pein, in an unpublished paper. I would like to acknowledge my debt to this paper, which was particularly helpful in clarifying the function of the narrative voice in "The Black Shawl."

14 One might (fairly) argue that Pushkin began with the meter and selected the content in accordance. I do not wish to enter into a "chicken or egg" discussion about poetic form and content. I would emphasize that, in Pushkin's creative mind, the content and the expression of that content were always inextricably linked.

15 Such studies led to the discovery of a Romanian song which bore remarkable resemblances to "The Black Shawl." However, the existence of such a song merely reflected the fact that Pushkin's poem had been translated into Romanian and, in this incarnation, become a part of the local folk culture. This issue is treated exhaustively in G. F. Bogach, *Pushkin i moldavskii fol'klor* (Kishinev: Kartia Moldoveniaske, 1967), pp. 37–62. It is curious to note that a corrupted version of Pushkin's text was recorded by a team of folklorists as recently as the 1970s and 1980s (in the villages of Russia's Northwest). See S. Adon'ev and N. Gerasimov (eds.), *Sovremennaia ballada i zhestokii romans* (St. Petersburg: Izdatel'stvo Ivana Limbakha, 1996), pp. 48–49.

16 First introduced to Russia at the turn of the nineteenth century, the shawl immediately became an immensely popular fashion item. See R. M. Kirsanova, *Kostium v russkoi khudozhestvennoi kul'ture 18–pervoi poloviny 20 vv.* (Moscow: Bol'shaia rossiiskaia entsiklopediia, 1995), pp. 322–24.

17 Using Russian Formalist terminology (from Boris Tomashevskii, *Teoriia literatury* [Leningrad: Gosudarstvennoe izdatel'stvo, 1925], pp. 136–46), one might say that the *siuzhet* coincides with the *fabula*.

18 As early as 1823, it was set to music by A. N. Verstovsky and, in this incarnation, became a popular song. For a detailed account, see Thomas P. Hodge, "*Chin china pochitai*: Zhukovskii and Pushkin in the Art-Song Enterprise," in Konstantin Polivanov, Irina Shevelenko, and Andrey Ustinov (eds.), *Themes and Variations in Honor of Lazar Fleishman* (Stanford Slavic Studies, 1994), pp. 146–51. The drawings are reproduced in S. A. Vengerov's Pushkin edition, Aleksandr Pushkin, *Sobranie sochinenii*, 6 vols. (St. Petersburg: Brokgauz-Efron, 1908), vol. II, p. 13.

19 This remarkable story, set in Venice, features a virtuous proletarian girl who is employed by a greedy capitalist in a Murano glass factory. When she is fired for not yielding to her employer's amorous attentions, her evil stepmother gives her a black shawl and sends her out to walk the streets. Fortunately, she is saved from this ignominy by a gondolier revolutionary. As they sail away from the iniquity of capitalism, she tosses the symbolic shawl overboard. The story, which first appeared in 1929, has been republished in I. Shurygina (ed.), *Lunnaia gost'ia: romany, povesti, rasskazy* (Moscow: Terra, 1997), pp. 572–91.

20 Pushkin's poem first appeared (in an unauthorized version, with mistakes) in *Syn otechestva* 15 (April 1821). The response appeared in *Vestnik evropy* 14 (July 1821).

21 See Aksakov's memoirs, in S. T. Aksakov, *Sobranie sochinenii*, 4 vols. (Moscow: Khudozhestvennaia literatura, 1956), vol. III, p. 128.

22 *Ibid.*, pp. 647–48.

23 This technique, reminiscent of how, in Greek tragedy, the murder always occurs offstage, was favored by Pushkin in ballads and narrative

poems. It occurs twice in "The Black Shawl" and can be found already in "Rusalka" (1819) as well as in the later "Southern Poems."

24 This version began with the line: "I look without a word at the black shawl" ("Gliazhu ia bezmolvno na chernuiu shal'"). See Pushkin, *Sobranie sochinenii* (St. Petersburg), vol. II, p. 553.

25 Aksakov, *Sobranie sochinenii*, vol. III, p. 51.

26 See the commentary in V. E. Gusev (ed.), *Pesni russkikh poetov*, 2 vols. (Leningrad: Sovetskii pisatel', 1988), vol. I, p. 294.

27 This particular couplet indicates an awareness of Pushkin's "Black Shawl" (lines 17–18) as well as Aksakov's poem. The complete text can be found in A. I. Polezhaev, *Stikhotvoreniia i poemy* (Leningrad: Sovetskii pisatel', 1957), pp. 79–80.

28 Polezhaev departs formally by not setting the rhymed couplets off graphically (that is, the poem appears as a single stanza) and by including one metrical irregularity and two truncated lines. The plot variation consists in the Cossack not yielding to the voice of Satan, which urges him to kill his wife, but instead turning to his icon of St. Nicholas and exclaiming: Никола, Никола, ты спас от войны, / Почто же не спас от неверной жены? ("Nicholas, Nicholas, you saved me from war, / Why could you not save me from my unfaithful wife?").

29 Pushkin, *Polnoe sobranie sochinenii* (Leningrad), vol. X, p. 23.

30 See the commentary of the poet and Pushkinist Vladislav Khodasevich: "The words about gloomy, heroic, Byronesque poetry are so obviously inappropriate for Del'vig that one could understand them as mockery. But this was not mockery, but [rather] the blindness of friendship, to which was added politics: Pushkin was seeking to form a new literary movement and he needed comrades-in-arms. Knowing Del'vig's sluggishness, he wanted to encourage him" (from the 1931 essay "Del'vig," reprinted in Vladislav Khodasevich, *Izbrannaia proza* [New York: Russica Publishers, 1982], p. 55).

31 A. A. Del'vig, *Polnoe sobranie stikhotvorenii* (Leningrad: Sovetskii pisatel', 1959), pp. 157–58.

32 In the Russian, this is accomplished through first-person singular verb endings (Pushkin) and the pronoun "I" (Del'vig).

33 "Lila," the name Del'vig gives to the unfaithful beloved, was one of the common conventional names in the love poetry of this time. See Pushkin's "Lile" ("To Lila," written in the period from 1817 to 1820), where Lila is the beautiful, cruel, and unattainable object of the poet's attention: Pushkin, *Polnoe sobranie sochinenii* (Leningrad), vol. I, p. 356.

34 Seemann ("Studien zum russischen Balladenvers," 331) notes that the pipe and nightcap function as surrogates for Pushkin's shawl.

35 Vinogradov (*Stil' Pushkina*, p. 355), noting the common rhythms and syntactic constructions, recognized Del'vig's poem as a parody. However, he did not consider the larger implications (perhaps because

he was unaware of the date of composition). The first to discuss the parodic nature of the poem in detail (though with observations and conclusions that differ from my own) was K. D. Seemann, "Studien zum russischen Balladenvers," 330–32.

36 M. Iu. Lermontov, *Polnoe sobranie sochinenii*, 5 vols. (Moscow: Academia, 1935–37), vol. 1, pp. 59–60.

37 *Ibid.*, p. 436.

38 Del'vig's poem lacks the violent conclusion, but its effect depends on the reader's expectation that the protagonist will murder his erstwhile beloved.

39 It is worth noting how frequently Lermontov's couplets end with commas (rather than full stops). This rather unpolished effect could have been avoided had the poem been cast in quatrains (as many other ballads were – though it is true that this would have resulted in an "orphan" couplet at the end) or even as a single stanza. Lermontov's otherwise inexplicable preference for couplets suggests that he had a specific model in mind (and no such model can be found in Schiller).

40 Of course, the German text is not completely ignored. Lermontov's poem is, after all, a translation, and it necessarily includes enough motivic elements taken directly from Schiller's ballad as to make the original recognizable. Thus, contrary to Pushkin's model but in keeping with the original, the male protagonist is the object (rather than the instrument) of vengeance.

41 Lermontov's writings before 1834 have been viewed as "the work of a juvenile graphomaniac who does not know where imitation stops and plagiarism begins": Simon Karlinsky, "Misanthropy and Sadism in Lermontov's Plays," in Julian W. Connolly and Sonia I. Ketchian (eds.), *Studies in Russian Literature in Honor of Vsevelod Setchkarev* (Columbus: Slavica, 1986), p. 166. On Lermontov's multifarious debts to Pushkin, see D. D. Blagoi, "Lermontov i Pushkin (problema istoriko-literaturnoi preemstvennosti)," in N. L. Brodskii, V. Ia. Kirpotin, E. N. Mikhailova, and A. N. Tolstoi (eds.), *Zhizn' i tvorchestvo M. Iu. Lermontova: issledovaniia i materialy* (Moscow: Goslitizdat, 1941), vol. 1, pp. 356–421.

42 On the other hand, certain elements suggest that Lermontov wanted his "Ballad" to be understood primarily as a poem in the Russian tradition, *not* as a translation from the German. In 1829, he undertook translations of five Schiller poems; in the four other cases, he translated the title literally and noted in parentheses beneath it "from Schiller." In the "Ballad," he neither indicated his source nor translated the title. Instead, he indicated only the genre (which itself was hardly necessary, given his meter's associations in Russia).

43 The Symbolist poet Fedor Sologub was particularly appreciative of this aspect of Lermontov's poetics: "Lermontov did nothing except rework other peoples' poems. That is what makes him a genius" (in M. M.

Pavlova and A. V. Lavrov [eds.], *Neizdannyi Fedor Sologub* [Moscow: Novoe literaturnoe obozrenie, 1997], p. 407).

44 I have omitted from discussion only Zhukovsky's 1820 "Tri putnika" ("Three Travelers"), a translation of Uhland's "The Innkeeper's Daughter" ("Der Wirtin Töchterlein"). This work had no apparent influence on subsequent Russian poets, yet it deserves mention because it is a ballad and thus confirms the connection of meter and genre we have observed elsewhere. In fact, *quatrains* of amphibrachic tetrameter (as against the couplets under investigation in this chapter) occur with relative frequency in Russian poetry, overwhelmingly in ballads – e.g., Zhukovsky's celebrated translation of Goethe's "Erlkönig."

45 V. M. Krasovskaia, "Siuzhety Pushkina v iskusstve russkoi khoreografii," *Pushkin: issledovaniia i materialy* 5 (1967), 260–61.

46 In A. A. Morozov (ed.), *Russkaia stikhotvornaia parodiia* (Leningrad: Sovetskii pisatel', 1960), pp. 309–10.

47 Both poems can be found in Gusev, *Pesni russkikh poetov*, vol. 1, pp. 365–66, 494–96.

48 A "rusalka," a nefarious water nymph (not to be confused with the innocuous mermaids of American popular culture), was a fixture of Slavic folklore. See Linda J. Ivanits, *Russian Folk Belief* (New York: M. E. Sharpe, 1989), pp. 75–82.

49 The first four lines have the rhyme scheme a-b-a-b, and occasional lines omit an unstressed syllable, turning the amphibrachic tetrameter into a *dol'nik*: e.g., the first line of the couplet "I iunyi gus*liar sto*it u vorot: / 'Poslushai, nevesta, chto arfa spoet!'"

50 Seemann ("Studien zum russischen Balladenvers," 334) lists several poems in similar meters from the latter half of the nineteenth century, but only one of them (M. L. Mikhailov's translation of a German poem by Chamisso) coincides completely with the formal model of "The Black Shawl." In this case, however, Pushkin's poem was irrelevant. The formal choices were clearly determined by Chamisso's *dol'nik* couplets with a strong amphibrachic tendency (i.e., a typical German ballad meter, as found, among other places, in Uhland's "Revenge"). For the Russian poem, see M. L. Mikhailov, *Sobranie stikhotvorenii* (Leningrad: Sovetskii pisatel', 1969), pp. 497–98.

51 A number of authors published poems, plays, and aphorisms under the fictitious name Koz'ma Prutkov. The "Romance" in question was the work of Vladimir Zhemchuzhnikov, but, in keeping with tradition, I will refer to the author as Prutkov.

52 Koz'ma Prutkov, *Polnoe sobranie sochinenii* (Moscow: Sovetskii pisatel', 1965), p. 71.

53 *Ibid.*, p. 430.

54 The term is somewhat of a misnomer, but it remains the most convenient way of designating the period. For a detailed discussion of its origins (and inadequacy), see Omry Ronen, *The Fallacy of the Silver Age*

in *Twentieth-Century Russian Literature* (Amsterdam: Harwood Academic Publishers, 1997).

55 Boris Gasparov, "Introduction," to Boris Gasparov, Robert P. Hughes, and Irina Paperno (eds.), *Cultural Mythologies of Russian Modernism* (Berkeley: University of California Press, 1992), p. 8.

56 Diana Burgin, "The Literary Ballad in the Symbolist Period," Ph.D. thesis, Harvard University (1973), pp. 260–62. Burgin also cites the Fofanov poem in its entirety.

57 To this list, one could add "Igry kentavrov" ("The Centaurs' Games," in free amphibrachs) and "Bitva kentavrov" ("The Centaurs' Battle," in amphibrachic trimeter quatrains with alternating rhymes). Except for "The Dream," which was first published in Bely's 1923 retrospective collection of poetry, all of these poems can be found in the "Obrazy" ("Images") section of Bely's first book of poetry, *Zoloto v lazuri* (Gold in the Azure).

58 Andrei Belyi, *Stikhotvoreniia* (Moscow: Kniga, 1988), p. 49.

59 See Alexander Lavrov, "Andrei Bely and the Argonauts' Mythmaking," in Irina Paperno and Joan Delaney Grossman (eds.), *Creating Life: The Aesthetic Utopia of Russian Modernism* (Stanford University Press, 1994), p. 112.

60 Kayser, *Geschichte der deutschen Ballade*, pp. 116–20.

61 It is curious that this refrain is not found in Bely's other centaur poems (i.e., it occurs only in the poem that precisely mirrors the form of "The Black Shawl").

62 This phrase is found in the memoirs of Blok's friend Modest Gofman: in Vadim Kreid (ed.), *Vospominaniia o serebrianom veke* (Moscow: Respublika, 1993), p. 368. For a detailed scholarly account of the subject, see Zara Mints, "Blok i Pushkin," *Trudy po russkoi i slavianskoi filologii* 21 (1973), 135–296.

63 For specific allusions to Nekrasov, see A. A. Blok, *Polnoe sobranie sochinenii i pisem v dvadtsati tomakh* (Moscow: Nauka, 1997–), vol. II, p. 677.

64 As early as 1833, Pushkin himself had complained about the predictability of this very rhyme: Pushkin, *Polnoe sobranie sochinenii* (Leningrad), vol. VII, p. 205. I cite and discuss this passage in chapter 2, p. 71.

65 Aleksandr Blok, *Stikhotvoreniia*, 3 vols. (St. Petersburg: Severo-Zapad, 1994), vol. III, p. 62.

66 Cf. the second poem of Blok's cycle, which begins with the line: "Ia gliazhu na tebia" ("I look at you"). On the importance of this motif and for a reading of the entire cycle, see David A. Sloane, *Aleksandr Blok and the Dynamics of the Lyric Cycle* (Columbus: Slavica, 1988), pp. 292–97.

67 Russian scholarship on Blok is remarkably persistent in its biographical readings of the poetry. Even Zara Mints, who clearly recognizes the symbolic nature of Blok's verse, views the "bytovye detali" ("everyday details") in "Black Blood" as a means of creating an autobiographical

effect: Zara Mints, *Lirika Aleksandra Bloka*, 4 vols. (Tartu: n.p., 1965–75), vol. IV, p. 84.

68 Anna Akhmatova, *Stikhotvoreniia i poemy* (Leningrad: Sovetskii pisatel', 1976), p. 44.

69 N. A. Nekrasov, *Polnoe sobranie sochinenii v trekh tomakh*, 3 vols. (Leningrad: Sovetskii pisatel', 1967), vol. I, p. 114.

70 "If a parody of a tragedy is a comedy, then a parody of a comedy can be a tragedy": Iu. N. Tynianov, *Arkhaisty i novatory* ([Leningrad]: Priboi, 1929), p. 455.

71 In his 1923 "Apocalypse in Russian Literature," republished in Aleksei Kruchenykh, *Kukish proshliakam* (Moscow: Gileia, 1992), p. 112.

72 Republished *ibid.*, p. 36.

73 A. E. Kručenych, *Selected Works* (Munich: Fink Verlag, 1973), p. 287.

74 *Ibid.*, p. 286. In Russian, this three-word phrase consists of the identical letters (with one barely noticeable alteration) and sounds remarkably similar (although, strictly speaking, it is not a homonym).

75 *Ibid.*, p. 292.

76 See Gerald Janecek, *The Look of Russian Literature: Avant-Garde Visual Experiments, 1900–1930* (Princeton University Press, 1984), pp. 69–121.

77 There were actual prototypes for both characters. Van'ka Kain was a famous criminal who terrorized Moscow in the middle of the eighteenth century, while Son'ka achieved notoriety through her bloody exploits in Odessa at the beginning of the twentieth century. For a thorough analysis of the poem and its social, historical, and literary context, see Ronald Vroon, "Aleksei Kruchenykh's 'Razboinik Van'ka-Kain' and the Literary Politics of LEF," *Slavic Review* 50, 2 (1991), 359–70.

78 For a short plot summary (itself no mean feat!), see *ibid.*, 359–60.

79 Kručenych, *Selected Works*, p. 407. All further references come from this edition, pp. 407–29.

80 Mercedes may be her surname (or an underworld nickname). See *ibid.*, p. 424, where she is called "Son'ka Mercedes."

81 A secondary connotation of the word "Mercedes," also developed by Kruchenykh, is that of the automobile (hence the comparisons "more impulsive than an auto, / thinner than an axle").

82 The phonic resemblance between shawl ("shal'") and scarf ("sharf") is stronger in Russian than in English.

83 She obviously would like to become his lover (Kručenych, *Selected Works*, p. 420) and it is conceivable that she is his former lover, since her first line to him (after a separation of presumably more than ten years) is "It's me . . . Mercedes" (p. 416). However, one must be cautious when drawing logical conclusions in a text that so assiduously eschews plot motivation.

84 *Ibid.*, p. 419.

85 For more on the "stepladder," see chapter 5, pp. 206–10.

86 Kručenych, *Selected Works*, p. 411.

87 *Ibid.*, p. 424.

88 Readers of Russian may recognize that the *phonetic* combination of "red" and "shawl" has been prepared in an earlier passage spoken by Kain himself: "Шалаши шатры / шальной гомон /туда сбежались со всех сторон! / в *красных* рубахах" (emphasis added). Vroon ("Aleksei Kruchenykh's 'Razboinik Van'ka-Kain'," 369) views the substitution of red for black in political terms.

89 Republished in Vladimir Markov (ed.), *Manifesty i programmy russkikh futuristov* (Munich: Fink Verlag, 1967), pp. 50–51.

90 Vladimir Maiakovskii, *Polnoe sobranie sochinenii v trinadtsati tomakh*, 13 vols. (Moscow: Khudozhestvennaia literatura, 1955–61), vol. XII, p. 338.

91 Mikhail Svetlov, *Stikhotvoreniia i poemy* (Moscow: Sovetskii pisatel', 1966), pp. 107–08.

92 In this line, one recognizes a rhythmic shift: Svetlov omits a weak stress (before "Nazem'"). Such variations – entirely absent from Pushkin's use of the meter, but not unusual in the context of twentieth-century Russian versification, where accentual verse was increasingly common – occur five times in the course of Svetlov's poem.

93 It may fairly be asked to what extent Svetlov was aware of his model. In 1957, Svetlov devoted a short essay to the circumstances that prompted the composition of his famous verses. He suggested that the entire poem was triggered by his seeing the sign in front of the "Grenada Hotel" in Moscow. In a way recalling Edgar Allen Poe's essay on the "Philosophy of Composition" (where the poet explained that "The Raven" arose from the sound of the single word "nevermore"), Svetlov claimed that the word "Grenada" supplied the impulse for the entire poem: "I saw the sign 'Hotel Grenada.' And a certain playful thought ("shal'naia mysl'") occurred to me." In the context of the generic and metrical connections I have demonstrated, one cannot help but wonder whether the "shal'naia mysl'" was related to the "shal'" of Pushkin's influential poem. See Svetlov, *Stikhotvoreniia*, p. 450. "Grenada" occupied a place of honor in Soviet literature and itself became a model for subsequent poets. Among the more creative rewritings of this poem is Naum Korzhavin's 1955 "Trubachi" ("Trumpeters"), which borrows Svetlov's form (altering the graphic layout, however) and political theme, but questions his naive patriotism: Naum Korzhavin, *Vremia dano: stikhi i poemy* (Moscow: Khudozhestvennaia literatura, 1992), p. 63.

94 Gerald S. Smith (ed.), *Contemporary Russian Poetry: A Bilingual Anthology* (Bloomington: Indiana University Press, 1993), p. 216.

95 Prigov is well aware of the way familiar rhymes call up specific intertextual associations. He has published a book in which all of the poems are based on the rhymes of famous poems of the past: Dmitrii Aleksandrovich Prigov, *Sobstvennye perepevy na chuzhie rifmy* (Moscow: Moskovskii gosudarstvennyi muzei Vladimira Sidura, 1996). On p. 16, there is a work that borrows the rhymes of Akhmatova's "Grey-Eyed

King." I have not been able to examine this rare book *de visu* and thank Igor' Smirnov for sending me a copy of this poem and the bibliographical data.

96 Del'vig's anticlimactic "anti-ballad" itself inspired a twentieth-century continuation entitled "Del'vig," a poem written in precisely the same form that comments directly on its predecessor. See Oleg Chukhontsev, *Stikhotvoreniia* (Moscow: Khudozhestvennaia literatura, 1989), pp. 42–43. I am grateful to Grigorii Kruzhkov for bringing this work to my attention.

97 Gotthold Ephraim Lessing, *Werke*, 8 vols. (Munich: Hanser Verlag, 1973), vol. v, pp. 389–90.

98 See John Hollander, "Romantic Verse Form and the Metrical Contract," in Harold Bloom (ed.), *Romanticism and Consciousness: Essays in Criticism* (New York: Norton, 1970), pp. 192–93.

99 In general, parody functions only when its double-voiced nature is perceptible: Gary Saul Morson and Caryl Emerson, *Mikhail Bakhtin: Creation of a Prosaics* (Stanford University Press, 1990), pp. 152–53.

2 THE BLANK VERSE LYRIC: "... AGAIN I VISITED" REVISITED

1 Baron Rozen, "O rifme," *Sovremennik* 1 (1836), 131.

2 M. L. Gasparov, *Ocherk istorii russkogo stikha* (Moscow: Nauka, 1984), p. 91.

3 *Ibid.*, p. 116. Zhukovsky first introduced the *rhymed* iambic pentameter (in 1811), and then, with the help of Hebel's German model, moved on to the unrhymed iambic pentameter without caesura.

4 All quotes from this poem are taken from V. A. Zhukovskii, *Zarubezhnaia poeziia v perevodakh V. A. Zhukovskogo*, K. N. Atarova and N. T. Beliaeva (eds.), 2 vols. (Moscow: Raduga, 1985), vol. II, pp. 253–61.

5 K. N. Batiushkov, *Sochineniia K. N. Batiushkova*, L. N. Maikov and V. I. Santov (eds.), 3 vols. (St. Petersburg: Tip. Kotomina, 1885–87), vol. III, p. 562.

6 A. S. Pushkin, *Polnoe sobranie sochinenii*, 10 vols. (Leningrad: Nauka, 1977–79), vol. VII, p. 58.

7 The effect of this verse was striking to contemporaries: "In the first issue [of the *Moscow Herald*] there first appeared the well-known fragment from *Boris Godunov.* The scene in the monastery between the chronicler Pimen and the monk Grigory made a profound impression on everyone through the simplicity, power, and harmony of the verses of unrhymed iambic pentameter; it seemed that we heard it for the first time, and we were amazed by it and rejoiced" (S. T. Aksakov, *Sobranie sochinenii*, 4 vols. [Moscow: Khudozhestvennaia literatura, 1956], vol. III, p. 116).

8 From "The Vision of Judgment," in Harold Bloom and Lionel Trilling (eds.), *Romantic Poetry and Prose* (New York: Oxford University Press,

1973), p. 395. See also Byron's "English Bards and Scotch Reviewers" and the dedication of *Don Juan: ibid.*, pp. 288–89, 316.

9 In that excerpt, Pushkin lauds Katenin's ballad "Ubiitsa" ("The Murderer"), comparing it with "the best works of Bürger and Southey": Pushkin, *Polnoe sobranie sochinenii* (Leningrad), vol. VII, p. 58. Pushkin's library contained four books by Southey. See B. L. Modzalevskii, *Biblioteka A. S. Pushkina* (St. Petersburg: Tip. Imperatorskoi Akademii Nauk, 1910), p. 340.

10 Robert Southey, *The Poetical Works of Robert Southey* (Paris: A. and W. Galignani, 1829), pp. 689–90.

11 Pushkin, *Polnoe sobranie sochinenii* (Leningrad), vol. III, p. 150.

12 Southey, *Poetical Works*, p. 197.

13 Pushkin, *Polnoe sobranie sochinenii* (Leningrad), vol. III, p. 195.

14 In one line of the "Hymn to the Penates" translation (and twice in an 1827 translation from the Italian dramatist Alfieri), Pushkin had not observed this caesura, but in "Madoc" he does so frequently enough to make clear that he no longer considers it essential. This caesura-free blank verse line becomes an invariant in Pushkin's work after 1830.

15 It has been argued – and I would tend to agree – that these radically shortened versions of Southey reflect not simply Pushkin's impatience, but rather the laconic quality so central to his poetics. Speaking about the truncated version of Southey's blank verse poem "Roderick" (as rendered in trochaic tetrameter quatrains by Pushkin in 1835), N. Iakovlev has written: "In this way, Pushkin translated only the very beginning of Southey's extremely long poem. Yet this represents an independent whole and does not demand a continuation or completion. Precisely in this way Pushkin took only the opening picture of Madoc's return to the homeland. He also shortened Southey's long 'Hymn to the Penates' without any loss to the integrity of that piece (because after that in Southey there are only prolixities)" (N. Iakovlev, "Iz razyskanii o literaturnykh istochnikakh v tvorchestve Pushkina," in *Pushkin v mirovoi literature: sbornik statei* [Leningrad: Gosudarstvennoe izdatel'stvo, 1926], pp. 158–59).

16 Pushkin, *Polnoe sobranie sochinenii* (Leningrad), vol. VII, p. 205. The passage comes from the essay "Journey from Moscow to Petersburg," which was begun in 1833 – curiously enough, the very year Pushkin started writing original lyric poetry in blank verse.

17 *Ibid.*, vol. III, pp. 313–14.

18 *Ibid.*, vol. X, p. 427.

19 It is noteworthy that the first draft of ". . . Again I visited" reflects Pushkin's discontent (and even anger) with the state of affairs, while the final version removes these details: *ibid.*, vol. III, pp. 427–29.

20 The term "stanza" ordinarily implies a fixed number of lines with a predictable rhyme scheme and is therefore, strictly speaking, inappropriate for blank verse. In this chapter, I have chosen to use the word

imprecisely (to designate a section of poetic text set off graphically by skipped lines before and after) rather than to introduce a term that might prove yet more confusing (e.g., "verse paragraph").

21 The same technique can be found in Wordsworth's "Tintern Abbey" (1798). This blank verse meditation shares with Pushkin's poem a number of themes (e.g., memory, change) and motifs (e.g., revisiting a familiar place after years of absence, a concluding apostrophe directed to another generation). Indeed, specific lines are remarkably close (e.g., "wilt thou remember me"). The extent of Pushkin's knowledge of Wordsworth remains unclear. The most complete, though by no means conclusive, account is found in Iakovlev, "Iz razyskanii," pp. 122–29, 132–37. In any case, it should be noted that the largely autobiographical speaker of Wordsworth's poem ("a worshipper of Nature") differs significantly from the largely autobiographical speaker of ". . . Again I visited." "Tintern Abbey," like so much of Wordsworth's poetry, is based on the contrast between the "din of towns and cities" and the "beauteous forms" of nature. In ". . . Again I visited," Pushkin's interest in Mikhailovskoe is connected less to the inherent beauty of that place than to its role as the backdrop of his early years. Moreover, Wordsworth's larger philosophical musings about the lost paradise of youth are foreign to Pushkin's poem and general world-view. All of this does not exclude the possibility that Pushkin borrowed selectively from Wordsworth's meditation.

22 It is curious that Zhukovsky himself introduced the motif of grandfather and grandson. In Hebel's poem, the dialogue takes place between father and son. See Zhukovskii, *Zarubezhnaia poeziia*, pp. 253–61.

23 The Russian "dedovskie" can mean either "belonging to one's grandfather" or simply "ancestral." I understand it in its more specific meaning, particularly since the estate in question was indeed bequeathed to Pushkin's grandfather. (Originally, Mikhailovskoe had been part of a larger parcel of land belonging to Pushkin's illustrious great-grandfather Avram Annibal. After Annibal's death, the land was divided among his sons.)

24 According to Stephanie Sandler's apt formulation, this is "a structure of endlessly repeating moments of retrospection": Stephanie Sandler, "Remembrance in Mikhailovskoe," in Boris Gasparov, Robert P. Hughes, and Irina Paperno (eds.), *Cultural Mythologies of Russian Modernism* (Berkeley: University of California Press, 1992), p. 241.

25 In this context, it is instructive to consider Lermontov's three poems entitled "Noch'" ("Night"). Written in blank verse in 1830, these are lyric meditations which – as Eikhenbaum has suggested (in his commentary to M. Iu. Lermontov, *Polnoe sobranie sochinenii*, 5 vols. [Moscow: Academia, 1935–37], vol. 1, p. 440) – have their source in Byron's lyric poems in blank verse ("The Dream" and "Darkness"). In other words, Zhukovsky's translations of Hebel might well have been

known to Lermontov, but they did not provide a sufficiently powerful model to influence the semantics of Lermontov's blank verse.

26 N. P. Ogarev, *Stikhotvoreniia i poemy* (Leningrad: Sovetskii pisatel', 1956), p. 170.

27 The basic idea of visiting the house of the beloved in her absence (and in the company of an old servant) may well be derived from another of Pushkin's influential texts: *Eugene Onegin*, where Tatiana visits Onegin's house in chapter VII.

28 I. S. Turgenev, *Stikhotvoreniia i poemy* (Leningrad: Sovetskii pisatel', 1970), pp. 104–05.

29 The likely suspects are named in I. Yampolsky's commentary: *ibid.*, pp. 406–07.

30 Apollon Grigor'ev, *Izbrannye proizvedeniia* (Leningrad: Sovetskii pisatel', 1959), pp. 110–11.

31 "The Phantom," Grigor'ev's other blank verse lyric, also ends with a question.

32 See B. O. Kostelianets' commentary to this poem in Grigor'ev, *Izbrannye proizvedeniia*, p. 533.

33 This image may have been inspired by Heinrich Heine's famous poem, "Ich, unglücksel'ger Atlas" ("I, unfortunate Atlas"), from the 1823–24 collection "Die Heimkehr" ("The Return Home").

34 From the 1859 essay "Vzgliad na russkuiu literaturu so smerti Pushkina," reprinted in Apollon Grigor'ev, *Literaturnaia kritika* (Moscow: Khudozhestvennaia literatura, 1967), p. 166.

35 By all accounts, Blok approached this scholarly task with the utmost gravity. See Aleksandr Blok, *Sobranie sochinenii v vos'mi tomakh*, 8 vols. (Moscow: Gosudarstvennoe izdatel'stvo khudozhestvennoi literatury, 1960–63), vol. V, pp. 765–66.

36 *Ibid.*, p. 499.

37 For a thorough study of the subject, see D. Blagoi, *Ot Kantemira do nashikh dnei*, 2 vols. (Moscow: Khudozhestvennaia literatura, 1972), vol. I, pp. 502–30.

38 Blagoi (*ibid.*, pp. 522–23) was the first to recognize this. The motif of "free thoughts" is only the most obvious instance of Grigor'ev's influence on Blok's cycle. As early as 1902, Blok had written (next to the poem "The Question" in the margins of his 1846 Grigor'ev edition), "Grigor'ev voobshche rassudochnyi" ("Grigor'ev is altogether rational"). A strikingly similar adjective "rassuditel'naia" ("calculating") describes the smile of the protagonist in the third line of Blok's cycle "Free Thoughts": A. A. Blok, *Zapisnye knizhki* (Moscow: Khudozhestvennaia literatura, 1965), p. 28.

39 L. Ia. Ginzburg, "O prozaizmakh v lirike Bloka," *Blokovskii sbornik* I (1964), 165.

40 The letter is published in Aleksandr Blok, *Pis'ma k zhene, Literaturnoe nasledstvo*, no. 89 (Moscow: Nauka, 1978), p. 199.

41 All citations from this particular poem are from A. A. Blok, *Polnoe sobranie sochinenii i pisem v dvadtsati tomakh* (Moscow: Nauka, 1997–), vol. II, pp. 205–09.

42 Nikolai Gumilev, *Sochineniia v trekh tomakh*, 3 vols. (Moscow: Khudozhest-vennaia literatura, 1991), vol. I, pp. 225–26.

43 One scholar has noted: "The last line . . . is left incomplete, but the word that obviously fits, both metrically and logically, is *umeret'*, to die" (Earl D. Sampson, *Nikolay Gumilev* [Boston: Twayne Publishers, 1979], p. 129). This is by no means as unambiguous as Sampson's apodictic tone suggests. In any case, the fact that Gumilev chose not to include the "obvious" final word brings his poem closer to Pushkin's example.

44 Scholars have tried valiantly to reconstruct the exact chronology suggested in this poem, but without complete success. Gumilev made several trips to Africa, and numerous sources suggest that he was in fact in a suicidal state over his relationship with Akhmatova. If the poem was written in 1917, then the recollections would coincide with Gumilev's first visit to Cairo to 1907. However, it seems equally plausible that the events described occurred in 1908. Moreover, the mystical vision of Ezbekieh recalls a passage in a letter (albeit an ironic one) that Gumilev sent to V. K. Shvarsalon from Cairo in 1909. (See Nikolai Bogomolov's commentary in Gumilev, *Sochineniia* (Moscow), vol. I, pp. 528–29, vol. III, p. 353, and Gleb Struve's gloss in N. Gumilev, *Sobranie sochinenii*, 4 vols. [Washington, D.C.: Victor Kamkin, 1962–68], vol. II, p. 291.) It seems to me quite possible that Gumilev's insistent repetition of "ten years" has less to do with precision of dates than with his desire to align the biographical circumstances of his own life with the temporal plan set out Pushkin's poem.

45 Blok himself apparently viewed these poems in this way and even tried to publish them in the leading journal of the "realists." See the commentary in Blok, *Polnoe sobranie sochinenii*, vol. II, pp. 866–69.

46 See, for example, David Bethea, *Khodasevich: His Life and Art* (Princeton University Press, 1983), pp. 160–61.

47 Vladislav Khodasevich, *Stikhotvoreniia* (Leningrad: Sovetskii pisatel', 1989), p. 112.

48 N. A. Bogomolov has written, "All of these poems are consciously based on the iambic pentameter blank verse of Pushkin ('. . . Again I visited')": *ibid.*, p. 26.

49 *Ibid.*, p. 108.

50 Of seven poems, the sole exception is "An Episode," which is in numerous other ways related to both Pushkin and Blok. At one point, for example, the poet looks at the mask of Pushkin that hangs on his wall. The Blokian elements extend to the final word of Khodasevich's poem: "wind" (a central symbol in Blok's poetic universe and, not coincidentally, the final word of "On Death").

51 As in Russian, these blank verse lines are hexameter (although the poem itself is primarily in pentameter).

52 The text is cited from Khodasevich, *Stikhotvoreniia*, pp. 116–18.

53 Other lexical details that can be traced to Blok's "On Death" include the noun "tribuna" ("tribune") and, more obviously, the adverb "vol'no" ("freely").

54 The Russian diminutive form "domik" has several connotations. It could simply mean "little house," which, in this context, is unlikely (the description of the house implies that it was fairly large). More probably, it adds a feeling of spiritual closeness, in English perhaps best rendered as "dear." Khodasevich had, after all, named an earlier collection of poetry "Schastlivyi domik" ("The Happy House"). This phrase, itself clearly borrowed from an early Pushkin poem ("Domovomu" ["To the House Spirit," 1819]), leads one to suspect that, in the later "The House," the same word again points to Pushkin. Khodasevich's first line ("zdes' domik byl" – literally: "here was a house") perhaps alludes to the line "vot opal'nyi domik" ("here's the house of exile") in Pushkin's ". . . Again I visited."

55 In an essay he was later to write on Pompeii, Khodasevich would use remarkably similar imagery to describe the ruined houses. Cf. Vladislav Khodasevich, "Pompeia," *Chast' rechi* 4–5 (1986), 32–33.

56 Iosif Brodskii, *Ostanovka v pustyne* (Ann Arbor: Ardis, 1989), pp. 166–68.

57 An English translation by George Kline, which was supervised by Joseph Brodsky, appeared in Joseph Brodsky, *Selected Poems* (New York: Harper & Row, 1973), pp. 131–33. For my purposes, however, it is necessary to rely on closer fidelity to the Russian text. I have therefore obtained permission from Farrar, Straus, & Giroux, Inc., and the Brodsky estate to produce my own translation, which borrows where possible from Kline's authorized translation (approximately ten lines of the concluding passage).

58 Formally speaking, Brodsky's realization of blank verse is more regular than virtually all of his predecessors. With one exception (a tetrameter in line 10), no lines are truncated or elongated. A lack of ellipsis and the limited use of enjambment create a rather static effect, particularly when compared with the earlier blank verse of Pushkin and Khodasevich.

59 Here Brodsky has in mind, among other things, Mandel'shtam's efforts to "hellenize" the Russian poetic language. In fact, the figure of Mandel'shtam, the quintessential "poet of culture" (whose most famous works include two poems celebrating non-Russian churches – "Notre Dame" and "Hagia Sophia") seems to haunt these deliberations. "Greece was always there, so was Rome, and so were the biblical Judea and Christianity. The cornerstones of our civilization, they are treated by Mandel'shtam's poetry in approximately the same way time itself would treat them: as a unity – and *in* their unity": Joseph Brodsky, *Less*

than One (New York: Farrar, Straus & Giroux, 1986), p. 127. Mandel'-shtam's syncretic view of culture stands in direct opposition to a "culture" that would actively destroy its links to the past.

60 Grigor'ev, of course, also concluded his blank verse meditation with a question, yet this similarity is surely nothing more than coincidence. The entire emphasis of Grigor'ev's poem is personal (i.e., the protagonist's unrequited love and undeserved sufferings). In contrast, Brodsky's questions, like his meditation as a whole, concern metaphysical and cultural issues, seen *sub specie aeternitatis*.

61 John Glad (ed.), *Conversations in Exile* (Durham: Duke University Press, 1993), p. 107.

62 See the first publication in *Sovremennye zapiski* 41 (1930), 170–72. In later publications, the poet changed the title to the more precise, yet less allusive "A Kishinev Funeral." See, for example, Dovid Knut, *Izbrannye stikhi* (Paris: Imprimerie moderne de la presse, 1949), pp. 107–10.

63 Vera Bulich, *Plennyi veter: stikhi* (Tallinn: J. & A. Paalmann'i trükk, 1938). All citations from Bulich's verse come from this edition.

64 For a discussion of this background and an introduction to the collection as a whole, see Catriona Kelly, *A History of Russian Women's Writing: 1820–1992* (Oxford University Press, 1994), pp. 326–32. For the Russian text and a full translation of the third part of "From [My] Diary," see Catriona Kelly (ed.), *An Anthology of Russian Women's Writing: 1777–1992* (Oxford University Press, 1994), pp. 307–08, 465–66.

65 "Icon" is not an exact translation. Russian "Plashchanitsa" refers to a life-sized representation of Christ after he was removed from the cross. According to Orthodox tradition, it is brought out from behind the iconostasis once a year – on Good Friday. It remains on a catafalque in the church until Easter Sunday, when it is carried back behind the iconostasis.

66 Susan Amert, *In a Shattered Mirror: The Later Poetry of Anna Akhmatova* (Stanford University Press, 1992), p. 166. Amert devotes almost twenty pages to a discussion of this crucial poem, discovering echoes from the Bible, St. Augustine, Shakespeare, and a host of Russian poets. However, she does not consider the significance of meter and thus neglects the tradition under consideration in this chapter.

67 I cite the text given in Anna Akhmatova, *Stikhotvoreniia i poemy* (Leningrad: Sovetskii pisatel', 1976), pp. 331–32.

3   THE ONEGIN STANZA: FROM POETIC DIGRESSION TO POETIC NOSTALGIA

1 A. S. Pushkin, *Polnoe sobranie sochinenii*, 10 vols. (Leningrad: Nauka, 1977–79), vol. v, pp. 86–87. Further references to this work will be given in the text, with Roman numerals designating chapter and Arabic numerals designating stanza (a reversal of Pushkin's convention).

2 Unless otherwise noted, all *verse* translations from Pushkin's novel will be taken from Aleksandr Pushkin, *Eugene Onegin: A Novel in Verse by Alexander Pushkin*, James E. Falen (trans.) (Carbondale: Southern Illinois University Press, 1990).

3 O. B. Kushlina (ed.), *Russkaia literatura XX veka v zerkale parodii* (Moscow: Vysshaia shkola, 1993), pp. 123–24.

4 The influential nineteenth-century critic Vissarion Belinsky, in a formulation known to every Russian schoolchild, called *Eugene Onegin* "an encyclopedia of Russian life." Dostoevsky, with characteristic disregard of Pushkin's genre designation, wrote of the work: "And so in *Eugene Onegin*, in that immortal poem which has yet to be surpassed, Pushkin revealed himself to be a great national writer . . . Incisively and perspicaciously he grasped the very essence of our being." See the relevant passages in Sona Stephan Hoisington (trans.), *Russian Views of Pushkin's Eugene Onegin* (Bloomington: Indiana University Press, 1988), pp. 17, 63. Further testimony to the role of *Onegin* as a national epic is reflected in Dmitri Minaev's Russian translation of Byron's "Childe Harold," in which he transformed the nine-line Spenserian stanzas of the original into fourteen-line stanzas that closely approximate Onegin stanzas. As M. L. Gasparov has pointed out, Minaev obviously felt that he was translating a quintessentially English form into its Russian equivalent: M. L. Gasparov, "Stikh nachala XX v.: stroficheskaia traditsiia i eksperiment," in V. A. Keldysh (ed.), *Sviaz' vremen: problemy preemstvennosti v russkoi literature kontsa XIX–nachala XX v.* (Moscow: Nasledie, 1992), p. 359.

5 I have in mind Aleksandr Pushkin, *Eugene Onegin: A Novel in Verse*, Vladimir Nabokov (trans.), 2 vols. (Princeton University Press, 1975), and Iu. M. Lotman, *Roman A. S. Pushkina "Evgenii Onegin": kommentarii* (Leningrad: Prosveshchenie, 1983).

6 It is interesting that Goethe's *Faust* (the only work *contemporary* to *Eugene Onegin* which could claim such a central position in its respective national culture) was composed in a variety of meters, most of which were chosen because of associations they already possessed.

7 Actually, there had been a precedent in a rather obscure eighteenth-century ode (with masculine and feminine rhymes reversed), but I regard this as coincidence rather than influence. See V. V. Sperantov, "Miscellanea poetologica: byl li kn. Shalikov izobretatelem 'oneginskoi strofy'?," *Philologica* 3, 5/7 (1996), 125–31.

8 Nabokov is but one of the enthusiasts. See his comments in Pushkin, *Eugene Onegin* (Nabokov edn.), vol. I, pp. 12–13. He may have been influenced by the arguments in Leonid Grossman, *Bor'ba za stil'* (Moscow: Nikitinskie subbotniki, 1927), pp. 75–80. In his *Poem Without a Subject* (to which we will return), Valery Pereleshin lends support to this view when he interrupts his own Onegin stanzas and "slips in" a

sonnet, as if by mistake: Valerii Pereleshin, *Poema bez predmeta* (Holyoke, MA: New England Publishing Co., 1989), pp. 47–48.

9 Pushkin had already mentioned the sonnet in a poem of 1815 ("A. I. Galichu" – "To A. I. Galich"), but in an unambiguously negative context. Throughout his career, he made light of Boileau's great claims for the sonnet. See B. V. Tomashevskii, "Pushkin – chitatel' frantsuzskikh poetov," in N. V. Iakovlev (ed.), *Pushkinskii sbornik pamiati professora Semena Afanas'evicha Vengerova* (Moscow: Gosudarstvennoe izdatel'stvo, 1923), p. 220. See also Boris Tomashevskii, "Pushkin i Bualo," in *Pushkin v mirovoi literature: sbornik statei* (Leningrad: Gosudarstvennoe izdatel'stvo, 1926), pp. 36, 353–54.

10 "Between 1800 and 1820, while in the Western literatures a new beginning in sonnet writing manifests itself in the work of Wordsworth, Keats, Ludwig Tieck, August Wilhelm Schlegel, and finally even – after some hesitation – Goethe, the sonnet in Russia is dead": Reinhard Lauer, "Das russische Sonett der Puškin-Zeit," in Hans-Bernd Harder and Hans Rothe (eds.), *Gattungen in den slavischen Literaturen: Beiträge zu ihren Formen in der Geschichte* (Cologne: Böhlau Verlag, 1988), p. 317.

11 Pushkin's first Onegin stanzas date from May 1823. In a letter to Del'vig of November 16, 1823, he reported having just encountered the sonnets: Pushkin, *Polnoe sobranie sochinenii* (Leningrad), vol. x, p. 58.

12 See the final tercet of his metapoetic "Sonnet" of 1830 ("Surovyi Dant ne preziral soneta"). Historically speaking, this view of Del'vig as the pioneering Russian sonnet writer is not entirely accurate. There had been an eighteenth-century tradition, but these earlier practitioners had a very different conception of the sonnet, and their work left virtually no mark on Pushkin's generation. See Lauer, "Das russische Sonett," pp. 316–18.

13 Given the dearth of Russian sonnets that predate *Onegin*, it is worth noting that Pavel Katenin also wrote (more precisely, translated) a sonnet in 1822 ("Italiia!"). In terms of rhyme, meter, and syntax, this poem conforms entirely to Del'vig's model.

14 A. A. Del'vig, *Polnoe sobranie stikhotvorenii* (Leningrad: Sovetskii pisatel', 1959), p. 163.

15 I am grateful to Eugene Gurarie for providing me with an equimetrical translation, which I have adapted slightly.

16 Tercets ordinarily use three rhymes. Those based on only two rhymes are generally considered a deviation from the canon. See Grossman, *Bor'ba*, p. 129.

17 The Shakespearean sonnet, developed for the (comparatively) rhyme-poor English language, has a simplified rhyme scheme and is, at least in this regard, closer to an Onegin stanza. However, this form was never popular in Russia, and it is doubtful that Pushkin had ever encountered it at the time he began work on *Onegin*. See J. Thomas Shaw, *Pushkin's Poetics of the Unexpected: The Nonrhymed Lines in the Rhymed*

Poetry and the Rhymed Lines in the Nonrhymed Poetry (Columbus: Slavica, 1994), p. 321.

18 This layout (with lines skipped after each quatrain and each tercet) is a convention of Russian sonnet writing. Shaw (*Pushkin's Poetics*, p. 321) sees this as yet another significant difference between the sonnet and Onegin stanza.

19 From "Natur und Kunst, sie scheinen sich zu fliehen" ("Nature and art appear to flee each other"), written between 1800 and 1802.

20 See Edward Stankiewicz, "The Onegin Stanza Revisited," in Simon Karlinsky, James L. Rice, and Barry P. Scherr (eds.), *O Rus! Studia litteraria slavica in honorem Hugh McLean* (Oakland: Berkeley Slavic Specialties, 1995), pp. 176–92. According to Stankiewicz, "the power and originality of the Onegin stanza lies not in the repeated violations of its chosen form . . . but in its systematic integration of diverse metrical forms" (p. 192). He argues that Pushkin's stanzas can be categorized as breaking down into semantic segments of *either* 4–4–4–2 *or* as 4–4–3–3. However, Stankiewicz himself admits that "a certain number" of Onegin stanzas fit neither of these patterns, and even some of his exemplary passages can be questioned (pp. 186–87). Tomashevsky's critique of Grossman can be applied to Stankiewicz as well. See B. V. Tomashevskii, *Pushkin: raboty raznykh let* (Moscow: Kniga, 1990), pp. 403–04.

21 For precise data on Pushkin's syntactic freedoms, see G. Vinokur, "Slovo i stikh v Evgenii Onegine," in A. M. Egolin (ed.), *Pushkin: sbornik statei* (Moscow: Ogiz, 1941), pp. 184–88.

22 M. Iu. Lermontov, *Sobranie sochinenii v chetyrekh tomakh*, 4 vols. (Moscow: Izdatel'stvo akademii nauk SSSR, 1962), vol. II, p. 433. All further citations from this work come from this edition.

23 Maksimilian Voloshin, *Stikhotvoreniia i poemy* (St. Petersburg: Nauka, 1995), p. 91. All further citations from this work come from this edition.

24 Igor' Severianin, *Sochineniia v piati tomakh*, 5 vols. (St. Petersburg: Logos, 1995), vol. III, p. 284. All further citations from this work come from this edition.

25 Russian readers should be amused at how Severianin puts the "shiftologist" Kruchenykh right where he belongs – in the genitive plural, modifying his fellow Cubo-Futurists, the Burliuk brothers. (In Russian, the proper name "Kruchenykh" looks like an adjective because of its genitive plural ending.)

26 Republished in Vladimir Markov (ed.), *Manifesty i programmy russkikh futuristov* (Munich: Fink Verlag, 1967), pp. 50–51.

27 Pereleshin, *Poema bez predmeta*, p. 35.

28 *Evgenii Vel'skoi, roman v stikhakh* (Moscow: Tip. S. Selivanovskogo, 1828–29), pp. v–vii.

29 The speaker is the hero's "starushka mat'" ("old lady-mother"), a somewhat odd designation, given that her son is not yet twenty. Yet

according to conventions of the time (e.g., Karamzin's "Poor Liza," Pushkin's own *Captain's Daughter*), exigencies of plot outweigh biological fine points. The author of *Eugene Velsky* needed to motivate the journey of his protagonist, and the simplest way was to show that his mother was too old to care for him.

30 Kirill Postoutenko has aptly called this a "*reductio ad absurdum* of the compositional principles of *Eugene Onegin*": K. Iu. Postoutenko, "Oneginskaia strofa v russkoi poezii (na materiale XIX–nach. XX v.)," dissertation, Moscow State University (1992), p. 70.

31 It might be noted that the word "sparkled" ("blistal") is also borrowed from *Onegin*, albeit from a more well-known passage (1, 2).

32 See, for example, the opening stanza of the third chapter, where Tambov fashions are lauded as the ideal costume for a masquerade party.

33 For a thorough discussion of the subject, with a somewhat different emphasis, see M. A. Peisakhovich, "Oneginskaia strofa v poemakh Lermontova," *Filologicheskie nauki* 1 (1969), 25–38.

34 Lermontov, *Sobranie sochinenii*, vol. II, pp. 545–46.

35 Dmitrii Blagoi, "Lermontov i Pushkin (problema istoriko-literaturnoi preemstvennosti)" in N. L. Brodskii, V. Ia. Kirpotin, E. N. Mikhailova, and A. N. Tolstoi (eds.), *Zhizn' i tvorchestvo M. Iu. Lermontova: issledovaniia i materialy*, vol. I (Moscow: Goslitizdat, 1941), p. 366.

36 Lermontov, *Sobranie sochinenii*, vol. I, p. 387.

37 *Ibid.*, vol. II, p. 159.

38 See Blagoi, "Lermontov i Pushkin," p. 385: "'The Tambov Treasurer's Wife' is written not only 'in the meter of *Onegin*,' but in the [same] light, sparkling, unforced-conversational style, with lyrical digressions . . . with asides to readers and friends that interrupt the narrative, with intentional sloppiness, incomplete stanzas, and so on."

39 In this regard, *Eugene Velsky* may provide the missing link between Pushkin's brief reference to Tambov and Lermontov's lengthy development of this motif. See Postoutenko, "Oneginskaia strofa," p. 109.

40 Postoutenko, "Oneginskaia strofa," pp. 14–50.

41 The only exceptions, it seems, are in consecutive stanzas of book v – stanza 28 (third syllable): "Вошел . . . Ах, новость, да какая" ("Stepped in . . . Oh, news – what news it is!"), and stanza 29 (sixth syllable): "Вдруг двери настежь. Ленкский входит / И с ним Онегин. Ах, творец ! " ("The doors are opened. Lensky enters / Onegin with him. Oh, my Lord! – ")

42 I have slightly altered Falen's translation here so that the word "oh" falls on the same syllable in the English as in the Russian. (See Pushkin, *Eugene Onegin* [Falen edn.], p. 87.)

43 Again I have slightly altered the Falen translation (*ibid.*, p. 124).

44 See Blagoi, "Lermontov i Pushkin," p. 387. Like Tatiana, Lermontov's hero – in the heat of the moment – suddenly switches his term of address from the formal to the informal (from "vy" to "ty").

45 Even Pushkin himself, turning to the form again in an unfinished poem of 1832–33 (called "Ezersky" in most modern editions), developed its comic potential. When he published a few stanzas in 1836, Pushkin added the genre designation "otryvok iz satiricheskoi poemy" ("fragment from a satiric [narrative] poem"): Pushkin, *Polnoe sobranie sochinenii* (Leningrad), vol. IV, p. 426. This comic/satirical quality is shared by the other extended nineteenth-century poem in Onegin stanzas, Dmitri Minaev's *Eugene Onegin of Our Time*. In this work (first published in the 1860s, but expanded in a later edition), the parody is directed not against Pushkin – "И лавр не сдвинулся с чела, / И слава та же, что была" ("And the laurel [wreath] has not moved from his forehead / And [his] glory remains the same as it was"), as the final lines state – but against the utilitarian literary critics of the 1860s (in particular, Pisarev). Lamenting his fate as a "поэт непоэтической эпохи" ("poet of an unpoetic age," [IV, 12]), Minaev rewrites Pushkin's plot in the spirit of the later time. The most notable changes include an Onegin based on Bazarov (the nihilist-hero of Turgenev's *Fathers and Sons*), a happy marriage of Lensky and Ol'ga, and an epilogue, in which the famous duel of Pushkin's text is played out in a battle of words: Lensky, lawyer for the defense, successfully defeats the prosecutor Onegin, who attempts to prove Tatiana's complicity in the death (by poison) of her elderly husband. See D. D. Minaev, *Sobranie stikhotvorenii* (Leningrad: Sovetskii pisatel', 1947), pp. 287, 306–08.

46 Kornei Chukovsky's "Today's Eugene Onegin" is, to my knowledge, the lone exception. As its title suggests, this work is a throwback to the earlier comic tradition. Published only in newspapers in Odessa, it had limited influence. For the first installments, see Kornei Chukovskii, "Nyneshnii Evgenii Onegin: roman v 4-kh pesniakh," *Odesskie novosti*, December 25, 1904, and January 1, 1905 (under the title "Sovremennyi Evgenii Onegin").

47 Cited by V. P. Kupchenko in his commentary in Voloshin, *Stikhotvoreniia*, p. 572.

48 The second letter is notably less strict, breaking away from the Onegin stanza toward the end. For an account of Voloshin's poetic freedoms in both "Letters," see Barry Scherr, "Maksimilian Vološin and the Search for Form(s)," *Slavic and East European Journal* 35, 4 (1991), 525–26. Voloshin's "Letters" were to influence Sergei Solov'ev, who soon thereafter wrote several epistles in Onegin stanzas. See M. L. Gasparov, "Stikh nachala XX v.," p. 359.

49 M. L. Gasparov, *Russkie stikhi 1890-kh–1925-go godov v kommentariiakh* (Moscow: Vysshaia shkola, 1993), p. 164.

50 Not only do both poets employ a similar construction, repeating the first two syllables and using antonyms to express the variegated quality of their work, but even the sounds are similar (repeated "p" and "u," chiasmic "ách" vs. "chá").

51 The "lengthened moment" (penultimate line) may also suggest one of the key lines of Goethe's *Faust*, where Mephistopheles tries to make Faust wish that the moment would linger ("Verweile doch, du bist so schön!"). For additional allusions to Tiutchev, see Scherr, "Maksimilian Vološin," 525.

52 The same phenomenon can be found in a number of Symbolist Onegin stanzas. Gasparov ("Stikh nachala XX v.," p. 359) notes how, in an epistle in Onegin stanzas, Sergei Solov′ev alludes to Lermontov rather than Pushkin. For a similar technique in Vyacheslav Ivanov's work, see Carol Culley Ueland, "Autobiographical *Poemy* of the Russian Symbolists: Aleksandr Blok's *Retribution*, Viacheslav Ivanov's *Infancy* and Andrei Bely's *The First Encounter*," Ph.D. thesis, Columbia University (1995), pp. 320–21.

53 Sergei Solov′ev, *Italiia: poema* (Moscow: Tip. V. I. Voronova, 1914). Strictly speaking, Onegin stanzas account for the vast majority of lines, but they are framed by Italian verse forms: octaves ("Introduction") and *terza rima* (in "Assisi," the concluding section).

54 Solov′ev's parents had taken him to Italy for six months when he was about five years old. Twenty-one years later, he returned and wrote the poem "Italy." See Igor′ Vishnevetskii, "Zhivye i 'blistatel′naia ten′": transformatsiia obraza Italii v pozdnei poezii Sergeia Solov′eva," in Daniela Rizzi and Andrei Shishkin (eds.), *Archivio italo-russo* (Trento: Dipartimento di Scienze Filologiche e Storiche, 1997), pp. 341–83.

55 Remarkable testimony to Pushkin's influence can be found in the "Venice" section, where Solov′ev develops the time-honored comparison of Venice and St. Petersburg by using the lexicon and phraseology not of *Eugene Onegin* (the formal model), but rather of Pushkin's St. Petersburg poem "The Bronze Horseman." To give but a single example: Solov′ev's line "Gde prezhnikh let moriak otvazhnyi" ("Where a daring sailor of former years") obviously reworks Pushkin's "Gde prezhde finskii rybolov" ("Where formerly a Finnish fisherman"). Throughout this section, Solov′ev contrasts the image of St. Petersburg in the introduction of Pushkin's poem (which rose from nothing to become a great city) with contemporary Venice (which has lost its grandeur and returned to a desolate state).

56 This translation is not ideal, but there is no exactly corresponding English word. "Mladenchestvo" refers to the first five or six years of life. "Childhood" might be a better rendering, except that this corresponds to the Russian "detstvo," and, in the Russian literary context, has a completely different set of associations. See Andrew Baruch Wachtel, *The Battle for Childhood: Creation of a Russian Myth* (Stanford University Press, 1990).

57 Viacheslav Ivanov, *Sobranie sochinenii*, 4 vols. (Brussels: Foyer Oriental Chrétien, 1971–86), vol. 1, p. 231. All further citations from this work come from this edition.

58 This was first noted, to my knowledge, in Carol Ueland, "Viacheslav Ivanov's Pushkin: Thematic and Prosodic Echoes of *Evgenii Onegin* in *Mladenchstvo*", in Boris Gasparov, Robert P. Hughes, and Irina Paperno (eds.), *Cultural Mythologies of Russian Modernism* (Berkeley: University of California Press, 1992), p. 347.

59 See Postoutenko, "Oneginskaia strofa," pp. 17, 66–67, 144; Ueland, "Viacheslav Ivanov's Pushkin," p. 349.

60 See Irina Paperno's contributions to Irina Paperno and Joan Delaney Grossman (eds.), *Creating Life: The Aesthetic Utopia of Russian Modernism* (Stanford University Press, 1994).

61 Aleksandr Blok *Novye materialy i issledovaniia, Literaturnoe nasledstvo*, no. 93 (Moscow: Nauka, 1980–93), bk. 3, p. 496.

62 Eugène Ternovsky, *Essai sur l'histoire du poème russe de la fin du XIXe et du début du XXe siècle: velikolepnaia neudacha* (Lille: Atelier national reproductions des thèses, 1987), pp. 170–76; Ueland, "Autobiographical *Poemy*," pp. 337–38.

63 See also stanzas 12 and 35 of "Infancy." I am indebted to M. L. Gasparov for referring me to a similar (yet more transparent) use of this image in another Ivanov poem contemporary to "Infancy." The poem was first published in Mikhail Gasparov, "Vera Merkur'eva – neizvestnaia poetessa kruga Viacheslava Ivanova," in Wilfried Potthoff (ed.), *Vjačeslav Ivanov: russischer Dichter – europäischer Kulturphilosoph* (Heidelberg: Universitätsverlag C. Winter, 1993), p. 113.

64 From Severianin's 1926 sonnet "Viacheslav Ivanov": Igor' Severianin, *Klassicheskie rozy: medal'ony* (Moscow: Khudozhestvennaia literatura, 1991), pp. 156–57. The hostile feelings were mutual; Ivanov considered Severianin unappreciative of the legacies of the past and compared him to "a prodigal son, who starts selling off his parents' books, which were collected over generations, and uses the money to buy liqueur": M. S. Al'tman, *Razgovory s Viacheslavom Ivanovym* (St. Petersburg: Inapress, 1995), pp. 24–25.

65 As Vladimir Markov has noted, Severianin's "propensity to classify" provides "a highly interesting attempt to emphasize genres when genres were already presumed dead": Vladimir Markov, *Russian Futurism: A History* (Berkeley: University of California Press, 1968), p. 93.

66 For an overview of these works, see Iu. V. Babicheva's introduction to Severianin, *Klassicheskie rozy*, pp. 15–16.

67 For a detailed plot summary and some excellent observations on the work as a whole, see Reinhard Lauer, "'Evgenij Onegin' à la Igor' Severjanin," *Arion: Jahrbuch der Deutschen Puschkin-Gesellschaft* 2 (1992), 97–108.

68 Using paronomasia, Severianin frequently links Lugne to the moon (in Russian, "luna"), thereby creating another similarity between his heroine and Pushkin's Tatiana (herself associated with the moon, e.g., in chapter v of *Eugene Onegin*).

69 Strictly speaking, Kiriena is her cousin, but Severianin uses the ambiguous term "sestra" (see III, 27) to emphasize the theme of two sisters, thereby supplying another link to Pushkin's novel.

70 See Markov, *Russian Futurism*, p. 96: "Toward the end [of Severianin's life], he almost got rid of his neologistic and barbaristic mannerisms and began to write in a traditional, neoclassical vein. Some of his best *émigré* poetry was written in this manner."

71 For additional examples, see Lauer, "'Evgenij Onegin' à la Igor' Severjanin," 104, and Boris Kats, "Uzh esli nastraivat' liru na push-kinskii lad . . . ," *Novoe literaturnoe obozrenie* 17 (1996), 284.

72 Severianin appears have been blissfully unaware not simply that the Symbolists had used Onegin stanzas for a strikingly similar purpose, but that the Symbolists had written them at all. In the third and fourth quatrains of the introduction to "Leander's Grand Piano," Severianin insists (and laments!) that no one writes Onegin stanzas: Severianin, *Sochineniia*, vol. III, p. 284.

73 Unlike Pushkin's novel, each canto has the identical number of stanzas (seventy-five).

74 Pereleshin, *Poema*, p. 132.

75 *Ibid.*, p. 185.

76 *Ibid.*, pp. 46, 53.

77 *Ibid.*, p. 215.

78 Karlinsky's comments are *ibid.*, pp. 20–21.

79 The image of Pegasus eating halvah – emphasizing the "Eastern" orientation of Pereleshin's work – has already appeared in the poem (*ibid.*, p. 185).

80 *Ibid.*, p. 218.

81 *Ibid.*, p. 264.

82 *Ibid.*, p. 400.

83 In Kushlina, *Russkaia literatura*, p. 352.

84 For example, "I was born on the banks of the Neva" comes directly from *Onegin*, I, 2. The passage about suffering ("for I was also here") alludes to *Onegin*, I, 50.

85 All of the documents requested of Onegin as well as his treatment at the hands of a housing department official would have been familiar to any Soviet citizen. The final phrase, a virtual rallying cry of the indolent worker, could be heard to the very end of the Soviet period in stores, post offices, etc.

86 It should be noted that Khazin was not alone in writing parodic Onegin stanzas in the Soviet period. However, other examples tended to reach a more limited audience (e.g., the members of Pushkin House or the science students at Moscow State University). For two such texts, see *Novoe literaturnoe obozrenie* 6 (1993–94), 167–71, 176–82.

87 Cited in Kushlina, *Russkaia literatura*, p. 468.

88 See, for example, Diana Lewis Burgin, *Richard Burgin: A Life in Verse*

(Columbus: Slavica, 1988), p. 13; Alicia Chudo, "The Onegin of Our Times: An Essay in Verse," *Formations*, 6, 1 (1991), 129–34; Vikram Seth, *The Golden Gate* (New York: Random House, 1986); D. M. Thomas, *Swallow* (New York: Viking, 1984), pp. 66–92.

89 Despite Seth's explicit comments to the contrary (*Golden Gate*, p. 102), the distinguished poet and critic D. J. Enright believes the work to be written in sonnets (see the blurb on the book's dust jacket). Another reviewer (John Gross, in the *New York Times*) seems to have assumed that Seth invented the form. See Douglas R. Hofstadter, *Le Ton beau de Marot* (New York: HarperCollins, 1997), p. 236. Hofstadter's iconoclastic book is, to my knowledge, the sole instance where a writer without a command of the Russian language devotes considerable attention (pp. 233–78) to the Onegin stanza.

90 Pushkin, *Eugene Onegin* (Nabokov edn.), "Foreword," vol. 1, p. x.

91 For an overview of Nabokov's thoughts on translation, see Judson Rosengrant, "Nabokov, *Onegin*, and the Theory of Translation," *Slavic and East European Journal* 38, 1 (1994), 13–27.

92 The phrase is Nabokov's own. See his foreword to Vladimir Nabokov, *The Gift* (New York: G. P. Putnam's Sons, 1963), p. 10.

93 Vladimir Nabokov, *Stikhi* (Ann Arbor: Ardis, 1979), p. 317. The edition appeared posthumously.

94 It is conceivable that the insistent masculine rhymes represent a deliberate attempt to bring the Onegin stanza closer to what Nabokov considered (erroneously, as I have argued) to be its formal model: the Shakespearean sonnet (which generally eschews feminine rhyme). I am grateful to Omry Ronen for bringing this possibility to my attention.

95 "Paraphrastic [translations offer] a free version of the original, with omissions and additions prompted by the exigencies of form, the conventions attributed to the consumer, and the translator's ignorance. Some paraphrases may possess the charm of stylish diction and idiomatic conciseness, but no scholar should succumb to stylishness and no reader be fooled by it": Pushkin, *Eugene Onegin* (Nabokov edn.), "Foreword," p. viii. Nabokov wrote this passage in 1963, two years after he completed work on the translation of *The Gift*.

96 He had attempted to compensate (a few hundred pages earlier) by closing his foreword with the laconic statement: "The epilogic poem mimicks [*sic*] an Onegin stanza" (Nabokov, *The Gift*, p. 11). In the translation of the Onegin stanza itself, the Russian "Evgenii" is replaced by English "Onegin," presumably to accentuate the connection to Pushkin's novel.

4 RUSSIAN ARCADIA: THE ELEGIAC DISTICH AND CLASSICAL STYLIZATION

1 A. S. Pushkin, *Polnoe sobranie sochinenii*, 10 vols. (Leningrad: Nauka, 1977–79), vol. III, p. 174.

2 *Ibid.*, p. 192.

3 The designation of Moscow as the "third Rome" is perhaps the best-known instance of this phenomenon. (Historically linked to the fall of Constantinople in the fifteenth century, the claim became a more general rallying cry in the nineteenth and early twentieth centuries.)

4 It would be fundamentally wrong to assume that this decision was "preordained" or even "correct." Both possibilities could in principle have been successful. The young Osip Mandel'shtam, for example, when writing on themes of antiquity, employed quatrains of iambic hexameter with caesura and rhymes (either alternating or in an "embracing" structure). There is nothing inherent to this form that would suggest classical metrics (about which Mandel'shtam was hardly an authority). Yet his success cannot be denied. By repeatedly grafting themes of antiquity onto a modern verse form, he *creates* in the mind of his readers a convincing association which, historically speaking, is groundless. See, for example, the poems "Est' ivolgi v lesakh" ("There are orioles in the woods"), "Bessonnitsa. Gomer. Tugie parusa" ("Sleeplessness. Homer. Taut sails"), "Priroda – tot zhe Rim" ("Nature is the same [as] Rome"), and even "Notre Dame." Indeed, so convincing are the results that Joseph Brodsky considered Mandel'stam's verse form "the nearest kin to [classical] hexameter." This argument has little scholarly merit, but it had profound practical implications for Brodsky. For Brodsky's view of Mandel'shtam's "classicism," see Joseph Brodsky, *Less than One* (New York: Farrar, Straus & Giroux, 1986), p. 126. For a discussion of Brodsky's creative adaptation of Mandel'shtam's "classical" form, see Ian K. Lilly, *The Dynamics of Russian Verse* (Nottingham: Astra Press, 1996), pp. 105, 111–13.

5 Richard Burgi, *A History of the Russian Hexameter* (Hamden, CT: Shoe String Press, 1954).

6 The precise extent of these substitutions has been studied exhaustively. See M. I. Shapir, "Geksametr i pentametr v poezii Katenina (o formal'no-semanticheskoi derivatsii stikhotvornykh razmerov)," *Philologica* I, 1/2 (1994), 43–114.

7 On the relationship of the classical pentameter to the hexameter, see M. L. Gasparov, *A History of European Versification* (Oxford University Press, 1996), p. 80.

8 Friedrich Schiller, *Werke und Briefe*, 12 vols. (Frankfurt am Main: Deutscher Klassiker Verlag, 1992–), vol. I, p. 283.

9 Theodore Ziolkowski, *The Classical German Elegy, 1795–1950* (Princeton University Press, 1980), pp. 57–58.

10 Henry Wadsworth Longfellow, one of the very few American poets whose metrical repertoire included elegiac distichs, paraphrased Schiller's famous metapoetic lines in his own "Elegiac Verse": "So the Hexameter, rising and singing, with cadence sonorous, / Falls; and in refluent rhythm back the Pentameter flows." In Longfellow's version, there are no trochaic substitutions whatsoever: Longfellow, *The Complete Poetical Works of Henry Wadsworth Longfellow*, Horace E. Scudder (ed.) (Boston: Houghton, Mifflin, 1893), p. 355.

11 Schiller, *Polnoe sobranie sochinenii Shillera v perevode russkikh pisatelei*, N. V. Gerbel' (ed.), 3 vols. (St. Petersburg, 1893), vol. 1, p. 95. It should be noted that Strugovshchikov's version is predicated on the reader's pronouncing the word "pentameter" in the German fashion (four syllables) rather than according to the rules of Russian pronunciation (where it has only three syllables). Such a reading is demanded by the meter, which does not tolerate substitutions in the second half of a pentameter line.

12 Schiller [Iogann Khristof Fridrikh Shiller], *Sobranie sochinenii*, 8 vols. (Moscow: Academia, 1936–50), vol. 1, p. 152.

13 Schiller [Fridrikh Shiller], *Sobranie sochinenii*, 7 vols. (Moscow: Gosudarstvennoe izdatel'stvo khudozhestvennoi literatury, 1955–57), vol. 1, p. 238.

14 Moreover, Trediakovsky's few distichs (in contrast to his hexameters) were rhymed – a blatant departure from the classical tradition. See his poems "Iz Argenidy," in Trediakovskii, *Sochineniia Tred'iakovskogo* (St. Petersburg: Aleksandr Smirdin, 1849), vol. 1, p. 451.

15 Ziolkowski, *German Elegy*, p. 56. See also Georg Luck's general introduction to the Roman love elegy in E. J. Kenney (ed.), *The Cambridge History of Classical Literature* (New York: Cambridge University Press, 1982), pp. 405–10.

16 Ziolkowski's book is devoted exclusively to this subject.

17 It should be emphasized that this was not the case in antiquity. The elegiac distich "was almost as popular in classical poetry as the pure hexameter. It was used for short poems (epigrams), medium-length poems (elegies), and also long poems": Gasparov, *European Versification*, p. 80.

18 The phrase first appeared in Winckelmann's 1755 treatise "Gedanken über die Nachahmung der griechischen Werke in der Malerei und Bildhauerkunst" ("Thoughts on the Imitation of Greek Works in Painting and Sculpture").

19 V. K. Kiukhel'beker, *Izbrannye proizvedeniia v dvukh tomakh*, 2 vols. (Moscow: Sovetskii pisatel', 1967), vol. 1, p. 81.

20 In this paragraph, I draw primarily on the explication of Bakhtin's thought in Gary Saul Morson and Caryl Emerson, *Mikhail Bakhtin: Creation of a Prosaics* (Stanford University Press, 1990), pp. 149–52.

21 Kiukhel'beker, *Izbrannye proizvedeniia*, vol. 1, p. 611. The passage comes from Kiukhel'beker's diary; the emphasis is in the original.

22 Characteristically, Pushkin recognized and took advantage of this possibility. In the epigraphs to this chapter (both written in 1830), one finds two poems on the subject of Gnedich's Homer translation, but containing diametrically opposed evaluations of it. The first is a stylization, the second a parody. It should be noted that the latter version came to light only through the exertions of textologists. Pushkin himself had made no effort to publish it and had even crossed it out in his notebooks. See the commentary in Pushkin, *Polnoe sobranie sochinenii* (Leningrad), vol. III, p. 457.

23 Kiukhel'beker, *Izbrannye proizvedeniia*, vol. I, pp. 79–82.

24 *Ibid.*, pp. 136–37.

25 *Ibid.*, p. 182.

26 *Ibid.*, p. 183.

27 "As he hurled lightning with his left hand and raised up his right": *ibid.*, p. 184. The two italicized words, referring to the left and right hands, are Church Slavonic in origin and thus quite distant from the standard poetic lexicon of the lyceum period. These words can also be found in Kiukhel'beker's unabashedly "archaic" poem "Prorochestvo" ("Prophecy," 1822): *ibid.*, p. 160.

28 This contrasts starkly with his twelve poems in hexameters, which contain 691 lines (on average, more than fifty lines per poem). See L. T. Senchina, "Metrika i strofika A. A. Del'viga," in M. L. Gasparov (ed.), *Russkoe stikhoslozhenie XIX v.: materialy po metrike i strofike russkikh poetov* (Moscow: Nauka, 1979), p. 274.

29 A. A. Del'vig, *Polnoe sobranie stikhotvorenii* (Leningrad: Sovetskii pisatel', 1959), p. 137.

30 See the discussion and commentary on this poem in S. A. Kibal'nik (ed.), *Venok russkim Kamenam: antologicheskie stikhotvoreniia russkikh poetov* (Moscow: Nauka, 1993), pp. 3, 267.

31 The word "neuviadaemye" is accented on the fourth syllable, yet the meter demands stresses on its first and final syllables (an impossibility in the Russian language, which does not permit secondary stress).

32 Del'vig, *Polnoe sobranie stikhotvorenii*, p. 134.

33 *Ibid.*, p. 158.

34 In this instance, Del'vig seconds Gnedich's own claims that, of all modern languages, Russian was best equipped to convey the quality of ancient Greek. See A. N. Egunov, *Gomer v russkikh perevodakh XVIII–XIX vekov* (Moscow: Nauka, 1964), p. 211.

35 This combination of theme and form probably gave Pushkin the impetus to write his own distichs on Gnedich's Homer translation, which serve as the epigraph to this chapter.

36 Historically speaking, Del'vig's distichs proved more influential than Kiukhel'beker's. The latter's involvement with the Decembrist uprising (and his subsequent exile) ensured that his name and works would remain obscure. Nonetheless, his distichs undoubtedly left a mark on

Pushkin. See S. A. Kibal'nik, "K voprosu ob istochnikakh pushkinskogo stikhotvoreniia 'Otrok,'" *Zeitschrift für Slawistik* 32, 1 (1987), 65–69.

37 This particular line, it seems, originally contained a metrical mistake ("Кто славянин молодой, духом грек, родом германец?"), which Pushkin corrected on the advice of a friend. If this story is true (and it is taken seriously enough to be noted among the variants in the most textologically authoritative Pushkin edition), then it would indicate just how novel the meter was for Pushkin. See A. S. Pushkin, *Polnoe sobranie sochinenii*, 17 vols. (Moscow: Izdatel'stvo Akademii nauk SSSR, 1937–49), vol. III, pt. 2, pp. 722, 1180. In any case, this rhythmic fault did not correspond to any uncertainty about the form's semantic associations. For a lengthy discussion of this particular "mistake" and a thorough account of all of Pushkin's work in classical meters, see "Pushkin i russkii gekzametr," in S. M. Bondi, *O Pushkine* (Moscow: Khudozhestvennaia literatura, 1978), pp. 310–71.

38 Pushkin, *Polnoe sobranie sochinenii* (Leningrad), vol. III, p. 110.

39 M. L. Gasparov (private communication of December 23, 1995) has noted that this particular statue still exists and that it is in fact a griffin rather than a sphinx. In his view, Pushkin consciously renamed the artwork in question in order to include the Oedipal theme of the riddle.

40 These biographical associations would recur in one of Pushkin's final poems in distichs: "Khudozhniku" ("To an Artist," 1836). In this case, Pushkin describes his ambivalent mood as he wanders through the atelier of an artist. He is delighted by the work he sees, but laments that Del'vig is no longer alive to enjoy it with him: "Весело мне. Но меж тем в толпе молчаливых кумиров – / Грустен гуляю: со мной доброго Дельвига нет; / В темной могиле почил художников друг и советник. / Как бы он обнял тебя! Как бы гордился тобой!" ("Happy am I. Nonetheless, in this crowd of idols all silent – / Sadly I wander: for now Del'vig is not at my side; / Friend and advisor of artists, he rests in the grave clothed in darkness. / He would embrace you for this! He would be proud of your work!") (Pushkin, *Polnoe sobranie sochinenii* [Leningrad], vol. III, p. 332).

41 "Stikhotvornaia tekhnika Pushkina," in Valerii Briusov, *Sobranie sochinenii v semi tomakh*, 7 vols. (Moscow: Khudozhestvennaia literatura, 1975), vol. VII, p. 87.

42 See L. G. Frizman, "A. S. Pushkin i 'Severnye tsvety,'" in Frizman (ed.), *Severnye tsvety na 1832 god* (Moscow: Nauka, 1980), pp. 326–28.

43 Pushkin, *Polnoe sobranie sochinenii* (Leningrad), vol. III, pp. 73–74.

44 *Ibid.*, p. 441.

45 *Ibid.*, p. 173.

46 It is revealing that Pushkin chose to publish these two metapoetic (Cornwall-inspired) "echo" poems together. Both appeared in the 1832 issue of *Northern Flowers*.

47 This was first recognized by Omry Ronen in the essay "Dva poliusa

paranomazii," in Barry P. Scherr and Dean S. Worth (eds.), *Russian Verse Theory: Proceedings of the 1987 Conference at UCLA* (Columbus: Slavica, 1989), p. 288.

48 "Pen*ei*a/M*ne*mozina" is an example of "wrenched rhyme," a phenomenon not uncommon in Western poetry, but rare in Russian verse (and completely absent from Russian poetry of the nineteenth century). See James Bailey, "Some Recent Developments in the Study of Russian Versification," *Language and Style* 5, 3 (1972), 162–63.

49 Pushkin, *Polnoe sobranie sochinenii* (Leningrad), vol. III, p. 175.

50 Translation by Vladimir Nabokov: Aleksandr Pushkin, *Eugene Onegin: A Novel in Verse*, Vladimir Nabokov (trans.), 2 vols. (Princeton University Press, 1975), vol. II, pt. 2, p. 384. It is curious that Nabokov truncates the cadence of the pentameter line, thus violating one of the cardinal rules of the distich.

51 Pushkin, *Polnoe sobranie sochinenii* (Leningrad), vol. III, p. 343.

52 V. A. Zhukovskii, *Sochineniia v trekh tomakh*, 3 vols. (Moscow: Khudozhestvennaia literatura, 1980), vol. I, pp. 316–17.

53 The lexical echoes are painstakingly traced in V. N. Toporov, "Iz issledovanii v oblasti poetiki Zhukovskogo," *Slavica Hierosolymitana* 1 (1977), 33–38.

54 Zhukovskii, *Sochineniia*, vol. III, pp. 509–10. This passage is probably the source of Dostoevsky's famous claim (at the conclusion of his Pushkin speech of 1880) that Pushkin carried a great secret to his grave, which his successors must try to guess.

55 It was first published in 1867.

56 A. A. Fet, *Stikhotvoreniia i poemy* (Leningrad: Sovetskii pisatel', 1986), p. 188.

57 Such frankly erotic passages incensed many contemporaries, one of whom suggested changing the name of the journal where these poems first appeared from "Die Horen" ("The Horae") to "Die Huren" ("The Whores"). Goethe himself saw the sensuality of these poems sanctioned by metrical semantics. As he told his amanuensis Eckermann, "In the various poetic forms there lie great and mysterious effects. If one wanted to translate the contents of my 'Roman Elegies' into the tone and verse form of Byron's 'Don Juan,' the effect would certainly be quite disgraceful [verrucht]": cited in the commentary to Goethe, *Gedichte* (Munich: C. H. Beck, 1982), pp. 580–81.

58 *Ibid.*, p. 160.

59 Apollon Grigor'ev noted in 1850 in regard to another of Fet's distichs: "Who but a talented student of Goethe could write such a poem?" (quoted in Fet, *Stikhotvoreniia*, p. 636). In the work in question ("Lozy moi za oknom razroslis' zhivopisno i dazhe" – "My vines have picturesquely grown out beyond the window and even . . . "), the overgrown plant life serves to hide the poet's beloved from his gossiping neighbors.

60 Fet's Goethe imitation was itself imitated. In 1848, Mikhail Mikhailov wrote a cycle of poems called "Zima" ("Winter"), which concludes with distichs on the subject of poetry and love. In the final lines, the poet turns to his beloved: "Znaiu, ditia: ty prekrasnyi poet, i usta tvoi zvuchno / K kazhdoi laske moei v rifmu tseluiut menia!" ("Child, I know that you are a wonderful poet whose lips are / Ready to answer in rhyme every caress that I give!") (M. L. Mikhailov, *Sobranie stikhotvorenii* [Leningrad: Sovetskii pisatel', 1969], p. 66).

61 The sole exception ("Tselyi zastavila den' menia promechtat' ty segodnia" ["Today you have forced me to dream all day long"], published in 1857), in no way departs from the generic and stylistic models of the earlier distichs. It should be noted that Fet, while refraining from using the distich in his own original poetry after this, continued to use the form in equimetrical translations from Latin: Fet, *Stikhotvoreniia*, p. 73.

62 Briusov, *Sobranie sochinenii*, vol. I, p. 544.

63 Pushkin, in fact, takes pride of place, since the poem is prefaced by an epigraph from his famous adaptation of Horace's "Exegi monumentum": "Dokol' v podlunnom mire / Zhiv budet khot' odin piit" ("As long as but a single poet shall be alive in the sublunar world").

64 The classical philologist F. F. Zielinski, who translated Ovid's distichs into Russian, included in that volume a detailed, three-page analysis of the principles of versification that he followed. His erudite discussion is prefaced by an acknowledgment of Ivanov's contributions. See Zielinski, "Russkii elegicheskii distikh," in Ovidii, *Ballady-Poslaniia* (Moscow: M. and S. Sabashnikov, 1913), pp. 312–15.

65 Among Ivanov's earliest verses (dating from his university years in Berlin) are German distichs. When, in the 1930s, he worked on a translation of his own long poem "Chelovek" ("Man") into German, he transposed the final verses of the first part (Russian iambic tetrameter quatrains) into German distichs. See Vjačeslav Ivanov, *Dichtung und Briefwechsel aus dem deutschsprachigen Nachlass* (Mainz: Liber Verlag, 1995), p. 282. For Greek and Latin distichs, see Viacheslav Ivanov, *Sobranie sochinenii*, 4 vols. (Brussels: Foyer Oriental Chrétien, 1971–86), vol. III, p. 60.

66 Sergei Averintsev has broached the subject, noting that Ivanov's distichs revive the epigram in the ancient sense of the word: S. S. Averintsev, "Gnomicheskoe nachalo v poetike Viach. Ivanova," *Studia Slavica: Academiae Scientiarum Hungaricae* 41 (1996), 5.

67 Ivanov, *Sobranie sochinenii*, vol. I, p. 635.

68 *Ibid.*, p. 642.

69 *Ibid.*, vol. II, p. 225.

70 See Pamela Davidson, *The Poetic Imagination of Vyacheslav Ivanov: A Russian Symbolist's Perception of Dante* (Cambridge University Press, 1989), pp. 195–200.

71 Ivanov, *Sobranie sochinenii*, vol. II, p. 504.

72 Schiller, *Werke und Briefe*, vol. I, p. 182.

73 Of particular interest is Verkhovsky's anthology of nineteenth-century poets, where distichs appear with frequency. In a lengthy introductory essay, Verkhovsky lauds Del'vig's contributions to Russian poetry, noting among other things that he "was the first to cultivate the distich on Russian soil": Iu. N. Verkhovskii (ed.), *Poety pushkinskoi pory: sbornik stikhov* (Moscow: M. and S. Sabashnikov, 1919), p. 26.

74 Republished in Kibal'nik, *Venok*, p. 246.

75 Republished *ibid.*, p. 250.

76 "Jealousy" belongs to a cycle called "Iz al'boma" ("From an Album") and takes its epigraph from Pushkin's "Rhyme." See Iu. N. Verkhovskii, *Solntse v zatochenii* (Petrograd: Mysl', 1922), p. 75.

77 The exceptions are themselves revealing. When a few mealy cucumbers miraculously appeared in her Stalinist prison cell, Eugenia Ginzburg celebrated this seemingly otherworldly event in distichs: Evgeniia Ginzburg, *Krutoi marshrut* (Moscow: Sovetskii pisatel', 1990), p. 137. In a later, considerably less dangerous period, Ol'ga Sedakova made an attempt at rejuvenating the distich in the cycle "Stely i nadpisi" ("Steles and Epigraphs," 1982). These poems, lapidary musings inspired by ancient gravestone inscriptions, are written in loose imitation of distichs (the first two lines of "Gospozha i sluzhanka" ["Mistress and Servant"], for example, take the form of a rhythmically irreproachable distich). As so often in Russian distichs, the stylization is clearly motivated by the classical subject matter. Sedakova's decision to depart from the metrical norms (often radically) reflects a certain conscious distancing between modernity and antiquity. In these poems, the poet guesses, as it were, at the meaning of the enigmatic markers of a lost world. While written in Russia in the Soviet period, this verse has virtually no connection to the thematic and stylistic canons of Soviet poetry: Ol'ga Sedakova, *Kitaiskoe puteshestvie, Stely i nadpisi, Starye pesni* (Moscow: Carte Blanche, 1990), pp. 25–33. For a discussion of the cycle in question, see Catriona Kelly, *A History of Russian Women's Writing 1820–1992* (Oxford University Press, 1994), pp. 427–29. A broken form of distichs can also be found in the work of Igor' Irten'ev, a non-conformist poet of the late Soviet period. In a poem called "Gekzametry" ("Hexameters"), Irten'ev uses a form somewhere between hexameters and distichs, taking advantage of the classical associations to give ironic commentary on Soviet history: Igor Irten'ev, *Povestka dnia* (France [*sic*]: AMGA, 1989), pp. 33–34.

78 The drafts of two humorous metapoetical poems in distichs can be found in Vladislav Khodasevich, *Stikhotvoreniia* (Leningrad: Sovetskii pisatel', 1989), p. 272.

79 *Ibid.*, pp. 188–89.

80 The conception of poetry as a "holy craft" can be traced to Karolina Pavlova. Briusov had used Pavlova's image as an epigraph to a section

of his 1912 book *Zerkalo tenei* (The Mirror of Shadows): Briusov, *Sobranie sochinenii*, vol. II, p. 65. In 1915, Briusov published an edition of Pavlova's poetry, which Khodasevich obviously read closely. In a review, he took some aspects of Pavlova's poetry to task, but praised its "many beautiful and edifying details": Vladislav Khodasevich, *Sobranie sochinenii*, 2 vols. (Ann Arbor: Ardis, 1983–90), vol. II, p. 218. This specific image obviously made a distinct impression on Khodasevich, since he repeated it again (citing Pavlova as his source) in a 1937 essay on Nabokov: Vladislav Khodasevich, *Literaturnye stat'i i vospominaniia* (New York: Izdatel'stvo imeni Chekhova, 1954), p. 248.

81 The theme of guessing recurs in diminutive form in the final stanza, where Khodasevich compares himself to a gambler. Even the Oedipal theme itself is strangely suggested in the second stanza, where the young Khodasevich examines his mother's bridal veil.

82 See the notes of John Malmstad and Robert Hughes, in Khodasevich, *Sobranie sochinenii*, vol. I, p. 385, and those of Nikolai Bogomolov in Khodasevich, *Stikhotvoreniia*, p. 404.

83 See the commentary in Aleksandr Blok, *Stikhotvoreniia*, 3 vols. (St. Petersburg: Severo-Zapad, 1994), vol. III, p. 381. On the classical sense of iambs, see Vyacheslav Ivanov's essay "Poet i chern'" ("The Poet and the Rabble"), in Ivanov, *Sobranie sochinenii*, vol. I, pp. 709–14.

5   HEIRS OF MAYAKOVSKY: THE POET AND THE CITIZEN

1 Vladimir Maiakovskii, *Polnoe sobranie sochinenii v trinadtsati tomakh*, 13 vols. (Moscow: Khudozhestvennaia literatura, 1955–61), vol. X, p. 279. In the translations in this chapter, one oblique (/) will indicate breaks at the end of each "step"; two obliques (//) will indicate breaks at the end of a line.

2 The only exceptions occur in posthumous publications of unfinished poems. Since *lesenka* belonged to the final stage of Mayakovsky's work, his drafts are in traditional graphic layout.

3 For an account of the evolution of Mayakovsky's graphic experiments, see Gerald Janecek, *The Look of Russian Literature: Avant-Garde Visual Experiments, 1900–1930* (Princeton University Press, 1984), pp. 207–47.

4 M. L. Gasparov, *Sovremennyi russkii stikh* (Moscow: Nauka, 1973), pp. 391–92.

5 The last word seems to belong to Mikhail Gasparov, who, by applying a rather complicated system of statistical analysis, has demonstrated that Mayakovsky used *lesenka* as a means of accentuating the syntactic structure of his verse: M. L. Gasparov, "Ritm i sintaksis: proiskhozhdenie 'lesenki' Maiakovskogo," in *Problemy strukturnoi lingvistiki – 1979* (Moscow: Nauka, 1981), pp. 149–68. However, Gasparov's conclusions have only peripheral application to the *lesenka* tradition *after* Mayakovsky. The focus of the present chapter concerns less the actual than

the perceived principles of Mayakovsky's graphic innovation, and it is highly unlikely that the poets who borrowed this technique were aware of the dimension that Gasparov has painstakingly traced. Most poets (and readers) viewed *lesenka* in terms of "freedom and unpredictability": Janecek, *Look of Russian Literature*, p. 236.

6 Maiakovskii, *Polnoe sobranie sochinenii*, vol. XII, p. 106.

7 Mayakovsky's contemporary Viktor Zhirmunsky devotes an entire chapter of his study of Russian rhyme to Mayakovsky. Zhirmunsky notes that Mayakovsky's inexact rhymes were not in themselves an innovation, but that their frequency and systematic application set Mayakovsky's rhyming practice off from that of his predecessors. See V. Zhirmunskii, *Rifma, ee istoriia i teoriia* (Petersburg: Academia, 1923), pp. 213–21.

8 Maiakovskii, *Polnoe sobranie sochinenii*, vol. XII, p. 113.

9 Cf. Mayakovsky's insistence that "today's slogan is above yesterday's *War and Peace*": *ibid.*, p. 162.

10 Semen Kirsanov, *Sobranie sochinenii*, 4 vols. (Moscow: Khudozhestvennaia literatura, 1976), vol. III, p. 104. Unless otherwise noted, further references will be to this edition.

11 "Chto Russkomu zdorovo, to Nemtsu smert'": V. Dal', *Poslovitsy russkogo naroda* (Moscow: Tip. universitetskaia, 1862), p. 344.

12 Mayakovsky's lines demand an imaginative leap on the part of the reader, who must recognize that the language of agitation propaganda (the concept of a "slogan") is applied to an abstract purpose (i.e., grabbing happiness from the future). In contrast, Kirsanov's verses belong – in terms of both lexicon and theme – exclusively to the military/political sphere.

13 From "How to Make Verses," in Maiakovskii, *Polnoe sobranie sochinenii*, vol. XII, p. 114.

14 From the 1927 essay "Rasshirenie slovesnoi bazy" ("Expansion of the Verbal Base"), *ibid.*, p. 163. This passage follows an untranslatable example in which Mayakovsky compares his own reading of a passage with that of the actor Vasily Kachalov.

15 Janecek, *Look of Russian Literature*, pp. 228–29.

16 M. L. Gasparov (*Sovremennyi russkii stikh*, pp. 436–37) has convincingly argued that Mayakovsky derived his *lesenka* from Andrei Bely's experiments in graphic layout. However, in the Soviet cultural context, it is safe to say that Bely's example would have lain dormant had it not been championed by Mayakovsky.

17 From the poem "Razgovor s Pushkinym" ("Conversation with Pushkin"), reprinted in O. B. Kushlina (ed.), *Russkaia literatura XX veka v zerkale parodii* (Moscow: Vysshaia shkola, 1993), pp. 272–74.

18 It is not clear whether Arkhangelsky would have yet known Mayakovsky's "Khorosho" ("It Is Good"). If so, he might have borrowed the technique of citing Pushkin in *lesenka* from Mayakovsky himself. The

fourth part of his long poem features a conversation between two enemies of the USSR (Ekaterina Kuskova and Pavel Miliukhov) which includes quotations from Tatiana's conversation with her nanny (*Eugene Onegin*, chapter III).

19 Iu. N. Tynianov, *Poetika. Istoriia literatury. Kino* (Moscow: Nauka, 1977), pp. 235–36. Mayakovsky, with his close ties to the Formalists, might well have known about this famous essay, which was written in 1922. That Tynianov viewed Mayakovsky as a twentieth-century odist is clear from numerous explicit statements. See, for example, *ibid.*, p. 501.

20 For an overview of the recollections of eyewitnesses, see Janecek, *Look of Russian Literature*, pp. 237–38. See also the description of the actor Vladimir Iakhontov's performances of Mayakovsky's poetry, in V. A. Katanian, "Ne tol'ko vospominaniia: k istorii izdaniia Maiakovskogo," *Druzhba narodov* 3 (1989), 225.

21 Cf. Mayakovsky's dictum: "Poetry begins where there is a tendency" (Maiakovskii, *Polnoe sobranie sochinenii*, vol. XII, p. 86).

22 *Ibid.*, p. 162.

23 *Ibid.*, p. 87. The concept of the "sotsial'nyi zakaz" (usually translated as "social demand" or "social order") was central to the ideology of LEF (the Left Front of Art), Mayakovsky's faction in the early period of Soviet literature. For a heated discussion of the term and its value, see the series of articles (by Vyacheslav Polonsky, Osip Brik, P. S. Kogan, and others) in *Pechat' i revoliutsiia* 1 (1929), 19–75.

24 After hearing Mayakovsky recite some of his post-revolutionary verse, Roman Jakobson is reputed to have said "Khorosho, no khuzhe Maiakovskogo" ("Good, but worse than Mayakovsky"): Victor Erlich, *Modernism and Revolution: Russian Literature in Transition* (Cambridge, MA: Harvard University Press, 1994), p. 274. See also Aleksandr Zholkovsky's concept of "plokhopis'" ("bad writing"), elaborated in part on the later poetry of Mayakovsky: Aleksandr Zholkovskii, *Inventsii* (Moscow: Gendal'f, 1995), pp. 123–25.

25 Maiakovskii, *Polnoe sobranie sochinenii*, vol. V, p. 54.

26 *Ibid.*, vol. VI, pp. 34–38.

27 The statement first appeared in an unsigned editorial in *Pravda*. For the background, see Katanian, "Ne tol'ko vospominaniia," 220–24.

28 The material for this chapter has been selected from the works of Mayakovsky's friends (Kirsanov, Aseev) and contemporaries (Aliger, Lugovskoi), as well as subsequent generations (Evtushenko, Rozhdestvensky, Voznesensky, Korzhavin).

29 William Mills Todd III, *Fiction and Society in the Age of Pushkin* (Cambridge, MA: Harvard University Press, 1986), pp. 52–54.

30 Maiakovskii, *Polnoe sobranie sochinenii*, vol. VIII, p. 43.

31 In the Soviet Union, the eighth of March was celebrated as a holiday ("International Woman's Day"). Mayakovsky associates this holiday with the genre of the ode; his own poem, however, which concerns an

individual woman's everyday life, uses a different vocabulary and style.

32 Nikolai Aseev, *Sobranie sochinenii v piati tomakh*, 5 vols. (Moscow: Khudozhestvennaia literatura, 1963–64), vol. I, p. 311.

33 *Ibid.*, vol. IV, p. 354.

34 See her essay "Maiakovskii prodolzhaetsia" ("Mayakovsky Continues"), in Margarita Aliger, *Sobranie sochinenii v trekh tomakh*, 3 vols. (Moscow: Khudozhestvennaia literatura, 1984–85), vol. III, pp. 365–79.

35 *Ibid.*, vol. I, p. 27.

36 One can find exceptions, but it takes some effort. Among the more highly regarded Soviet poets, both Ol'ga Berggol'ts (1910–75) and Rimma Kazakova (born 1932) have used *lesenka*. In Berggol'ts' work, it is usually found in the civic verse that made her famous (e.g., the poems about the Second World War or, more specifically, the heroism of Leningrad). See, for example, Ol'ga Berggol'ts, *Izbrannye proizvedeniia* (Leningrad: Sovetskii pisatel', 1983), pp. 188–91, 221–23, 233–34. In the case of Kazakova, it is somewhat harder to understand, since she is generally a lyric poet who shies away from overtly patriotic themes. Her use of *lesenka* in poems about partisans or about Cuba is not surprising, but there is the occasional poem where individual verses are set in *lesenka* solely as a means of emphasis and apparently without any political or civic significance. See Rimma Kazakova, *Izbrannye proizvedeniia*, 2 vols. (Moscow: Khudozhestvennaia literatura, 1985), vol. I, pp. 240–41, 257–58, 284–86, 305–06. It should be emphasized that *lesenka* accounts for only a tiny percentage of Kazakova's verse.

37 See, for example, numerous passages in her long poem "Zoia" ("Zoya"), about the heroism of a Komsomol girl who, as a partisan, sacrifices herself so that the Soviets can triumph over the Nazis: in Aliger, *Sobranie sochinenii*, vol. I, pp. 277–321.

38 For a study of this genre of Mayakovsky's work (with comparisons to Pindar), see the article by M. L. Gasparov and I. Iu. Podgaetskaia, "Griadushchei zhizni godovshchiny: kompozitsiia i topika prazdnichnykh stikhov Maiakovskogo," reprinted in M. L. Gasparov, *Izbrannye trudy*, 2 vols. (Moscow: Iazyki russkoi kul'tury, 1997), pp. 241–71.

39 It is an amusing irony that Lenin himself was unenthusiastic about Mayakovsky's poetry, preferring nineteenth-century classics to contemporary experiments. See E. I. Naumov, "Lenin o Maiakovskom (novye materialy)," in *Literaturnoe nasledstvo*, no. 65 (*Novoe o Maiakovskom*) (Moscow: Nauka, 1958), pp. 208–09.

40 Maiakovskii, *Polnoe sobranie sochinenii*, vol. VI, p. 267.

41 From the 1930 poem "Lenintsy" ("Leninites"): *ibid.*, vol. X, pp. 171–74.

42 *Ibid.*, vol. VI, p. 233.

43 Semen Kirsanov, *Stikhotvoreniia* (Moscow: Khudozhestvennaia literatura, 1951), pp. 43–44.

44 Evgenii Evtushenko, *Poet v Rossii – bol'she, chem poet* (Moscow: Sovetskaia Rossiia, 1973), p. 157.

45 Andrei Voznesenskii, *Sobranie sochinenii*, 3 vols. (Moscow: Khudozhest-vennaia literatura, 1983), vol. I, p. 386.

46 Robert Rozhdestvenskii, *Radius deistviia* (Moscow: Sovetskii pisatel', 1965), p. 216.

47 A similar usage can be found in "Stantsiia 'Maiakovskaiia'" ("Metro Station Mayakovsky"), in Kirsanov, *Sobranie sochinenii*, vol. III, p. 65.

48 Aseev's interesting long poem "Maiakovskii nachinaetsia" ("Maya-kovsky Begins," written 1937–39) is the exception that confirms the rule. Rather than using *lesenka*, Aseev writes in *stolbik* (column construction), the graphic technique that Mayakovsky had favored before moving to *lesenka*. Aseev's formal choice was semantically motivated, for his poem took the daring (for the time) position that Mayakovsky was essentially a Futurist and that his roots could be found in that earlier period. For a detailed discussion of the history of this poem (but without any comments on its graphic form), see A. M. Kriukova, "K tvorcheskoi istorii poemy 'Maiakovskii nachinaetsia,'" in *Literaturnoe nasledstvo*, no. 93 (*Iz istorii sovetskoi literatury 1920–1930-kh godov*) (Moscow: Nauka, 1983), pp. 438–530.

49 Maiakovskii, *Polnoe sobranie sochinenii*, vol. VII, p. 87.

50 Kirsanov, *Stikhotvoreniia*, pp. 144–45.

51 Kirsanov, *Sobranie sochinenii*, vol. III, pp. 118–19. The poem is called "Tank 'Maiakovskii'" ("Mayakovsky the Tank").

52 Kirsanov, *Sobranie sochinenii*, vol. III, p. 105.

53 Nikolai Aseev, *Stikhotvoreniia* (Leningrad: Sovetskii pisatel', 1967), p. 201.

54 Aseev, *Sobranie sochinenii*, vol. IV, p. 377–78.

55 Maiakovskii, *Polnoe sobranie sochinenii*, vol. VI, p. 54.

56 Vladimir Lugovskoi, *Sobranie sochinenii*, 3 vols. (Moscow: Khudozhest-vennaia literatura, 1971), vol. II, p. 284.

57 From a factual point of view, this is curious, for Mayakovsky never joined the Party after the Revolution – indeed, this was one of the biographical details that Soviet critics tended to sidestep. Mayakovsky always showed deep respect for the Party, yet he stubbornly resisted joining it – even at the end of his life, when he came under frequent attack in this regard.

58 Mayakovsky's formal technique acted as a type of "Midas touch" even here: the poem about the great poet's mother ("Mat' Maiakovskogo," 1954) is written in *lesenka*. See Evgenii Evtushenko, *Stikhotvoreniia i poemy*, 3 vols. (Moscow: Sovetskaia Rossiia, 1987), vol. I, p. 28.

59 *Ibid.*, p. 448.

60 "The tradition of public poetry readings, introduced earlier by Maya-kovsky and then interrupted, was reconstructed": Evgenii Evtushenko, *Avtobiografiia* (London: Flegon Press, 1964), p. 100. The theme of mass

poetry readings comes up in many of Evtushenko's poems, e.g., "Nasledniki Stalina" ("Heirs of Stalin," 1962).

61 In certain editions, Evtushenko used this as the final poem in the cycle. He originally published it as a separate poem. The following citations come from Evtushenko, *Stikhotvoreniia i poemy*, vol. I, pp. 517–19.

62 The last four lines of this passage are not included in some editions of this work. I cite them from George Reavey (ed.), *The New Russian Poets: 1953 to 1968* (New York: October House, 1966), p. 102.

63 In the 1985 poem "Fuku," one finds a passage in which Evtushenko suggests that he himself is Mayakovsky's "son": Evtushenko, *Stikhotvoreniia i poemy*, vol. III, p. 482. In a brief autobiographical statement of 1995, Evtushenko intimates that he is distantly related (by blood) to Mayakovsky: Evgenii Evtushenko (ed.), *Strofy veka* (Minsk and Moscow: Polifakt, 1995), p. 767.

64 Whereas Mayakovsky had used a crude and scatalogical term ("sh—t," an unpublishable word in the 1960s), Rozhdestvensky opts for a slangy interjection ("Hey") – which, not coincidentally, can also be found in the conclusion of "About That" (Maiakovskii, *Polnoe sobranie sochinenii*, vol. IV, p. 178).

65 See the part of Korzhavin's memoirs entitled "Maiakovskii i nasha zhizn' (vstavnoe esse)" ("Mayakovsky and Our Life [An Interpolated Essay]"): Naum Korzhavin, "V soblaznakh krovavoi epokhi," *Novyi mir* 8 (1992), 144–47.

66 Naum Korzhavin, *Vremia dano: stikhi i poemy* (Moscow: Khudozhestvennaia literatura, 1992), p. 49.

67 Evtushenko always kept apace of Party policy, being careful never to overstep the boundary of the permissible. He clearly recognized the difference between himself and Korzhavin, writing that the latter was "the only poet who wrote and openly read poems against Stalin during Stalin's lifetime." See Evtushenko, *Avtobiografiia*, p. 86.

68 Personal communication. Republications of his works nonetheless retain *lesenka*. See Korzhavin, *Vremia dano*. It is curious that, in his memoirs, Korzhavin cites (with respect, if not admiration) a poem by Aseev and specifically notes that he is quoting it without *lesenka* (Korzhavin, "V soblazniakh," 156). On the one hand, he does so presumably because he is interested in the passage's ideological thrust, not its poetic qualities. But it is likely that he also wishes to lessen its official Soviet connotations.

AFTERWORD: THE MEANING OF FORM

1 A. P. Sumarokov, *Izbrannye proizvedeniia* (Leningrad: Sovetskii pisatel', 1957), p. 135.

2 N. M. Karamzin, *Pis'ma russkogo puteshestvennika* (Leningrad: Nauka, 1984), p. 185. There is a curious irony here. As Karamzin remarks in a

footnote, Baggesen did not keep his word for long. Yet Karamzin himself ultimately renounced poetry (and prose fiction) in favor of history, saying, "for the mature mind, truth has a special charm which does not exist in fictions": "Istoricheskie vospominaniia i zamechaniia na puti k Troitse," in N. M. Karamzin, *Sochineniia Karamzina*, 8 vols. (Moscow: Tip. S. Selivanovskogo, 1803–04), vol. VIII, p. 377.

3 Sigmund Freud, *Der Witz und seine Beziehung zum Unbewussten* (Frankfurt: Fischer Verlag, 1975), p. 65.

4 William Wordsworth, "Preface to Lyrical Ballads," in Harold Bloom and Lionel Trilling (eds.), *Romantic Poetry and Prose* (New York: Oxford University Press, 1973), p. 596. As Trilling points out in his note to the passage in question, even Wordsworth himself qualifies this statement.

5 Briusov is said to have improvised sonnets, but this indicates less the natural element of poetic language than the aesthetization of everyday life so characteristic of Russian Symbolism. In any case, the fact that there is a variant to the published version of a supposedly improvised sonnet makes one wonder about its "spontaneity." See Valerii Briusov, *Sobranie sochinenii v semi tomakh*, 7 vols. (Moscow: Khudozhestvennaia literatura, 1975), vol. III, pp. 44, 556.

6 For a study of some of the smaller forms, see Reinhard Lauer, *Gedichtform zwischen Schema und Verfall* (Munich: Fink Verlag, 1975).

7 W. H. Auden displays commendable candor when he states: "Russians are unanimous in regarding him [Pushkin] as their greatest poet, but I have yet to read a translation which, if I did not know this, would lead me to suppose that his poems had any merit whatsoever": in "Foreword," to Andrei Voznesensky, *Antiworlds and "The Fifth Ace"* (New York: Doubleday, 1967), p. v.

8 In this instance, there already exists an exemplary reading which places Kuzmin's poem in the context of Blok's "Free Thoughts." See Omry Ronen, "A Functional Technique of Myth Transformation in Twentieth-Century Russian Lyrical Poetry," in Andrej Kodjak, Krystyna Pomorska, and Stephen Rudy (eds.), *Myth in Literature* (Columbus: Slavica, 1985), pp. 114–16.

9 M. L. Gasparov, *Ocherk istorii russkogo stikha* (Moscow: Nauka, 1984), pp. 118–19.

10 Several poets, rather than using Pushkin's precise form, created a variation of it, by altering the rhyme scheme or the meter. It would be instructive to do a systematic study of these works and their relationship to *Onegin*. I am thinking of Baratynsky's "Bal" ("The Ball"), Sukennikov's "Fedor Volgin," Nabokov's "Universitetskaia poema" ("University Poem"), and passages from Iazykov's "Lipy" ("The Lime Trees") and Pavlova's "Kadril'" ("The Quadrille").

11 It is in this context that one should understand the curious case of Jurgis Baltrushaitis, a Symbolist who wrote several poems in the form of a single Onegin stanza. See M. L. Gasparov, *Russkie stikhi 1890-kh–1925-go*

godov v kommentariiakh (Moscow: Vysshaia shkola, 1993), p. 164. For an example of a work that consists of only a few Onegin stanzas (in which nostalgia again plays a dominant role), see Georgii Shengeli's 1916 poem "Domik" ("The [Dear] House"): Georgii Shengeli, *Inokhodets: sobranie stikhov* (Moscow: Sovpadenie, 1997), pp. 52–54.

12 Leonid Timofeev, *Slovo v stikhe* (Moscow: Sovetskii pisatel', 1982), p. 145.

13 A number of subsequent poems suggest that this tradition continues. See Ian K. Lilly, *The Dynamics of Russian Verse* (Nottingham: Astra Press, 1996), p. 81. The fact that examples can be found in the work of a poet/ scholar like Aleksandr Kushner prompts the unusual question as to whether the impulse came from Lermontov's poem or from Taranovsky's essay. See Kushner's "L'etsia svet. Voda bredet vo mrake" ("Light flows. Water wanders in the darkness"), in Gerald S. Smith (ed.), *Contemporary Russian Poetry: A Bilingual Anthology* (Bloomington: Indiana University Press, 1993), pp. 120–22.

14 Taranovsky had claimed that, in poems of trochaic pentameter, a verb of motion at the beginning of the line is connected to the theme of the journey (e.g., Lermontov's "Vykhozhu" ["I step forth"]). Gasparov has proved that there are no statistical grounds for such a claim (M. L. Gasparov, "The Semantic Halo of the Russian Trochaic Pentameter: Thirty Years of the Problem," *Elementa* 2, 3–4 [1996], 204–06). However, this does not exclude the possibility that individual poets sensed and cultivated such a link in their own verse. Nabokov's 1929 poem on the death of the critic Iulii Aikhenval'd (not mentioned in Taranovsky's essay) begins: "Pereshel ty v novoe zhilishche" ("You have stepped into another dwelling"). Curiously, the final line of the poem is truncated – by a foot – and indented, as if to emphasize visually that very step into the world beyond. The fact that this device appears in the very first word of Nabokov's poem (and that the fateful step is indicated graphically in the final line) strongly suggests the influence of Lermontov's "rhythmical-syntactic figure." Statistical evidence, in short, does not outweigh actual poetic practice, even if this practice concerns only a very small number of poets. See Vladimir Nabokov, *Stikhi* (Ann Arbor: Ardis, 1979), p. 224.

15 To a certain extent, this can be explained by the pioneering nature of the enterprise. Taranovsky did recognize and apply the interpretive possibilities of his approach in a later essay: "Vdal' vlekomye: odin sluchai poeticheskoi polemiki Bloka i Belogo s Viach. Ivanovym," *Slavica Hierosolymitana* 5–6 (1981), 289–96.

16 For a discussion of the significance of these repetitions, see I. P. Smirnov, *Porozhdenie interteksta* (Vienna: Wiener Slawistischer Almanach, 1985), pp. 83–88.

17 For Bely's influence on Khodasevich, see K. F. Taranovskii, "Chetyrekhstopnyi iamb Andreia Belogo," *International Journal of Slavic Linguistics and Poetics* 10 (1966), 145–47. For later poets, see V. V. Ivanov, "Iz

nabliudenii nad chetyrekhstopnym iambom sovremennykh poetov," in Roman Jakobson, C. H. van Schooneveld, and Dean S. Worth (eds.), *Slavic Poetics: Essays in Honor of Kiril Taranovsky* (The Hague: Mouton, 1973), pp. 231–38.

18 The term comes from John Hollander, "The Metrical Emblem," *Kenyon Review* 21, 1 (1959), 294.

19 On the cultural significance of these events and of this poem in particular, see Robert Hughes, "Pushkin in Petrograd, February 1921," in Boris Gasparov, Robert P. Hughes, and Irina Paperno (eds.), *Cultural Mythologies of Russian Modernism* (Berkeley: University of California Press, 1992), pp. 204–13.

20 M. Kuzmin, *Stikhotvoreniia* (St. Petersburg: Akademicheskii proekt, 1996), p. 425.

21 Sergei Esenin, *Sin', upavshaia v reku* (Moscow: Pravda, 1985), p. 291.

22 Z. N. Gippius, *Stikhotvoreniia: zhivye litsa* (Moscow: Khudozhestvennaia literatura, 1991), pp. 158–59. Gippius was not against free verse as such, but against the way it "enslaved" those unprepared for it. (The poem is dedicated to "young poets" and has a distinctly didactic emphasis.)

23 See "Vesennii lepet ne raznezhit" ("The spring babble will not soften") and "Ne iambom li chetyrekhstopnym" ("Should I not in iambic tetrameter"), in Vladislav Khodasevich, *Stikhotvoreniia* (Leningrad: Sovetskii pisatel', 1989), pp. 156–57, 410–11. On the former, see David Bethea, *Khodasevich: His Life and Art* (Princeton University Press, 1983), pp. 279–82. For a discussion of the latter, see Robert P. Hughes, "Reflections on Khodasevich's Ode to the Russian Iambic Tetrameter," in Simon Karlinsky, James L. Rice, and Barry P. Scherr (eds.), *O Rus! Studia litteraria slavica in honorem Hugh McLean* (Oakland: Berkeley Slavic Specialties, 1995), pp. 470–84.

24 Khodasevich, *Stikhotvoreniia*, p. 156.

25 The image of "lowing trans-rationally" in this line is surely directed against a specific Futurist – Mayakovsky, who had provocatively entitled a 1916 book of poetry *Simple as Lowing* (*Prostoe kak mychanie*). In a vicious attack penned after Mayakovsky's suicide, Khodasevich was to write that Mayakovsky "filled in the emptiness, the zero significance of trans-rational poetry with a new content: the beastly 'simple, like lowing' [*sic*] . . . He dragged out to the bazaar the riches that human thought had accumulated – and he vulgarized the refined, simplified the complicated, made the subtle coarse, made the deep shallow, belittled the sublime, and stamped it into the mud": Vladislav Khodasevich, *Izbrannaia proza* (New York: Russica Publishers, 1982), pp. 184–85.

26 Gasparov, *Ocherk istorii russkogo stikha*, p. 97.

27 According to the fullest account of eighteenth-century verse forms, this specific odic stanza is found only four times: twice in Bogdanovich, once in Derzhavin, and once anonymously. Only in the anonymous poem does the placement of masculine and feminine rhymes coincide

with that of Khodasevich's poem. See G. S. Smith, "The Stanza Forms of Russian Poetry from Polotsky to Derzhavin," Ph.D. thesis, University of London (1977), pp. 435–36. I am indebted to Ian Lilly for supplying this reference.

28 In the context of this general resemblance, some readers may note a few direct references to Pushkin's verse: Iu. I. Levin, "Zametki o poezii Vl. Khodasevicha," *Wiener Slawistischer Almanach* 17 (1986), 55–56.

29 Marina Tsvetaeva's cycle "Stikhi k Pushkinu" ("Verses to Pushkin," 1931) supplies an impressive counterexample. Using a variety of forms with distinctly twentieth-century resonances, Tsvetaeva presents "her" (characteristically idiosyncratic) Pushkin.

30 This subject, together with readings of the entire series of poems under consideration, is treated in depth in Lev Loseff and Barry Scherr (eds.), *A Sense of Place: Tsarskoe Selo and Its Poets* (Columbus: Slavica, 1993).

31 A. S. Pushkin, *Polnoe sobranie sochinenii*, 10 vols. (Leningrad: Nauka, 1977–79), vol. III, p. 171.

32 See Roman Jakobson's essay "The Statue in Puškin's Poetic Mythology," in Roman Jakobson, *Language in Literature* (Cambridge, MA: Harvard University Press, 1987), pp. 318–67.

33 Lev Loseff, "The Toy Town Ruined," in Loseff and Scherr, *Sense of Place*, p. 40. See also Jakobson's essay "Stikhi Pushkina o deve-statue, vakkhanke i smirennitse," republished in Roman Jakobson, *Raboty po poetike* (Moscow: Progress, 1987), pp. 187–88.

34 A. K. Tolstoi, *Sobranie sochinenii*, 4 vols. (Moscow: Khudozhestvennaia literatura, 1963), vol. I, p. 665. The date of Tolstoi's poem is unknown.

35 For a thorough analysis of this cycle, see Nancy Pollak, "Annensky's 'Trefoil in the Park' (Witness to Whiteness)," in Loseff and Scherr, *Sense of Place*, pp. 171–90.

36 Innokentii Annenskii, *Stikhotvoreniia i tragedii* (Leningrad: Sovetskii pisatel', 1990), p. 122.

37 M. L. Gasparov, *Ocherk istorii russkogo stikha*, pp. 58–60.

38 Emphasis added. Pushkin, *Polnoe sobranie sochinenii* (Leningrad), vol. III, p. 340.

39 See M. L. Gasparov, *Russkie stikhi 1890-kh–1925-go godov v kommentariiakh*, pp. 152–53. Still more relevant to the present context, Tomas Venclova has noted in regard to two poems of Vasily Komarovsky: "Both the texts are written in strict Alexandrines. The very choice of this meter refers us to Pushkin and to Pushkin's time. Although Alexandrines are not uncommon in Annensky's works, and later in Akhmatova's, they still stand out sharply among the poetry at the beginning of the twentieth century" (Tomas Venclova, "The Exemplary Resident of Tsarskoe Selo and the Great Pupil of the Lycée: Some Observations on the Poetics of Count Vasily Alekseevich Komarovsky," in Loseff and Scherr, *Sense of Place*, p. 265. Komarovsky is in numerous respects an essential link in the sequence of Tsarskoe Selo poems, but since his

alexandrine verses rely explicitly on Annensky's model, he is not essential for my purposes. See also V. N. Toporov, "Dve glavy iz istorii russkoi poezii nachala veka: I. V. A. Komarovskii – II. V. K. Shileiko (k sootnosheniiu poetiki simvolizma i akmeizma)," *Russian Literature* 7, 3 (1979), 266–67.

40 Anna Akhmatova, *Stikhotvoreniia i poemy* (Leningrad: Sovetskii pisatel', 1976), pp. 101–02.

41 Wendy Rosslyn, "Remodelling the Statues at Tsarskoe Selo: Akhmatova's Approach to the Poetic Tradition," in Loseff and Scherr, *Sense of Place*, p. 156.

42 For precise figures of metrical frequency, see M. L. Gasparov, *Sovremennyi russkii stikh* (Moscow: Nauka, 1973), pp. 53–57. See also M. L. Gasparov, "Semanticheskii oreol pushkinskogo chetyrekhstopnogo khoreia," in S. G. Isakov (ed.), *Pushkinskie chteniia* (Tallinn: Eesti raamat, 1990), p. 5.

43 M. Volkova and S. Dovlatov (eds.), *Ne tol'ko Brodskii: russkaia kul'tura v portretakh i anekdotakh* (Moscow: Kul'tura, 1992), p. 46.

44 From the 1913 essay "O sobesednike" ("On the Interlocutor"), Osip Mandel'shtam, *Slovo i kul'tura* (Moscow: Sovetskii pisatel', 1987), pp. 49–50.

45 "The Nobel Laureates of Literature: An Olympic Gathering. Panel Discussion I," *Georgia Review* 49, 4 (1995), 850.

46 John Glad (ed.), *Conversations in Exile* (Durham: Duke University Press, 1993), p. 110.

Bibliography

PRIMARY LITERATURE

Adon'ev, S. and Gerasimov, N. (eds.), *Sovremennaia ballada i zhestokii romans*, St. Petersburg: Izdatel'stvo Ivana Limbakha, 1996.

Akhmatova, Anna, *Stikhotvoreniia i poemy*, Leningrad: Sovetskii pisatel', 1976.

Aksakov, S. T., *Sobranie sochinenii*, Moscow: Khudozhestvennaia literatura, 1956.

Aliger, Margarita, *Sobranie sochinenii v trekh tomakh*, Moscow: Khudozhestvennaia literatura, 1984–85.

Annenskii, Innokentii, *Stikhotvoreniia i tragedii*, Leningrad: Sovetskii pisatel', 1990.

Aseev, Nikolai, *Sobranie sochinenii v piati tomakh*, Moscow: Khudozhestvennaia literatura, 1963–64.

Stikhotvoreniia, Leningrad: Sovetskii pisatel', 1967.

Batiushkov, K. N., *Sochineniia K. N. Batiushkova*, L. N. Maikov and V. I. Santov (eds.), St. Petersburg: Tip. Kotomina, 1885–87.

Belyi, Andrei, *Stikhotvoreniia*, Moscow: Kniga, 1988.

Berggol'ts, Ol'ga, *Izbrannye proizvedeniia*, Leningrad: Sovetskii pisatel', 1983.

Blok, A. A. [Aleksandr], *Novye materialy i issledovaniia*, *Literaturnoe nasledstvo*, no. 93, Moscow: Nauka, 1980–93.

[Blok, Aleksandr], *Pis'ma k zhene*, *Literaturnoe nasledstvo*, no. 89, Moscow: Nauka, 1978.

Polnoe sobranie sochinenii i pisem v dvadtsati tomakh, Moscow: Nauka, 1997–.

Sobranie sochinenii v vos'mi tomakh, Moscow: Gosudarstvennoe izdatel'stvo khudozhestvennoi literatury, 1960–63.

[Blok, Aleksandr], *Stikhotvoreniia*, St. Petersburg: Severo-Zapad, 1994.

Zapisnye knizhki, Moscow: Khudozhestvennaia literatura, 1965.

Bloom, Harold and Trilling, Lionel (eds.), *Romantic Poetry and Prose*, New York: Oxford University Press, 1973.

Briusov, Valerii, *Sobranie sochinenii v semi tomakh*, Moscow: Khudozhestvennaia literatura, 1975.

Brodskii, Iosif, *Ostanovka v pustyne*, Ann Arbor: Ardis, 1989.

[Brodsky, Joseph], *Selected Poems*, New York: Harper & Row, 1973.

306

Bulich, Vera, *Plennyi veter: stikhi*, Tallinn: J. & A. Paalmann'i trükk, 1938.
Burgin, Diana Lewis, *Richard Burgin: A Life in Verse*, Columbus: Slavica, 1988.
Chudo, Alicia, "The Onegin of Our Times: An Essay in Verse," *Formations* 6, 1 (1991), 129–34.
Chukhontsev, Oleg, *Stikhotvoreniia*, Moscow: Khudozhestvennaia literatura, 1989.
Chukovskii, Kornei, "Nyneshnii Evgenii Onegin: roman v 4-kh pesniakh," *Odesskie novosti*, December 25, 1904, and January 1, 1905.
Del'vig, A. A., *Polnoe sobranie stikhotvorenii*, Leningrad: Sovetskii pisatel', 1959.
Dzhangirov, Karen (ed.), *Antologiia russkogo verlibra*, Moscow: Prometei, 1991.
Esenin, Sergei, *Sin', upavshaia v reku*, Moscow: Pravda, 1985.
Evgenii Vel'skoi, roman v stikhakh, Moscow: Tip. S. Selivanovskogo, 1828–29.
Evtushenko, Evgenii, *Avtobiografiia*, London: Flegon Press, 1964.
    Poet v Rossii – bol'she, chem poet, Moscow: Sovetskaia Rossiia, 1973.
    Stikhotvoreniia i poemy, Moscow: Sovetskaia Rossiia, 1987.
Evtushenko, Evgenii (ed.), *Strofy veka*, Minsk and Moscow: Polifakt, 1995.
Fet, A. A., *Stikhotvoreniia i poemy*, Leningrad: Sovetskii pisatel', 1986.
Ginzburg, Evgeniia, *Krutoi marshrut*, Moscow: Sovetskii pisatel', 1990.
Gippius, Z. N., *Stikhotvoreniia: zhivye litsa*, Moscow: Khudozhestvennaia literatura, 1991.
Goethe, *Gedichte*, Munich: C. H. Beck, 1982.
Grigor'ev, Apollon, *Izbrannye proizvedeniia*, Leningrad: Sovetskii pisatel', 1959.
Gumilev, Nikolai, *Sobranie sochinenii*, Washington, D.C.: Victor Kamkin, 1962–68.
    Sochineniia v trekh tomakh, Moscow: Khudozhestvennaia literatura, 1991.
Gusev, V. E. (ed.), *Pesni russkikh poetov*, Leningrad: Sovetskii pisatel', 1988.
Irten'ev, Igor, *Povestka dnia*, France [*sic*]: AMGA, 1989.
Ivanov, Viacheslav [Vjačeslav], *Dichtung und Briefwechsel aus dem deutschsprachigen Nachlass*, Mainz: Liber Verlag, 1995.
    Sobranie sochinenii, Brussels: Foyer Oriental Chrétien, 1971–86.
Karamzin, N. M., *Pis'ma russkogo puteshestvennika*, Leningrad: Nauka, 1984.
    Sochineniia Karamzina, Moscow: Tip. S. Selivanovskogo, 1803–04.
Kazakova, Rimma, *Izbrannye proizvedeniia*, Moscow: Khudozhestvennaia literatura, 1985.
Kelly, Catriona (ed.), *An Anthology of Russian Women's Writing: 1777–1992*, Oxford University Press, 1994.
Khodasevich, Vladislav, *Literaturnye stat'i i vospominaniia*, New York: Izdatel'stvo imeni Chekhova, 1954.
    Sobranie sochinenii, Ann Arbor: Ardis, 1983–90.
    Stikhotvoreniia, Leningrad: Sovetskii pisatel', 1989.
Kibal'nik, S. A. (ed.), *Venok russkim Kamenam: antologicheskie stikhotvoreniia russkikh poetov*, Moscow: Nauka, 1993.
Kirsanov, Semen, *Sobranie sochinenii*, Moscow: Khudozhestvennaia literatura, 1976.

Stikhotvoreniia, Moscow: Khudozhestvennaia literatura, 1951.

Kiukhel'beker, V. K., *Izbrannye proizvedeniia v dvukh tomakh*, Moscow: Sovetskii pisatel', 1967.

Knut, Dovid, *Izbrannye stikhi*, Paris: Imprimerie moderne de la presse, 1949.

Korzhavin, Naum, "V soblaznakh krovavoi epokhi," *Novyi mir* 8 (1992), 130–93.

Vremia dano: stikhi i poemy, Moscow: Khudozhestvennaia literatura, 1992.

Kruchenykh, Aleksei, *Kukish proshliakam*, Moscow: Gileia, 1992.

[Kručenych, A. E.], *Selected Works*, Munich: Fink Verlag, 1973.

Kushlina, O. B. (ed.), *Russkaia literatura XX veka v zerkale parodii*, Moscow: Vysshaia shkola, 1993.

Kuzmin, M., *Stikhotvoreniia*, St. Petersburg: Akademicheskii proekt, 1996.

Lermontov, M. Iu., *Polnoe sobranie sochinenii*, Moscow: Academia, 1935–37.

Sobranie sochinenii v chetyrekh tomakh, Moscow: Izdatel'stvo akademii nauk SSSR, 1962.

Lessing, Gotthold Ephraim, *Werke*, Munich: Hanser Verlag, 1973.

Longfellow, Henry Wadsworth, *The Complete Poetical Works of Henry Wadsworth Longfellow*, Horace E. Scudder (ed.), Boston: Houghton, Mifflin, 1893.

Lugovskoi, Vladimir, *Sobranie sochinenii*, Moscow: Khudozhestvennaia literatura, 1971.

Maiakovskii, Vladimir, *Polnoe sobranie sochinenii v trinadtsati tomakh*, Moscow: Khudozhestvennaia literatura, 1955–61.

Markov, Vladimir (ed.), *Manifesty i programmy russkikh futuristov*, Munich: Fink Verlag, 1967.

Mikhailov, M. L. *Sobranie stikhotvorenii*, Leningrad: Sovetskii pisatel', 1969.

Minaev, D. D., *Sobranie stikhotvorenii*, Leningrad: Sovetskii pisatel', 1947.

Morozov, A. A. (ed.), *Russkaia stikhotvornaia parodiia*, Leningrad: Sovetskii pisatel', 1960.

Nabokov, Vladimir, *The Gift*, New York: G. P. Putnam's Sons, 1963.

Stikhi, Ann Arbor: Ardis, 1979.

Nekrasov, N. A., *Polnoe sobranie sochinenii v trekh tomakh*, Leningrad: Sovetskii pisatel', 1967.

"Novye perevody," *Novoe literaturnoe obozrenie* 6 (1994), 278–79.

Ogarev, N. P., *Stikhotvoreniia i poemy*, Leningrad: Sovetskii pisatel', 1956.

Pasternak, Boris, *Sobranie sochinenii v piati tomakh*, Moscow: Khudozhestvennaia literatura, 1989–92.

Pereleshin, Valerii, *Poema bez predmeta*, Holyoke, MA: New England Publishing Co., 1989.

The Poetical Works of Milman, Bowles, Wilson, and Barry Cornwall, Paris: A. and W. Galignani, 1829.

Polezhaev, A. I., *Stikhotvoreniia i poemy*, Leningrad: Sovetskii pisatel', 1957.

Prigov, Dmitrii Aleksandrovich, *Sobstvennye perepevy na chuzhie rifmy*, Moscow: Moskovskii gosudarstvennyi muzei Vladimira Sidura, 1996.

Prutkov, Koz'ma, *Polnoe sobranie sochinenii*, Moscow: Sovetskii pisatel', 1965.

Pushkin, Aleksandr, *Eugene Onegin: A Novel in Verse by Alexander Pushkin*, James E. Falen (trans.), Carbondale: Southern Illinois University Press, 1990.

Eugene Onegin: A Novel in Verse, Vladimir Nabokov (trans.), Princeton University Press, 1975.

Polnoe sobranie sochinenii, Moscow: Izdatel'stvo Akademii nauk SSSR, 1937–49.

Polnoe sobranie sochinenii, Leningrad: Nauka, 1977–79.

Pushkin Threefold, Walter Arndt (trans.), New York: E. P. Dutton, 1972.

Sobranie sochinenii, St. Petersburg: Brokgauz-Efron, 1908.

Reavey, George (ed.), *The New Russian Poets: 1953 to 1968*, New York: October House, 1966.

Reiser, S. A. (ed.), *Vol'naia russkaia poeziia XVIII–XIX vekov*, Leningrad: Sovetskii pisatel', 1988.

Rozhdestvenskii, Robert, *Radius deistviia*, Moscow: Sovetskii pisatel', 1965.

Schiller, Friedrich, *Polnoe sobranie sochinenii Shillera v perevode russkikh pisatelei*, N. V. Gerbel' (ed.), St. Petersburg, 1893.

[Shiller, Iogann Khristof Fridrikh], *Sobranie sochinenii*, Moscow: Academia, 1936–50.

[Shiller, Fridrikh], *Sobranie sochinenii*, Moscow: Gosudarstvennoe izdatel'stvo khudozhestvennoi literatury, 1955–57.

Werke und Briefe, Frankfurt am Main: Deutscher Klassiker Verlag, 1992–.

Sedakova, Ol'ga, *Kitaiskoe puteshestvie, Stely i nadpisi, Starye pesni*, Moscow: Carte Blanche, 1990.

Seth, Vikram, *The Golden Gate*, New York: Random House, 1986.

Severianin, Igor', *Klassicheskie rozy: medal'ony*, Moscow: Khudozhestvennaia literatura, 1991.

Sochineniia v piati tomakh, St. Petersburg: Logos, 1995.

Shengeli, Georgii, *Inokhodets: sobranie stikhov*, Moscow: Sovpadenie, 1997.

Shurygina, I. (ed.), *Lunnaia gost'ia: romany, povesti, rasskazy*, Moscow: Terra, 1997.

Smith, Gerald S. (ed.), *Contemporary Russian Poetry: A Bilingual Anthology*, Bloomington: Indiana University Press, 1993.

Solov'ev, Sergei, *Italiia: poema*, Moscow: Tip. V. I. Voronova, 1914.

Southey, Robert, *The Poetical Works of Robert Southey*, Paris: A. and W. Galignani, 1829.

Sumarokov, A. P., *Izbrannye proizvedeniia*, Leningrad: Sovetskii pisatel', 1957.

Svetlov, Mikhail, *Stikhotvoreniia i poemy*, Moscow: Sovetskii pisatel', 1966.

Thomas, D. M., *Swallow*, New York: Viking, 1984.

Tolstoi, A. K., *Sobranie sochinenii*, Moscow: Khudozhestvennaia literatura, 1963.

Tred'iakovskii, V. K., *Sochineniia Tred'iakovskogo*, St. Petersburg: Aleksandr Smirdin, 1849.

Turgenev, I. S., *Stikhotvoreniia i poemy*, Leningrad: Sovetskii pisatel', 1970.

Verkhovskii, Iu. N., *Solntse v zatochenii*, Petrograd: Mysl', 1922.

Voloshin, Maksimilian, *Stikhotvoreniia i poemy*, St. Petersburg: Nauka, 1995.

Voznesenskii, Andrei, *Sobranie sochinenii*, Moscow: Khudozhestvennaia literatura, 1983.

Zhukovskii, V. A., *Sochineniia v trekh tomakh*, Moscow: Khudozhestvennaia literatura, 1980.

    Zarubezhnaia poeziia v perevodakh V. A. Zhukovskogo, K. N. Atarova and N. T. Beliaeva (eds.), Moscow: Raduga, 1985.

SECONDARY LITERATURE

Al'tman, M. S., *Razgovory s Viacheslavom Ivanovym*, St. Petersburg: Inapress, 1995.

Amert, Susan, *In a Shattered Mirror: The Later Poetry of Anna Akhmatova*, Stanford University Press, 1992.

Auden, W. H., "Foreword," in Andrei Voznesensky, *Antiworlds and "The Fifth Ace"*, New York: Doubleday, 1967.

Averintsev, S. S., "Gnomicheskoe nachalo v poetike Viach. Ivanova," *Studia Slavica: Academiae Scientiarum Hungaricae* 41 (1996), 3–12.

Bailey, James, "Some Recent Developments in the Study of Russian Versification," *Language and Style* 5, 3 (1972), 155–91.

Bethea, David, *Khodasevich: His Life and Art*, Princeton University Press, 1983.

Blagoi, Dmitrii, "Lermontov i Pushkin (problema istoriko-literaturnoi preemstvennosti)," in N. L. Brodskii, V. Ia. Kirpotin, E. N. Mikhailova, and A. N. Tolstoi (eds.), *Zhizn' i tvorchestvo M. Iu. Lermontova: issledovaniia i materialy*, vol. 1, Moscow: Goslitizdat, 1941.

    Ot Kantemira do nashikh dnei, Moscow: Khudozhestvennaia literatura, 1972.

Bogach, G. F., *Pushkin i moldavskii fol'klor*, Kishinev: Kartia Moldoveniaske, 1967.

Bondi, S. M., *O Pushkine*, Moscow: Khudozhestvennaia literatura, 1978.

Brodsky, Joseph, *Less than One*, New York: Farrar, Straus & Giroux, 1986.

Burgi, Richard, *A History of the Russian Hexameter*, Hamden, CT: Shoe String Press, 1954.

Burgin, Diana, "The Literary Ballad in the Symbolist Period," Ph.D. thesis, Harvard University, 1973.

Dal', V., *Poslovitsy russkogo naroda*, Moscow: Tip. universitetskaia, 1862.

Davidson, Pamela, *The Poetic Imagination of Vyacheslav Ivanov: A Russian Symbolist's Perception of Dante*, Cambridge University Press, 1989.

Egunov, A. N., *Gomer v russkikh perevodakh XVIII–XIX vekov*, Moscow: Nauka, 1964.

Eikhenbaum, Boris, *O poezii*, Leningrad: Sovetskii pisatel', 1969.

Erlich, Victor, *Modernism and Revolution: Russian Literature in Transition*, Cambridge, MA: Harvard University Press, 1994.

Freud, Sigmund, *Der Witz und seine Beziehung zum Unbewussten*, Frankfurt am Main: Fischer Verlag, 1975.

Frizman, L. G. (ed.), *Severnye tsvety na 1832 god*, Moscow: Nauka, 1980.

Gasparov, Boris, "Introduction," to Gasparov, Hughes, and Paperno, *Cultural Mythologies of Russian Modernism*.

Gasparov, Boris, Hughes, Robert P. and Paperno, Irina (eds.), *Cultural Mythologies of Russian Modernism*, Berkeley: University of California Press, 1992.

Gasparov, M. L., *A History of European Versification*, Oxford University Press, 1996.

Izbrannye stat'i, Moscow: Novoe literaturnoe obozrenie, 1995.

Izbrannye trudy, Moscow: Iazyki russkoi kul'tury, 1997.

Ocherk istorii evropeiskogo stikha, Moscow: Nauka, 1989.

Ocherk istorii russkogo stikha, Moscow: Nauka, 1984.

"Ritm i sintaksis: proiskhozhdenie 'lesenki' Maiakovskogo," in *Problemy strukturnoi lingvistiki – 1979*, Moscow: Nauka, 1981.

Russkie stikhi 1890-kh–1925-go godov v kommentariiakh, Moscow: Vysshaia shkola, 1993.

"The Semantic Halo of the Russian Trochaic Pentameter: Thirty Years of the Problem," *Elementa* 2, 3–4 (1996), 191–214.

"Semanticheskii oreol pushkinskogo chetyrekhstopnogo khoreia," in S. G. Isakov (ed.), *Pushkinskie chteniia*, Tallinn: Eesti raamat, 1990.

Sovremennyi russkii stikh, Moscow: Nauka, 1973.

"Stikh nachala XX v.: stroficheskaia traditsiia i eksperiment," in V. A. Keldysh (ed.), *Sviaz' vremen: problemy preemstvennosti v russkoi literature kontsa XIX–nachala XX v.*, Moscow: Nasledie, 1992.

"V poiskakh 'nastoiashchego verlibra,'" *Literaturnaia ucheba* 6 (1980), 208–11.

"Vera Merkur'eva – neizvestnaia poetessa kruga Viacheslava Ivanova," in Wilfried Potthoff (ed.), *Vjačeslav Ivanov: russischer Dichter – europäischer Kulturphilosoph*, Heidelberg: Universitätsverlag C. Winter, 1993.

Ginzburg, L. Ia., "O prozaizmakh v lirike Bloka," *Blokovskii sbornik* 1 (1964), 157–71.

Glad, John (ed.), *Conversations in Exile*, Durham: Duke University Press, 1993.

Grigor'ev, Apollon, *Literaturnaia kritika*, Moscow: Khudozhestvennaia literatura, 1967.

Grossman, Leonid, *Bor'ba za stil'*, Moscow: Nikitinskie subbotniki, 1927.

Gukovskii, Gr., "Iz istorii russkoi ody XVIII veka," *Poetika* 3 (1927), 129–47.

Hodge, Thomas P., "*Chin china pochitai*: Zhukovskii and Pushkin in the Art-Song Enterprise," in Konstantin Polivanov, Irina Shevelenko, and Andrey Ustinov (eds.), *Themes and Variations in Honor of Lazar Fleishman*, Stanford Slavic Studies, 1994.

Hofstadter, Douglas R., *Le Ton beau de Marot*, New York: HarperCollins, 1997.

Hoisington, Sona Stephan (trans.), *Russian Views of Pushkin's Eugene Onegin*, Bloomington: Indiana University Press, 1988.

Hollander, John, "The Metrical Emblem," *Kenyon Review* 21, 1 (1959), 279–96.

"Romantic Verse Form and the Metrical Contract," in Harold Bloom (ed.), *Romanticism and Consciousness: Essays in Criticism*, New York: Norton, 1970.

Hughes, Robert, "Pushkin in Petrograd, February 1921," in Gasparov, Hughes, and Paperno, *Cultural Mythologies of Russian Modernism*.

"Reflections on Khodasevich's Ode to the Russian Iambic Tetrameter," in Karlinsky, Rice, and Scherr, *O Rus!*

Iakovlev, N., "Iz razyskanii o literaturnykh istochnikakh v tvorchestve Pushkina," in *Pushkin v mirovoi literature.*

"Poslednii literaturnyi sobesednik Pushkina," *Pushkin i ego sovremenniki* 28 (1917), 5–28.

Ivanits, Linda J., *Russian Folk Belief*, New York: M. E. Sharpe, 1989.

Ivanov, V. V., "Iz nabliudenii nad chetyrekhstopnym iambom sovremennykh poetov," in Roman Jakobson, C. H. van Schooneveld, and Dean S. Worth (eds.), *Slavic Poetics: Essays in Honor of Kiril Taranovsky*, The Hague: Mouton, 1973.

Jakobson, Roman, *Language in Literature*, Cambridge, MA: Harvard University Press, 1987.

Raboty po poetike, Moscow: Progress, 1987.

Janecek, Gerald, *The Look of Russian Literature: Avant-Garde Visual Experiments, 1900–1930*, Princeton University Press, 1984.

Karlinsky, Simon, "Misanthropy and Sadism in Lermontov's Plays," in Julian W. Connolly and Sonia I. Ketchian (eds.), *Studies in Russian Literature in Honor of Vsevolod Setchkarev*, Columbus: Slavica, 1986.

Karlinsky, Simon, Rice, James L. and Scherr, Barry P. (eds.), *O Rus! Studia litteraria slavica in honorem Hugh McLean*, Oakland: Berkeley Slavic Specialities, 1995.

Katanian, V. A., "Ne tol'ko vospominaniia: k istorii izdaniia Maiakovskogo," *Druzhba narodov* 3 (1989), 220–27.

Kats, Boris, "Uzh esli nastraivat' liru na pushkinskii lad . . . ," *Novoe literaturnoe obozrenie* 17 (1996), 279–95.

Katz, Michael R., *The Literary Ballad in Early Nineteenth-Century Russian Literature*, London: Oxford University Press, 1976.

Kayser, Wolfgang, *Geschichte der deutschen Ballade*, Berlin: Junker und Dünnhaupt Verlag, 1936.

Geschichte des deutschen Verses, Munich: Francke Verlag, 1981.

Kelly, Catriona, *A History of Russian Women's Writing: 1820–1992*, Oxford University Press, 1994.

Kenney, E. J. (ed.), *The Cambridge History of Classical Literature*, New York: Cambridge University Press, 1982.

Khodasevich, Vladislav, *Izbrannaia proza*, New York: Russica Publishers, 1982.

"Pompeia," *Chast' rechi* 4–5 (1986), 29–35.

Kibal'nik, S. A., "K voprosu ob istochnikakh pushkinskogo stikhotvoreniia 'Otrok,'" *Zeitschrift für Slawistik* 32, 1 (1987), 65–69.

Kirsanova, R. M., *Kostium v russkoi khudozhestvennoi kul'ture 18–pervoi poloviny 20 vv.*, Moscow: Bol'shaia rossiiskaia entsiklopediia, 1995.

Krasovskaia, V. M., "Siuzhety Pushkina v iskusstve russkoi khoreografii," *Pushkin: issledovaniia i materialy* 5 (1967), 255–77.

Kreid, Vadim (ed.), *Vospominaniia o serebrianom veke*, Moscow: Respublika, 1993.

Kriukova, A. M., "K tvorcheskoi istorii poemy 'Maiakovskii nachinaetsia,'" in *Literaturnoe nasledstvo*, no. 93 *(Iz istorii sovetskoi literatury 1920–1930-kh godov)*, Moscow: Nauka, 1983.

Lauer, Reinhard, "'Evgenij Onegin' à la Igor' Severjanin," *Arion: Jahrbuch der Deutschen Puschkin-Gesellschaft* 2 (1992), 97–108.

    Gedichtform zwischen Schema und Verfall, Munich: Fink Verlag, 1975.

    "Das russische Sonett der Puškin-Zeit," in Hans-Bernd Harder and Hans Rothe (eds.), *Gattungen in den slavischen Literaturen: Beiträge zu ihren Formen in der Geschichte*, Cologne: Böhlau Verlag, 1988.

Lavrov, Alexander, "Andrei Bely and the Argonauts' Mythmaking," in Paperno and Grossman, *Creating Life*.

LeSage, Laurent, *The Rhumb Line of Symbolism: French Poets from Sainte-Beuve to Valéry*, University Park: Pennsylvania State University Press, 1978.

Levin, Iu. I., "Zametki o poezii Vl. Khodasevicha," *Wiener Slawistischer Almanach* 17 (1986), 43–129.

Lilly, Ian K., *The Dynamics of Russian Verse*, Nottingham: Astra Press, 1996.

Lilly, Ian K. and Scherr, Barry P., "Russian Verse Theory, 1982–1988: A Commentary and Bibliography," *International Journal of Slavic Linguistics and Poetics* 41 (1997), 143–91.

Loseff, Lev, "The Toy Town Ruined," in Loseff and Scherr, *A Sense of Place*.

Loseff, Lev and Scherr, Barry (eds.), *A Sense of Place: Tsarskoe Selo and Its Poets*, Columbus: Slavica, 1993.

Lotman, Iu. M., *Roman A. S. Pushkina "Evgenii Onegin": kommentarii*, Leningrad: Prosveshchenie, 1983.

Mandel'shtam, Osip, *Slovo i kul'tura*, Moscow: Sovetskii pisatel', 1987.

Markov, Vladimir, *Russian Futurism: A History*, Berkeley: University of California Press, 1968.

Matiash, S. A. "Stikhotvornyi perenos: k probleme vzaimodeistviia ritma i sintaksisa," in Dmitrii Bak, James Bailey, Iurii Orlitskii, and Kirill Postoutenko (eds.), *Russkii stikh: metrika, ritmika, rifma, strofika*, Moscow: Rossiiskii gosudarstvennyi gumanitarnyi universitet, 1996.

Mints, Zara, "Blok i Pushkin," *Trudy po russkoi i slavianskoi filologii* 21 (1973), 135–296.

    Lirika Aleksandra Bloka, Tartu: n. p., 1965–75.

Modzalevskii, B. L., *Biblioteka A. S. Pushkina*, St. Petersburg: Tip. Imperatorskoi Akademii Nauk, 1910.

Morson, Gary Saul and Emerson, Caryl, *Mikhail Bakhtin: Creation of a Prosaics*, Stanford University Press, 1990.

Naumov, E. I., "Lenin o Maiakovskom (novye materialy)," in *Literaturnoe nasledstvo*, no. 65 (*Novoe o Maiakovskom*), Moscow: Nauka, 1958.

Neumann, Friedrich Wilhelm, *Geschichte der russischen Ballade*, Königsberg: Ost-Europa-Verlag, 1937.

"The Nobel Laureates of Literature: An Olympic Gathering. Panel Discussion 1," *Georgia Review* 49, 4 (1995), 832–56.

Paperno, Irina and Grossman, Joan Delaney (eds.), *Creating Life: The Aesthetic Utopia of Russian Modernism*, Stanford University Press, 1994.

Pavlova, M. M. and Lavrov, A. V. (eds.), *Neizdannyi Fedor Sologub*, Moscow: Novoe literaturnoe obozrenie, 1997.

Peisakhovich, M. A., "Oneginskaia strofa v poemakh Lermontova," *Filologicheskie nauki* 1 (1969), 25–38.

Pollak, Nancy, "Annensky's 'Trefoil in the Park' (Witness to Whiteness)," in Loseff and Scherr, *Sense of Place*.

Postoutenko, K. Iu., "Oneginskaia strofa v russkoi poezii (na materiale XIX–nach. XX v.)," dissertation, Moscow State University, 1992.

Pushkin v mirovoi literature: sbornik statei, Leningrad: Gosudarstvennoe izdatel'stvo, 1926.

Ronen, Omry, "Dva poliusa paranomazii," in Barry P. Scherr and Dean S. Worth (eds.), *Russian Verse Theory: Proceedings of the 1987 Conference at UCLA*, Columbus: Slavica, 1989.

  The Fallacy of the Silver Age in Twentieth-Century Russian Literature, Amsterdam: Harwood Academic Publishers, 1997.

  "A Functional Technique of Myth Transformation in Twentieth-Century Russian Lyrical Poetry," in Andrej Kodjak, Krystyna Pomorska, and Stephen Rudy (eds.), *Myth in Literature*, Columbus: Slavica, 1985.

Rosengrant, Judson, "Nabokov, *Onegin*, and the Theory of Translation," *Slavic and East European Journal* 38, 1 (1994), 13–27.

Rosslyn, Wendy, "Remodelling the Statues at Tsarskoe Selo: Akhmatova's Approach to the Poetic Tradition," in Loseff and Scherr, *Sense of Place*.

Rozen, Baron, "O rifme," *Sovremennik* 1 (1836), 131–54.

Sampson, Earl D., *Nikolay Gumilev*, Boston: Twayne Publishers, 1979.

Sandler, Stephanie, "Remembrance in Mikhailovskoe," in Gasparov, Hughes, and Paperno, *Cultural Mythologies of Russian Modernism*.

Scherr, Barry, "Maksimilian Vološin and the Search for Form(s)," *Slavic and East European Journal* 35, 4 (1991), 518–36.

  Russian Poetry: Meter, Rhythm, and Rhyme, Berkeley: University of California Press, 1986.

Seemann, K. D., "Studien zum russischen Balladenvers 1," *Zeitschrift für slavische Philologie* 46 (1986), 318–35.

Senchina, L. T., "Metrika i strofika A. A. Del'viga," in M. L. Gasparov (ed.), *Russkoe stikhoslozhenie XIX v.: materialy po metrike i strofike russkikh poetov*, Moscow: Nauka, 1979.

Shapir, M. I., "Geksametr i pentametr v poezii Katenina (o formal'no-semanticheskoi derivatsii stikhotvornykh razmerov)," *Philologica* 1, 1/2 (1994), 43–114.

"Iz istorii 'parodicheskogo balladnogo stikha,'" in N. Bogomolov (ed.), *Anti-mir russkoi kul'tury*, Moscow: Ladomir, 1996.

"'Semanticheskii oreol metra': termin i poniatie," *Literaturnoe obozrenie* 12 (1991), 36–40.

Shaw, J. Thomas, *Pushkin's Poetics of the Unexpected: The Nonrhymed Lines in the Rhymed Poetry and the Rhymed Lines in the Nonrhymed Poetry*, Columbus: Slavica, 1994.

Sloane, David A., *Aleksandr Blok and the Dynamics of the Lyric Cycle*, Columbus: Slavica, 1988.

Smirnov, I. P., *Porozhdenie interteksta*, Vienna: Wiener Slawistischer Almanach, 1985.

Smith, G. S., "The Stanza Forms of Russian Poetry from Polotsky to Derzhavin," Ph.D. thesis, University of London, 1977.

Sperantov, V. V., "Miscellanea poetologica: byl li kn. Shalikov izobretatelem 'oneginskoi strofy'?," *Philologica* 3, 5/7 (1996), 125–31.

Stankiewicz, Edward, "The Onegin Stanza Revisited," in Karlinsky, Rice, and Scher, *O Rus!*.

Stein, Leonard (ed.), *Style and Idea: Selected Writings of Arnold Schoenberg*, Berkeley: University of California Press, 1984.

Taranovskii, K. F., "Chetyrekhstopnyi iamb Andreia Belogo," *International Journal of Slavic Linguistics and Poetics* 10 (1966), 127–47.

"O vzaimootnoshenii stikhotvornogo ritma i tematiki," in *American Contributions to the Fifth International Congress of Slavists*, The Hague: Mouton, 1963.

[Taranovskii, Kiril], "Some Problems of Enjambement in Slavic and Western European Verse," *International Journal of Slavic Linguistics and Poetics* 7 (1963), 80–87.

"Vdal' vlekomye: odin sluchai poeticheskoi polemiki Bloka i Belogo s Viach. Ivanovym," *Slavica Hierosolymitana* 5–6 (1981), 289–96.

Ternovsky, Eugène, *Essai sur l'histoire du poème russe de la fin du XIXe et du début du XXe siècle: velikolepnaia neudacha*, Lille: Atelier national reproductions des thèses, 1987.

Timofeev, Leonid, *Slovo v stikhe*, Moscow: Sovetskii pisatel', 1982.

Todd, William Mills III, *Fiction and Society in the Age of Pushkin*, Cambridge, MA: Harvard University Press, 1986.

Tomashevskii, B. V., "Pushkin – chitatel' frantsuzskikh poetov," in N. V. Iakovlev (ed.), *Pushkinskii sbornik pamiati professora Semena Afanas'evicha Vengerova*, Moscow: Gosudarstvennoe izdatel'stvo, 1923.

"Pushkin i Bualo," in *Pushkin v mirovoi literature*.

[Tomashevskii, Boris], *Pushkin: raboty raznykh let*, Moscow: Kniga, 1990.

Teoriia literatury, Leningrad: Gosudarstvennoe izdatel'stvo, 1925.

Toporov, V. N., "Dve glavy iz istorii russkoi poezii nachala veka: 1. V. A.

Komarovskii – II. V. K. Shileiko (k sootnosheniiu poetiki simvolizma i akmeizma)," *Russian Literature* 7, 3 (1979), 249–326.

"Iz issledovanii v oblasti poetiki Zhukovskogo," *Slavica Hierosolymitana* I (1977), 32–101.

Tsiavlovskii, Mstislav, "Pushkin i angliiskii iazyk," *Pushkin i ego sovremenniki* 17 (1913), 48–73.

Tynianov, Iu. N., *Arkhaisty i novatory,* [Leningrad]: Priboi, 1929.

Poetika. Istoriia literatury. Kino, Moscow: Nauka, 1977.

Ueland, Carol Culley, "Autobiographical *Poemy* of the Russian Symbolists: Aleksandr Blok's *Retribution,* Viacheslav Ivanov's *Infancy* and Andrei Bely's *The First Encounter,*" Ph.D. thesis, Columbia University, 1995.

"Viacheslav Ivanov's Pushkin: Thematic and Prosodic Echoes of *Evgenii Onegin* in *Mladenchstvo,*" in Gasparov, Hughes, and Paperno, *Cultural Mythologies of Russian Modernism.*

Unbegaun, Boris, *Russian Versification,* Oxford University Press, 1956.

Venclova, Tomas, "The Exemplary Resident of Tsarskoe Selo and the Great Pupil of the Lycée: Some Observations on the Poetics of Count Vasily Alekseevich Komarovsky," in Loseff and Scherr, *Sense of Place.*

Verkhovskii, Iu. N. (ed.), *Poety pushkinskoi pory: sbornik stikhov,* Moscow: M. and S. Sabashnikov, 1919.

Vinogradov, V. V., *Stil' Pushkina,* Moscow: Goslitizdat, 1941.

Vinokur, G., "Slovo i stikh v Evgenii Onegine," in A. M. Egolin (ed.), *Pushkin: sbornik statei,* Moscow: Ogiz, 1941.

Vishnevetskii, Igor', "Zhivye i 'blistatel'naia ten'": transformatsiia obraza Italii v pozdnei poezii Sergeia Solov'eva," in Daniela Rizzi and Andrei Shishkin (eds.), *Archivio italo-russo,* Trento: Dipartimento di Scienze Filologiche e Storiche, 1997.

Volkova, M. and Dovlatov, S. (eds.), *Ne tol'ko Brodskii: russkaia kul'tura v portretakh i anekdotakh,* Moscow: Kul'tura, 1992.

Volm, Matthew, *W. A. Zhukovskii als Uebersetzer,* Ann Arbor: Edwards Brothers, 1945–47.

Vroon, Ronald, "Aleksei Kruchenykh's 'Razboinik Van'ka-Kain' and the Literary Politics of LEF," *Slavic Review* 50, 2 (1991), 359–70.

Wachtel, Andrew Baruch, *The Battle for Childhood: Creation of a Russian Myth,* Stanford University Press, 1990.

Wagenknecht, Christian, *Deutsche Metrik: eine historische Einführung,* Munich: Verlag C. H. Beck, 1981.

Würzbach, Natascha, "Tradition and Innovation: The Influence of Child Ballads on the Anglo-American Literary Ballad," in Joseph Harris (ed.), *The Ballad and Oral Literature,* Cambridge, MA: Harvard University Press, 1991.

Zhirmunskii, V., *Rifma, ee istoriia i teoriia,* Petersburg: Academia, 1923.

Teoriia stikha, Leningrad: Sovetskii pisatel', 1975.

Zholkovskii, Aleksandr, *Inventsii,* Moscow: Gendal'f, 1995.

Zielinski, F. F., "Russkii elegicheskii distikh," in Ovidii, *Ballady-Poslaniia*, Moscow: M. and S. Sabashnikov, 1913.

Ziolkowski, Theodore, *The Classical German Elegy, 1795–1950*, Princeton University Press, 1980.

Index

Zholkovsky, Aleksandr, 261 n. 9, 262 n. 26,
   297 n. 24
Zhukovsky, Vasily, 60, 175, 198, 268 n. 44, 274
   n. 25
   and ballad, 21, 22–24, 38, 39, 56
   on death of Pushkin, 189–92
   in works of Pushkin, 25–27, 65–66, 70, 242
   "Motionless he lay" ("On lezhal bez
     dvizhen'ia"), 189–92

"Perishability" ("Tlennost'"), 60–65, 75,
   76–77, 78
"Revenge" ("Mshchenie"), 22–24, 25, 26,
   27, 29, 39
Zielinski, Faddei, 293 n. 64
Zinov'eva-Annibal, Lidiia Dmitrievna, 197
Ziolkowski, Theodore, 174